FRANCE AND THE GERMAN QUESTION, 1945–1990

FRANCE AND THE GERMAN QUESTION, 1945–1990

Edited by
FRÉDÉRIC BOZO AND CHRISTIAN WENKEL

berghahn
NEW YORK · OXFORD
www.berghahnbooks.com

First published in 2019 by
Berghahn Books
www.berghahnbooks.com

Library of Congress Cataloging-in-Publication Data

Names: Bozo, Frédéric, editor. | Wenkel, Christian, editor.
Title: France and the German Question, 1945–1990 / edited by Frédéric Bozo and
    Christian Wenkel.
Description: New York: Berghahn Books, 2019. | Includes bibliographical references and
    index.
Identifiers: LCCN 2019007659 (print) | LCCN 2019011546 (ebook) |
    ISBN 9781789202274 (ebook) | ISBN 9781789202267 (hardback: alk. paper)
Subjects: LCSH: France—Foreign relations—Germany. | Germany—Foreign relations—
    France. | German reunification question (1949–1990) | Cold War. | France—Foreign
    relations—1945–
Classification: LCC DC59.8.G3 (ebook) | LCC DC59.8.G3 F685 2019 (print) |
    DDC 327.4404309/045—dc23
LC record available at https://lccn.loc.gov/2019007659

British Library Cataloguing in Publication Data

A catalogue record for this book is available from the British Library

ISBN 978-1-78920-226-7 hardback
ISBN 978-1-78920-227-4 ebook

CONTENTS

Abbreviations

AAPD	*Akten zur Auswärtigen Politik der Bundesrepublik Deutschland*
ACDP	Archiv für Christlich-Demokratische Politik, Sankt Augustin
AdsD	Archiv der sozialen Demokratie, Bonn
AMAE	Archives du ministère des Affaires étrangères, La Courneuve
AMSZ	Archive of the Polish Ministry for Foreign Affairs, Warsaw
AnF	Archives nationales de France, Pierrefitte-sur-Seine
AP	Archives parlementaires, Paris
ASD	Affaires stratégiques et du désarmement, MAE
AVPRF	Arkhiv Vneshnei Politiki Rossiiskoi Federatsii, Moscow
BKA-AA	Österreichisches Staatsarchiv, Archiv der Republik, Vienna
BKAH	Bundeskanzler-Adenauer-Haus, Rhöndorf
CADN	Centre des Archives diplomatiques de Nantes, MAE
CAEF	Centre des archives économiques et financières, Savigny-le-Temple
CAS	Centre d'archives socialistes, Paris
CSU	Christlich-Soziale Union
DBPO	*Documents on British Policy Overseas*
DDF	*Documents diplomatiques français*
EM	Entretiens et Messages, AMAE
FNSP	Fondation nationale des sciences politiques, Paris
FRUS	*Foreign Relations of the United States*
IPMF	Institut Pierre Mendès France, Paris
MAE	Ministère des Affaires étrangères, Paris
NA	National Archives Records Administration, Washington
PA/AA	Politisches Archiv des Auswärtigen Amts, Berlin
PEF	*Politique étrangère de la France. Textes et documents*
RFA	République fédérale d'Allemagne
RGANI	Rossiiskii Gosudarstvennyi Arkhiv Noveishei Istorii, Moscow
TNA	National Archives, The, Kew
WBA	Willy–Brandt–Archiv, AdsD, Bonn

INTRODUCTION

FRÉDÉRIC BOZO AND CHRISTIAN WENKEL

Is the German question once again an open one? Against the backdrop of the euro-crisis of the past few years and Germany's newly gained prominence in Europe, many scholars and pundits seem to have come to that conclusion. "There is a new German question," wrote Timothy Garton-Ash at the height of the crisis in 2013, adding, "It is this: Can Europe's most powerful country lead the way in building both a sustainable, internationally competitive Eurozone and a strong, internationally credible European Union?"[1] Two years later, with the crisis lingering, Hans Kundnani, in his much-acclaimed analysis of *The Paradox of German Power*, agreed: "The 'German question' has re-emerged in a new form," he wrote—a form that once again derives from the country's size and centrality on the continent.[2] This alleged reemergence of the German question has been a matter of concern in France, too; during the presidential campaigns of 2012 and 2017 a central issue was how to deal with Germany.

More than twenty-five years after Germany's unification, such concerns are astonishing. For most contemporaries, the events of 1989–90—spanning those 329 days that led from the fall of the Berlin Wall on 9 November 1989 to the new day of German national unity on 3 October 1990[3]—had been a subject of amazement. Because by the end of the 1980s ending Germany's four decades of division had come to be seen as either requiring an indefinite period or involving the risk of a major disruption of the European order, such a brisk and peaceful development had come as a huge surprise. Yet in the aftermath of the country's unification most observers believed that the German question in effect was closed, since all the sensitive issues deriving from it—for example, the country's borders or its politico-military status—had been solved, first and foremost within the Treaty on the Final Settlement with Respect to Germany signed in Moscow on 12 September 1990—also known as the Two Plus Four Agreement.

This was no small achievement. The German question had been central to the European system since the beginning of the modern era—in fact, since the very emergence of that system in the wake of the 1648 Peace of Westphalia. During the course of the following three centuries, the centrality of the German question was never in doubt. The French Revolution and the Napoleonic era contributed to no small extent to the process that led to the emergence of the modern German nation-state. In the wake of the dissolution of the Holy Roman Empire of the German nation in 1806, France became the "other" that helped forge the German national sentiment, as illustrated by the campaign to end French occupation and the 1813 Battle of the Nations. The creation of a German confederation by the Congress of Vienna in 1814–15 did not solve the German question, satisfying neither Prussia's imperial ambitions nor the German bourgeoisie's aspiration to a German federal state. Thereafter, the country's unification remained the order of the day, whether peacefully and democratically at Frankfurt in 1848–49 or by "iron and blood" under Bismarck in 1864–71. Between 1870 and 1944, imperial and then Nazi Germany invaded France three times, leading General Charles de Gaulle to state, in the wake of the liberation of France, that Germany's "fate" was a "question of life and death" for France and—no less—the "central problem of the universe."[4]

The Cold War emerged at least partly from the victors' inability, in the wake of the Potsdam Conference of July–August 1945, to reach agreement on the terms of a peace treaty with defeated Germany. By the late 1940s, the nascent Cold War opened a new and decisive chapter in the protracted history of the German question. That chapter was determined by a seemingly unescapable dialectic. On the one hand, the division of Europe and, at its center, of Germany, offered a solution (temporary at least) to the German question: German power was tamed as a result of the country's partition and diminished sovereignty, and its territorial limits were embedded in the status quo of the bloc system, itself guaranteed by the nuclear balance of terror. On the other hand, precisely because Germany (and particularly Berlin) was at the center of the Cold War system, any calling into question of the German status quo could well lead to a major disruption of the European order, if not World War III—hence the difficulty for most contemporaries until 1989–90 to imagine a peaceful and swift settlement. "The German problem," de Gaulle famously remarked in 1965, had become "the European problem par excellence."[5]

This volume covers the period that stretches from the defeat of Nazi Germany in 1945 to the country's unification in 1990. Although it is a relatively brief chapter— less than half a century—in the multisecular history of the German question, it is a uniquely distinctive and portentous period precisely because of the inextricability between the latter and the wider international context of East-West relations. It is distinctive because the Cold War, together with its German variation, represents a coherent and distinct phase of Europe's international history, with a beginning and an end as well as an organizational principle running throughout it; and it is portentous because the German question, throughout this period, was the epicenter of the European and international system—and the condition of its sustainability as well as the possible cause of its collapse.

We focus specifically on France and the German question for two reasons.

First, the German question—which, for France, had been existential for decades— remained critical in the country's European and international policies throughout the Cold War. In spite of its weakness at the end of War World II compared to the other three victors—the United States and the Soviet Union of course, but also the United Kingdom—France in 1945 was recognized as one of the four victorious powers with rights and responsibilities with regard to Berlin and Germany as a whole. This, together with its status as a permanent member of the United Nations Security Council and as a nuclear power since the early 1960s, remained until 1990 a major component of France's claim to international rank. In fact, France's major international concerns and priorities during the Cold War were, for the most part, addressed through its relationships with the other three powers involved in the German question, whether the United States (key to the defense of France and of the West at large), the Soviet Union (central to East-West relations and European security), and—somewhat less crucially—the United Kingdom (France's alter ego and rival West European would-be Great Power). The German question, in other words, was at the crossroads of France's policies during this period.

Yet France looked at the German question and its possible evolution primarily through the prism of Franco-German relations, characterized over centuries not only by mutual occupations and wars, but also by a broad range of cultural transfers spanning multiple domains—from industry to philosophy—and involving a characteristic mixture of mutual attraction and rejection. The image of Germany as a home of philosophers and writers, an image once captured by Germaine de Staël, was partly destroyed by Prussian invaders in 1870–71, and coexisted since then with the perception of Germany as a threat.[6] Due to this intertwined history, the German question had become a distinctly French question, even obsession. For French politicians, intellectuals, or public opinion, it was a much more complicated issue than for their British or American counterparts. The French use of the expression "German problem" (a choice of words preferred, for instance, by de Gaulle) testifies to the highly psychological dimension of that issue as well as its characteristic *longue durée*.[7]

Franco-German relations thus remained central in France's European and international policies in the second half of the twentieth century. Given its past enmity with Germany, France in 1945 was justifiably concerned with the evolution of the German question. The experience of the first post–world war period and the failure of French objectives after 1918 loomed large in the immediate aftermath of the 1944–45 victory. Yet, in spite of a public discourse that by and large remained in line with that of the earlier era, the lessons had been learned and were transformed, partly under American pressure, into pragmatic policy. The intuitions of the 1920s—that Europe's reconstruction could only happen through Franco-German reconciliation—were quickly elevated to a political principle that it fell on France to fulfill. Robert Schuman famously accomplished this at the very beginning of the 1950s; by then de Gaulle himself unequivocally characterized Franco-German reconciliation as a primary objective of French policy. In short, no country other than France had such a decisive stake in giving life to Chancellor Konrad Adenauer and his successors' notion that German unification could only take place under a European roof—echoing Thomas Mann's famous call for "a European Germany" rather than "a German Europe."[8]

As a result of the foregoing, France's role in the German question was decisive throughout the period under consideration—this is the second reason why we focus specifically on France in this volume. As one of the four victorious powers, France held a veto over any evolution in the German status quo. From Potsdam in 1945 to the ratification of the Bonn–Paris convention in 1955, a peace treaty proved unattainable and the country's division became a fact of life, leading the three Western powers to devise a partial and temporary settlement involving the economic, political, and military integration of the Federal Republic of Germany (FRG, or West Germany) into the Western bloc while reserving their rights until a final settlement became workable. In order to preserve the leverage of the Four Powers' rights, French diplomacy from then on nurtured a small group of Berlinologists whose task was to ensure respect for Berlin's quadripartite status by both German states as well as by the two superpowers, who were less inclined toward this legal formalism. While throughout the following decades the Cold War status quo made any radical departure from the German status quo unlikely, France, including through its quadripartite prerogatives, kept a keen eye on possible evolutions, in particular those that might result from the FRG's new *Ostpolitik* once it was launched in the late 1960s. And when in the wake of Mikhail Gorbachev's coming to power in 1985 events in the East eventually led to the fall of the wall, creating the conditions for ending four decades of Germany's division, France—eager once again to make use of its rights and responsibilities if need be—was determined to have a say on how to finally solve the German question and to contribute to shaping the definitive settlement that was reached in 1990.

Beyond the strictly legal aspects, what made France a key player in the German question from beginning to end was the country's ability to mobilize its diplomatic resources to that effect, whether through its relations with the United States, the Union of Soviet Socialist Republics (USSR, or Soviet Union), or other East European countries like Poland. Yet the most important vehicle for France's influence on the evolution of the German question was its relations with the FRG and, starting in the early 1970s, the German Democratic Republic (GDR, or East Germany). The Franco-West German relationship, throughout the four decades of Germany's division, progressively emerged as the backbone of the European project, and the completion of that project had come to be seen in Paris—like in Bonn—as the precondition for solving the German question and Germany's return to some sort of unity; as a result, by the 1980s France was in a position to exert considerable leverage on the German question and on the European integration process. In fact, France's role faced with the effective prospect of Germany's unification in 1989–90 could be summarized by a willingness to ensure that the latter would not hinder or slow down European unification. This strategy culminated in the Maastricht Treaty, signed in 1991–92 in the wake of German unification. That a unified Germany henceforth would remain embedded in European construction as well as in the Atlantic alliance can legitimately be considered as a success of more than four decades of an active French policy in search of a satisfactory answer to the German question.

France's important role in framing and, ultimately, bringing about the final settlement of the German question in the period 1945 to 1990 has to a large extent been neglected by the historiography, at least until quite recently. Although historians have focused in depth on specific junctures—in particular the early years and, lately, the final ones—no comprehensive study of France and the German question throughout the period under scrutiny in this volume exists so far in the otherwise increasingly rich literature that covers the Cold War and the German question. When France's role is discussed, two features characterize existing accounts. First, that role is often seen as limited compared to that of the other major players, beginning with the two superpowers and West Germany. France is usually described as a secondary player with limited influence on the evolution of the German question. Second, France's contribution to framing, managing, and eventually solving the latter between 1945 and 1990 has been, until recently, widely seen in negative terms. To the extent France is recognized in a role, that role is generally seen as one of obstruction, be it in the formative years (through its alleged opposition to West Germany's reemergence and then integration into the Western bloc, culminating in France's rejection of the European Defence Community [EDC] in 1954), in the period of the East-West and German status quo (as reflected in France's purported defiance toward the FRG's Ostpolitik and its alleged ulterior motives), and, last but not least, against the backdrop of Germany's unification in 1989–90 (as made clear by France's supposed attempt at delaying if not at obstructing it altogether).

These traits of the historiography can easily be explained. That France's role in the German question throughout the Cold War has long been dismissed reflects a historiography that has predominantly focused on, to the detriment of other actors, the role played by the superpowers and, of course, by West Germany. The Cold War has long been seen as essentially a U.S.–Soviet affair, leaving little room for European players—except for Germany itself, the central object of the bipolar confrontation. As to the predominantly negative rendition of France's role, it stems to a large extent from the foregoing: France's contribution has mostly been seen through the lenses of the other actors, creating a bias. At no juncture is this in fuller display than when it comes to German unification in 1989–90, whose accounts have mostly been written through the prism of U.S., West German, and to some extent Soviet policies—all of which differed somehow from French policy. Where the United States was predominantly concerned with German unification within NATO, France was less sanguine; and where West German leaders, starting in the early weeks of 1990, wagered on a quick unification while paying limited attention to the international setting, French leaders—in line with the doctrine formulated by de Gaulle since 1959— stressed the need for a controlled process as well as a robust international framework for solving the German question.

These differences on the best way to deal with the German question at its various stages and the fact that, in that regard too, France pursued an independent policy, explain to a large extent the negative perceptions that have long been associated with France's role—a phenomenon that is also amplified by the well-known phenomenon of source bias: France's role has most often been construed through the exploration of U.S., Soviet, or German archives, memoirs, and other types of documents, rather than French ones. This source bias is particularly felt in the case of German sources: because German decision makers throughout the period—whether in the early period, at the time of Ostpolitik and, of course, at the time of unification—have almost systematically proved to be suspicious of French motives and objectives in dealing with the German question (an attitude that can be explained by many factors, including the reminiscence of the post–World War I period), the German negative perception of France's role has often been seen as effectively reflecting the truth rather than an opinion, if not a prejudice.

We believe the time has come to revisit this issue to reflect the current state of the evolving historiography. Two main factors explain this historiographical evolution. First, a growing access to sources: almost three decades after the fall of the Berlin Wall, archival documents have become available for the whole duration of the period under scrutiny, including its decisive, final phase. This is the case not least in France, where scholars investigating the country's approach to the German question now have access to the foreign ministry's archives on a normal basis and, increasingly, to the presidential archives. As a result, France's role can now be understood on the basis of the appropriate French documentation rather than through the distorted prism of other, non-French sources. (Of course, international sources, which are also increasingly accessible, are nevertheless important to situate French policy in the appropriate multinational framework. Together with French archival sources, the available collections of documents from Germany, the United Kingdom, the United States, and Russia, in particular, now make it possible to investigate the German question from 1945 to 1990 along a truly multinational approach.[9]) The second factor allowing historians to revisit the issue is, as always, the passage of time. By and large, this history is now closed. Whether or not a new German question has effectively emerged in recent years, the German question, as understood in this volume, is clearly over. In other words, nearly thirty years after the end of the Cold War and German unification (i.e., the time of a generation), collective memories and the political stakes associated with it are increasingly blurred, making it possible for scholars to engage in a dispassionate and de-ideologized analysis.

The result is that historians in France, Germany, and elsewhere have recently begun to change their views on France's role in the German question, in essence both reevaluating its significance and its nature and showing that it was far more decisive and constructive than long averred. It was decisive because from the early period onward, France's status as one of the Four Powers, its role in the evolution of the Cold War, and, even more crucially, its increasingly close cooperation with West Germany in the emerging European project in effect gave it a say over key issues or developments pertaining to the German question—be it in the formative period from the late 1940s to the early 1950s, during the long status quo from the 1960s to the 1980s, or in the final period in the late 1980s. And it was constructive precisely because all the foregoing—not least the Franco-German and European dimensions—were key factors that throughout the period led France to understand, perhaps more acutely than other international actors, that the German question in essence did (and should) remain an open one until a final settlement had been reached—a settlement that had to be devised primarily in European terms, as confirmed by the Maastricht Treaty.

Embedding the German question in a European framework was, in other words, France's constant objective throughout the period. To the extent that there is nowadays a new German question, as Garton Ash posits, it is, ironically, to an extent the result of France's approach to solving the old question: Has the very European Germany that the French had long seen as the ultimate response to the German question now given way to a German Europe that such a European Germany was meant to prevent from emerging? Providing an answer to this question exceeds the scope of this volume. Suffice it here to remark that the mere fact of asking the question proves, in hindsight, France's centrality in the German question during the Cold War and in its final settlement.

The following contributions reflect this evolving historiography. In order to cover the key issues and junctures that relate to France's approach to the German question from 1945 to 1990, the individual chapters are both chronologically and thematically organized. In Part I "From Capitulation to Cooperation" we look at the early postwar period. From the defeat of Nazi Germany to the creation of the FRG, France was faced with a clean slate when it came to dealing with the German question. While the dominant narrative has long stressed the allegedly coercive approach evolved by de Gaulle and his immediate successors, recent historiography has largely disproved this. In chapter 1 ("France and the German Question, 1945–1949: On the Interdependence of Historiography, Methodology, and Interpretations"), Rainer Hudemann revisits the evolving historiography of the early postwar period and explains how and why the long-held view of France's punitive attitude has now been superseded by a more positive rendering of the country's attitude in these crucial years. Although France in some quarters still has the reputation of having led a revenge policy in Germany in these years, Hudemann shows that French international policies started to change as early as 1945, creating a paradigm of cooperation that has characterized Franco-German relations until the present. In a similar vein but within a more specifically economic (though equally crucial) purview, Françoise Berger, in chapter 2 ("Economic and Industrial Issues in France's Approach to the German Question in the Postwar Period"), explores the evolving historical knowledge on France's postwar economic aims and policies toward Germany, an indispensable step—given the vital character of economic issues in the occupation of Germany and the reconstruction of both countries—to understand France's evolving approach to the German question at large. By 1955 France and Germany had become each other's number one trading partner, making the Franco-German couple, from now on, the economic engine of European integration.

In part II, "The Emergence of the Bloc System," we turn to an examination of France's attitude toward the German question in the formative years of the Cold

War. With the partition of Germany and the integration of the FRG and the GDR into two opposing military blocs, the German question, against the backdrop of the emerging bipolar order, gained no less than systemic significance—acquiring the potential to degenerate into a new world war. In chapter 3 ("France, German Rearmament, and the German Question, 1945–1955"), Michael H. Creswell analyzes how France, against the backdrop of the emerging East-West military confrontation, was forced to devise a strategy to respond to the increasing Soviet threat and contribute to solving the German question. While the historiography has long described France's reaction to West Germany's rearmament as one of foot-dragging if not hostility, he shows that the French Fourth Republic was committed to devising a constructive response by including Germany in the politico-military structures of Western Europe, thus ensuring the "double security" on which the country would from then rely on. In chapter 4 ("Impossible Allies? Soviet Views of France and the German Question in the 1950s"), Geoffrey Roberts explores the parallel issues of Franco-Soviet relations and the German question in the formative period of the Cold War. While courtship of France—a country Moscow saw as sharing a common security interest faced with a possible resurgence of German militarism—was undoubtedly at the center of the Soviet Union's strategy for the containment of Germany in the 1950s, Roberts observes that France consistently failed to live up to Soviet expectations, at no point breaking ranks with the British and Americans on European collective security and the German question, here again correcting a widespread belief that Paris, ever since the early Cold War, was eager to establish a de facto alliance with Moscow to keep a divided Germany under control.

In Part III, "The de Gaulle Factor," we turn our attention to how the first president of the French Fifth Republic durably shaped his country's approach to the German question. By recognizing, as mentioned above, that the German question was at the center of the bipolar system and that only its definitive and peaceful settlement—including the overcoming of Germany's division—would bring about the possibility of transcending the Cold War status quo on the divided continent, de Gaulle, in this realm too, proved to be prescient. In chapter 5 ("An Arbiter between the Superpowers: Charles de Gaulle and the German Question, 1958–1969"), Garret J. Martin reminds us that, for de Gaulle, the German question remained a major preoccupation throughout his presidency because it fundamentally intersected with his ambitions both for enhancing France's rank and for transforming the continent, if not the international system as a whole. For him, Germany presented both a problem to be solved and a vehicle to foster dramatic changes in Europe—hence his firm belief that its eventual return to unity was desirable in order to bring about a new European security order even though such a settlement had to be tightly controlled to reassure and address the concerns of the other countries on the continent. In chapter 6 ("The German question in the Eastern policies of France and Germany in the 1960s"), Benedikt Schoenborn further explores this theme by looking more specifically at the interplay between France and West Germany in their approaches toward the

East against the backdrop of the still looming German question. While the German leaders were intrigued by de Gaulle's approach, their suspicions of his ulterior motives impeded a common Franco-German policy. Still, the French president's sustained dialogue with Moscow clearly was one of the influences that led to a change of course in the FRG, first in December 1966 when the Grand Coalition government moved toward a more active policy to the East, and then in 1969 when the social-liberal government under Willy Brandt embarked on a new Ostpolitik.

Exploring "The Era of Ostpolitik" is the purpose of Part IV of the volume. Starting in 1969, the FRG emerged as a key—perhaps the key—actor in East-West relations in Europe and the privileged interlocutor of the Soviet Union, a role once played by de Gaulle's France. The new Ostpolitik was a potential game changer for the German question, though it was an ambivalent game changer: on the one hand, Germany's division was now recognized as a durable fact; on the other, a realistic path toward its eventual overcoming was now open. This new situation was bound to affect France's approach toward the German question as well as its role in East-West relations. In chapter 7 ("Perceptions of Ostpolitik: French–West German Relations and the Evolving German Question under Willy Brandt and Georges Pompidou"), Gottfried Niedhart explores both the French perceptions of Brandt's Ostpolitik and the way in which the FRG believed its Ostpolitik was perceived by the French government—involving mirror-imaging and inevitable distortions. While the French were concerned with some aspects of Ostpolitik (not least its impact on the rights of the Four Powers and on the FRG's Westbindung), Paris, contrary to a long-held perception that emerged early on in Bonn, was not opposed to West Germany's new course even though it came together with its rapid reemergence as a major international actor. In chapter 8 ("France, the CSCE, and the German Question"), Nicolas Badalassi looks at the interaction, in France's policies, between the German question and the emerging Helsinki process. Because Germany was the epicenter of the East-West conflict in Europe, its status was naturally at the heart of the negotiations that culminated in the drafting of the 1975 Final Act—hence the considerable interest Paris showed in the aspects of the Conference on Security and Cooperation in Europe (CSCE) that involved the German question. For French diplomats, the CSCE was a way to deal with the latter in accordance with their dynamic vision of East-West relations and the objective of overcoming Yalta: beyond channeling Ostpolitik and preserving the Four Powers' rights, keeping the German question open, accordingly, was a major objective of French diplomacy in the CSCE. In chapter 9 ("The Economic and Monetary Dimensions of the German Question: A French Perspective, 1969–1979"), Guido Thiemeyer develops the economic aspects of the German question as seen from Paris in the 1970s. In addition to the status of the two Germanys and their possible unification, there was, he argues, a second dimension to the German question in the 1970s as seen from Paris: due to its economic success, the FRG was emerging as the most influential economic power in Western Europe and within the European Economic Community (EEC), hence creating another challenge for the neighboring countries, not least France. In response, the French government evolved a strategy that involved embedding Germany in the EEC, binding it through bilateral economic and industrial ties and, last but not least, modernizing France in order to restore an economic balance between the two states and deny Germany the exclusive leadership in economic and monetary affairs in Western Europe.

In Part V "The End Game," we turn our attention to the last decade of the Cold War, culminating with the fall of the Berlin Wall and Germany's unification in 1989–90—an outcome unforeseen by most players but that cannot be explained without looking at the return to the foreground of the German question throughout the 1980s. In chapter 10 ("The French 'Obsession' with the German Question: Willy Brandt, François Mitterrand, the German Question, and German Unification, 1981–1990"), Bernd Rother examines the ongoing conversation between French President François Mitterrand and former West German Chancellor and President of the Socialist International Willy Brandt on this matter. Before 1989 Mitterrand rightly sensed the importance of this theme for the Germans in general and the Social Democratic Party (SPD) in particular—in spite of the Social Democrats' claim to the contrary. Mitterrand had thus at least prepared himself for the possibility of German unification, but his constant preoccupation with the German question raised some incomprehension on the German side, in particular from Brandt. This, however, did not result in a real split due to Mitterrand and Brandt's common objective of deepening European integration. In chapter 11 ("All about Europe? France, Great Britain, and the Question of German Unification, 1989–1990"), Ilaria Poggiolini looks at the reactions of Germany's two main European partners and their interactions faced with the reopening of the German question and the prospect of German unification at the end of the 1980s. Although the dominant narrative of German unification typically equates Mitterrand's attitude with the hostility displayed by UK Prime Minister Margaret Thatcher, Ilaria Poggiolini clearly differentiates the French approach and shows that Thatcher's hope of a Franco-British common front were ill-founded. In the end, it was "all about Europe": France's commitment to Franco-German reconciliation and European integration, in contrast to Thatcher's growing rejection of the European project, made a new Franco-British entente cordiale all but impossible. In chapter 12 ("Franco-Soviet Relations, German Unification, and the End of the Cold War"), Frédéric Bozo sees a similar pattern being played out between France and the Soviet Union. Although Soviet leaders—including Mikhail Gorbachev—had long banked on a shared Franco-Soviet interest to thwart any German unification, Bozo shows that Moscow's expectations derived from a misinterpretation of the Gaullist design (as described above) and an underestimation of the strength of Franco-German relations. In spite of shared concerns with regard to the pace and international consequences of German unification, Mitterrand and Gorbachev did not share a common vision of the European response of the challenge, making a Franco-Soviet entente impossible.

Part VI, "Enduring Concerns: Anschluss, Borders, and the two Germanys," concludes the volume by discussing some key themes that permeate France's approach to the German question throughout the period at hand. In chapter 13 ("Towards a new Anschluss? France, the German and the Austrian Questions 1945–1955"), Thomas Angerer argues that understanding France's attitude toward the German question and, in particular, Germany's possible unification during the early Cold War and after requires taking into account the *longue durée* of France's historical experience with the Habsburg monarchy and the more recent trauma of Austria's 1938 Anschluss, in other words the nightmare of a pan-German hegemony at the center of Europe. (Reciprocally, France's Austrian policies after 1945 were influenced by France's objectives in the German question.) To prevent Austria from rejoining (West) Germany in a common state or group of states was part and parcel of French strategies for dealing with the German question after World War II as much as it had been after World War I. In chapter 14 ("France, Poland, and Germany's Eastern Border, 1945–1990: The Recurrent Issue of the German Question in French-Polish Relations"), Pierre-Frédéric Weber reminds us that the German question during the Cold War revolved around not only the issue of Germany's eventual return to unity, but also its territorial limits, especially to the East. In fact, the issue of the FRG's recognition of the Oder-Neisse line was, until the very end of the period, one of the most sensitive aspects of the German question. Because Poland was in that regard the most concerned of Germany's neighbors and because of France's keenness to ensure a durable settlement of this issue—including, as de Gaulle had called for as early as 1959, the definitive character of the border—relations between France and Poland remained, until the very end of the period and France's crucial involvement in the final settlement of this issue, a determining factor. In chapter 15, the volume's final chapter ("A Surprising Continuity: The French Attitude and Policy toward the GDR, 1949–1990"), Christian Wenkel explores the continuity in the way French diplomacy dealt with the Second German state throughout the period, thus illustrating the permanence of France's attitude and policies with regard to the German question as a whole from the 1950s to the 1980s. Even the establishment of diplomatic relations between France and the GDR in 1973 did not alter this continuity. It was a small step in a long process of normalization of Franco–East German relations that had become necessary in the context of détente and the CSCE. In fact, it was a precondition to achieve the kind of progressive and controlled return to a unified German nation that can be considered one of French foreign policy's long-term goals during the Cold War.

This volume would not exist without the support of the Sorbonne Cold War History Project (Universities Panthéon Sorbonne – Paris 1 and Sorbonne Nouvelle – Paris 3, with funding from the French National Research Agency) and the German Historical Institute in Paris. These organizations helped to bring together many of the volume's contributors in February of 2013 to present preliminary research, and they have remained supportive of our efforts since then. The editors want to thank all those involved in the organization of the 2013 event and the subsequent editorial process, in particular Dr. Nicolas Badalassi (Sorbonne Cold War History Project, Paris), Dr. N. Piers Ludlow (London School of Economics), Dr. Stefan Martens (German Historical Institute, Paris), Professor Hélène Miard-Delacroix (University Paris Sorbonne – Paris 4), Professor Marie-Pierre Rey (University Panthéon Sorbonne – Paris 1), Professor Mary Elise Sarotte (University of Southern California, Los Angeles), Dr. Johannes Schmid (German Historical Institute, Paris), and Professor Andreas Wilkens (University of Lorraine).

Frédéric Bozo is professor of contemporary history at the Sorbonne Nouvelle (University of Paris 3, Department of European Studies). He was educated at the École Normale Supérieure, at the Institut d'études politiques de Paris and at Harvard University. He received his PhD from the University of Paris-Nanterre (1993) and his habilitation from the Sorbonne Nouvelle (1997). His publications include *Mitterrand, the End of the Cold War, and German Unification* (2009), *Visions of the End of the Cold War in Europe, 1945–1990* (coedited with N. Piers Ludlow, Marie-Pierre Rey, and Bernd Rother, 2012) and *French Foreign Policy since 1945: An Introduction* (2016), all with Berghahn Books. His most recently published book is *A History of the Iraq Crisis: France, the United States, and Iraq, 1991–2003* (2016).

Christian Wenkel is associate professor of contemporary history at Artois University. After receiving a PhD from the University of Munich and Sciences Po Paris, he was a senior research fellow at the German Historical Institute in Paris from 2009 to 2016. His research interests cover the Franco-German relationship, French foreign policy, the Cold War, and European integration. Relevant publications in the context of this book include *Auf der Suche nach einem "anderen Deutschland." Das Verhältnis Frankreichs zur DDR im Spannungsfeld von Perzeption und Diplomatie* (2014) and *La diplomatie française face à l'unification allemande. Archives inédites réunies* (with Maurice Vaïsse, 2011).

Notes

1. Ash, "The New German Question."
2. Kundnani, *The Paradox of German Power*, 6.
3. Teltschik, *329 Tage*.
4. De Gaulle, *Discours et messages*, vol. 1, 483.
5. De Gaulle, *Discours et messages*, vol. 4, 338.
6. Caro, "Les deux Allemagnes"; Digeon, *La crise allemande*.
7. Note that this choice of words is not limited to the French: see, e.g., Rödder, *Wer hat Angst vor Deutschland?*, 15.
8. Mann, *Schriften zur Politik*, 206.
9. On the end of the period, see, e.g., Bozo, Rödder, and Sarotte, *German Reunification*.

Bibliography

Ash, T. Garton. 2013. "The New German Question." *New York Review of Books*, 15 Aug., https://www.nybooks.com/articles/2013/08/15/new-german-question/ (accessed 12 Feb. 2019).

Bozo, F., A. Rödder, and M. Sarotte, eds. 2017. *German Reunification: A Multinational History*. London: Routledge.

Caro, E.-M. 1871. "Les deux Allemagnes. Madame de Staël et Henri Heine." *Revue des deux mondes* 96, 5–20.

De Gaulle, C. 1970. *Discours et messages*. Vol. 1, *Pendant la guerre*. Paris: Plon.

———. 1970. *Discours et messages*. Vol. 4, *Pour l'effort*. Paris: Plon.

Digeon, C., 1959. *La crise allemande de la pensée française*. Paris: Presses universitaires de France.

Kundnani, H. 2015. *The Paradox of German Power*. London: Hurst & Company.

Mann, T. 1970. *Schriften zur Politik*. Frankfurt, Germany: Suhrkamp.

Rödder, A. 2018. *Wer hat Angst vor Deutschland? Geschichte eines europäischen Problems*. Frankfurt, Germany: S. Fischer.

Teltschik, H. 1991. *329 Tage. Innenansichten der Einigung*. Berlin: Siedler.

PART I

FROM CAPITULATION TO COOPERATION

CHAPTER 1

FRANCE AND THE GERMAN QUESTION, 1945–1949

ON THE INTERDEPENDENCE OF HISTORIOGRAPHY, METHODOLOGY, AND INTERPRETATIONS

RAINER HUDEMANN

France still has the widespread reputation of having led a pure revenge policy in Germany in the early postwar years.[1] According to many authors, it was Allied pressure on France at the Moscow conference of foreign ministers in 1947, or Robert Schuman's plan for the European Coal and Steel Community (ECSC) in 1950, or the Elysée Treaty signed by General de Gaulle and Federal Chancellor Konrad Adenauer in 1963, that subsequently led to change in French policy, eventually allowing Franco-German reconciliation. The Nobel Committee referred to such a narrative when it awarded its Peace Prize to the European Union in 2012.[2]

Yet this image of French policy has been profoundly revised by broad historical research conducted over more than three decades.[3] It had long been underestimated how profoundly French international policies started to change from 1944–45 onward, creating the paradigm of crisis and cooperation that has characterized Franco-German relations until the present. This change resulted from French decision makers' efforts to understand the origins of the two world wars and from their willingness to determine the conditions for restoring France's international position. As early as late summer 1945, the democratization of Germany, aimed at preventing new wars by transforming German society, became the third pillar of French security policy alongside the traditional goals of military security and economic enhancement, which had failed to establish a durable Franco-German peace after 1919. From summer 1945 on, a partition of Germany was looming as a result not only of the emerging Cold War, but also of the creation of two reparation zones at the Potsdam

Conference and the rapid transformation of eastern German society by the Soviets. This only underlined the importance of a French contribution to forging a peaceful Western German society; international relations and reform of German society were thus intimately intertwined in the French approach to the German question, which from then on went far beyond the sheer issue of Germany's division.

It gradually emerged that historical analysis of France's attitude toward the German question after 1944–45 had to take into account a very large variety of domains simultaneously instead of isolating them from each other: from domestic to international politics, from diplomatic and military decisions to decision-making processes on the ground, from the dismantling of industrial plants to the physiology of nutrition, from currency and economic order theory to cultural policy, from informal structures of communication to specific decision-making processes, from so-called public opinion to administrative structures, from long-term experiences and stereotypes to innovative ideas and their origins after the two world wars. Only broad historical research of this kind can meet the methodological challenge of such complex situations and explain former misinterpretations.[4]

This chapter will first outline the advancement of this highly complex research process. We will then describe the contents of France's constructive policies in Germany, which are less widely known than its policies on the international level. The following section will analyze the underpinnings of the constructive political concepts and practices that characterized France's German policies. Finally, we will explore the interconnections between the international and the binational levels of these policies. As the international level is the priority in this volume, basic level and fundamental consequences of occupation policy, which are less known but have generated fundamental findings relevant to the international level, will be emphasized.[5]

Traditional Interpretations and Their Limits

According to the traditional approach, French policy essentially included the following components: dismembering Germany, separating the left bank of the Rhine, taking revenge for German warfare and war crimes, reinstating the security measures of 1919,[6] resorting to obstruction in the Allied Control Council (the quadripartite governing body in Berlin) regarding measures concerning Germany as a whole, and strictly controlling German politics and administration.

Wilfried Loth summarized the traditional assumptions in 1983 by distinguishing between two contrary concepts: domination, following the *Erbfeindschaft* (hereditary enmity) tradition, and integration, represented by de Gaulle and the French resistance.[7] But in reality, it was precisely the interconnection and interaction between such apparently contradictory elements that created the dynamics of Franco-German rapprochement and cooperation in the second half of the twentieth century. Already in 1962, the first general survey of French occupation by Frank Roy Willis differentiated among the various policies pursued by France after 1945.[8] Raymond

Poidevin and, in the following generation, Georges-Henri Soutou, among others, have discussed the validity of some of these elements early on.[9] Over time, most of the features that have been attributed to French policy proved to be if not outright wrong, then at least far more complex or ambivalent, and reflecting only a minor part of France's actual policies on the ground.[10]

Several factors explain this. "Filters of perception," a term used by Hélène Miard-Delacroix in analyzing how, in the 1950s, old stereotypes (*les vieux démons*, or the old demons) fundamentally handicapped senior French officials in comprehending the profound changes Germany had been undergoing since the war, as illustrated first and foremost by French high commissioner André François-Poncet himself.[11] But such filters were (and continue to be) effective on the German side as well. They have multiple origins. The myth of Franco-German Erbfeindschaft (which was of course an invention of the 1870s) was a powerful factor in German expectations toward French behavior after the German capitulation on 8 May 1945, and it remained strong in German and French media as well as in aspects of historiography for a long time. Nazi propaganda had anticipated a policy of annihilation, if not extermination, in case of Allied victory, a policy that had in fact been Nazi policy throughout great parts of Europe just previously. So when a famine occurred in Germany in 1946, even the Hartmannbund (the leading group representing German doctors) denounced what they represented as an Allied war by famine against Germany. In fact, the exact opposite was the case. Famine and black market were the consequence of the total breakdown of the hidden, silent, and amateurish Nazi economic and financial policies, and of the end of the exploitation of the occupied countries during the war.[12] France, itself suffering from scarce nutrition, could not provide nutrition parcels as did the United States, a situation that seemed to confirm the erroneous interpretation of French exploitation policy. The destruction of southwestern Germany in the seventeenth century Palatine wars of Louis XIV—the ruins of the Heidelberg castle are famous throughout the world—was as rooted in collective memory as the struggles with Napoleon and the sometimes authoritarian behavior of French troops during the occupation of the Rhineland after 1919. These and other deeply engrained memories prepared the ground for efficient filters of perception: people often saw the policy they expected to see, and in their discourses of memory many recounted what they "saw," and not what was really happening.

A second issue relates to sources. The interpretation of French policy with regard to Germany has indeed been widely influenced by the use of American documents on post-1945 Germany (published from 1960 onward), creating at least two series of problems. First, the American perception of French policies has long been influenced by the French defeat of 1940, which turned the country into a minor partner in American—though less so in British—eyes, by an underestimation of French resistance against the Vichy regime (which the United States supported for a long time), and by the severe conflicts that pitted de Gaulle against the Anglo-Saxons in 1944–46 (whether during the invasion of Germany, in the conflict over Aosta, or in Lebanon and Syria). Because French archives were not yet accessible in the 1960s, American documents (and therefore U.S. positions) often served as a source for understanding French ideas and policies, thereby creating an important bias.

Second, Soviet policy and the process leading to the Cold War was analyzed more accurately by French diplomacy than by American diplomacy in 1945. Some historians like Ernst Deuerlein (whose erroneous idea of a systematic French policy of obstruction in the Allied Control Council is still influential) were prone to read these American sources based on their own prejudices while, in fact, a thorough reading and evaluation of these documents could and should have led much sooner to a far more nuanced view of French policy on an international level.[13] The discovery that the French government in its own zone implemented certain important decisions of the Allied Control Council that the British and Americans had refused—for example, the fundamental reform of social security concerning the whole population—gave the impetus for a thorough reexamination of French texts and policy on the quadripartite level, taking seriously the French conception of central Allied offices for administering a unified Germany.[14] At the same time, Paris was—like London but unlike Washington—acutely aware of Soviet efforts to secure unilateral control of the German-headed central agencies they had created starting in June 1945 in Berlin.

A third issue stems from translation and ambivalence. Filters of perception are more difficult to identify when they contribute to simplified or inaccurate translations. One characteristic example is de Gaulle's famous 1945 statement, "Plus de Reich centralisé" (no more centralized Reich), which has been frequently used as evidence of an alleged French policy of dismembering Germany. Although a grammatically accurate reading of this phrase points to the acceptance of a Reich, albeit one with a decentralized, federal structure, the fear of a dismembering of Germany often (and wrongly) influenced—and still influence—interpretations of the phrase in the sense of an annihilation of the Reich altogether, followed by the installation of a federation of independent states. But, in fact, establishing several independent German states was primarily an American concept, not a French one.[15]

A fourth issue revolves around discourse and actual policies. A main criterion for interpreting the former must be analyzing the latter; texts alone are not sufficient. It is therefore important to distinguish between the public proclamations that are relevant for policy, and those that are not significant. When the public speeches of de Gaulle in the occupation zone in October 1945 giving orders for Franco-German cooperation in order to materially and morally reconstruct Germany were followed by precise orders of the military government and a long series of concrete realizations, such speeches were not mere rhetoric, but must be taken seriously.[16] De Gaulle often used voluntarily ambiguous formulations aiming at maintaining his future freedom of action; for historians, the use of such language by de Gaulle reinforces the obligation to take into account effective policy (more on this below). And decision-making processes were multilevel in Paris, as Hüser analyzes. Some isolated quotations are therefore not sufficient for explaining highly complex political evolutions.

Finally, a fifth issue concerns state-building and circular arguments. France was a fully functioning state in 1945, while Germany was in a state of complete defeat (*debellatio* in international law); it was only in 1949 that two new German states were created.[17] As a result there was no capital in Germany before 1949, which reinforced a tendency—particularly at the level of research on international relations—to consider 1945–49 as a rather unimportant period. This has fed a circular reasoning on the bilateral as well as on the international level of analysis in which the profound innovation that took place in French policies during these years was systematically underestimated. All these complexities contribute to the explanation of why the topic remains controversial.

A Body of Constructive Work under Conditions of Occupation and Conflict[18]

The evolution of historiography was not only (and in the beginning not even primarily) a consequence of the increasing access to archives; methodological innovation, a better understanding of the politicized character of contemporary judgements, and a growing mental distance from old stereotypes were also significant factors. Yet most of the new parameters for analysis simply came from the sources.

Immediately after 1945 a decisive shift in French reflections about Germany took shape. Joseph Rovan (who had survived the Dachau concentration camp and took over responsibility for adult education in the military government of the French zone) and Alfred Grosser (who launched the Comité français d'échanges avec l'Allemagne nouvelle), became and remained for decades leading figures when it came to supplying information that did not rely on old stereotypes, but instead analyzed contemporary West Germany. Among other intellectuals and academics, they gradually began to gain a profound influence on politics and civil society.[19] The monthly review *Documents/Dokumente*, providing information about the two countries, started appearing on 1 August 1945, and continues in German until the present.

Culture is a domain that has constituted the main field of investigation since the 1960s and 1970s and has been assessed the most positively by contemporaries and researchers. French cultural policy in occupied Germany included profound democratic school reform, high-quality theatre, the intensive use of cinema, the creation of the radio stations Südwestfunk and Saarländischer Rundfunk (which both, e.g., greatly encouraged contemporary composers), the early reopening of the universities of Tübingen and Freiburg—on personal order of de Gaulle—and the (re-)founding of the universities of Mainz (which had declined after 1800) and the Saarland. French cultural achievements in postwar Germany thus were spectacular. The Directorate of Fine Arts, headed by the esteemed medievalist Michel François, was established within the central military government of the zone in fall 1945. It organized—using the internal justification of the government's order to democratize Germany in order to get the necessary credits—fifty exhibitions on literature, history, art history, and modern art from 1945 to 1949. The main exhibition of contemporary painting alone attracted more than one hundred thousand visitors in all zones of occupation.[20] Heinrich Küppers for school reform, Monique Mombert and Jacqueline Plum for the youth movements, and Corine Defrance for the general framework of cultural policy and later the universities rank as particularly productive authors in this field.[21]

Trade unions did not constitute just a means of control, but also an important instrument for democratizing German society and politics, as Alain Lattard has shown for Rheinland-Pfalz and Hans-Christian Herrmann for Saarland.[22] Anne-Katrin Kusch and subsequently Edgar Wolfrum have produced important research on political parties in which they have shown that control was equally interwoven with deliberate democratization. Democratic constitutions for the newly created Länder (regional states) and communal institutions were a central issue for the French government, preparing since 1945–46 in detail a future federal constitution for the Western zones before the British and Americans did.[23] Stephan Schölzel made clear early on that censorship was not the main characteristic of press policy, whose priorities were, by contrast, to support pluralism and democratization.[24]

Investigating social policy has provided a particularly broad perspective on the interdependence of a multitude of levels: the international level in the Allied Control Council, the regional level of the zone, and the local level. Except for Saarland, this aspect of French policy was until the 1960s and 1970s completely forgotten.[25] France started a fundamental reform of the German social security system in 1945, dismantling class differences inherited from the nineteenth century, with a direct impact on the whole population; the FRG cancelled that system in 1949-52 under pressure from special interests, but applied it de facto little by little during the following decades until the final health insurance reform in 1994. Support for war victims (aimed at demilitarization), the disabled, and victims of Nazism, as well as worker participation in industry, were some of many tangible results of these policies. (The exception was worker participation in Saarland, where French entrepreneurial traditions prevented it while family policies were particularly generous in accordance with French domestic policies.) Most of these social reform policies went far beyond the achievements of the British and American military governments in those fields; in some areas, such as social security, worker participation, or compensation for war victims, they went even farther than the policies of the FRG in the 1950s and1960s.

These and many other achievements were illustrations of what increasingly became a vast array of social and democratization policies—policies that were at the core of France's willingness to influence German society and must be seen in retrospect as a fully fledged component of post-1945 French security policy toward Germany occurring under conditions of strict control and in a conflictual context. True, Klaus-Dietmar Henke, in his study on denazification, claims that the constructive elements in French policies really amounted to a "Politik des als ob" (the policies of "as if")—in other words, policies designed to appear constructive in order to disguise an even harsher exploitation and control; and Angelika Ruge-Schatz criticized the new school text books as reactionary and full of zealous Jacobinism.[26] Still, the mass of new findings and subsequent research in additional fields have confirmed the new interpretations from the late 1980s on; thus Rainer Möhler showed that denazification enhanced democratization through a particularly interesting approach, one that refused American formalism and searched to encourage individual responsibility independently of administrative positions.[27]

So how are these initiatives to be explained? Some of them were simply incompatible with the image of pure economic exploitation because they were extremely costly, such as care for war victims, a program that ran the risk of amounting to half of the budget of the Land of Baden, thus contradicting French economic interests as a result of skyrocketing direct occupational costs. Other initiatives were incompatible with the contemporary perception of French obstruction in the Allied Control Council. As we can see, more and more questions were raised by those who started working in the archives in the 1970s and 1980s as they continuously uncovered new elements in French policy toward occupied Germany.

Basic Structures of Constructive Policies

By the mid-1980s the state of research allowed historians to systematize a wide spectrum of factors contributing to an explanation of these policies. Motivation of administrators on the ground is a classical phenomenon: from Roman pro-consuls to General Resident Hubert Lyautey in Morocco in the 1910s and 1920s, they have frequently tended to defend their "subjects" against central directives. Likewise, on the level of the French zone, individuals in charge have worked constructively and intelligently. Often they were young and aspired to enhancing their careers—and starving the population they administered would not have been the best evidence of their efficiency. Meanwhile strict control of German administration and policies often provided a good knowledge of the country, producing a sort of Franco-German socialization under conflictual conditions. Many former occupation officers still recalled this phenomenon decades later. Occupation thus forged a human capital in—conflictual or nonconflictual—cooperation on extremely difficult matters during the reconstruction of a largely devastated Europe and particularly of France and Germany. Thousands of administrators participated in this process, and many of them would succeed in brilliant careers subsequently. Most of these careers were not confined to the Franco-German sphere in the narrow sense; indeed, the occupation forged the background for wider Franco-German cooperation in the following decades, be it in the construction of European integration, in diplomacy, industry, culture, military, and many other activities. Having known this partner and his problems in difficult circumstances created the base for further common work, resulting particularly in the Elysée Treaty in 1963.

The French zone of occupation had been carved out after Yalta at the expense of the initially projected British and American zones, and it was made of two geographically separate parts; it had no central administration at its disposal, and all existing administrations were located in one of the other three zones. While the British and Americans could use the German administrative structures in their own zones, the French military government was forced to act directly; administrators were therefore in a position to put innovative ideas into practice, for instance by encouraging functionalist urban planning according to Le Corbusier in opposition to Nazi architecture and urban planning, or by transferring to Germany the social security reforms being simultaneously implemented in France.

The economic prerequisite for a German contribution to the reconstruction of France was the prior reconstruction of German industrial plants, railways, roads, tunnels, and bridges; a majority of this work on infrastructure, which constituted the key element for unblocking German economic recovery, was done by the French army. The very controversial dismantling of industry—decided on not by France but by the Allied Control Council, except for wild dismantling during the first weeks of 1945—in fact did not greatly benefit France, as Sylvie Lefèvre has shown. Christoph Buchheim has even established that France, which paid for 80 percent of all the products imported from the zone in dollars and paid 100 percent from 1947 onward (a fact largely overlooked by research for decades), in many senses exploited itself: with its scarce dollars, it could have purchased many products, needed more urgently than the goods imported from its German zone, on the world market.[28] In French entrepreneurial activities in Germany and in general economic policy, Jean-François Eck and Martial Libera have detected a fundamental opposition between the government and entrepreneurs, deepening our general knowledge of French positions and concrete measures: many leading French industrialists hoped to conquer the German market, sometimes producing long-term structures of cooperation (structures that remained particularly efficient in the Saarland region analyzed by Armin Heinen); these industrialists were often more interested in gains from their plants than in such constructive structures, however. Meanwhile, from 1945 onward important forces in Paris as well as in the military government in the occupation zone pursued a long-term policy based on preserving the economic potential of the zone instead of plundering it. To senior officials as to de Gaulle himself, it was self-evident that France needed Franco-German structures in the future in order to maintain its own position as a Great Power; thus reconstruction in Germany served reconstruction in France as well as French interests generally, which led to the 1950 Schuman Plan.[29] Bureaucratic control, perceived by the German side as further evidence of a policy of exploitation, in fact struck French and German entrepreneurs in the same way: it was intended to protect the zone's industrial potential and to take care of foreign currency supply through exports, a supply that was indispensable for allowing the German population to survive.[30]

Decentralization and geographic differences must also be taken into account. The separation of the French zone from the other zones and the separation between the Länder that were founded in the French zone was in fact much less rigid than portrayed in public discourse. Ministers of the zone held regular joint conferences, deputies of the French zone participated in the debates of the Länder Council (provisional parliament) of the American zone located in Stuttgart, and so on.[31] Meanwhile French policy differed between the Länder of its zone. In Saarland, Paris hoped that, by means of self-determination, France would win over the population for long-term incorporation into France. While annexation was universally expected in French public debates but carefully avoided at the level of government policy, the Saarland's economy and currency were linked to the French system in 1948, maintaining an ambivalent political semiautonomy and separating it from the zone of occupation. On the international level, this constituted around 1954 the main unsolved problem between France and the FRG, hampering any advance in European integration; a majority rejected a European status in a referendum in 1955, and the territory was incorporated into the FRG in 1957.[32] Armin Heinen has shown the close connections among the regional, binational, and international levels, and in industry, economy, politics, society, mentalities, and memory. The particularly constructive but nevertheless controversial policy in this territory reflects a considerable French commitment to future cross-border structures, which continue to function even now. In Rheinland-Pfalz (created by France in 1946 on the left bank of the Rhine), as well as in southern Baden, Paris hoped to maintain a long-term influence. Paris wanted to integrate southern Baden with the northern part, situated in the U.S. zone, in exchange for the southern part of Württemberg in which France had no long-term interest. (In 1952 all parts were integrated in the newly created Land of Baden-Württemberg.)

The often complex relationships between the army and the administration also played an important role. Hardships resulting from requisition, particularly of food, were often attributable to the army, which was strongly criticized for this by senior officials like Claude Hettier de Boislambert, governor of Rheinland-Pfalz and personally very close to general de Gaulle, who regarded his colleagues as "locusts" constituting a danger to the entire French reconstruction policy in Germany—and he was right.[33] The conflicts between the army and the military government in charge of civil administration are one of the keys when explaining German and historiographic perceptions, particularly since these conflicts were kept hidden from the German public, which consequently imputed all hardships to official French policy and often continues to do so to this day. After 1949 these hardships were, for instance, frequently and furiously called in when the Bundestag discussed politics toward France.

As already mentioned, France did not obstruct the work of the Allied Control Council. Yet it (rightly) criticized the contradiction in the Potsdam agreement between the aims of political decentralization and economic unity of Germany, especially since the economic administration of Germany was to be entrusted to state secretaries, which are political positions in American and German terminology, while political centralization was refused according to the same Potsdam protocol. Administering a zone unable to subsist on its own production, France in its own interest wanted economic unity and thus central economic agencies, but not agencies headed by Germans. France's counterproposal of *bureaux alliés* (Allied offices) for these agencies was not accepted by its partners, though London agreed with Paris on the basic Potsdam contradictions. Both also feared that the Soviets would gain control of these agencies (whose foundation they had started in Berlin from June 1945 on) if they were headed by Germans—and subsequent East-West controversies in the Allied Control Council confirmed this apprehension. The view of French policy as one of obstruction derived from the above-mentioned American perceptions, particularly on the part of the charismatic but impatient General Clay, American deputy commander in chief, who wanted to get rid of technical complications in administering Germany.[34]

Paris or the French Zone?

When intensive historiographical debates started in the 1980s, it seemed to some historians—including this author—that the constructive aspects of French occupation were the result of an opposition, even a confrontation between intelligent people on the ground and intransigent policies at the level of the government in Paris. Subsequently, historical research focused again on the top level of government. In 1984 the French central government directives for French policy in Germany immediately after the war, which had been thought to be nonexistent, were discovered in the government archives. Until his resignation on 20 January 1946, they were drafted under de Gaulle's presidency as head of the Provisional Government of the French Republic (GPRF), the first of these on 20 July 1945.[35] Reconstituting the whole series, which is spread over several archives, brought to light almost fifty directives up to March 1946, covering all policy areas. Of course, these directives were not enacted word for word; the decision-making processes were much too convoluted for that to happen. Yet a considerable amount of constructive French measures in the zone turned out to have in effect been supported by Paris, if not ordered by de Gaulle himself. In the light of these directives, de Gaulle's long-forgotten first public speeches in Germany held after the war and, as mentioned above, when he visited the French zone on 3–5 October 1945, which might have been taken for pure rhetoric, appeared to have been decisive after all.[36] To the complete surprise of the heads of German governments, de Gaulle had appealed for cooperation in reconstruction, defining the latter as material, moral, political, and legal. Intentionally, he did not speak about the past, but about the future and old—particularly Napoleonic—traditions of shared Franco-German experiences. Two weeks later the military government had transformed these speeches into orders for all senior French agents throughout the zone as mentioned above: democratization was from then on a central term and aim of French policy in Germany.

In 1996 Dietmar Hüser published the first comprehensive analysis of the issue.[37] He included all diplomatic and official papers that were by then accessible, showing the impact of international conditions on French policy toward Germany as well as the multiple and often contradictory policy-making levels of that policy and the heavy influence of public opinion on it. He delineated the administrative structures and decision-making processes of these years in all their complexity and their voluntary or inevitable ambiguities. He showed that France had had a double German policy: a tough public discourse, reflecting the expectations of the French public and formulating maximalist negotiation positions vis-à-vis the Allies on the one hand, and highly differentiated and gradually evolving concepts combined with very constructive and concrete measures to achieve the two real priority goals of France on the other: these goals were the decentralization of Germany, and participation in the control of the potential of German heavy industry, particularly in the Ruhr basin (which was part of the British zone). French policy in the end did not constitute a failure: decentralization was achieved with the 1949 Grundgesetz, and economic control was enacted first via the International Authority for the Ruhr in 1949 and then via European integration policy as per the 1950 Schuman Plan, leading to the ECSC in 1952. This analysis seems all the more convincing since it clarifies many of the contradictions and ambiguities in the perception and practice of French policy that research had been struggling with previously. It confirms the narrow interdependence of French international policy and the policies applied in Germany itself since 1945. Ever since these fundamental findings were made, research has continued to enhance our knowledge in a wide range of domains. On the diplomatic level, for instance, Geneviève Rouche-Maelstaf, as well as Michael Creswell and Marc Trachtenberg have confirmed earlier findings.[38] Similarly, in recent years civil society has become a major topic in the study of Franco-German relations.[39]

Conclusion

In conclusion, in spite of profound internal political divisions, the French government expected the foundation of a West German state to take place very soon, and preparing a federalist structure for it counted among its two main political goals, together with ensuring access to the Ruhr production for itself. Both goals were achieved in 1949. The Cold War had made the partition of Germany very probable early on and, in effect, soon achieved it; meanwhile, Paris remained extremely suspicious of Soviet goals. Franco–(West) German rapprochement has been to some extent the work of motivated, often highly qualified, and sometimes visionary individuals. The long-term effectiveness of the results of their commitment is to be explained by a wide variety of clearly identifiable factors, contributing to a growing structural rapprochement. French concepts about security dating from 1919 had fundamentally evolved after World War II; the military and the economy were complemented as main pillars of security by a third pillar: democratization, conceived as a means to change the German soul—thought to be by nature militaristic, authoritarian, and imperialist—into that of good democrats who would consequently stop attacking their neighbors.[40] This explains the importance of cultural and social policies and in particular the considerable financial means invested in them. The multiple constructive elements in French "double policy" toward Germany were often hidden from the public as a result of the harsh rhetoric developed under the pressure of French public opinion, socioeconomic crisis, and hostile communist propaganda, yet they appear clearly in internal political concepts and in actual policy.[41] As early as summer and fall 1945, ideas and their implementation—voluntarily or not—gradually produced a conflictual but in the final analysis constructive cooperation, thereby initiating a process of forging the two countries together whose effects proved long-lasting.

Analysis of Franco-German relations has to simultaneously take into account the interdependency of all concerned domains: diplomacy, the military, Great Power politics and France's position in the world, economics, industry, mentality, and culture. The effectively implemented policies in Germany in all these fields must be understood as part of a very broad spectrum in which democratization pervaded society and political culture. Crisis and compromise, confrontation and cooperation, constitute an intrinsic element of Franco-German relations since 1945. The dynamics of this relationship owe a great deal to these apparently contradictory elements as they have emerged over the decades following the war. It could almost be stated as a general rule that, in the middle and longer term from 1945 on, conflicts have often produced an even deeper cooperation as a result of the intense work of compromise necessary to overcome them.

Rainer Hudemann is emeritus professor of contemporary history of Germany and German-speaking countries at Sorbonne University, Paris; and emeritus professor of contemporary history at the Saarland University, Saarbrücken, Germany. After studies of history, political science, and roman literatures and languages in Heidelberg, Kiel, Paris, and Trier, he received his PhD on the origins of parliamentary groups in France 1871–75 at Trier University (1976) and his habilitation on French occupation in Germany after 1945 (1984). Other fields of interest include transnational processes and memories, elites in international comparison, and international transfer in urban history from the nineteenth to the twenty-first century.

Notes

I thank Dr. Andrea Caspari, Princeton, MA, and Frédéric Bozo for the English language revisions of the script.

1. Leading historians have followed such perceptions, e.g., when Hans-Peter Schwarz characterized it as a "pitiless policy of revenge and security" (xxxvi), or when Theodor Eschenburg, speaking about

the French occupation zone where he had served as a deputy minister, characterized it as a "colony to be exploited."). See Schwarz, *Vom Reich*; Eschenburg, *Jahre der Besatzung*, 96. See also Ziebura, *Die deutsch-französischen*, 32–38.

2. The Nobel Peace Prize 2012 presentation speech reads in part: "In the first years after 1945, it was very tempting to continue along the same track, emphasizing revenge and conflict. Then, on the 9th of May 1950, the French Foreign Minister Robert Schuman presented the plans for a Coal and Steel Community." See the Nobel Peace Prize 2012 presentation speech by Thorbjørn Jagland, Chairman of the Norwegian Nobel Committee, Oslo, 10 Dec. 2012, "Award Ceremony Speech," http://www.nobelprize.org/nobel_prizes/peace/laureates/2012/presentation-speech.html (retrieved 28 Apr. 2016). The integrated Franco-German school textbook is another example, with biased quotations from de Gaulle ignoring his constructive public speeches (Le Quintrec and Geiss, "Deutschland und Frankreich - wie aus Feinden Partner wurden [1954–1963]").

3. For an early reappraisal, see Hudemann, "Französische Besatzungszone." At this time it still—wrongly—seemed that constructive policies in the occupation zone differed from international policies on the Paris level.

4. Dietmar Hüser has applied the broadest methodical approach to these years based on archival research (Hüser, *Frankreichs "doppelte Deutschlandpolitik"*). For an early multidimensional approach see Hudemann, *Sozialpolitik*. Because this was the first book based on German and French archives simultaneously, restriction to a sectoral approach was necessary; social policy was chosen because it touched nearly every aspect of French policy at the time.

5. Detailed bibliographies and analyses are presented in Defrance and Pfeil, *Entre guerre froide*, and Miard-Delacroix, *Le défi européen* (both also published in German as part of the Franco-German History project, edited by the German Historical Institute Paris). See also Françoise Berger's contribution in this volume, coordinated with the present chapter.

6. The security measures were supposed to include the prioritization of military security and the weakening of the German economy and industry, favoring French superiority and European reconstruction through the exploitation of the occupation zone and the imposition of a rigorous decentralization, including the rejection until 1949 of any trans-zonal institutions and even communications within the zone as well as on the inter-zone level.

7. Loth, "Die Franzosen."

8. As a Californian, Willis may have had a more detached view of the subject than Loth. See Willis, *The French in Germany*; and Schreiner, *Bidault*.

9. See Bariéty and Poidevin, *Frankreich und Deutschland*; Poidevin, *Robert Schuman*; Poidevin, "Frankreich und die Ruhrfrage"; Poidevin, "Die französische Deutschlandpolitik"; Poidevin, "La politique allemande de la France"; Soutou, *La Guerre de cinquante ans*; Soutou, *L'Alliance incertaine*; and many other works, including Soutou, "Frankreich und die Deutschlandfrage"; Grosser, *Affaires extérieures*; Kessel, *Westeuropa und die deutsche Teilung*; Kraus, *Ministerien für das ganze Deutschland?*; Guillen, *La question allemande*. For additional information about these early findings and new approaches, see Hudemann, "Revanche ou partenariat?"; Hudemann, "L'occupation française." For the internal French debates, see Loth, *Sozialismus und Internationalismus*.

10. The published French diplomatic documents enable a large readership to follow this complex evolution based on first-hand sources: MAE, DDF.

11. Miard-Delacroix, *Question nationale allemande*.

12. See Hudemann, *Sozialpolitik*, 49–107. For a theory of the black market as partial explanation of political reactions and stereotypes, see Hudemann, "Techniques de la politique."

13. Deuerlein, "Frankreichs Obstruktion."

14. Hudemann, *Sozialpolitik*, 140–206; Hudemann, "La France et le Conseil de Contrôle"; Hüser, *Frankreichs "doppelte Deutschlandpolitik,"* 518–59.

15. For details about the complex discussions and President Roosevelt's evolving positions, see, e.g., Backer, *The Decision to Divide Germany*, 16–27.

16. See the detailed analysis by Hüser, *Frankreichs "doppelte Deutschlandpolitik,"* 433–51.

17. Thus the edition by Klaus Hildebrand and Horst Möller begins in 1949 (Hildebrand and Möller, *Die Bundesrepublik Deutschland*). For an analysis on the diplomatic level, see Lappenküper, *Die deutsch-französischen Beziehungen*.

18. A variety of major conferences since the 1970s have revealed the findings of many more scholars than can be quoted in this article: Scharf and Schröder, *Die Deutschlandpolitik Frankreichs*; Vaillant, *La dénazification par les vainqueurs*; Institut français de Stuttgart, *Die französische*; Knipping, Le Rider, and Mayer, *Frankreichs Kulturpolitik*; Manfraß and Rioux, *France–Allemagne*; Loth and Picht, *de Gaulle, Deutschland*; Hudemann and Poidevin, *Die Saar*; Jurt, *Die "Franzosenzeit"*; Jurt, *Von der Besatzungszeit*; Rauh-Kühne and Ruck, *Regionale Eliten zwischen*; Martens, *Vom "Erbfeind" zum "Erneuerer"*; Clemens, *Kulturpolitik*; Krebs and Schneilin, *L'Allemagne*; Wilkens, *Die deutsch-französischen Wirtschaftsbeziehungen*; Hudemann, Jellonnek, and Rauls, *Grenz-Fall*; Miard-Delacroix and Hudemannn, *Wandel und Integration*; Defrance, *Wege der Verständigung*.

19. Grosser, *L'Allemagne*; Grosser, *La joie et la mort*; Picard, *Des usages de l'Allemagne*.

20. Schieder, *Im Blick des Anderen*.

21. Defrance, *La politique culturelle*; Defrance, "Eléments d'une analyse"; Defrance, *Les Alliés occidentaux*; Heinen and Hudemann, *Universität des Saarlandes*; Mombert, *Sous le signe*; Zauner, *Erziehung und Kulturmission*; Baginski, *La politique religieuse*; Fassnacht, *Universitäten am Wendepunkt?*; Küppers, *Bildungspolitik im Saarland*; Plum, *Französische Kulturpolitik*; Woite, *Zwischen Kontrolle und Demokratisierung*; Zimmermann, Hudemann, and Kuderna, *Medienlandschaft Saar*. For additional titles see Françoise Berger's contribution in this book.

22. Lattard, *Gewerkschaften und Arbeitgeber*; Herrmann, *Sozialer Besitzstand*.

23. Hudemann, "Zentralismus und Dezentralisierung.

24. Kusch, *Die Wiedergründung*; Wolfrum, *Französische Besatzungspolitik*; Küppers, *Staatsaufbau*; Heil, "*Gemeinden sind wichtiger*"; Schölzel, *Die Pressepolitik*. For economy and industry, see the contribution of Françoise Berger in this volume.

25. Hudemann, *Sozialpolitik*; Hudemann, "Anfänge der Wiedergutmachung."

26. Ruge-Schatz, *Umerziehung und Schulpolitik*.

27. Henke, *Politische Säuberung*; Henke, "Politik der Widersprüche"; Möhler, *Entnazifizierung*; Grohnert, *Die Entnazifizierung*.

28. Lefèvre, *Les relations économiques*; Buchheim, *Die Wiedereingliederung*; Lorentz, *La France et les restitutions allemandes*.

29. Broad evidence in Hüser, *Frankreichs "doppelte Deutschlandpolitik,"* 316–65 (for the economic department of the Quai d'Orsay), 365–404 (for the responsible ministries).

30. Eck, *Les entreprises françaises*; Libera, *Un rêve de puissance*; Heinen, *Saarjahre*.

31. Hudemann, "Zentralismus und Dezentralisierung."

32. Hudemann and Poidevin, *Die Saar*; Heinen, *Saarjahre*.

33. Memorandum by Governor Hettier de Boislambert; private archives of Claude Hettier de Bolislambert.

34. Hudemann, *Sozialpolitik*, 140–206; Hudemann, "La France et le Conseil de Contrôle"; Hüser, *Frankreichs "doppelte Deutschlandpolitik,"* 518–28. This is one example of many fields where the published American archives had clearly shown much more differentiated French positions than appeared in historiography.

35. Source published by Hudemann, "Gouvernement provisoire de la République française"; published online: Hudemann, "Lehren aus dem Krieg"; source also published in MAE, DDF 1945, 116–31; broad contextualization in Hüser, *Frankreichs "doppelte Deutschlandpolitik,"* 405–33.

36. The first of them, in Saarbrücken on 3 October 1945, is published in the *Le Monde*; see Hudemann, Heinen, Großmann, and Hahn, *Das Saarland zwischen Frankreich*, 238–39.

37. Hüser, *Frankreichs "doppelte Deutschlandpolitik."*

38. Maelstaf, *Que faire de l'Allemagne?*; Creswell and Trachtenberg, "France and the German Question."

39. Defrance, *Wege der Verständigung*.

40. Hudemann, "Kulturpolitik im Spannungsfeld."

41. Hüser, *Frankreichs "doppelte Deutschlandpolitik."*

Bibliography

Backer, J. H. 1978. *The Decision to Divide Germany: American Foreign Policy in Transition*. Durham, NC: Duke University Press.

Baginski, C. 1997. *La politique religieuse de la France en Allemagne occupée 1945–1949*. Villeneuve-d'Ascq, France: Septentrion.

Bariéty, J., and R. Poidevin. 1982. *Frankreich und Deutschland: Die Geschichte ihrer Beziehungen 1815–1975*. Munich, Germany: Beck.

Buchheim, C. 1990. *Die Wiedereingliederung Westdeutschlands in die Weltwirtschaft 1945–1958*. Munich, Germany: Oldenbourg.

Buffet, Cyril, 1991. *Mourir pour Berlin. La France et l'Allemagne 1945–1949*. Paris: Colin.

Clemens, G., ed. 1994. *Kulturpolitik im besetzten Deutschland 1945–1949*. Stuttgart, Germany: Steiner.

Creswell, M., and M. Trachtenberg. 2006. "France and the German Question, 1945–1955." *Journal of Cold War Studies* 5, no. 3: 5–28.

Defrance, C. 1991. "Eléments d'une analyse de la politique culturelle française en Allemagne à travers son financement." *Revue d'Allemagne* 4, no. 23: 499–518.

———. 1994. *La politique culturelle de la France sur la rive gauche du Rhin 1945–1955*. Strasbourg, France: Presses universitaires de Strasbourg.

———. 2000. *Les Alliés occidentaux et les universités allemandes 1945–1949*. Paris: Editions du Centre national de la recherche scientifique (CNRS).

———, ed. 2010. *Wege der Verständigung zwischen Deutschen und Franzosen nach 1945. Zivilgesellschaftliche Annäherungen*. Tübingen, Germany: Narr.

Defrance, C., and U. Pfeil. 2012. *Entre guerre froide et intégration européenne: Reconstruction et rapprochement 1945–1963*. Villeneuve d'Asq, France: Presses du Septentrion.

Deuerlein, E. 1971. "Frankreichs Obstruktion deutscher Zentralverwaltungen 1945." *Deutschland-Archiv* 4: 466–91.

Eck, J.-F. 2003. *Les entreprises françaises face à l'Allemagne de 1945 à la fin des années 1960*. Paris: Comité pour l'histoire économique et financière de la France.

Eschenburg, T. 1983. *Jahre der Besatzung 1945–1949*. Stuttgart, Germany: Deutsche Verlags-Anstalt.

Fassnacht, W. 2000. *Universitäten am Wendepunkt? Die Hochschulpolitik in der französischen Besatzungszone 1945–1949*. Munich, Germany: Alber.

Grohnert, R. 1991. *Die Entnazifizierung in Baden 1945–1949*. Stuttgart, Germany: Kohlhammer.

Grosser, A. 1953. *L'Allemagne de l'Occident*. Paris: Gallimard.

———. 1984. *Affaires extérieures. La politique de la France 1944–1984*. Paris: Flammarion.

———. 2011. *La joie et la mort. Bilan d'une vie*. Paris: Presses de la Renaissance.

Guillen, P. 1996. *La question allemande 1945–1995*. Paris: Imprimerie nationale.

Heil, P. 1997. *"Gemeinden sind wichtiger als Staaten" Die kommunale Neuordnung in Rheinland-Pfalz 1945–1957*. Mainz, Germany: v. Haase & Koehler.

Heinen, A. 1996. *Saarjahre. Politik und Wirtschaft im Saarland 1945–1955*. Stuttgart, Germany: Steiner.

Heinen, A., and R. Hudemann, eds. 1989. *Universität des Saarlandes 1948–1988*. Saarbrücken, Germany: Universität des Saarlandes.

Henke, K.-D. 1981. *Politische Säuberung unter französischer Besatzung. Die Entnazifizierung in Württemberg-Hohenzollern*. Stuttgart, Germany: Deutsche Verlags-Anstalt (DVA).

———. 1982. "Politik der Widersprüche. Zur Charakteristik der französischen Militärregierung in Deutschland nach dem Zweiten Weltkrieg." *Vierteljahrshefte für Zeitgeschichte* 30, no. 3: 500–37.

Herrmann, H.-C. 1996. *Sozialer Besitzstand und gescheiterte Sozialpartnerschaft. Sozialpolitik und Gewerkschaften im Saarland 1945 bis 1955*. Saarbrücken, Germany: Kommission für saarländische Landesgeschichte und Volksforschung.

Hildebrand, K., and H. Möller. 1997–99. *Die Bundesrepublik Deutschland und Frankreich. Dokumente 1949–1963*, 4 vols. Munich, Germany: Saur.

Hudemann, R. 1981. "Französische Besatzungszone 1945–1952." *Neue politische Literatur* 26, 325–60.

———. 1987a. "Anfänge der Wiedergutmachung: Französische Besatzungszone 1945–1950." *Geschichte und Gesellschaft* 13, no. 2: 181–216.

———. 1987b. "Kulturpolitik im Spannungsfeld der Deutschlandpolitik. Frühe Direktiven für die französische Besatzung in Deutschland." In Knipping, Le Rider, and Mayer, *Frankreichs Kulturpolitik*, 15–31.

———. 1987c. "Zentralismus und Dezentralisierung in der französischen Deutschland- und Besatzungspolitik 1945–1947." In *Die Kapitulation von 1945 und der Neubeginn in Deutschland*, edited by W. Becker, 181–209. Cologne, Germany: Böhlau.

———. 1988. *Sozialpolitik im deutschen Südwesten zwischen Tradition und Neuordnung 1945–1953. Sozialversicherung und Kriegsopferversorgung im Rahmen französischer Besatzungspolitik*. Mainz, Germany: v. Hase & Koehler.

———. 1989. "La France et le Conseil de contrôle interallié en Allemagne 1945–1947." *Revue d'Allemagne* 21, 235–56.

———. 1990. "Gouvernement provisoire de la République française. Document No. 1 (20 juillet 1945). Directives pour notre action en Allemagne." In *L'Allemagne occupée 1945–1949*, edited by H. Ménudier, 169–182. Brussels, Belgium: Complexe.

———. 1996. "Revanche ou partenariat? A propos des nouvelles orientations de la recherche sur la politique française à l'égard de l'Allemagne après 1945." In Krebs and Schneilin, *L'Allemagne 1945–1955*, 127–52.

———. 1997. "L'occupation française d'après-guerre dans les relations franco-allemandes depuis 1945." *Vingtième siècle* 14, no. 55: 58–68.

———. 2006. "Lehren aus dem Krieg. Neue Dimensionen in den deutsch-französischen Beziehungen nach 1945." http://www.europa.clio-online.de/2006/Article=160 (retrieved 28 Apr. 2016).

———. 2014. "Techniques de la politique économique et financière nazie, marché noir et émotions dans la mémoire Franco-allemande depuis 1945." In *Mémoire et émotions. Au cœur des relations internationales*, edited by A. Marès, M.-P. Rey, and A. Wieviorka, 31–40. Paris, Publications de la Sorbonne.

Hudemann, R., A. Heinen, J. Großmann, and M. Hahn. 2007. *Das Saarland zwischen Frankreich, Deutschland und Europa 1945–1957. Ein Quellen- und Arbeitsbuch*. Saarbrücken, Germany: Kommission für Saarländische Landesgeschichte und Volksforschung.

Hudemann, R., B. Jellonnek, and B. Rauls, eds. 1997. *Grenz-Fall: Das Saarland zwischen Frankreich und Deutschland 1945–1960*. St. Ingbert, Germany: Röhrig.

Hudemann, R., and R. Poidevin, eds. 1995. *Die Saar 1945–1955. Ein Problem der europäischen Geschichte/La Sarre 1945–1955. Un problème de l'histoire européenne*. Munich, Germany: Oldenbourg.

Hüser, D. 1996. *Frankreichs "doppelte Deutschlandpolitik": Dynamik aus der Defensive—Planen, Entscheiden, Umsetzen in gesellschaftlichen und wirtschaftlichen, innen- und außenpolitischen Krisenzeiten 1944–1950*. Berlin: Duncker & Humblot.

Institut français de Stuttgart, ed. 1987. *Die französische Deutschlandpolitik zwischen 1945 und 1949*. Tübingen: Attempto.

Jurt, J., ed. 1992. *Die "Franzosenzeit" im Lande Baden von 1945 bis heute. Zeitzeugnisse und Forschungsergebnisse*. Freiburg, Germany: Rombach Verlag.

———, ed. 1993. *Von der Besatzungszeit zur deutsch-französischen Kooperation/De la période d'occupation à la coopération franco-allemande*. Freiburg, Germany: Rombach Verlag.

Kessel, M. 1989. *Westeuropa und die deutsche Teilung. Englische und französische Deutschlandpolitik auf den Außenministerkonferenzen von 1945 bis 1947*. Munich, Germany: Oldenbourg.

Knipping, F., J. Le Rider, and K. J. Mayer, eds. 1987. *Frankreichs Kulturpolitik in Deutschland 1945–1950*. Tübingen, Germany: Attempto.

Kraus, E. 1990. *Ministerien für das ganze Deutschland? Der Alliierte Kontrollrat und die Frage gesamtdeutscher Zentralverwaltungen*. Munich, Germany: Oldenbourg.

Krebs, G., and G. Schneilin, eds. 1996. *L'Allemagne 1945–1955. De la capitulation à la division*. Asnières, France: Presses de la Sorbonne Nouvelle.

Küppers, H. 1984. *Bildungspolitik im Saarland 1945–1955*. Saarbrücken, Germany: Kommission für saarländische Landesgeschichte und Volksforschung.

———. 1990. *Staatsaufbau zwischen Bruch und Tradition. Geschichte des Landes Rheinland-Pfalz 1946–1955.* Mainz, Germany: v. Haase & Koehler.

Kusch, K. 1989. *Die Wiedergründung der SPD in Rheinland-Pfalz nach dem Zweiten Weltkrieg 1945–1951.* Mainz, Germany: v. Haase & Koehler.

Lappenküper, U. 2001. *Die deutsch-französischen Beziehungen 1949–1963: Von der "Erbfeindschaft" zur "Entente élémentaire,"* 2 vols. Munich, Germany: Oldenbourg.

Lattard, A. 1988. *Gewerkschaften und Arbeitgeber in Rheinland-Pfalz unter französischer Besatzung 1945 bis 1949.* Mainz, Germany: v. Haase & Koehler.

Lefèvre, S. 1998. *Les relations économiques Franco-allemandes de 1945 à 1955. De l'occupation à la coopération.* Paris: Comité pour l'histoire économique et financière de la France.

Libera, M. 2012. *Un rêve de puissance. La France et le contrôle de l'économie allemande 1942–1949.* Brussels, Belgium: Peter Lang.

Lorentz, C. 1998. *La France et les restitutions allemandes au lendemain de la seconde guerre mondiale 1945–1954.* Paris: Direction des archives et de la documentation du ministère des Affaires étrangères.

Loth, W. 1977. *Sozialismus und Internationalismus. Die französischen Sozialisten und die Nachkriegsordnung Europas 1940–1950.* Stuttgart, Germany: Deutsche Verlags-Anstalt (DVA).

———. 1983. "Die Franzosen und die deutsche Frage 1945–1949." In Scharf and Schröder, *Die Deutschlandpolitik Frankreichs,* 27–48.

Loth, W., R. Picht, eds. 1991. *De Gaulle, Deutschland und Europa.* Opladen, Germany: Springer.

Maelstaf, G., 2000. *Que faire de l'Allemagne? Les responsables français, le statut international de l'Allemagne et le problème de l'unité allemande 1945–1955.* Paris: La documentation française.

Manfraß, K., and J.-P. Rioux, eds. 1990. "France–Allemagne 1944–1947. Akten des 22. Deutsch-französischen Historikerkolloquiums." In *Institut d'histoire du temps présent , ed. Les Cahiers de l'Institut d'histoire du temps présent 13–14.* Paris: Institut d'histoire du temps présent.

Martens, S., ed. 1993. *Vom "Erbfeind" zum "Erneuerer": Aspekte und Motive der französischen Deutschlandpolitik nach dem Zweiten Weltkrieg, Sigmaringen.* Germany: Thorbecke.

Miard-Delacroix, H. 2004. *Question nationale allemande et nationalisme. Perceptions françaises d'une problématique allemande au début des années cinquante.* Villeneuve d'Asq, France: Septentrion.

———. 2011. *Le défi européen de 1963 à nos jours.* Villeneuve d'Asq, France: Presses du Septentrion.

Miard-Delacroix, H., and R. Hudemann, eds. 2005. *Wandel und Integration. Deutsch-französische Annäherungen der fünfziger Jahre/Mutations et intégration. Les rapprochements franco-allemands dans les années cinquante.* Munich, Germany: Oldenbourg.

Ministère des Affaires étrangères (MAE). 2003. *Documents diplomatiques français, 1944–1954* (DDF). Paris: Imprimerie nationale.

Möhler, R. 1992. *Entnazifizierung in Rheinland-Pfalz und im Saarland unter französischer Besatzung von 1945 bis 1952.* Mainz, Germany: v. Hase & Koehler.

Mombert, M. 1995. *Sous le signe de la rééducation. Jeunesse et Livre en Zone Française d'Occupation 1945–1949.* Strasbourg, France: Presses universitaires de Strasbourg.

Picard, E. 1999. *Des usages de l'Allemagne. Politique culturelle française en Allemagne et rapprochement Franco-allemand 1945–1963. Politique publique, trajectoires, discours.* http://tel.archives-ouvertes.fr/tel-002 67294/fr/ (retrieved 28 Apr. 2016).

Plum, J. 2007. *Französische Kulturpolitik in Deutschland 1945–1955. Jugendpolitik und internationale Begegnungen als Impulse für Demokratisierung und Verständigung.* Wiesbaden, Germany: Deutscher Universitäts-Verlag.

Poidevin, R. 1979. "Frankreich und die Ruhrfrage 1945–1951." *Historische Zeitschrift* 120, no. 2: 317–34.

———. 1983. "Die französische Deutschlandpolitik 1943–1949." In Scharf and Schröder, *Die Deutschlandpolitik Frankreichs,* 15–25.

———. 1985. "La politique allemande de la France en 1945." In *La victoire en Europe: 8 mai 1945,* edited by M. Vaïsse, 221–38. Paris: Editions Complexes.

———. 1986. *Robert Schuman, homme d'Etat 1886–1963.* Paris: Imprimerie nationale.

Rauh-Kühne, C., and M. Ruck, eds. 1993. *Regionale Eliten zwischen Diktatur und Demokratie: Baden und Württemberg 1930–1952.* Munich, Germany: Oldenbourg.

Ruge-Schatz, A. 1977. *Umerziehung und Schulpolitik in der französischen Besatzungszone 1945–1949.* Frankfurt, Germany: Peter Lang.

Le Quintrec, G., and P. Geiss, eds. 2006. "Deutschland und Frankreich - wie aus Feinden Partner wurden (1954–1963)." In *Histoire/Geschichte*, Vol. 3, *Europa und die Welt seit 1945*, edited by P. Geiss, D. Henri, and G. Le Quintrec, 296–297. Stuttgart, Germany: Klett.

Scharf, C., and H.-J. Schröder, eds. *Die Deutschlandpolitik Frankreichs und die Französische Zone 1945–1949.* Wiesbaden, Germany: Steiner.

Schieder, M. 2005. *Im Blick des Anderen: Die deutsch-französischen Kunstbeziehungen 1945–1959.* Berlin: Akademie Verlag.

Schölzel, S. 1986. *Die Pressepolitik in der französischen Besatzungszone 1945–1949.* Mainz, Germany: v. Haase & Koehler.

Schreiner, R. 1985. *Bidault, der MRP und die französische Deutschlandpolitik 1944–1948.* Frankfurt, Germany: Peter Lang.

Schwarz, H.-P. 1980. *Vom Reich zur Bundesrepublik Deutschland im Widerstreit der außenpolitischen Konzeptionen in den Jahren der Besatzungsherrschaft 1945–1949.* Neuwied, Germany: Luchterhand.

Soutou, G.-H. 1995. "Frankreich und die Deutschlandfrage 1943 bis 1945." In *Ende des Dritten Reiches— Ende des Zweiten Weltkriegs*, edited by H.-E. Volkmann, 75–116. Munich, Germany: Piper.

———. 1996. *L'Alliance incertaine. Les rapports politico-stratégiques Franco-allemands, 1954–1996.* Paris: Fayard.

———. 2001. *La Guerre de cinquante ans. Les relations Est-Ouest 1943–1990.* Paris: Fayard.Vaillant, J., ed. 1981. *La dénazification par les vainqueurs. La politique culturelle des occupants en Allemagne 1945–1949.* Lille, France: Septentrion.

Wilkens, A., ed. 1997. *Die deutsch-französischen Wirtschaftsbeziehungen 1945–1960/Les relations économiques Franco-allemandes 1945–1960.* Sigmaringen, Germany: Thorbecke.

Willis, F. 1962. *The French in Germany 1945–1949.* Stanford, CA: Stanford University Press.

Woite, S. 2001. *Zwischen Kontrolle und Demokratisierung. Die Sportpolitik der französischen Besatzungsmacht in Südwestdeutschland 1945–1950.* Schorndorf, Germany: Hofmann.

Wolfrum, E. 1991. *Französische Besatzungspolitik und deutsche Sozialdemokratie. Politische Neuansätze in der "vergessenen Zone" bis zur Bildung des Südweststaates 1945–1952.* Düsseldorf, Germany: Droste.

Zauner, S. 1994. *Erziehung und Kulturmission. Frankreichs Bildungspolitik in Deutschland 1945–1949.* Munich, Germany: Oldenbourg.

Ziebura, G. 1970. *Die deutsch-französischen Beziehungen seit 1945. Mythen und Realitäten.* 2e éd. Pfullingen, Germany: Günther Neske.

Zimmermann, C., R. Hudemann, and M. Kuderna, eds. 2010. *Medienlandschaft Saar von 1945 bis in die Gegenwart.* 3 vols. Munich, Germany: Oldenbourg.

CHAPTER 2

Economic and Industrial Issues in France's Approach to the German Question in the Postwar Period

Françoise Berger

Evaluating French policies toward Germany during the Allied occupation period after the war has long been difficult because of both countries' sensitivity toward economic and industrial issues. These aspects were seldom studied apart from their negative consequences in the French Zone of Occupation (ZFO). This contribution aims to review the existing research and knowledge on France's postwar economic policies toward Germany from the wartime Free France projects up to 1955.[1] It will highlight the importance of economic issues, which were far from being secondary for France. If a certain number of facts and explanations have long been established, recent historiography has enhanced the understanding of this policy area in the context of the beginnings of the Cold War.

Studying the economic aspects of France's attitude toward postwar Germany necessitates a multiplicitous approach. Such an approach must cover France's economic policies in relation to Germany, the economic problems related to the national and European reconstruction and its interferences with the Marshall Plan, the policy regarding control of Germany in the context of the Allied occupation—necessarily a policy of compromise—as well as the more autonomous economic policy practiced in the ZFO. This involves multiple, more or less autonomous scales of decision and action. It is also necessary to include the question of reparations (including coal deliveries), which were very important for a French economy that was facing many difficulties during the reconstruction period, in particular before the announcement of the Marshall Plan. The question of restitutions, which also involved economic consequences, is also concerned, though in a more marginal way.[2] Finally, we must consider the problem of foreign trade and the creation of new bilateral economic relationships in the context of the reconstruction and normalization of Europe.

Research on these economic issues started early and is still ongoing. With time, our understanding of the internal debates between the decision makers was deepened and prompted new perspectives on the periodization of these events. The context of the Cold War is clearly one of the reasons for the rather quick evolution of the French position, but the influence of the Europeanist circles was also important, leading to fast changes in the economic policy France carried out toward Germany. The position of economic milieus was also revised.

The first seminal writings on the topic showed that the French projects of 1945 had to adapt because of political and, above all, economic circumstances. First, it was necessary to take account of the three other Allies for the control of Germany (quadripartite agreements); then, starting in 1947, it became necessary to make concessions to the United States, which had set up the Marshall Plan. French historians initially presented French policy as eventually having had to yield to Anglo-Saxon pressure after a useless resistance.[3]

In the 1980s the opening of the French archives[4] allowed a certain number of advances in knowledge, and also led, in the 1990s, to some partial reconsideration of the former analyses. While some historians continued to highlight French concerns[5] about Germany, other authors[6] relativized this fear and insisted on equally major and early fears in relation to the behavior of the Union of Soviet Socialist Republics (USSR, or Soviet Union) as early as July 1945[7]—in other words, even before the real start of the Cold War.

Explanations must take the considerable complexity of the issue into account.[8] Contrary to the nonrealistic vision of French policy still defended by some, it should be stressed that political actors were in effect completely aware of the realities, even if this did not lead to a change in the official position of France, which—in a realistic way—had to take various elements into account, starting with public opinion and the country's urgent reconstruction needs.[9] Other works, focusing on the economic aspects, have explored the apparent ambiguities of a French policy caught between domestic and Allied constraints.[10] These works nuanced predatory interpretations[11] of the French attitude[12] by showing, for example, that if the production of the ZFO was partly oriented toward French needs, it was also partly focused on the needs of the ZFO itself. The question of the reparations and compensations was also linked to the general principles of French economic policy toward Germany.[13] Finally, we now know much more about the evolution of the French project for Germany up to 1949.[14]

Apart from the official approach, the actions of the economic milieus have also been studied, showing hesitations but also a certain amount of goodwill from French entrepreneurs, albeit slowed down by or lacking support from the French authorities.[15] This discrepancy between the political and industrial circles is particularly noticeable in the iron and steel industry, where, as early as 1946, relatively short-term objectives were being set regarding the rebuilding of an industrial cartel with Germany.[16] In 1949, when the Federal Republic of Germany (FRG, or West Germany) was created, what the French entrepreneurs feared above all was not German competition but the interventionism of the public authorities.[17]

These successive and complementary works thus refined and complexified the understanding of French economic policy toward Germany, first and foremost in terms of the chronology of the evolution (both public and secret) of France's approach to the German question, but also concerning the influence of the context, the constraints, and the objectives. These works made it possible to gain insight into the debates and the divergences among politicians as well as ministries. They also showed the differences between the various levels of French intervention (foreign policy, inter-Allied policy, policy in the ZFO). Finally, they led to a more realistic assessment (in spite of the persistent stereotypes) of the actual results of French policy, particularly in the ZFO.

Taking these elements into account, as well as the above-mentioned discrepancies between declared objectives and perceived realities, and the strong—internal and external—constraints, we are able to present a revised periodization of French economic policy toward Germany, whose evolutions do not follow the same rhythm as the more political aspects of the German question as seen from France. The broad outlines of this multiform economic policy are well-known even if the policy has not been studied as comprehensively as the security aspects. However, recent research has contributed to a better understanding of the question, and it brings to light the dichotomy between the discourse aimed at influencing French public opinion—which, in addition to a feeling of revenge, showed concern and lassitude facing the economic difficulties of the first postwar period—and the semiofficial but real evolutions taking place in the occupied zones, including secret negotiations with the Anglo-American Allies. Consequently, the general characterization of France's policies toward Germany has not been completely revised, but rather has been split into two categories: discourse and reality. We can find several examples of these discrepancies between official texts or declarations, and internal documents from the various ministries and authorities.[18]

What also arises is the need for parallel observation on the various levels of French economic policy. Such observation tends to reinforce the idea of an apparent ambiguity of that policy, but it also partly explains the contradictions by showing the different constraints on each level, and the amount of leeway given to the actors in the field. This constant change of scale must be accompanied by a fine periodization, which is not exactly the same for the general policy and for the policy concerning the ZFO. We can distinguish four main phases, including the last part of the war period, because that is the moment when the first French economic project for Germany was drawn up.

The Prehistory of the French Economic Project for Germany, 1942–45

We now know that, from 1942–43 to 1945, the National French Council, which was chaired by General Charles de Gaulle, gave rise to many projects with regard to France's policies toward Germany. These projects converged to some extent; priority was given to security, an aspect that seems to have been almost obsessional for de Gaulle[19] and for most of the political actors of the Resistance—an aspect that obviously was related to Germany's potential heavy industry production and, thus, of armament. As a result, attention was focused on the main economic areas, in particular the Ruhr, but also the whole of Rhineland-Westphalia as well as the Saarland. In these neighboring territories, the French state had ambitions of control, even of annexation, but it also had needs for coke supply. This simple equation was a source of friction: How could Germany compensate France, Belgium, or Great Britain without rousing fear of the reawakening of the industrial power that had led to the war? These interrogations took past experiences into account, because no one wanted a solution that could be harmful in the long term, as had happened in 1919.

By 1942 some possible solutions were outlined.[20] From 1943 onward the examination of the economic outlooks for the postwar period resulted in about ten projects.[21] Do these projects in effect amount to an overall policy of economic disarmament?[22] Be that as it may, security was the main focus, involving military disarmament and economic measures that would prevent any future rearmament of Germany.[23] The men and networks in charge of these various projects formed a rather homogeneous group of decision makers, in London or Algiers, but also in Paris, in the various administrations, which took part.[24]

Although the economic question was at the heart of these projects, contrary to what was long affirmed[25] no industrialists nor economists were consulted, not unlike what happened in the first postwar period when the government's plans were little appreciated in business circles because they did not take account of European geoeconomic realities.[26] The detachment of the Ruhr from German territory was undoubtedly the element that received the most support until February 1945, both among the French and among the Allies within the Inter Allied Armistice Study Committee.[27] Only the project carried by Pierre Mendès France did not involve this separation, yet it fell under an economic imperialist aim, like many of the other French projects, as it hoped to reverse the balance of power in the iron and steel-making industry to the benefit of France.[28] The case of Saarland, a major coal-providing territory (hence a very important asset for the European economy), was also in question, but it was treated in another way: the Saarland was separated from the German territory, and put under a French governor until the Saarland people chose in 1956, after long bilateral negotiations, to join Germany.[29]

All these projects wanted to weaken the defeated country, but René Mayer and Hervé Alphand's projects were definitely more moderate in scope. Among the lot, only one project clearly stood out, namely that of Jean Monnet, who advocated, from

1943 onward, an equal treatment with the objective of a complete European over-haul. Monnet's project, however, was too innovative to be taken seriously given the situation of France in 1943.[30] With the final victory against Germany in May 1945, the French provisional government (GPRF) could publicly proclaim its ambitions (i.e., to rebuild France's industry, particularly its steel industry) thanks to German coal and to the production limitations of defeated Germany—an approach that was similar to the one that France adopted after World War I.[31]

French Requirements and Allied Constraints, May 1945–May 1948

After the fall of the Third Reich, the economic policy that France was planning to carry out in Germany was already quite different from the early projects, but the debates continued: from July to September 1945 four other plans were refined.[32] Clearly, those advocating a very firm position had the upper hand, but they were far from the position of total intransigence that some continued to recommend.[33] Discussions with the Allies within the Inter Allied Armistice Study Committee also led to a note by the GPRF dated 7 July 1945, "Note on the economic and financial disarmament of Germany."[34] Following the very convincing argumentation of Creswell and Trachtenberg, we can make the assumption that while it advocated a very uncompromising stance, such a stance in fact no longer reflected the conceptions of the time, which had already moved to a more moderate approach to policies with regard to Germany; the meaning of disarmament has been somewhat inaccurately interpreted along the lines of a "total (both military and economic) disarmament." Similarly, the plans to separate the Ruhr area, at least after May 1945, were no longer taken very seriously.[35]

It was during the Potsdam Conference (17 July to 2 August 1945) that the new French authorities, having just gained control of the ZFO that was allotted to them, issued a first series of directives.[36] In them, they tried to define the priorities of France's action in Germany; the principal problem therein was the choice between helping reconstruction and maintaining security—in other words, between the possibility of counting on German reparations that left the possibility for a German economic recovery in the medium term, and the possibility of decreeing the economic disarmament of the country in order to obtain security in the long term.[37] French economic policy toward Germany was caught for months in this hesitation, even if, officially, it was the security requirement that prevailed.

Among the decisions made within the Allied Control Council was the industrial plan of 28 March 1946 that limited Germany's total industrial production to 50 percent of its level of 1938 (this level had not been reached yet). This question of the maximum level of German production was recurrent, because it quickly became obvious that production had to be increased in order for the German territories to attain self-sufficiency while still being able to ensure deliveries as compensations. The Allies did not want to finance Germany's subsistence in any way, but that country's economic and social situation was extremely difficult. This situation also led the French to develop their own position regarding reparations pursuant to the decisions made at the Potsdam Conference. True, French policy in this field was still not clearly defined in January 1947.[38] Yet a few months later, with the Cold War now under way (and after the French communist ministers had been ousted in May 1947), the French position seemed to evolve significantly and get closer to the U.S. and British positions: on 2 December 1947 Foreign Minister Georges Bidault explained that France "allows the principle of reparations to be taken from the current production, under the condition . . . that they not be used as a pretext for an excessive increase of the level of German industry."[39] Though Germany's competitive potential was undoubtedly one of the reasons—though not officially acknowledged—for the fear of such an "excessive increase," the limitation of Germany's industrial production was also seen as having potentially fatal consequences on the French and European industrial needs. In fact, on 5 December 1947 Bidault officially agreed to ease the restrictions and allow a production of 10 million–12 million tons of steel, whereas in March of the same year he had claimed that "steel [whose production was set at 7.5 million tons in March 1946] is among the first industries that will be permanently limited."[40]

French concerns with regard to German competition did not always appear in an obvious way in the public discourse. True, in March 1947 Bidault explained that the limitation of German steel production was justified not only for security reasons, but also "by the need to allow the peaceful countries to increase their own production and to reinforce their industrial power." He added, "If Germany needs more steel, its neighbors will be able to provide it."[41] Yet internal documents reflect, from very early on, a realistic understanding that it was simply not possible to block German industry for too long.

Meanwhile, on the question of creating a customs union between the Ruhr area and France, the French faced a wall of opposition from the Allies, who offered Saarland as a concession.[42] On 30 March 1947 Bevin declared himself favorable to the economic union of Saarland and France, and he reiterated this proposal to General Marshall, the U.S. secretary of State, on 10 April 1947.[43]

French Economic Policy in the ZFO

In the meantime, since the end of the war the French command had been facing concrete problems in the ZFO that were quite different from the concerns of the government in Paris. The military government of the ZFO was responsible, from September 1945 onward, of the "control of the German economy as a whole, within the French zone,"[44] with very broad powers in all economic sectors. The economic policy of the ZFO theoretically depended entirely on him. Thus, the French military authorities had designed, from the very first moments of the occupation, an economic policy and precise methods to carry it out. Implementation of the policy was not free of hesitations or blunders, but it was far from the accusations of being completely improvised or wanting to transform the ZFO into a kind of autarky.

The French military authorities aimed at a balanced management of the ZFO, both in order to allow deliveries to France and to prove that they were able to face this responsibility. The serious economic difficulties of the ZFO required compromises. Control of the German economy had a dual dimension: first, the French exercised tight control over all economic activities of the area, and second, they had the monopoly over foreign trade. But the head of the civil administration of the ZFO, Emile Laffon, also had to control the economy of the ZFO.[45] Therefore, there was a double set of internal tensions. Measures concerning the ZFO itself, divided between the military government led by General Koenig and the civil administration led by Laffon, often followed different priorities. The military government was more independent in its action[46] and furthermore, the two men were often in personal conflict. Thus, tensions between the official directives coming from Paris and the on-site needs led to situations that were difficult to manage. There emerged two types of policies for the ZFO: those decided in Paris, and the actions in the ZFO themselves by both Koenig and Laffon.

There were also a couple of local factors that made this situation even more complex. The administrative fragmentation of the ZFO, which comprised eight different units, made it much more difficult to manage than the other Allied zones. It was made up of whole or parts of preexistent regional units that did not have any administrative structure in common.[47] And there was another difficulty: even though, from a political point of view, France was opposed to an administrative centralization of Germany,[48] from an economic standpoint, the French authorities felt the need for a measure of coordination with the two other Western zones. Because the Potsdam agreements stipulate that "during the period of occupation, Germany shall be treated as an economic unit," a note from the French military headquarters stated as early as 15 December 1945, that "allowing excessive economic disparities to develop between our zone and its neighboring zones would be counterproductive and these disparities would most likely be interpreted as divergences of policy. Such divergences, indeed, should not occur, since the aims we are pursuing are the same ones as our Allies." The document also specified that the decisions made during the negotiations in Berlin would be strictly enforced in the ZFO.[49] Moreover, the same document explained that, insofar as the French did not have the necessary staff, it would be in France's best interest to allow a German administration to emerge, especially because they would be more able to impose "the obligations resulting from defeat" on the population. Economic disarmament was also mentioned; its main goal was the destruction of war factories and any factories essential in times of war.[50] Finally, because of the relatively low industrial potential of the FZO, it was necessary to maintain relationships with the other zones. Yet this made the situation even more complex, because the Allies used the French economic requests to gain leverage on political issues.[51]

The creation of the Anglo-American Bizone in January 1947, without French participation, is a perfect example of the contradictions between these two levels of action. France did not join the Bizone until June 1948: Although such a move was long hoped for by the administration in the ZFO, mostly for economic reasons, it was opposed by many in Paris. In January 1948 René Massigli, France's ambassador to London, complained to Jean Chauvel, the secretary general of the minister of foreign affairs, about Paris's attitude concerning the plan of merging the Allied zones.[52] General Koenig seemed open to the negotiation, but he did not want to precipitate it because the fusion would also have undesirable political consequences. When a reorganization plan of the Bizone was drawn up, the European department of the French Ministry of Foreign Affairs complained that it had not been consulted even though the planned reorganization, though primarily economic in scope, could, in the long term, have consequences on the political organization of Germany.[53] Massigli argued that, if France was interested in the Bizone, it should join it or else stop complaining about not being included. The ministry shared his opinion on the subject: "It is eminently regrettable that we delayed the fusion of our zone and the Bizone."[54] Even though the economic fusion between the ZFO and the two other Allied zones did not take place until June 1948, considerable changes in the objectives and discourses had started to appear in early 1948.

Observing the New Germany and Beginning Cooperation, June 1948–May 1952

From the agreement of 1 June 1948,[55] which initiated the process of the creation of a German federal state, the French position evolved quickly, both generally speaking as well as regarding economic policy in particular. Realism was now the order of the day: "The aim of the London agreements was the political and economic restoration of Germany," Robert Schuman declared.[56] The production restrictions (decreed for security reasons) were not abandoned; they would be facilitated by the new statute of occupation, starting from the creation of the FRG in May 1949.[57] The International Authority for the Ruhr, created on 28 December 1948, marked the beginning of a Franco-German economic and financial cooperation, in particular in the ZFO. From this time on, industrial dismantling in the name of reparations was clearly slowed down in the Bizone; France nevertheless continued this practice in spite of German protests—yet another ambiguous policy.

Starting in May 1948, and as a consequence of the Marshall Plan and the pressure from the Americans to include the Western part of Germany in the Western camp, we notice a complete reversal in the French official position on economic policy.[58] A note from the French Ministry of Foreign Affairs urged a change in the economic policy toward Germany and highlighted the importance of seeking European economic solidarity.[59] Almost at the same moment, the plan drawn up by the French Planning Commission (Commissariat au Plan) considered the potential contribution of a rebuilt Germany with which egalitarian economic relations could be restored.[60]

The European option was clearly favored, thanks not only to the Europeanist convictions of the majority of the decision makers of the time and to the growing influence of this thinking in public opinion, but also to realism. The new foreign minister starting in September 1948, Robert Schuman, was not a naive Europeanist: he remained on the defensive toward Germany. Yet Schuman was ready to implement a radical new policy; his arrival at the Quai d'Orsay, which quickly involved a change of staff, transformed the situation. His appointment (official as of 15 December 1948) of André François-Poncet, a close acquaintance of his, as adviser to General Koenig, was instrumental in changing French policies. (François-Poncet became high commissioner with the creation of the FRG, a position that he kept until the end of the occupation statute in 1955. He was the only one of the Allied high commissioners to remain in office throughout all this period.) As France's former ambassador to Berlin, François-Poncet knew prewar Germany quite well, and he was particularly interested in the economic issues.[61] He was experienced in negotiations in this field and was well informed about the evolution of Germany's economic situation from the beginning of the Allied occupation.[62] As a long-time Europeanist activist, he was representative of the dominant positioning of Schuman's entourage—and of their contradictions, because they were at the same time wary of a German recovery and intent on building a pacified Europe based on economic cooperation. In May 1948 François-Poncet took part in the Hague Conference that founded the European Movement, of which he was a very active member. His abundant diplomatic correspondence reflects the interrogations of an engaged Europeanist about French policy priorities and their evolution.[63] It shows that, from 1949 onward, things had clearly changed from an economic standpoint: the prospects for European construction were already present— particularly in the Schuman Plan, which counted on German economic power to be a pillar of this construction. The will for economic cooperation was stressed, but, at the same time, the fear of competition remained very present, in particular after the monetary reform that helped stabilize the German economy.

The French point of view is indeed often ambiguous concerning this cooperation. What dominates, however, in the writings of the ambassador are the security concerns. Schuman spoke of an "increasing discomfort" felt after the Petersberg agreements (November 1949): "We applied a new policy with old methods: i.e., we made many very large, important and well-intentioned concessions, but always bitterly negotiated, concessions wrest away from the reticent and mistrustful winners by a nation which had been defeated and was humiliated by having to beg for them."[64] In the economic domain, this resulted in the growing focus around the Ruhr problem (even though Germany had reluctantly agreed to join the International Authority for the Ruhr as a result of the Petersberg Agreement). Plans for dismantling German industry became even more controversial, especially toward the end of 1949. The French leaders were well informed of the agitation caused by the plans, in particular in Berlin, agitation that was encouraged by the widely divergent views of the Western Allies on this question. "In our opinion, it is quite likely that the imminent dismantling of the Borsig plants in Berlin will raise a wave of indignation against us and will be likely to cause incidents. Furthermore, the protest movement has the support of the industrialists and even of local civil servants."[65] Despite complaints, the French continued the dismantling (which shows the limits of American pressure), even if they did not directly reap any benefits from it, arguing that they were only applying the Allied group decisions. However, the French high commissioner's comments show that he understood Adenauer's position quite well: Adenauer was asking, in a moderate way, for a slowing down of the dismantling. François-Poncet wrote that Adenauer "was looking forward to starting negotiations with the Allies, and particularly with France, with the objective of substituting the dismantlings with a system which would establish a balance between Allied concerns on security issues, i.e., limiting Germany's war potential, and Germany's ability to fund the reparations."[66] This report, written in the characteristic style of François-Poncet, was his way of diplomatically calling for a change in the government's position and of pointing out the gap with the Allies on this issue.

At the time of the devaluation of the mark in October 1949, France was able to impose its point of view: it successfully recommended a rate of about 20.5 percent whereas the German federal government, backed by the American and British high commissioners had proposed a rate of 25 percent. The French found benefits in limiting the fall of the value of the mark for obvious trade reasons: the lower the mark, the more German products would be competitive against French products. The French high commissioner considered that, "without a doubt, this is a success for us."[67] The affair caused some tension within the high commission because it was a decision of major importance for the country "whose economic activity it must control and guide."[68] The actions taken by the high commission clearly show that France and its representative were able to maintain certain room for maneuver, particularly concerning economic affairs, in spite of the constraints previously discussed.

Even if German foreign trade was never really interrupted (although this issue had been a source of permanent conflict since the beginning of the French occupation)[69] it was then officialized and the new partners joined the negotiating table. It gave Germany a form of equality that was difficult for the French to accept, especially because Germany's quick economic recovery worried France, which was facing economic difficulties of its own. However, France required outlets for its agricultural and industrial production and wanted to purchase capital equipment produced in Germany, which, thanks to the quick recovery of the country's solid infrastructure, was of good quality and sold at competitive prices. Pushed by this need, it was therefore very tempting to turn to the FRG, in spite of the fear of helping it to reinforce its industry.[70] The easing of tensions happened very gradually. In consequence, although "the German authorities really wanted the first agreement that they were authorized to negotiate to be a Franco-German agreement,"[71] the first negotiations, similar to those that would follow throughout this period, were particularly tense, with sharp discussions, aggressive language, session adjournments, threats, and ultimatums of all kinds, with the Germans seen as the eternal culprit. These negotiations were difficult.[72] They nevertheless led to the first Franco-German trade agreement signed on 18 February 1950 (not yet a true treaty because German foreign trade was still under allied control) which provided for strictly defined quotas of product imports on both sides. This system was highly criticized by the Germans for its lack of economic liberalism and because they felt that the quota constraints would tamper with fair competition. The German economic liberal model was already quite different from the more statist French model.[73] Still, nearly 60 percent of the exchanges were liberalized, their full amount was doubled, the procedures were simplified and—this was the great innovation—the two countries used their respective currencies, the franc and the mark, which reduced the deficits in dollars to which they both were confronted (the dollar was used only as an accounting currency).[74] This agreement, which was valid for only six months (but thereafter regularly renewed for an identical period of time), was greeted with approval; the German press presented it as "a general rehearsal before free trade."[75] Even if this assertion was a little premature, bilateral exchanges quickly represented a significant part of both countries' foreign trade.[76]

The declaration of 9 May 1950 was the solution finally found by Schuman and Monnet to ease the tensions and put an end to the balancing act between negotiations and outdated requirements.[77] After almost a year of difficult negotiations,[78] it led to the signature of the Treaty of Paris creating a European Coal and Steel Community (ECSC) on 18 April 1951. After this date, there was a significant change of attitude illustrated, for example, by a clear evolution of the attitude of the Allied high commissioners toward German authorities, giving the federal government almost complete control and partly becoming a rubber stamp.

A Slow Normalization of Relations and the Final European choice, May 1952–May 1955

On 26 May 1952 the three Western powers signed a convention on the statute of the FRG, which granted it full sovereignty not only on national affairs, but also on international relations as a result of its entry into the new European Defence Community (EDC). The end of the occupation statute was swiftly anticipated and the French high commissioner even announced his impending departure months in advance.[79]

Yet in spite of the change of tone effective since the Schuman proposal, French public opinion remained opposed to the German rearmament under the guise of European projects, and this eventually led to the rejection of the EDC after long months of waiting (on 30 August 1954). Consequently, the agreement could not come into force and it was necessary to quickly find another solution. To that end, the agreements of Paris (October 1954) enabled the regularization of this situation as of the following year. In the meantime, the situation was rather strange. In practice,

Germany had already gained its equal treatment in the economic domain, and the ECSC had come into force 23 July 1952, but the Allied high commission was still not dissolved, even if its role was now reduced to keeping record of the decisions. As for the Saarland question, it remained present over the whole period because the problem was only solved in 1956 in favor of Germany. The economic questions were obviously decisive in this dispute, but they were far from being the only decisive ones. On 5 May 1955 the agreements of Paris of October 1954, which gave the new German republic its sovereignty, came into effect. The Allied high commissioners became ambassadors. From the commercial point of view, the two countries become each other's largest trading partners. The page of the postwar period could be turned.

To summarize, one must highlight the great disparities between the very rigid official discourses on France's economic approach toward defeated and occupied Germany, and the more realistic policies implemented by the French Ministry of Economy and in the ZFO. The image given by the harshness of French demands, at the beginning of the occupation period, simply does not correspond to the actual practices.

In this respect, the most recent research has made it possible to refine knowledge on the constraints brought by the nascent Cold War, on the apparent contradictions between the official objectives and the necessary adaptations on site, on the perception of the various scales of the implementation, as well as the internal dissensions between the decision makers, including the French administrations themselves. The Soviet danger—contrary to what was long asserted—was perceived quite early on (1945–46) and its influence on French policy is very clear, from the Marshall Plan onward. In other words, decision makers understood early on that the part played by the German economy in Europe's recovery and security (indirectly, through its financial contributions), was essential, considering Western Europe's new situation faced with the Soviet threat. If the French discourse remained very firm, it was not because of ideological differences, but because, even under those conditions, France did not want to give up anything it deemed necessary to its economic development and because politicians and decision makers believed that public opinion was still not ready for change.

Conclusion

France's economic policy toward Germany during the decade following the war has been reevaluated. It has been shown that it was a lot more constructive than we long thought, involving a quick and pragmatic acceptance of Germany's economic recovery starting in the beginning of the postwar period, because France (and Europe) definitely needed it for its own restoration. Thus, the context of the Cold war and anti-Soviet mistrust[80]—except among the communist circles—as well as the pressure from Europeanist groups, led the French governments to revise their policy in order to enable a true economic cooperation whose effects were felt rather quickly, as early as the first months of the FRG. In 1955 France thus became Germany's number one trading partner, and reciprocally. Furthermore, as of the following year the widened European economic project was promoted jointly by the Franco-German couple, which subsequently became the economic engine of European construction.

Françoise Berger is associate professor of contemporary history at the Institute of Political Studies (Grenoble, France). She is a member of the Commission for the Publication of French Diplomatic Documents (on World War II). Research topics: Franco-German economic and diplomatic relations in the twentieth century, economic and diplomatic aspects of World War II, European economic constructions, European industrial history. Recent publications: "Le haut-commissariat français et la nouvelle Allemagne (1949–1955)," in *Frankreich in Deutschland seit 1870: 150 Jahre diplomatische Präsenz*, edited by M. Aballea and M. Osmont (2017); "Le ministère français des Affaires étrangères face au blocus économique contre l'Allemagne: objectifs et stratégie," in *L'Industrie française dans la Grande Guerre*, edited by Fridenson (2018).

Notes

1. This contribution is complementary to Rainer Hudemann's contribution in this volume, which also covers the general historiography.
2. Unlike reparations, which were determined by an Allied commission to compensate for the losses of the victorious powers, the term "restitutions" refers to goods plundered during the war that are returned to their owners.
3. See Creswell and Trachtenberg, "France and the German Question."
4. France has the custody of the archives of the Allied Command (in Colmar until 2011, now in La Courneuve). See the very relevant remarks of Hudemann on the use of the archives in his contribution to this volume.
5. Poidevin, "Plan Marshall et problème allemand."
6. See, e.g., Hudemann, "L'occupation française en Allemagne."
7. Ibid., 232; Creswell and Trachenberg, "France and the German Question," 7–8.
8. Rainer Hudemann has insisted on this for a long time in various articles, and so have I in my previous research (see, e.g., Berger, *La France, l'Allemagne*). This point of view has been recently confirmed by Michael Creswell and Marc Trachenberg, even if their position does not enjoy unanimous support. See Creswell and Trachtenberg, "France and the German Question"; and Creswell and Trachtenberg, "New Light on an Old Issue?" See, in the same special issue of *Journal of Cold War Studies*, three contradictory answers to the former article.
9. Creswell and Trachenberg, "France and the German Question."
10. Hüser, *Frankreichs "doppelte Deutschlandpolitik."*
11. This vision was primarily developed by German authors. The feelings of the population influenced German historians because German sources, in particular the press, were negative.
12. Lefèvre, *Les relations économiques.*
13. Maelstaf, *Que faire de l'Allemagne?*
14. Libera, *Un rêve de puissance.* Libera presents a fine synthesis of the evolutions until 1949, in particular the large variety of the first projects that had been elaborated before the middle of 1945. Gérard Bossuat had already mentioned ten projects dating back before December 1944, and four more plans between July and September 1945; see Bossuat, "Les conceptions françaises," 27.

15. Eck, *Les entreprises françaises*; see also Berger, *La France, l'Allemagne*, 809–11.
16. Such a cartel was not considered to be immediately convenient, but only because France had not yet reconquered enough market shares to hold a sufficiently strong position in an international negotiation. In 1948 semiofficial negotiations to that end nevertheless started; see Berger, *La France, l'Allemagne*, 871–872.
17. Berger, *La France, l'Allemagne*, 866.
18. Gaps of the same type were also pointed for the United States and Great Britain, undoubtedly less important but quite real; see Creswell and Trachtenberg, "France and the German Question."
19. Yet if de Gaulle did play a central role in the decision-making process, he hardly participated in the development of these projects, whose authors were, essentially, senior officials; see Libera, *Un rêve de puissance*, 71.
20. "Problèmes économiques de l'après-guerre, un point de vue français," note by Hervé Alphand (director of economic affairs in the French Ministry of Foreign Affairs), quoted in Bossuat, "Les conceptions françaises," 26.
21. See a useful chart in Bossuat, "Les conceptions françaises," 26; and a fine analysis of the projects in Libera, *Un rêve de puissance*, 73–103.
22. Bitsch, "Un rêve français," n2.
23. The project evoked by Marie-Thérèse Bitsch was refined in 1944 within the French delegation to the London-based Inter Allied Armistice Study Committee (CIEA), which included ministers of foreign affairs and experts from various Allied nations; see Conway and Gotovitch, *Europe in Exile*, 117, n53. This committee, which was created on 23 October 1942, according to Martial Libera was in charge of studying the "necessary measures to ensure the military, naval and air disarmament of the enemy and to prevent its rearmament, in particular through the implementation of economic measures" (Libera, *Un rêve de puissance*, 49). Specialized subcommittees focused on the industrial, financial or commercial questions and were in charge of working out proposals for the European Advisory Commission (EAC), which had been agreed on at the Moscow Conference of Oct. 1943; in charge of the study of the postwar political problems in Europe and the drafting of recommendation to the three major allied governments, it was terminated in Aug. 1945. See FRUS 1945, European Advisory Commission, Austria, Germany, vol. 3, 883–1147.
24. For this period, Libera's contribution is essential because he studies in detail these various projects and the men and networks who designed them: see Libera, *Un rêve de puissance*, 39–134.
25. According to Libera, *Un rêve de puissance*, 141–43: "In 1945, there is no doubt that the majority of the decision-makers were fully aware of the prominent role of the economy as a deciding factor of power. Paradoxically, however, it was the defenders of the traditional designs . . . who imposed their views."
26. See Berger, "Les relations entre les sidérurgies," 172.
27. See Libera, *Un rêve de puissance*, 145.
28. Ibid., 137.
29. See Hudemann and Poidevin, *Die Saar*.
30. Ibid., 100.
31. See Berger, "Les relations entre les sidérurgies."
32. Bossuat, "Les conceptions françaises."
33. This included Pierre Mendès France.
34. See Bitsch, "Un rêve français," (xx).
35. Creswell and Trachtenberg, "France and the German Question."
36. "Gouvernement provisoire de la république française: Directives pour notre action en Allemagne," 20 Jul. 1945 (Hudemann, "L'Occupation française en Allemagne," 169–82).
37. Libera, *Un rêve de puissance*, 147–150.
38. Bossuat, "Les conceptions françaises," 32.
39. Siegfried, *L'année politique*, 251.
40. Ibid., 55.
41. Ibid., 55–56.

42. "The Anglo-Saxons give the impression that, to draw us away from the Ruhr, they want to satisfy us in Saarland" (Siegfried, *L'année politique*, 82).

43. Ibid.

44. Ordinance no. 5 of the French commander in Germany, 4 Sept. 1945 (Libera, *Un rêve de puissance*, 227).

45. Libera, *Un rêve de puissance*, 227.

46. Dietmar Hüser explained this very well: From the beginning, the objectives of France were moderate despite national pressure (domestic politics) or international constraints (the need to negotiate with the Allies). See Hüser, *Frankreichs "doppelte Deutschlandpolitik."*

47. Abelshauser, "Wirtschaft und Besatzungspolitik," 114.

48. France's opposition to administrative centralization derived not only from the fear of a resurgent Reich, but also, according to recent work (see, e.g., Creswell and Trachtenberg, "France and the German Question"), from the fear of a Soviet takeover of German central administrations that would thus put the Soviet danger at the French border. (The debate on this subject was still important in 1945.)

49. Directives de politique économique et financière, 15 Dec. 1945, AnF, 462 AP, box 26.

50. Ibid.

51. R. Hudemann describes "the swift, uninterrupted fight carried out by General Koenig to improve the food supply of his zone" against all the French and Allied administrations (see Hudemann, "L'occupation française en Allemagne," 237).

52. Letter by Massigli to Chauvel, 10 Jan. 1948, MAE, DDF 1948, vol. 1, 56–57.

53. Note of the Division of European Affairs, 12 Jan. 1948, DDF 1948, vol. 1, 63–65.

54. Ibid.

55. The London Conference from February to June 1948 agreed on 1 June 1948 to initiate a process of creating a German federal state with broad legislative and administrative powers that was nevertheless demilitarized and under occupation statute. The London Conference also agreed to create an International Authority for the Ruhr in charge of coordinating and controlling its economic activity in the Ruhr area.

56. Robert Schuman's speech on the origins and the development of the European Steel and Coal Community (ECSC) in Bruges, Belgium, on 22 Oct. 1953, can be found at the Centre Virtuel de la Connaissance sur l'Europe (CVCE; Virtual Centre for Knowledge on Europe), http://www .cvce.eu/obj/discours_de_robert_schuman_sur_les_origines_et_sur_l_elaboration_de_la_ceca_brug es_22_23_octobre_1953-fr-91c347fc-ab32-4e8d-a31f-f8e244362705.html (accessed 13 Mar. 2017).

57. The Washington Agreement of 8 April 1949 ratified the creation of the FRG and a revision of the occupation statute. It was followed on 8 May 1949 by the promulgation of the Fundamental Law of the FRG. On 9 November 1949, in Paris, the conference of the three Western powers integrated the FRG into the Western bloc by allowing it to join the various international organizations of the West: the Organisation for European Economic Co-operation (OEEC), the Council of Europe, and the International Authority for the Ruhr. To allow for this, the Petersberg Agreement was signed on 22 November 1949 between the three Allied high commissioners and Konrad Adenauer.

58. After the May 1947 dismissal of the four communist ministers, it took some time for the government to make a real change in its priorities: the main enemy became the USSR rather than Germany, even if public opinion was reluctant to follow this new position (the communists voters were nearly 30 percent in 1947).

59. Note of 21 May 1948, quoted by Bossuat, "Les conceptions françaises," 33.

60. Ibid., 34.

61. See Berger, "André François-Poncet."

62. For example, on 15 December 1945 he received from the military headquarters a folder on the situation and on the economic policy in the ZFO, perhaps to prepare a leading article or one of the lectures which he readily gave on these subjects in the years to follow (AnF, 462 AP, box 26).

63. See his monthly reports starting in May 1949 published by Hans Manfred Bock (Bock, *Les rapports mensuels*).

64. Robert Schuman's speech on the origins and the development of the ECSC in Bruges, 22 Oct. 1953.

65. Report of the French high commissioner, 19 Oct. 1949 (Bock, *Les rapports mensuels*, vol. 1, 191–92).
66. Ibid., 193.
67. Ibid.
68. Ibid.
69. See Libera, *Un rêve de puissance*, 416–28; Eck, *Les entreprises françaises*, 17–61.
70. Berger, *Les relations économiques*.
71. 29 Nov. 1949, AMAE, Europe 4.22.2, box 357.
72. French reluctance seemed to be the result of pressure by French protectionist circles, though the French accused the Germans of delaying the signature in order to put pressure on France in the Saarland issue. The agricultural problem was not the only one to create tensions between France and Germany. In the German iron and steel industry, the new trade agreement, which opened the doors of the German market to some iron and steel French products, received very little support (Director Georgen's letter to the six factories of the iron group, 8 Mar. 1950, Bundesarchiv, B 109/97, WVESI).
73. See Berger, "France-Allemagne."
74. *Journal Officiel*, 14 Feb. 1950.
75. 16 Feb. 1950, CAEF, B 33890.
76. Berger, *Les relations économiques*.
77. In a context where the French knew that they would not go on controlling German production for much longer—particularly steel production—it was a compromise designed to keep some control in the future and, at the same time, doing a neighborly act opening the way to a European construction including Germany.
78. These negotiations started in 1950 under an unequal statute and were marked by concessions gradually wrested by the German delegation to obtain equal treatment. See Berger, "Le compromis Franco-allemand."
79. See Extracts of press, 3 Jan. 1952, AnF, 462 AP, box 29.
80. This was particularly clear in André François-Poncet's view, which makes his writings interesting, because he struggled—as most of the French people did—between a rather primary anticommunism and a defensive standpoint against a Prussian Germany, which he had known before and during the war.

Bibliography

Abelshauser, W. 1983. "Wirtschaft und Besatzungspolitik in der Französischen Zone 1945–1949." In *Die Deutschlandpolitik Frankreichs und die französische Zone 1945–1949*, edited by C. Scharf and H.-J. Schröder, 111–39. Wiesbaden, Germany: Franz Steiner.

Berger, F., 1991. *Les relations économiques de la République française avec la République fédérale d'Allemagne sous statut d'occupation*. Master thesis, University of Paris 1, under the supervision of René Girault.

———. 2000. *La France, l'Allemagne et l'acier 1932–1952. De la stratégie des cartels à l'élaboration de la CECA*. Doctoral diss., University of Paris 1, under the supervision of René Girault.

———. 2004. "Le compromis Franco-allemand dans l'industrie sidérurgique." In *Die Bundesrepublik Deutschland und die europäische Einigung 1950–2000. Bewegende Kräfte und politische Akteure*, edited by M. König and M. Schulz, 379–99. Stuttgart, Germany: Franz Steiner Verlag.

———. 2005. "André François-Poncet, des réseaux intellectuels à l'expérience du journalisme économique au service des entrepreneurs." In *Les permanents patronaux. Eléments pour l'histoire de l'organisation du patronat en France dans la première moitié du XXe siècle*, edited by O. Dard and G. Richard, 75–92. Metz, France: Centre régional universitaire lorrain d'histoire.

———. 2007. "Les relations entre les sidérurgies française et allemande de 1870 à la CECA." *Revue d'Allemagne et des pays de langue allemande* 39, no. 2: 163–99.

———. 2012. "France-Allemagne. Stratégies comparées sur la longue durée." *Outre-Terre* 33–34, 213–31.

Bitsch, M.-T. 1987. "Un rêve français. Le désarmement économique de l'Allemagne 1944–1947." *Relations internationales* 51: 313–29.

Bock, H. M., ed. 1996. *Les rapports mensuels d'André François-Poncet, haut-commissaire français en Allemagne 1949–1955*, 2 vols. Paris: Imprimerie nationale.

Bossuat, G. 1997. "Les conceptions françaises des relations économiques avec l'Allemagne 1943–1960." In *Die deutsch-französischen Wirtschaftsbeziehungen 1945–1960/Les relations économiques Franco-allemandes 1945–1960*, edited by A. Wilkens, 25–62. Sigmaringen, Germany: Thorbecke.

Conway, M., and J. Gotovitch, eds. 2001. *Europe in Exile: European Exile Communities in Britain 1940–1945*. New York: Berghahn Books.

Creswell, M., and M. Trachtenberg. 2003. "France and the German Question 1945–1955." *Journal of Cold War Studies* 5, no. 3: 5–28.

———. 2003. "New Light on an Old Issue?" *Journal of Cold War Studies* 5, no. 3: 46–53.

Eck, J.-F. 2003. *Les entreprises françaises face à l'Allemagne de 1945 à la fin des années 1960*. Paris: Comité pour l'histoire économique et financière de la France.

Hudemann, R. 1990. "L'occupation française en Allemagne. Problèmes généraux et perspectives de recherche." In *L'Allemagne occupée 1945–1949*, edited by H. Ménudier, 221–42. Brussels, Belgium: Complexe.

Hudemann, R., and R. Poidevin, eds. 1992. *Die Saar 1945–1955. Ein Problem der europäischen Geschichte*. Munich, Germany: Oldenbourg.

Hüser, D. 1996. *Frankreichs "doppelte Deutschlandpolitik." Dynamik aus der Defensive: Planen, Entscheiden, Umsetzen in gesellschaftlichen und wirtschaftlichen, innen- und außenpolitischen Krisenzeiten 1944–1950*. Berlin: Duncker & Humblot.

Lefèvre, S. 1998. *Les relations économiques Franco-allemandes de 1945 à 1955. De l'occupation à la coopération*. Paris: Comité pour l'histoire économique et financière de la France.

Libera, M. 2012. *Un rêve de puissance. La France et le contrôle de l'économie allemande 1942–1949*. Brussels, Belgium: Peter Lang.

Maelstaf, G. 1999. *Que faire de l'Allemagne ? Les responsables français, le statut international de l'Allemagne et le problème de l'unité allemande 1945–1955*. Paris: Imprimerie nationale.

Poidevin, R. 1993. "Plan Marshall et problème allemand: les inquiétudes françaises 1947–1948." In *Le plan Marshall et le relèvement économique de l'Europe*, edited by R. Girault and M. Lévy-Leboyer, 87–96. Paris: Comité pour l'histoire économique et financière de la France.

Siegfried, A., ed. 1948. *L'année politique 1947*. Paris: Grand siècle.

Part II

The Emergence of the Bloc System

CHAPTER 3

France, German Rearmament, and the German Question, 1945–1955

Michael H. Creswell

One of the most important international issues of the twentieth century was the so-called German question, that is, how to treat Germany,[1] a country that possessed the ability and, at times, the ambition to dominate the rest of Europe both economically and militarily. While this question had long preoccupied policymakers and military officials on both sides of the Atlantic, it attracted special attention in France, especially in the wake of World War II. Having fought three debilitating wars against its powerful neighbor in seventy years, France urgently sought an answer to this question.[2]

The Allied victory in World War II raised hopes that a permanent solution to the German question had been found, as the Nazis' dream of dominating Europe collapsed under the weight of Allied arms. But although Germany in 1945 was in no position to threaten any other country, the Union of Soviet Socialist Republics (USSR, or Soviet Union) posed an immediate and potentially deadly threat to Europe. Although many French officials believed that Germany continued to present France with a long-term economic and military problem, they considered it less of a concern than the threat then posed by Moscow. The challenge for France, therefore, was to devise a strategy that would solve both of these problems. Ultimately France developed such a strategy, which involved the diplomatic and military initiatives discussed below.

France Confronts the Postwar Environment

For France, the Soviet threat and the German question were linked and defied resolution independently of each other. Paris could not blunt the Soviet menace unless it also devised an answer to the German question, nor could it solve the German question without also confronting the Soviet threat. Indeed, it was the Soviet problem that rendered the German question so acute. From France's standpoint, remaining at odds with both Federal Republic of Germany (FRG, or West Germany) and the USSR could lead to a rapprochement between Bonn and Moscow.[3] France's security would be imperiled if the Soviets came to dominate both halves of Germany, thereby bringing Soviet power to the Franco-German border. Conversely, were France to adopt a pro-German policy, it would offer Paris the strategic benefit of forward defense—in other words, increasing the odds that France would not be the battle-ground should East-West conflict occur. France's growing fear of Soviet ambitions thus forced French officials to view the German question in a new light.

Even before World War II ended, prominent French officials had begun to reas-sess their nation's anti-German policy. This reassessment stemmed from their deep concern about Soviet intentions toward Europe. For example, in April 1945 U.S. Ambassador to France Jefferson Caffery reported that General Charles de Gaulle, the head of the Provisional Government of the French Republic (GPRF), Foreign Minister Georges Bidault, and other "highly placed French authorities" were "frankly apprehensive" about the Soviet menace. In fact, de Gaulle believed it was "very pos-sible that Russia will take over the entire continent of Europe in due course." Given the Soviet threat, it was very important, he told Caffery, for France to work with America. De Gaulle was nonetheless pessimistic about enlisting American support: "You are far away and your soldiers will not stay long in Europe. . . . It is a matter of life and death for us; for you, one interesting question among others."[4]

French doubts about the United States' commitment to Europe led France to adopt a new approach to the German question. Absent a tangible, long-term Ameri-can commitment to Western Europe's defense, France would have to find other ways to ensure that all of Germany did not fall under Soviet domination. Adoption of a hardline approach toward Germany, such as dismembering the country, would have to be avoided. Dismemberment might prompt the Soviets to exploit the situation, perhaps by offering German reunification in return for neutrality.

Motivated by the belief that they could not count on a robust long-term Amer-ican commitment to European security, French officials sought support from their regional partners.[5] Like France, the other Western European powers had yet to re-cover from the recent war and were individually unable to deter a Soviet attack. They therefore decided that banding together would be the best method to ensure their security. This strategy would also help persuade the United States to commit militar-ily to the defense of Europe, because the Europeans would be engaging in self-help, a key American demand. The Europeans recognized that without the participation of America, they stood no chance against the USSR militarily.[6] By 1947 the nations of Western Europe had embraced a new geostrategic calculus. They regarded the Soviet Union as the primary security threat on Europe's horizon.

To this end, France took a step toward collective defense on 4 March 1947 when it concluded the Treaty of Dunkirk with Britain. According to the text, the signatories were "Determined to collaborate . . . with the object of preventing Germany from becoming again a menace to peace."[7] Although the treaty's language formally identified Germany as the target, the actual though unacknowledged threat was that posed by the Soviet Union. In a nod to caution, the document's drafters hid its true purposes. These were to assemble a Western European military bloc in response to the Soviet threat and, until that bloc took shape, to avoid antagonizing the communist world while Western Europe remained vulnerable to attack or subversion. At this time Western Europe remained weak and there existed no definite United States commitment to its defense.[8] While the treaty was being negotiated, British Foreign Minister Ernest Bevin noted, "Any suggestion that the Treaty was not primarily directed against Germany would rouse suspicion and perhaps opposition not only in Moscow but in . . . the Communist Party in France."[9]

Bidault underscored Bevin's assertion. According to U.S. Secretary of State George C. Marshall, Bidault told him in April 1947, "To the American question, 'Can we rely on France?' the answer is 'Yes.'" But France needed time and must avoid a civil war.[10] Indeed, the French Communist Party was the largest and best-organized political party in France. Convinced that the Party obeyed Moscow, many French officials feared a potential fifth column. In addition, at the time four members of the Party were in the French cabinet. Thus, both domestic political considerations and the Soviet threat weighed heavily on France's approach to the German question.[11]

The Treaty of Dunkirk, however, hardly solved France's security problem, because Soviet power and influence continued to spread over the continent. An Anglo-French combination was simply not powerful enough to stop the Soviets. The advance of communism convinced France and the other West European states that they needed to take further steps to defend themselves. Agreement on a formal alliance proved elusive, however, because differing national interests stymied their efforts. In particular, both Britain and France sought to assume the role of leader of Western Europe, while Belgium and the Netherlands wanted to avoid French domination of a larger framework and sought to be treated as a unit with Luxembourg.[12]

But the February 1948 communist coup d'état in Czechoslovakia, the suspicious death of Czech Foreign Minister Jan Masaryk on 10 March, and continued American pressure all pushed the Western Europeans toward an agreement. French Ambassador Maurice Dejean's 12 March 1948 dispatch from Prague warned Paris about "France's extremely alarming predicament" in the absence of any "common defense" with United States participation.[13] Nevertheless, despite increasing Cold War tensions, the Europeans first had to put their own house in order, or they could not expect America to temper its deep suspicion of alliances.[14]

Prompted in part by the Prague coup, on 17 March Britain, France, and the Benelux countries signed the Treaty of Brussels (also known as the Brussels Treaty or the Brussels Pact), which called for cooperation between the contracting parties in several areas. Yet, like the Treaty of Dunkirk, the document's clauses identified Germany as the main threat and made no mention of the Soviet Union.[15] The Brussels Treaty, too, was a calculated act of misdirection designed to avoid provoking Moscow. French domestic politics also played a role, because many French people still feared Germany.[16]

The Brussels Pact also had an important secondary purpose of drawing the United States into the defense of Western Europe. In fact, the Truman administration encouraged the Europeans to take the first step in creating a defense organization in order to demonstrate to the U.S. Congress that Europe was willing to play an active role in its own defense, rather than relying solely on the United States. The Truman administration indicated that it would then be ready to discuss a defense organization in which America would take part.[17] Quite simply, until and unless the Western European democracies secured an American commitment to their defense, it would be foolhardy to provoke the much stronger Soviet Union. In the meantime, Europe remained at risk militarily. As Bidault put it in 1948, "If the Russians are smart, they will attack right away."[18]

Bidault was correct to imply that Western Europe was incapable of stopping a Soviet military assault. Although exact figures are hard to come by, contemporary Western observers believed that Soviet ground forces greatly outnumbered Western forces: 175 Soviet divisions compared with only 16 Allied divisions.[19] To remedy this manpower deficiency, France sought to shift the balance of power by enlisting the great latent strength of the United States. In line with the United States' wishes noted above, in 1948 the British and French foreign ministers requested formal talks with the Americans for the establishment of an Atlantic collective security organization.

Because French military officials believed that the Brussels Pact failed to meet all of France's essential security needs, it was extremely important to them that the proposed Atlantic defense organization meet those needs.[20] It was up to Henri Bonnet, France's ambassador in Washington, DC, to make the case to the Allies. Although the French wanted a security organization, they were adamant that if war did occur, the United States would guarantee that Europe would be defended; mere support would not do.[21] According to some participants in the meetings over this issue, Bonnet was strident. Nicholas Henderson, Foreign Minister Ernest Bevin's private secretary, noted, "M. Bonnet, of course, was not inhibited by any Anglo-Saxon notion of team spirit. He was there to state the French case, and nothing but it." Oliver Franks, who was part of the British delegation, suggested that Bonnet would have been better served had he refrained from the "language of conditions."[22]

Despite the sometimes contentious negotiations, in April 1949 the North Atlantic Treaty Organization (NATO) was born.[23] While France appreciated the creation of NATO, which bound the United States and other countries in a collective security arrangement, other important French concerns remained unresolved. One immediate concern was the poor overall state of Western defense. Indeed, NATO was more of an alliance on paper than in fact. Even the United States had distinct limits on the help it was able and willing to provide.[24] Finding the personnel and materiel to bridge the gap would pose a huge political and economic challenge for the organization.[25]

For France, NATO's military weakness meant that both the German and the Soviet problems remained. French policy toward occupied Germany was complex because it existed in a much larger political context. Although France's civilian leadership saw a resurgent Western Germany as a challenge, they also viewed it as a boon to other French objectives, including fostering European economic recovery and advancing the cause of European unity, which was itself a way to deal with the Soviet danger. One way to square the circle was to bring Western Germany into a European framework. As Jacques Tarbé de Saint-Hardouin, a French political adviser in Germany, put it, France needed to accentuate the European character of its policy in order to solve the German question in a way that defended French interests.[26]

The creation of West Germany the following year reflected a step in the direction toward a European solution to the German question. A further step was taken in 1950 by Jean Monnet, head of the Commissariat for the Plan (Commissariat Général au Plan), who was charged with directing French economic reconstruction. Monnet had both economic and foreign policy considerations in mind when he authored a plan that would pool the coal and steel production of France and Germany. In the first instance, this Monnet Plan would allow France to advance its own plans for domestic modernization and recovery.[27] But the proposal would also be a way to help solve the German question by establishing joint control over the Ruhr, Germany's industrial heartland. Taking the resources of the Ruhr out of national hands and putting them instead in the hands of a supranational authority would remove the material basis for war.[28]

Monnet's idea attracted support from many officials in the French Foreign Ministry, including Foreign Minister Robert Schuman. The two men believed that a harsh anti-German policy would be counterproductive. Moreover, the Monnet Plan offered the possibility of French ideas shaping the new Europe. Harsh French policies toward Germany would be ignored by London and Washington, who would then deal with the German question on their own terms. Announced by Schuman on 9 May 1950, the European Coal and Steel Community (ECSC), also known as the Schuman Plan, attempted to remove a longstanding source of tension between France and Germany. The ECSC would, in Schuman's words, make war between France and Germany "not merely unthinkable, but materially impossible."[29] As an added benefit to a Franco-German economic and political entente, the ECSC would, by being open to other countries, help to raise the standard of living throughout Europe and thereby strengthen the European idea.

At this point, the vast majority of French officials saw no need to rearm Germany. Once in place, the ECSC would, they believed, stifle any potential German threat. Moreover, diverting a key element of Western Germany's material resources to the service of Europe would promote economic recovery and, because military might rests largely on economic might, Western Europe would be better able to defend itself against the Soviet Union. In France's view, West Germany would thus provide resources and not soldiers to the defense of Europe.

In addition to planning European security arrangements, France was also busy prosecuting the Indochina War (1946–54), in which French forces were pitted against the Viet Minh. This conflict would make solving the German question even more complex, as we shall see.

On 10 October 1950 France suffered a major military defeat at Cao Bằng, on the northern border with China. Although France's leaders doubted the country could defeat the Viet Minh, they nevertheless responded to Cao Bằng by increasing the country's commitment to the conflict. Equally surprising, French leaders made this commitment even knowing that it would impair France's military commitment to Western Europe.

The French government embraced this strategic contradiction out of the fear that if France conceded defeat in Indochina it would be seen as the new "sick man of Europe."[30] Staying the course in the face of difficult odds while simultaneously meeting its commitments in Europe would certify France's status as a Great Power.[31] Embracing this contradiction, though, meant that there would be an even greater need for German ground forces in Europe in order to compensate for the shortfall in French troops.

In fact, France's Radical Party leader, Pierre Mendès France, a consistent critic of French colonialism, argued that sending more French forces to Indochina would come at the expense of an August 1950 commitment France had made to NATO to undertake a large-scale rearmament program. But French Prime Minister René Pleven's government rejected the advice of Mendès France. Instead, the government decided to both prosecute the Indochina War and keep the August 1950 commitment.[32]

The Pleven government had made that commitment in the hope that its own effort to rearm would lessen American interest in German rearmament. France thought that the deployment of ten French divisions in Western Europe in 1951 would impress the Americans. The French government also suspected that because of the great importance the Americans assigned to France's role in European security arrangements, they would subsidize the cost of French rearmament.[33] When it became apparent that the Indochina conflict would make it impossible to meet the rearmament schedule established in August 1950, the French calculated that the United States so valued the French war against communism in Indochina that Washington would tolerate delays in French rearmament (and hence European rearmament) without pushing for Germany to be rearmed immediately. However, France's desire to commit militarily to two theatres simultaneously failed to impress its alliance partners, and rendered the question of German rearmament even more pressing for the Americans. From Washington's standpoint, German forces would be needed to compensate for France's military weakness in Western Europe.

The Question of German Rearmament

But given widespread and lingering doubts about obtaining a lasting American military commitment to the continent's security,[34] some French officials sought other, more-controversial ways to shore up Europe's defense and thus solve both the Soviet and the German questions. For Bidault and other highly placed French officials, one logical step France and its partners could take against the Soviet threat would be to place Germans in their occupation zones under arms. In light of France's concerns about the United States' commitment to its defense, these French officials believed that recruiting the human and material resources of West Germany made sense.[35]

France's military leadership was an early advocate of rearming Germany. Its justification for making this politically contentious recommendation rested on purely military grounds. If Europe were to be safeguarded from the Red Army and French soil spared the ravages of modern conventional war, the front line had to be pushed as far east as possible. The Germans in the Western zones of occupation, therefore, had to bear their share of the defense burden. During the negotiations for the Brussels Pact, two leading French officers, General Paul Ely[36] and Colonel Paul Stehlin, told Prime Minister Schuman[37] that the Germans should pay the "blood price" for their own safety. Stehlin contended, "A Germany that remains neutralized and demilitarized would soon fall under Soviet dependence and the frontier of the Western world would soon be on the Rhine."[38]

Ely and Stehlin were far from alone in holding these views. In November 1948, for example, Vice Admiral André Lemonnier, chief of staff of the French Navy, echoed their assessment. He asked that France's general staff place the issue of German rearmament on its agenda, deeming it a matter of "primordial importance."[39]

But although the French military leadership had begun to rally behind the idea of German rearmament, most French civilian officials rejected the idea. However, the outbreak of the Korean War in June 1950 cast this issue in a new light. The conflict infused the German question with an urgent military dimension. Believing that North Korea's attack on South Korea foreshadowed a Soviet attack on an unprepared Western Europe, American officials concluded that the European members of NATO needed to bolster their collective defense quickly in order to deter Soviet aggression or defeat it if deterrence failed. They also believed that Germany should be rearmed.

At a September 1950 meeting of the North Atlantic Council (NAC) in New York, Secretary of State Dean Acheson bluntly presented the Allies with the so-called package proposal: in exchange for receiving American financial and military aid, the Europeans would be obliged to quickly create a European army that would include several German ground divisions.[40] Acheson had thus thrown the issue of German rearmament on the table in a very public way.

Despite his objections to the brusque manner in which Acheson presented the package,[41] Foreign Minister Schuman agreed with his logic. "Regarding the participation of Germany in the defense effort," Schuman told his British and American counterparts at the start of the conference, "it would seem illogical for us to defend Western Europe, including Germany, without contributions from Germany."[42]

But there was a serious "psychological problem to be faced, particularly in France." Schuman "did not think this was an obstacle to all action"; indeed, in his view, "it was really only a question of timing." But if the French government "were forced to take a stand on this issue before French public opinion was ready, everything might go wrong." The answer, he thought, was to take a step-by-step approach, with the first step being to build up the military strength of the NATO countries so that they could defend themselves should the Soviet Union respond militarily to efforts to arm West Germany. After NATO had begun to move ahead in this area it would be easier, Schuman said, to "reach a decision on German participation." NATO would then be more than just an alliance on paper: it would have the power to deter the Soviets and the organizational infrastructure to ensure that any German military contribution would be tightly controlled and thus unable to act independently. "The difficulties confronting the French Government would" by then, in Schuman's view, "largely have been removed." He stressed the point that the delay he had in mind would not be lengthy; in his opinion it was "only a question of a few months," and maybe even less than that.[43]

Ultimately, Acheson dismissed Schuman's objections. Although France continued to protest, the American position prevailed. At the final meeting of the NAC, convened on 26 September, the members agreed to establish an integrated military force within NATO that would include German divisions serving under an American Allied Supreme Commander for Europe. After the meeting, Schuman, mindful of French public opinion, suggested that France should not appear to be "dragged on the end of a chain." In other words, the French public would react negatively if it believed that the Allies had coerced France into agreement on this issue. This suggestion notwithstanding, Schuman did not reject the German rearmament proposal in principle.[44] The French government, in fact, had now given its provisional blessing to German rearmament.[45]

Schuman was not the only top French civilian official who saw the need to rearm West Germany. Other French officials also conveyed to London and Washington that they, too, accepted the need for German rearmament. Oliver Harvey, then Britain's ambassador to France, reported that Roland de Margerie, political director of the Quai d'Orsay, had admitted that from France's standpoint, the results of the meetings in New York "had not been unsatisfactory."[46] And after meeting with French officials in late December 1950, State Department counselor Charles "Chip" Bohlen reported to Washington, "[the] French government has recognized the necessity of [a] German contribution to [a] European defense force."[47] By the end of 1950 Paris and Washington were in agreement that Germany should be rearmed.

Obtaining complete French acceptance of German rearmament would, however, require more than the support of just a handful of senior French political and military officials. Indeed, rearming Germany could have important spillover effects in other areas of French policy. For example, French leaders worried that if Germany were rearmed, it would then have less incentive to cooperate with the Western Allies, which would threaten the Schuman Plan's initiative to pool the coal and steel resources of Western Europe within an ECSC. Monnet, therefore, wanted to delay German rearmament until the ECSC Treaty was signed. As he confided to one of his associates in October 1950, "You well understand . . . that if we rearm [Germany], there is no longer a Schuman Plan."[48]

To avoid being painted as obstructionist, and to buy time, the French government responded to the NAC decision by proposing the Pleven Plan, conceived by Monnet and named after Prime Minister René Pleven. Presenting the plan to the National Assembly on 24 October 1950, Pleven called for "the creation, for the purposes of common defense, of a European army tied to the political institutions of a united Europe." The project envisioned the creation of a hundred-thousand-man European force that would include divisions from the Benelux countries, France, West Germany, and Italy integrated "at the level of the smallest possible unit." Modeled after the Schuman Plan, this army would blend the manpower and materiel of the various countries into a unified force. Member governments would name a European minister of defense answerable to a European Assembly, and his power would include the creation and implementation of the force's armament and equipment programs. The army's funds would emanate from a common budget. In addition, the European contingents would be placed at the disposal of NATO and would function according to the contractual obligations of the North Atlantic pact.[49]

There were two major problems with the Pleven Plan. First, it would have created a fighting force that was militarily ineffective. Integration at the smallest level would create polyglot units unable to communicate. Second, its supranational character would place limitations on the employment of French forces by forbidding France from withdrawing them for use in its colonial empire.

The main positive attribute of the Pleven Plan was that it would be politically acceptable to France's parliament.[50] Hervé Alphand, France's deputy representative to the NAC, told the British that the Pleven Plan was the best compromise available.[51] The French cabinet had already given its blessing to the plan on 21 October, and the National Assembly followed suit by a vote of 343 to 225.[52]

Although many observers suspected that the Pleven Plan was actually intended to prevent German rearmament—Monnet had crafted it without input from French military officials—this was not the case. Even Defense Minister Jules Moch, the French cabinet minister who most publically opposed West German rearmament, admitted that under certain conditions German rearmament would be acceptable to France. When asked at the NATO Defense Committee in late October 1950 if France's government accepted "the principle of the creation of German military units," Moch said yes, "but only under the condition that the creation of these units be not or tend not to become a risk which might be mortal to the democracies. In other words, that these units be not large units, but be integrated into European Divisions."[53] At the same time Moch warned that while France would contribute its fair share, it must not become the "infantry of Europe."[54] France would play its part, but it would not undertake this role without sufficient support from the other West European countries.

Far from agreeing with his allies simply in order to buy time for France to derail German rearmament, Moch held to the same position during internal French discussions conducted in late 1950. As he advised at a mid-December meeting of France's National Defense Committee, "the error to be avoided" was to accept West German rearmament "while Western forces are still not ready." In short, Moch believed that the Western bloc could accept German rearmament once it had built up its own power. The question concerning German rearmament was thus not "whether?" but "under what conditions?"[55]

For French officials, the question of timing was crucial. It would take time to augment the military power of the Western bloc to the point that it could credibly deter the Soviet Union. Rearming Germany before that point was reached could provoke the Soviet Union. Western military power had to be built up first. It was also a question of the political consolidation of the Western bloc, and especially the integration of Germany into that bloc via the ECSC. Indeed, Monnet's priority was to save the ECSC, and not to promote further military consolidation. Schuman believed that the concerns of Monnet, like those of Moch, could be met by proper timing.

But whereas Paris had agreed to create a European army that would include a German military component, differences with the Allies over the Pleven Plan's details soon arose. In late November 1950 the two sides reached a compromise. The Spofford Plan, named after Charles Spofford, the U.S. deputy representative to the NAC, laid out an interim period during which German forces would be limited to regimental combat teams of five thousand to six thousand men, or one third of a division, and would not exceed 20 percent of NATO forces serving in the European army. Neither of these strictures would apply to France, thus ensuring that French forces would maintain a numerical superiority over German forces. This was the key to gaining political support for the Spofford Plan in France.[56]

Despite having adopted the Spofford Plan, disagreement remained over whether Germany would be rearmed on a national basis within NATO, or on a supranational basis within a European army. Thus at its meetings on 18 and 19 December, the alliance set up two parallel conferences to begin in 1951, with the aim of reconciling these opposing institutional frameworks. The Petersberg Conference, to be held in Bonn, would discuss a way for bringing German troops into an integrated NATO force, while the Paris Conference would discuss the Pleven Plan's solution to the problems posed by German rearmament—in other words, creating a European army that included German forces. Ultimately, the NAC decided that while Germany would contribute troops to the West, it would not take part in NATO. Eventually, the Allies officially adopted the European army plan, which later became known as the European Defence Community (EDC).[57]

The European Defence Community

Thus by 1951 the Pleven Plan had evolved into a proposal for an EDC. There was, nonetheless, significant domestic and international opposition to the EDC. General Dwight Eisenhower, who had just become supreme commander of NATO, condemned the European army plan as militarily ineffective. Most high-ranking Allied military officials agreed with him. But at the urging of U.S. high commissioner to Germany John J. McCloy, Eisenhower met with Monnet to discuss the EDC. Based on his conversation with Monnet, Eisenhower became a convert to the EDC, testifying on its behalf before the Senate Foreign Relations Committee. Eisenhower's stature meant that his support carried great weight among civilian and military officials throughout the alliance.[58] The so-called Eisenhower Conversion thus gave an important boost to the European army plan, as the United States switched from supporting the NATO solution to backing the EDC.

After long and difficult negotiations, a treaty establishing the EDC was signed in May 1952. Yet despite signing the treaty, the French government would not submit it to the National Assembly. From France's standpoint, loose ends remained. One was the absence of a long-term, ironclad, and robust Anglo-American troop commitment to Europe's defense. France sought this commitment because it would provide a balance to a revitalized West Germany. Some French officials viewed British participation in European affairs as a key pillar of France's strategy for solving the German question. Even British officials admitted that one of the main reasons why successive French governments failed to submit the EDC Treaty to the National Assembly was "the fact that the U.K. was not a member of the community and the lack of a clear definition of her relationship with it."[59] Despite this admission, Britain continued to refuse the key French demand: a binding guarantee to maintain a substantial number of British troops on the European continent.

As previously discussed, the conflict in Indochina complicated matters for NATO and the EDC, because it drained the French treasury and diverted French forces from Europe. As long as that conflict continued, France's government would be unlikely to submit the EDC Treaty to its parliament. In response to Allied criticism that the Indochina War diverted France's human and material resources from the defense of Europe, French officials argued that Indochina was an important theatre in the struggle against international communism, and that France deserved continuing support for its effort there. Accordingly, France sought to count the Indochina War as a part of its general effort within NATO.[60]

But the other members of NATO disagreed with France on this, and they in turn began to question France's commitment to the defense of Western Europe.[61] Then, in November 1952, France announced that it would fail to meet its force goals for 1953.[62] This announcement dramatically underscored the fact that the cost of France's empire represented a direct drain on French resources and an indirect one on NATO's. This situation heightened the importance of finding a way to bring the Indochina War to a close. An end to the Indochina entanglement could potentially pave the way for a solution to the question of German rearmament by enabling France to devote greater human and material resources to the defense of Europe (thereby balancing German military power, and hence influence, in this critical region). Events would soon force France to make a decision.

In early May 1954 the siege of Điện Biên Phủ ended in a French surrender. France's Indochina policy was in shambles. In the wake of this defeat, Mendès France, who believed that continuing the war was not worth the human and material costs, was elected prime minister. At the Geneva Conference in July 1954, the Mendès France government reached an agreement to end the conflict.[63] France under Mendès France also began to wean itself off American financial aid, thus gaining greater freedom over its own affairs and avoiding what many of the French people believed was the humiliation of begging for money from the Americans.[64]

Mendès France next decided to put the EDC to a vote. Finally, after four years of debate and false starts, France's National Assembly killed the project on 30 August 1954. German Chancellor Konrad Adenauer, British Prime Minister Winston Churchill, and U.S. President Dwight D. Eisenhower all expressed anger at the National Assembly's vote, saying it placed Western security in jeopardy.[65]

Yet within days an alternative plan was in the works. Policymakers in Britain and France suggested substituting a simpler alliance arrangement for the EDC's complex and controversial one. The substitute would be the dormant Brussels Treaty Organization, which would be revamped and renamed the Western European Union (WEU). Meeting in London from 28 September to 3 October 1954, all of the interested parties reached general agreement on the outstanding issues. Final adjustments to the agreements reached in London were hammered out at a conference convened in Paris on 20 October. There France made concessions, including an agreement allowing Germany to enter the WEU and NATO simultaneously. Paris obtained some of its key requirements in return. These included German renunciation of the manufacture of atomic, biological, and chemical weapons on its soil, and Anglo-American military assurances to the WEU.[66] It seemed that a solution to the problem of integrating German forces into the Western alliance had finally been found.

However, on 24 December the National Assembly unexpectedly rejected a key section of the Paris Accords.[67] Although once again furious at France, Eisenhower decided to avoid placing pressure on Paris. His patience was soon rewarded, and on 30 December 1954 the National Assembly ratified the London-Paris Accords by a vote of 287 to 260. This vote revived and amended the 1948 Brussels Treaty. Recast as the WEU, this new military alliance featured the same lineup as the ill-fated EDC, but with the addition of Great Britain. West Germany went on to gain membership in NATO in May 1955, after the other parties had ratified the London-Paris accords. For France one crucial aspect of the German question seemed settled, at least for the time being. Mendès France, for one, was more than satisfied with the arrangements that the Allies struck in December 1954. He later wrote, "In the final analysis we came out rather well."[68]

Conclusion

The vastly changed geostrategic environment after World War II forced France to reassess its international position and adapt itself to new circumstances. Key French policymakers, along with the military high command, recognized early on that the Soviet Union posed the primary threat to France's security, rather than a defeated and divided Germany. While recognizing that West Germany presented a long-term concern to France, many French officials came to believe that West Germany could help to advance French interests.

Still weakened by the war and unsure of the United States' commitment to defend Europe militarily, France sought safety in collective security arrangements. The most important of these efforts was the creation of NATO in 1949. But while NATO went a long way toward ensuring France's security, the organization was initially more an alliance on paper than in fact. It was the outbreak of the Korean War that forced NATO's members to turn the organization into a true military alliance.

To this end, at the September 1950 NAC meeting the United States pushed the alliance to rearm Germany. Although France balked at the public way in which Secretary of State Acheson raised the issue, it did not reject the proposal itself. Foreign Minister Schuman admitted privately that the American proposal was logical. His main concern was over timing: Europe first needed to repair its defenses, and the French public needed to be prepared psychologically.

Due in large part to domestic opposition, France presented the EDC Treaty to its parliament only in late 1954. Although the National Assembly initially rejected the treaty, Mendès France offered to replace it with the 1948 Brussels Treaty. The agreement was revamped to include Italy and West Germany, and renamed the WEU. In return, West Germany agreed to renounce the production of atomic, biological, and chemical weapons on its soil. At the end of December 1954, France ratified the Paris Accords. The fruit of this agreement ripened in May 1955, when West Germany joined NATO. The German question, at least for the foreseeable future, had been solved.

In the years to come both France and Germany would work to deepen their new relationship. Despite its negative historical reputation, the French Fourth Republic found a satisfactory answer to the German question by including Germany in the economic, political, and military structures of postwar Western Europe. Among France's many accomplishments in the international arena, this one is surely not the least.

Michael H. Creswell, a graduate of Indiana University and the University of Chicago, has served as the Annenberg Visiting Assistant Professor of History at the University of Pennsylvania. He is currently associate professor of history at Florida State University and adjunct professor of strategy for the U.S. Naval War College. The author of *A Question of Balance: How France and the United States Created Cold War Europe* (2006), Creswell's planned next book will examine the evolution of France's arms strategy after World War II.

Notes

Parts of this chapter have been previously published in Creswell and Trachtenberg, "France and the German Question," by the president and fellows of Harvard College and the Massachusetts Institute of Technology, published by the MIT Press. Used with permission from the *Journal of Cold War Studies* and the MIT Press.

In addition to the editors of the volume, I thank Jon Harrison and Mark Thompson for their valuable suggestions on earlier drafts of this chapter.

1. This chapter deals specifically with the Federal Republic of Germany (FRG, or West Germany), which was founded in 1949.
2. "The German question" has meant different things to different groups at different times. Here the German question refers to the geostrategic debate in France regarding the role of German economic and military power from 1945 to 1955.
3. Historical precedents for a Russo–German entente included the Reinsurance Treaty of 1887–90, the Treaty of Rapallo of 1922, and the Molotov-Ribbentrop Pact of 1939–41.
4. Caffery to secretary of state, 3 Nov. 1945, FRUS 1945, vol. 3, 890.
5. These regional partners included Britain and the Benelux countries. For France's many attempts to enlist the military support of London and Washington, see Creswell, "With a Little Help."
6. The United States' unwillingness to commit to Europe until the Europeans took the first step can also be seen as American pressure for European integration.
7. For the text of the Treaty of Alliance and Mutual Assistance between the United Kingdom and France, see Centre Virtuel de la Connaissance sur l'Europe (CVCE; Virtual Centre for Knowledge on Europe), http://www.cvce.eu/obj/treaty_of_alliance_and_mutual_assistance_between_the_united_king dom_and_france_dunkirk_4_march_1947-en-1fb9f4b5-64e2-4337-bc78-db7e1978de09.html.
8. Young, *France, the Cold War*.
9. Telegram, 23 Jan. 1947, TNA, Kew, FO 371/67670.
10. "Bidault-Marshall Meeting," 20 Apr. 1947, FRUS 1947, vol. 2, 369–70.
11. In May 1947 France's socialist prime minister, Paul Ramadier, ejected the four communist ministers from his cabinet, thus ending tripartisme, which was the alliance of communists, socialists, and Christian democrats that had governed France since 1944.
12. See Svik, "The Czechoslovak Factor," 150–51.
13. Melandri and Vaïsse, "France: From Powerlessness,"464; Svik, "The Czechoslovak Factor."
14. The only previous alliance the United States had entered into was the Treaty of Alliance with France in 1778.
15. For the text of The Treaty of Economic, Social and Cultural Collaboration and Collective Self-Defence, see The Brussels Treaty, 17 Mar. 1948, CVCE, https://www.cvce.eu/en/obj/the_brussels_ treaty_17_march_1948-en-3467de5e-9802-4b65-8076-778bc7d164d3.html.
16. According to France's *Etat-Major de la Défense nationale*, the Brussels Pact met "an immediate need to deal with a Soviet attack." "Note sur les négociations du Pacte Atlantique et ses aspects militaires," 31 Jan. 1949, SHAA, E2924.
17. Trachtenberg, *A Constructed Peace*, 86.
18. Bidault quoted in Demory, *Georges Bidault*, 275.
19. It should be noted, however, that a Russian division was smaller than an American or European division. See Bitzinger, "Assessing the Conventional Balance," 4–6.
20. France's *Etat-Major de la Défense nationale* stated that the Brussels Pact had "shortcomings and serious gaps." Quote found in "Note sur les négociations," E2924.
21. Kaplan, *NATO 1948*, 113; Bothwell, *Alliance and Illusion*, 68.
22. Henderson and Franks are quoted in Kaplan, *NATO 1948*, 113.
23. Signing the treaty were Belgium, Canada, Denmark, France, Italy, Iceland, Luxembourg, Netherlands, Norway, Portugal, the United Kingdom, and the United States.
24. According to Article 5 of the NATO treaty, in the event of an attack on one of its members, the other members "will assist the Party or Parties so attacked by taking forthwith, individually and in concert

with the other Parties, *such action as it deems necessary, including the use of armed force*, to restore and maintain the security of the North Atlantic area" (italics added). In other words, the use of armed force is not automatic. See the North Atlantic Treaty, 4 Apr. 1949, Brussels, Belgium, North Atlantic Treaty Organization (NATO) website, https://www.nato.int/cps/en/natohq/official_texts_17120 .htm.

25. May, "The American Commitment."

26. Saint-Hardouin to Pierre de Leusse, 5 Sept. 1948, AMAE, Y-Internationale, 1944–49, vol. 312.

27. As Monnet stated in Mar. 1946, "The development of our industrial capacity, and of steel in particular, would be impossible if we were not assured of regular supplies of at least 20 million tons of coal annually from Germany." Quoted in Lynch, *France and the International Economy*, 30.

28. Monnet, *Memoirs*, 288–317.

29. The text of Schuman's declaration is reprinted in Poidevin, *Robert Schuman*, 261–62.

30. General Jean de Lattre de Tassigny told the National Defense Committee, "As long as we hold in Indochina, we will remain a great power. . . . On the contrary, if we lose, we will be the 'sick man' of the second half of the twentieth century." Minutes of the National Defense Committee, 20 Feb. 1951 AnF, 552 AP 45, 4AU/Dr. 3.

31. See Thompson, "Defending the Rhine."

32. Ibid., 477–79.

33. Ibid., 479.

34. See Creswell, "With a Little Help," 6–7.

35. See Creswell and Trachtenberg, "France and the German Question," 14–16.

36. In 1949 Ely would be named the French representative on the Military Committee of the Brussels Pact; Stehlin served as France's military attaché to London from 1947 to 1950. In Jun. 1953 he became head of France's permanent military delegation to the Atlantic Alliance.

37. Robert Schuman served as prime minister from 24 Nov. 1947 to 26 Jul. 1948.

38. Ely and Stehlin quoted in Guillen, "Les chefs militaires français," 4.

39. Raflik, "La IVe République," 85.

40. "United States Minutes, Private Meeting of the Foreign Ministers," New York, 12 Sept. 1950, FRUS 1950, vol. 2, 1199.

41. British foreign secretary Ernest Bevin also regretted Acheson's hardball tactics, counseling him, "You've got the right idea, me lad, but you're goin' about it the hard way." See Acheson, *Present at the Creation*, 442.

42. Acheson-Schuman-Bevin meeting, 12 Sept. 1950, FRUS 1950, vol. 3, 1200.

43. Bevin to foreign office, 13 Sept. 1950, DBPO, series 2, vol. 3, 36.

44. See " The Secretary of State to the Acting Secretary of State," 26 Sept. 1950, FRUS 1950, vol. 3, 350, 52; and "Memorandum of Conversation, by the Assistant to the Secretary of State," FRUS 1950, vol. 3, 352, 53.

45. Provisional because the National Assembly, France's main legislative body, had to first be consulted.

46. Telegram, 18 Oct. 1950, TNA, FO 371/85089.

47. Telegram, 28 Dec. 1950, Library of Congress, Washington, Averell Harriman Papers, Trip, Correspondence, box 301.

48. Quoted in Vial, "Limites et contradictions," 23.

49. Pleven's quotes in this paragraph found at "Statement by René Pleven on the Establishment of a European Army (24 October 1950)," CVCE, https://www.cvce.eu/en/obj/statement_by_rene_ pleven_on_the_establishment_of_a_european_army_24_october_1950-en-4a3f4499-daf1-44c1- b313-212b31cad878.html.

50. This European army would have included soldiers from Belgium, France, Germany, Italy, Luxembourg, and the Netherlands, and would have been integrated down to units as small as brigades and even battalions.

51. Churchill Archives Centre, Cambridge University, Gladwyn Jebb papers, 19 Nov. 1951, GLAD 1/1/1.

52. *L'Année Politique, 1950*, 222–24.

53. "Minutes of the Fourth Meeting, First, Second, and Third Sessions Held on 28–31 Oct. 1950," NATO Archives, Brussels, Record-DC-004.
54. "The United States Deputy Representative on the North Atlantic Council to the Secretary of State," 26 Jul. 1950, FRUS 1950, 143.
55. "Minutes of the National Defence Committee," 16 Dec. 1950. AnF, 552 AP 44, 4AU 5/Dr 1.
56. Ibid. For the provisions of the Spofford Plan, see FRUS 1950, vol. 3, 457–64.
57. Schwartz, *America's Germany*, 150.
58. Creswell, *A Question of Balance*, 64.
59. "The European Defence Community," 28 Oct. 1953. North Atlantic Treaty Organization, OV178/2; 11 Feb. 1953–12 Aug. 1958, The Bank of England Archive, London, CBP887v4-9.
60. Thompson, "Defending the Rhine," 476–77.
61. Raflik, "La IVe République," 216.
62. "NATO: Disappointing Performance," *Time* 60, 8 Dec. 1952, 28–29.
63. Mendès France, *Œuvres complètes*, vol. 2, 541–47; Mendès France, *Œuvres complètes*, vol. 3, 54–56; Cesari, "The Declining Value."
64. See Raflik, "Les dissensions Franco-américaines."
65. Creswell, *A Question of Balance*, 158–59.
66. The United Kingdom committed itself to stationing four divisions and a tactical air fleet on the European mainland, and it agreed not to withdraw them against the wishes of the other members. The United States had already committed additional divisions to Europe by 1951.
67. The rejected section would have modified the Brussels Treaty Organization to permit the membership of Germany and Italy.
68. Mendès France quoted in Creswell and Trachtenberg, "France and the German Question," 26.

Bibliography

Acheson, D. 1987. *Present at the Creation: My Years in the State Department*. New York: W. W. Norton.
Bitzinger, R. A. 1989. "Assessing the Conventional Balance in Europe, 1945–1975." RAND Note N-2859-FF/RC.
Bothwell, R. 2007. *Alliance and Illusion: Canada and the World, 1945–1984*. Vancouver, Canada: University of British Columbia Press.
Cesari, L. 2007. "The Declining Value of Indochina: France and the Economics of Empire, 1950–1955." In *The First Vietnam War: Colonial Conflict and Cold War Crisis*, edited by M. A. Lawrence and F. Logevall, 175–95. Cambridge: Harvard University Press.
Creswell, M. 2002. "With a Little Help from Our Friends: How France Secured an Anglo-American Continental Commitment, 1945–54." *Cold War History* 3, no. 1: 1–28.
———. 2006. *A Question of Balance: How France and the United States Created Cold War Europe*. Cambridge: Harvard University Press.
Creswell, M., and M. Trachtenberg. 2003. "France and the German Question, 1945–1955." *Journal of Cold War Studies* 5, no. 3: 5–28.
Demory, J.-C. 1995. *Georges Bidault*. Paris: Editions Julliard.
Guillen, P. 1983. "Les chefs militaires français, le réarmement de l'Allemagne et la CED 1950–1954." *Revue d'histoire de la Seconde Guerre mondiale et des conflits contemporains* 129: 3–33.
Kaplan, L. S. 2007. *NATO 1948: The Birth of the Transatlantic Alliance*. Lanham, MD: Rowman & Littlefield Publishers.
Lynch, F. 2006. *France and the International Economy: From Vichy to the Treaty of Rome*. London: Routledge.
May, E. R. 1989. "The American Commitment to Germany, 1949–55." *Diplomatic History* 13, no. 4: 431–60.
Melandri, P., and M. Vaïsse. 1986. "France: From Powerlessness to the Search for Influence." In *Power in Europe? Great Britain, France, Italy and Germany in a Postwar World, 1945–1950*, edited by J. Becker and F. Knipping, 461–74. Berlin: De Gruyter.

Mendès France, P. 1985. *Œuvres complètes*. Vol. 2, *Une politique de l'économie 1943–54*.
———. 1986. Œuvres complètes. Vol. 3, *Gouverner, c'est choisir 1954–55*.
Monnet, J. 1978. *Memoirs*. Garden City, NJ: Doubleday.
Poidevin, R. 1986. *Robert Schuman, homme d'Etat, 1886–1963*. Paris: Imprimerie nationale.
Raflik, J. 2005. "Les dissensions Franco-américaines face à la politique indochinoise de la France. 1950–1954," paper presented at "Cold War France and America: New Perspectives," Florida State University.
———. 2009. "La IVe République et l'OTAN: fidélité à l'Alliance ou revendications nationales?" *Bulletin de l'Institut Pierre Renouvin* 30: 77–90.
Schwartz, T. A. 1991. *America's Germany: John J. McCloy and the Federal Republic of Germany*. Cambridge: Harvard University Press.
Svik, P. 2016. "The Czechoslovak Factor in Western Alliance Building, 1945–1948." *Journal of Cold War Studies* 18, no. 1: 133–60.
Thompson, M. 2015. "Defending the Rhine in Asia: France's 1951 Reinforcement Debate and French International Ambitions." *French Historical Studies* 38, no. 3: 473–99.
Trachtenberg, M. 1999. *A Constructed Peace: The Making of the European Settlement, 1945–1963*. Princeton, NJ: Princeton University Press.
Vial, P. 2002. "Limites et contradictions d'une méthode: Monnet et les débuts de la construction communautaire 1950–1954." In *Cinquante ans après la déclaration Schuman, histoire de la construction européenne*, edited by M. Catala, 45–101. Nantes, France: Ouest Editions.
Young, J. W. 1990. *France, the Cold War, and the Western Alliance, 1944–49: French Foreign Policy and Post-War Europe*. Basingstoke, UK: Palgrave Macmillan.

CHAPTER 4

IMPOSSIBLE ALLIES?
SOVIET VIEWS OF FRANCE AND THE GERMAN QUESTION IN THE 1950S

GEOFFREY ROBERTS

At the center of the Union of Soviet Socialist Republics' (USSR, or Soviet Union) strategy for the containment of Germany in the 1950s was courtship of France—a state that Moscow saw as sharing a common interest in security from German militarism and aggression. Nowhere in Western Europe was Soviet political influence as great as it was in France. The French Communist Party (PCF) was a major force in the country and France was the bastion of a powerful, communist-led international peace movement. The movement's founding congress in Paris in April 1949 attracted more than two thousand delegates claiming to represent 600 million people, while the 1950 Stockholm Appeal calling for the prohibition of nuclear weapons garnered half a billion signatures worldwide, including 15 million in France. Among the movement's French luminaries were the scientist and Nobel laureate Frédéric Joliot-Curie, who was the president of the World Peace Council (WPC); the writer Jean Lafitte, who was WPC secretary; and former Air Minister and radical deputy Pierre Cot. Ilya Ehrenburg, the leading Soviet representative on the WPC, spent almost as much time in Paris in the 1950s as he did in Moscow. The Soviet leadership followed events in France avidly and the Soviet embassy in Paris was a frequent channel of communication between Moscow and the leaders of the PCF and the peace movement.[1]

There was a long history of Soviet efforts to woo France. In the 1930s France was at the center of the Soviet struggle for a collective security front against Hitler. During World War II Moscow established relations with de Gaulle's Free French Movement and in December 1944 the general traveled to Moscow to sign a mutual assistance pact between the Soviet Union and liberated France. After the war, Moscow remained highly interested in the Gaullist movement and cultivated contacts with its leaders. In the 1950s the Soviets followed closely the fortunes of the Gaullist splinter group, Les Républicains sociaux, headed by Jacques Chaban-Delmas and Gaston Palewski, a group seen as striving for rapprochement between France and the Soviet Union. De Gaulle was also seen as sympathetic to the Soviet Union; the Soviets noted with approval the general's statement in April 1954 that France should play an independent role in international affairs and work to facilitate coexistence and agreement between the two Cold War blocs.

Central to Moscow's postwar perspective was an alliance with France based on an assumed common antipathy to Germany. However, this outlook was rendered redundant by Paris's embrace of Western Cold War policies. France joined NATO in 1949 and thereafter increasingly identified the Soviet Union as the main threat to French security.[2] In May 1952 France signed a treaty to establish a European Defence Community (EDC), including the rearmament of West Germany. In August 1954 the French parliament refused to ratify the EDC but German rearmament went ahead anyway. Moscow retaliated by repudiating the 1944 pact and by establishing the Warsaw Treaty Organization as a counter to NATO.

The threads of these troubled relations were drawn together by Soviet officials in an April 1956 briefing paper on the history of Franco-Soviet relations, prepared for Soviet leaders in advance of a visit to Moscow by a delegation of French Socialist Party leaders. The paper was sanguine about the future of Franco-Soviet relations. It pointed to the impact in France of recent Soviet peace initiatives, notably the Geneva Summit of July 1955, which had swayed public opinion in favor of a rapprochement with the Soviet Union. Crucially, the coming to power in February 1956 of a socialist-led government headed by Guy Mollet augured the possibility of significant improvements in Franco-Soviet relations.[3]

Soviet policy toward France in the 1950s was akin to Romain Rolland's maxim: pessimism of the intellect, optimism of the will. The Soviets placed great hopes on enlisting Paris in a campaign for European collective security but saw French foreign policy as weak and without much influence relative to Britain and the United States. Soviet conversations with French diplomats and politicians were generally friendly but the anti-communism and anti-Sovietism of Fourth Republic leaders was self-evident, as was their strong commitment to an alliance with the United States.

The view from Moscow was that the main obstacle to a Franco-Soviet alliance was a fundamental difference about the solution to the German question. While Moscow wanted to unify Germany as a peaceful and democratic state, the French preferred a divided and weak Germany, or so the Soviets believed. By 1956 French and Soviet policies on the German question had begun to converge. However, this incipient Franco-Soviet détente was blown away by the fallout from the Suez and Hungarian crises.

From the Stalin Notes to European Collective Security

Soviet policy on the German question was framed by the so-called Stalin Notes of March–April 1952 that proposed a peace treaty for Germany that would unify, neutralize, and disarm the country. In response, Western states, including France, called for all-German elections to elect a government that would then negotiate a peace treaty. The Soviets were willing to consider elections but with the precondition that a united Germany would remain unarmed and would not join either Cold War bloc.[4]

When in May 1952 the Western powers established the EDC, Stalin lost interest in the proposals that bear his name. But when Vyacheslav Molotov—the true author of the Stalin Notes—became foreign minister again after Stalin's death he revived the peace treaty proposal, a project he pursued doggedly until he was ousted from office by the new party leader, Nikita Khrushchev.

The French response to the Stalin Notes was, to use Georges-Henri Soutou's word, *méfiance* (mistrust).[5] French officials viewed the Notes as an attempt to disrupt Western military integration and the proposed peace treaty as a device to enhance Soviet influence in Germany. But the French foreign minister, Robert Schuman, with an eye to the attractiveness of the Soviet proposals to German and French public opinion, favored serious negotiations with the Soviet Union about Germany, including the possibility of its reunification.

Schuman's inclination to negotiate with the Soviets was abandoned when Georges Bidault returned as foreign minister in January 1953. Unlike Schuman, Bidault shared his officials' view that the least bad solution to the German question was the country's continued division. In Bidault's diplomacy the demand for all-German elections became a tactic to preclude serious negotiations with the Soviets. Only when Bidault was replaced by Pierre Mendès France in June 1954 was there a partial return to the idea of real, albeit prudent, negotiations with the Soviet Union.

Moscow's policy on the German question took a new turn when it began to agitate for European collective security. The launch pad for the campaign was the Berlin conference of the foreign ministers of Britain, France, the Soviet Union, and United States in January 1954.

On the eve of the conference Soviet Foreign Ministry analysts assessed the positions of the Western powers, highlighting that the official French stance would be no different from that of Britain and the United States. However, they reported, too, that Soviet political and diplomatic contacts in France indicated a wide range of opinion in favor of a more independent foreign policy and for collaboration with the Soviet Union in relation to Germany. In November 1953, for example, Palewski had told the Soviet ambassador in Paris, S. A. Vinogradov, that "for the resolution of the German question a rapprochement between France and the USSR was necessary. In this connection our group considers it very important to conclusively settle the question of Germany's border along the Oder-Neisse line and for the four powers to guarantee this frontier."[6] There were also reports from Soviet diplomatic sources that former prime minister—Édouard Daladier—and de Gaulle were hostile to the EDC and in favor of a rapprochement with the Soviet Union.

Bidault was, according to the Soviet analysts, pro-American and favored the EDC as a way of containing Germany, fearing that a united but neutral German state would come under Soviet influence. Bidault favored participation in the four-power conference in Berlin only to demonstrate that it was not possible to reach agreement with the Soviet Union. Even more hostile to negotiations with the Soviet Union was Deputy Prime Minister Paul Reynaud, but he also believed a five-power conference (i.e., including China and the Soviet Union) was necessary to end the war in Indochina.

On the basis of this somewhat contradictory picture, the briefing concluded that France was more open to serious discussion with the Soviet Union about the German question than either Britain or the United States. There was even the possibility of separate Soviet-French negotiations about Germany.[7]

Soviet proposals on the German question and European collective security were presented to the conference by Molotov. The essence of the Soviet position was that there should be a pan-European collective security agreement guaranteeing mutual assistance against aggression. Under the umbrella of European collective security, there could be negotiations for a German peace treaty leading to the reunification of the country as a neutral and pacific state. The Western alternative to this proposal, strongly backed by France, was the Eden Plan (named after British Foreign Secretary Anthony Eden) involving general elections in Germany whose government would then be free to decide its foreign policy—a proposal unacceptable to the Soviets who insisted on advance commitments to Germany's disarmament and neutralization.

Collective security was rejected by the West on grounds that the Soviet proposals were aimed at undermining NATO. At the conference Bidault and Eden badgered Molotov about this issue. Indeed, according to Alexei Filitov, it was Bidault "who most furiously attacked his Soviet counterpart."[8]

The Soviets had anticipated this objection in a briefing paper drawn up on the eve of the conference in January 1954. Moscow's answer, if the issue was raised, would be that the proposed European collective security system was certainly incompatible with the EDC—because it would divide Europe into opposing blocs—but was not necessarily incompatible with NATO.[9]

On 17 February Molotov told the conference that European collective security was an alternative to the EDC, and that "regarding the question of its compatibility with the North Atlantic Pact we are prepared to study this question. Don't forget that in relation to [NATO] there are different views. Eden has more than once emphasised that in his view it has a defensive character. Bidault also spoke about this. The Soviet government has a different estimation. . . . It is not to be excluded that [NATO] could be amended and the differences about the character of the pact eliminated."[10]

Although the Soviets were disappointed by Western rejection of their proposals, they were not surprised, nor were they disheartened. They were encouraged by reports of a positive public response to their European collective security idea, especially in France. Not long after his return from the conference, Molotov wrote to the Soviet leadership: "According to reports from Soviet embassies and missions and in the foreign press, the Soviet draft of a General European Agreement on Collective Security in Europe has provoked positive responses from quite wide public circles abroad, including such French press organs as *Le Monde*."[11]

Among the opponents of the Soviet proposal, noted Molotov, were those who feared that European collective security was a device to dislodge the United States from Europe. Molotov cited a statement by Palewski to Vinogradov that the Soviet proposal was unacceptable because it excluded the United States. Another argument against the proposal was that it was designed to secure the liquidation of NATO.

To meet these objections Molotov proposed a radical response: Moscow would shelve its objections to American participation in European collective security and would consider the possibility of the Soviet Union joining NATO. Molotov was pessimistic that anything would come of these proposals but he did not exclude the possibility that NATO could change with the Soviet Union becoming a member of the organization in the context of a wider collective security framework.[12]

The Soviet proposals were published in March 1954 and, as expected, were rejected by the Western powers; nevertheless, Moscow's campaign for European collective security continued.

The Geneva Conferences

After the Berlin Conference the main topic of Franco-Soviet diplomatic conversations was Indochina. It had been agreed in Berlin to convene an international conference on Indochina and Korea. This internationalizing of discussions on the war in Indochina was a significant success for French diplomacy as Paris strove to involve Moscow in extricating France from its military quagmire in Vietnam. The Soviets were happy to oblige, calculating that by playing a constructive role they would enhance the prospects for Franco-Soviet détente and collaboration on European problems.[13]

At the somewhat prolonged conference in Geneva (May–July 1954) France was initially represented by Bidault, but following a governmental crisis in June 1954 Pierre Mendès France became prime minister and foreign minister. By the end of the third week of July there was agreement on peace in Indochina.[14] The Americans suspected that Molotov and Mendès France had concocted a deal for the French to sabotage the EDC in return for Soviet help in resolving the Indochina conflict. But this supposition is not supported by either the French or Soviet diplomatic records.[15]

At the end of the conference, on 21 July, Molotov and Mendès France did have a long conversation about the German question and European security but there was little agreement between the two men.

The French record of the meeting states that the conversation began at Molotov's suggestion. According to the Soviet report, however, the discussion began with a declaration by Mendès France that now peace in Indochina had been achieved it was time to move to other questions. Molotov agreed and said that a rapprochement between French and Soviet views on European security and the German question was vital. When Mendès France interjected that other countries had an interest in these matters and that many ideas needed to be considered, Molotov responded that France and the Soviet Union were especially interested in the German question. Anglo-American proposals on Germany represented a serious threat to security in Europe, argued Molotov, and the division of the country would strengthen reactionary forces in West Germany. Molotov urged Mendès France to adopt a more independent foreign policy and asserted that a convergence in French and Soviet positions on the German question could prevent Germany's rearmament.

Mendès France replied that France was not a free agent. The British and Americans were intent on German rearmament and he urged Molotov to put forward "a new constructive proposal that would provide a basis for optimism on the part of the western powers." France was "in a difficult position," Mendès France told Molotov. "Of course France was independent but there was a reality to consider when taking decisions. It had to take into account the position of America and England on the German question."[16] Molotov appreciated France's complex position but reiterated that France faced a choice: whether or not to act in the interests of peace.

During the conversation Mendès France suggested the Soviet Union should launch a new initiative on nuclear disarmament and pointed out the importance of this question to French public opinion. But Molotov felt the more important issue was European collective security.[17]

Molotov's conversation with Mendès France was typical of the robust exchanges between French and Soviet officials about European security and the German question, "Le premier secrétaire du parti emploie un language direct" (the first secretary of the party uses a direct language), reported the French ambassador, Louis Joxe, after a bruising encounter with Khrushchev at a reception in Moscow in November 1954, "Il n'est pas précisement brutal, il est rude" (he is not exactly brutal, he is rough). Khrushchev berated Joxe about the recently signed London-Paris agreements on the direct admission of West Germany into NATO, demanding to know against what threat the Federal Republic of Germany (FRG, or West Germany) was being rearmed. But the conversation concluded on a more diplomatic note: "Together we Russians and French could do a lot for peace," Khrushchev told Joxe.[18]

While it is unlikely that Molotov derived much hope from his conversation with Mendès France, the success of the Geneva conference did provide an opening for the Soviet collective security campaign. On 24 July 1954 the Soviets published a diplomatic note proposing an agreement on economic and political cooperation in Europe and the convening of an international conference to discuss collective security.[19]

The French National Assembly's rejection of the EDC Plan by a large majority on 30 August 1954 was a considerable boost to the Soviet diplomatic campaign; on 10 September Moscow welcomed "the collapse of this projected military bloc" and reiterated its proposals for European collective security and the reunification of Germany as a peaceful and democratic state.[20]

What the Soviets did not anticipate was the London-Paris agreements. In a briefing paper the foreign ministry informed the Soviet leadership that this was a worse outcome for Moscow than the EDC Plan. Under the agreements, the FRG would enter NATO as an equal member and would have much more control over its rearmament than it would have had within the EDC, including in relation to atomic weapons research. In negotiations with the British and Americans the French had tried, but failed, to place controls on German rearmament. The result was that France had received "no serious guarantees against a revival of German aggression."[21]

This ominous development coincided with the tenth anniversary of the Franco-Soviet Pact. Moscow used the anniversary to celebrate the treaty and to attack the London-Paris agreements as incompatible with its mutual assistance obligations. This was the start of what Joxe described as a violent propaganda campaign.[22]

At a public meeting in Moscow on 10 December, Ehrenburg was greeted with stormy applause when he said, "The pen that ratified the Paris agreements will strike out the Franco-Soviet treaty. Every French man must know: either alliance with the Soviet Union against the resurgence of German militarism or alliance with the German militarists."[23] On 16 December the Soviet Union issued a note to France stating that ratification of the London-Paris agreements would render the Franco-Soviet Pact "null and void."[24]

The process of ratifying the London-Paris agreements was completed on 5 May 1955. That same day Joxe met the Soviet premier, Nikolai Bulganin. His mission was to assure the Soviets the agreements were defensive and that France wanted to maintain friendly relations with the Soviet Union. "The London-Paris agreements have opened the path to war and revanchism," Bulganin told Joxe. While Bulganin was unimpressed by Joxe's argument that West Germany's admission to NATO was a means to control German rearmament, he was more receptive to the idea there should be a four-power summit.[25]

In the Soviet mind the London-Paris agreements were linked to another series of threatening developments: the Schuman Plan, the establishment of the European Coal and Steel Community (ECSC), and the ongoing process of European economic integration. Moscow did not view European integration benignly. It viewed the ECSC, for example, as a device to facilitate the revival of Germany's industrial power as the basis for its rearmament. In France were to be found many prominent proponents of European federalism—advocates of an integrated West European political, economic, and military bloc that Moscow saw as directed against the Soviet Union.[26]

In 1955 Soviet policy turned toward creating a defensive glacis to counter the threat of a rearmed West Germany integrated into the Western military bloc. When the Bonn parliament ratified the London-Paris agreements on West Germany's admission to NATO the Soviet Union and its communist allies met in the Polish capital and signed the collective security agreement that was the basis for the Warsaw Treaty Organization.

Not long after the signature of the Warsaw Pact, the Soviets agreed with the Western powers to convene a summit of heads of state in Geneva. European collective security was the first item on the Soviet agenda for the meeting.

In the diplomatic sphere, the Soviet campaign for European collective security had been on the back foot since the London-Paris agreements. But politically the Soviet Union approached the Geneva summit in a far stronger position. By the middle of 1955 a plurality of Western public opinion supported collective security arrangements in Europe, while only a small minority favored the retention of NATO. An analysis of public opinion polling data from several West European countries, including France, prepared for the Eisenhower administration, concluded that the results "raise disquieting doubts about the future of NATO. . . . NATO, in fact, appears highly vulnerable from the opinion point of view. . . . At the least, it appears the people of Western Europe are now willing to consider security arrangements alternative to NATO."[27]

The Soviet peace campaign also reached its peak in mid-1955. The World Assembly for Peace in Helsinki at the end of June was the most diverse and broadly based of all the WPC's international gatherings. The Helsinki Appeal called for international differences to be resolved by discussion and negotiation. In August, on the tenth anniversary of the atomic bombing of Hiroshima, the WPC organized a petition calling for the prohibition of weapons of mass destruction that secured an astonishing 665,963,811 signatures, including one-third of Japan's population.[28]

In its pre-Geneva briefing for the Soviet leadership, the foreign ministry noted a strong tendency in French foreign policy toward an agreement with the Soviet Union about Germany, together with a deal on collective security. However, the French did not really want a united Germany, argued the briefing; they preferred some kind of federal solution that would keep the country divided.[29] As it happened, similar sentiments had been expressed by French peace activists at the Helsinki Assembly, who were not convinced that a united Germany was a good solution from the point of view of European security.[30]

The directive to the Soviet delegation to the summit summarized Moscow's policy toward France: the Soviet Union wanted to maintain and improve good relations with France but did not intend to damage France's relations with other countries. Moscow was prepared to replace the Franco-Soviet Pact with a new agreement and would refrain from doing anything that would add to France's difficulties in North Africa.[31]

Another paper sent to the Soviet leadership around the same time dealt with French difficulties in North Africa and their likely impact on France's policy at the Geneva summit. Just as the crisis in Indochina had weakened the French position at the Berlin foreign ministers conference, so France's colonial problems in Algeria, Morocco, and Tunisia would undermine its influence at Geneva. These problems were also weakening the French position within the Western bloc, especially since Paris was transferring French troops from Europe to North Africa. Internal political divisions within France were deepening and France's economic and strategic dependence on the United States was growing. The paper concluded that the French might seek Soviet help in resolving their problems in North Africa, the implication being that in those circumstances France might be more cooperative in relation to other matters.[32]

Very little of a concrete character resulted from the Geneva summit, except for an agreement to hold a foreign ministers' conference in the same venue. But the political atmosphere was good and there was much talk in the press about the so-called spirit of Geneva—the hope the summit would lead to a prolonged Soviet-Western détente. Expectations were high that there could be a Soviet-Western agreement on the German question and European collective security.

In a pre-conference briefing on the Geneva foreign ministers' meeting, the Soviet analysts noted that while the Western powers were united on Germany, there were divisions in relation to collective security, with Britain and especially France more inclined than the United States to seek an agreement with the Soviet Union. The French were expected to propose guarantees that would make the London–Paris agreements nonthreatening toward the Soviet Union, such as the inclusion of a united Germany in a pan-European collective security organization. However, according to the Soviet analysts, the French did not really want a united Germany, France's official position notwithstanding. They preferred an agreement between the Soviet Union and West Germany as the basis for a modus vivendi in Europe that would include restrictions on the armed forces of the two German states.[33]

The Soviets approached the Geneva conference of November–December 1955 confident their proposals on Germany and European collective security would make some headway. To reach agreement they were prepared to compromise, including allowing a long transition to a full-blown system of European collective security. These expectations were met when the Western powers presented proposals for a European Security Pact that, in effect, guaranteed the Soviets against a NATO attack. But this offer was linked to implementation of the Eden Plan—in other words, all-German elections leading to a united Germany that was then expected to remain in NATO.

Halfway through the conference Molotov hosted a friendly and relaxed dinner for the French delegation. Toward the end of the evening the talk turned to politics. When Foreign Minister Pinay said there could be no stability in Europe while Germany remained divided it provoked a tirade from Molotov against Germany in general and the FRG in particular: Do you really think you can keep the Germans in your bloc if they want to leave it? Do you really believe they will not try to dominate the alliance for their own purposes? We do not want a Germany governed by the Junkers. If the Germans ever decide to go to war again it would be a fight to the finish and we cannot accept guarantees from a military grouping that includes Germany. Molotov insisted that the division of Germany would take time to overcome and required a gradual rapprochement of the two German states. He was, he stressed, a supporter of elections in Germany but they could not be held in the immediate future. In response, Pinay said that France shared Soviet preoccupations but the division of Germany was the principal cause of insecurity in Europe.[34]

Shortly after the meeting Molotov returned to Moscow to try to persuade the Soviet leadership to accept Western proposals for all-German elections as a basis for negotiation. He was overruled by Khrushchev, who shared the French preference for a divided Germany, as long as the Soviet Union kept control of communist East Germany.

When Molotov returned to Berlin he gave a speech that closed the door to elections and hence to an agreed settlement of the German question. With the Soviets now insisting on the de-linkage of European collective security and the German question (previously the Soviets had insisted the two were inextricably linked) the Geneva conference closed without agreement.[35]

Khrushchev's rejection of Molotov's policy on the German question signified that Moscow now accepted that two Germanys were better than one. Because the Soviet Union possessed nuclear weapons, including the hydrogen bomb, Khrushchev was more sanguine than Molotov about German revanchism, but West Germany's potential military power threat to the Soviet Union could not be ignored. The campaign for European collective security continued, as did Soviet efforts to woo the French.

The Franco-Soviet Mini-Détente of Mid-1956

Even after the failure of the foreign ministers' conference and the dissipation of the spirit of Geneva, the Soviets remained optimistic about the future. A foreign ministry briefing paper of January 1956 emphasized the continuing popularity of Soviet proposals for collective security, especially in France.[36]

The outlook was particularly bright when it came to Franco-Soviet relations. The combative Joxe had been succeeded by Maurice Dejean in December 1955. While Dejean also had "une attitude méfiante" (a suspicious attitude) toward the Soviet Union, he saw the possibilities for a political evolution of the Soviet regime and favored a constructive dialogue with the Soviets.[37]

When Dejean called on Andrei Gromyko in January 1956, he told the Soviet deputy foreign minister that despite recent difficulties there had been progress in discussions on disarmament and European security. Gromyko responded that progress had been blocked by the Western position on the German question. Dejean countered by saying that he did not think there were fundamental differences between the West and the Soviet Union with regard to Germany, given the common interest in preventing a revival of German aggression. This was a short, protocol meeting with a new ambassador but Gromyko took the trouble to circulate his report to the Soviet leadership.[38]

The biggest beneficiary of the January 1956 elections in France was the PCF, which increased its parliamentary mandates to 150. In February a socialist-led government headed by Guy Mollet came to power, but its parliamentary majority depended on the communists, who were now the biggest party in the National Assembly.

In 1956 Moscow abandoned Molotov's complex multilateral diplomacy and pursued bilateral relations with Western states.[39] This new strategy also served to cement Khrushchev's and Bulganin's control of Soviet foreign policy. In January 1956 Bulganin proposed a U.S.-Soviet treaty of friendship and cooperation. At the twentieth party congress in February, Khrushchev proposed nonaggression pacts and friendship treaties as a means to regulate relations between states. In spring 1956 the Soviets had a series of meetings with Scandinavian leaders aimed at loosening that region's ties with the Western bloc. In April 1956 Bulganin and Khrushchev traveled to Britain on a battleship and conducted the first Anglo-Soviet summit since the war.

The culmination of this diplomatic offensive was the arrival in Moscow of a high-powered delegation headed by Mollet and Foreign Minister Christian Pineau—the first such Western government visit to the Soviet Union since the end of World War II.

Mollet's journey to Moscow in May 1956 followed a significant expansion of Soviet-French cultural, scientific, economic, and political contacts that had begun even before Stalin's death in March 1953. At the Moscow International Economic Conference in April 1952, the largest delegation was from France, including many business leaders. The aim of the conference was to break the Cold War economic blockade of the Soviet Union and the most generous offer on trade relations was made to the French. Soviet-French trade grew from 77 million roubles in 1952 to 481 million in 1957.[40]

The Soviets were also keen on developing cultural ties. French culture was big in the Soviet Union, especially the classics of French literature. In February 1952 fifteen hundred people attended a celebration in Moscow of the 150th anniversary of Victor Hugo's birth. In 1954 the Comédie-Française toured the Soviet Union.[41] More than fifty Soviet delegations or groups traveled to France in 1955 and thirty French delegations to the Soviet Union. French tourists were beginning to visit the Soviet Union in large numbers and Soviet cultural initiatives in France—in film and dance, for example—had been well received. In January 1957 there were nearly 123 million copies of books by French authors, translated into Russian, in circulation in the Soviet Union.[42]

In April 1956 a French Socialist Party delegation arrived in the Soviet Union on a fact-finding mission. Invited by the Soviet Communist Party, the delegation proposed to conduct an independent investigation of political and economic conditions in post-Stalin Russia. The delegation included many prominent French socialists, and its highly publicized tour visited Moscow, Leningrad, and Tbilisi, as well as a labor/prison camp at Tula.[43] In May the Soviet peace committee received a French parliamentary delegation to the Soviet Union that visited Moscow, Leningrad, and Kiev. That same month Moscow—and later Leningrad and Kiev—hosted an exhibition of French books by leading Parisian publishers. This was followed by an exhibition of French nineteenth-century art in Moscow and Leningrad and a broadcast by Soviet television of a history of French film. May also saw the publication of a new, biweekly French-language publication devoted to foreign and internal political affairs—*Nouvelles de Moscou.*

As Mikhail Narinski reports, the Soviets prepared intensively for the Franco-Soviet summit, which took place in Moscow from 16–19 May. A foreign ministry briefing paper designated the summit a trust-building exercise that would help improve relations and develop cooperation with France. In relation to Germany, the directives to the Soviet delegation stated that German reunification could come about only as a result of direct negotiations between the FRG and the German Democratic Republic (GDR, or East Germany).[44]

The summit took the form of a series of wide-ranging discussions of international questions.[45] According to Pineau, he had "never taken part in an international conference where the discussions were so frank and blunt."[46] Both sides agreed that allaying mutual suspicions was essential to a Franco-Soviet détente. In relation to Germany the French thought that an agreement on nuclear disarmament would facilitate German reunification. Such linkage was resisted by the Soviets, who wanted to keep the two issues separate. In their view the way forward was rapprochement between the two German states leading to eventual reunification.

The Franco-Soviet summit was the last major diplomatic duty performed by Molotov, who was fired as foreign minister in June 1956. In one of his more forceful contributions to the discussion, Molotov corrected Pineau's characterization of Soviet policy as being hostile to reunification: "We are not against it. But German rearmament, especially with nuclear arms, is as great a menace to France as it is to the USSR."[47]

While there was no convergence of French and Soviet positions on the German question during the Moscow conversations, after the summit there was some movement in the Soviets' position when, in July, they published proposals for a phased withdrawal of foreign armed forces from Germany as part of a process of European disarmament. In the same package were proposals for a nonaggression pact between NATO and the Warsaw Pact and an agreement on the nonuse of force by the two blocs.[48] Such suggestions were not novel but they did take the Soviets closer to the French emphasis on the importance of disarmament and arms control to the resolution of the German question.

Khrushchev was the main Soviet speaker at the summit and he harped on his favorite theme: Why did the French not play a more forceful role in international affairs? "The voice of France in international politics is weak. . . . In Geneva I had an unpleasant experience: we almost couldn't hear the voice of France. Do not see what I say to you as interference in your affairs. If France spoke with full awareness of its power and prestige, it wouldn't be for our benefit, but for the cause of peace, and the balance of forces in the world would be quite different."[49]

At the end of the summit the two sides issued a joint communiqué that spoke of conversations that had taken place in an atmosphere of friendship, warm sincerity, and mutual comprehension. Both governments pledged to work for a reduction of international tensions, for the improvement of Franco-Soviet relations and in support of peace and international security. There were also specific commitments on the improvement of trade, cultural, scientific, and sporting relations.[50]

The French delegation was welcomed with enthusiasm by the Moscow public. According to Reuters, Soviet and French leaders were mobbed by hundreds of cheering Russians when they emerged from an embassy reception. The summit was front-page news for days in the Soviet press. Reporters covered the French delegation's tourist activities as well as official functions such as a ceremony dedicating a plaque to forty-two French pilots who had died fighting on the Soviet-German front.[51] After the French departed, *Pravda* published a front-page editorial lauding the success of the summit and its positive impact on the international atmosphere.[52]

There was some discussion of Middle East issues at the summit but not about the crisis that was brewing in Egypt, which bubbled over when Nasser nationalized the Suez Canal Company in July 1956. Moscow was a staunch supporter of Egypt throughout the ensuing crisis, calling for a peaceful resolution of Nasser's dispute with Britain and France. The Soviets listened politely to French representations but rebuffed any suggestion that Moscow should modify its position on the crisis. When Dejean met Dmitry Shepilov on 7 August, the new Soviet foreign minister reminded him that Mollet and Pineau had agreed to work with Moscow to reduce international tensions in the Near and Middle East. Yet now France and Great Britain were acting in opposition to that common goal.[53]

In September Gromyko met Dejean and Edgar Faure, the former prime minister, who was a Russian speaker and a noted Slavophile. Faure told Gromyko that while he did not agree with military action against Egypt, Nasser's actions were wrong, dangerous, and reminiscent of Hitler. The two Frenchmen argued that from a trade point of view the Soviet interest in a stable Suez Canal regime was as great as that of the French. They suggested the Soviet Union could be given guarantees about access to the canal. But Gromyko was unimpressed and reiterated Soviet support for Egypt.[54]

When Britain, France, and Israel attacked Egypt at the end of October, the Soviet Union was forthright in its condemnation and rallied international support for the Nasser regime. On 4 November the Soviets made what Aleksandr Fursenko and Timothy Naftali describe as "a toothless call for a ceasefire."[55] The next day the Kremlin came out with a much stronger line in the form of messages from Bulganin to the British and French that famously threatened to use force and rocket attacks to stop the invasion of Egypt. The content of the two messages was broadly similar but there were some differences, indicating that Moscow was mindful of French public opinion and was trying not to burn all its bridges to Paris.

Bulganin's message to Mollet recalled that when they met in Moscow the French leader had spoken about his socialist ideas. "How can we reconcile the ideas of socialism with a treacherous attack by France on a country that only recently gained its independence and which does not have enough armaments for its defense?" But Bulganin's appeal for French restraint was more conciliatory than in his letter to the British: "It is time to show reason, to stop, not to allow belligerent forces to prevail"[56]

The Suez crisis was virtually over by the time Mollet replied to Bulganin on 8 November but that did not stop the French premier from attacking the Soviet Union's bloody suppression of the popular revolt in Hungary.

Soviet military action in Hungary provoked a highly negative reaction in France. There were massive popular demonstrations against the Soviet Union and both the

PCF and the peace movement were split by events in Budapest. When leaders of the peace movement met in Helsinki, they were unable to agree to a position on the Hungarian events. The best they could come up with was a neutral resolution that blamed the bloodshed on the Cold War.[57]

The Mollet government had fallen by the time Franco-Soviet relations had recovered from the twin crises of Suez and Hungary. There would be many more attempts to secure a Franco-Soviet détente, some more successful than others, but none that came close to the hopes entertained by Moscow in the mid-1950s.

Conclusion

France presented an enticing political and diplomatic target for the Soviets but consistently failed to live up to Moscow's expectations. At no point did the French break ranks with the British and Americans on European collective security and the German question. The Soviets wielded some influence within French politics but not enough to detach Paris from its united front with Britain and the United States.

It is tempting to conclude that a Franco-Soviet alliance was always impossible to achieve. But, as George-Henri Soutou has noted, neutrality was very fashionable in Europe in 1954–55 and the Soviet policy of neutralizing Germany within a collective security framework was not without its supporters in France.[58] In 1955 Molotov came quite close to securing a deal with the West on Germany and European collective security—an outcome that would have revolutionized the context of Soviet-French relations. The Franco-Soviet mini-détente of 1956 has been overlooked by historians, but Moscow's near rapprochement with Mollet's government is not to be lightly dismissed. Without the intervention of the Egyptian and Hungarian events it is quite possible there would have developed a significant Franco-Soviet détente.

The Soviets thought that France and the Soviet Union had many common interests and concerns in relation to the German question. The problem was that the French feared a Soviet influenced Germany more than a united Germany. While Moscow saw pan-European collective security as a solution to its fears of a German revival, the French saw it as a device that could destabilize their security situation. For Paris the resolution of the German question was only one key to European security, while the other was the containment of Soviet power.

Geoffrey Roberts, senior fellow, Helsinki Collegium for Advanced Studies (2018–19) is emeritus professor of history at University College Cork, and a Member of the Royal Irish Academy. His many books include *Stalin's Wars: From World War to Cold War, 1939–1953*; *Molotov: Stalin's Cold Warrior*; *Stalin's General: The Life of Georgy Zhukov*; and *Churchill and Stalin: Comrades in Arms during the Second World War*.

Notes

1. On the peace movement in France, see Santamaria, *Le parti de l'ennemi?*; Brogi, *Confronting America*; and Buton, "Le Mouvement des partisans."
2. See Soutou, "La perception de la menace soviétique."
3. *Ot Atlantiki do Urala*, 27–33.
4. On the Stalin note see Bjornstad, *The Soviet Union and German Reunification*; Filitov, *Germaniya v Sovetskom*, 138–73; and Loth, *Die Sowjetunion*, 101–57.
5. Soutou, "La France et les notes soviétiques."
6. "Pozitsiya Frantsii po Voprosu o Predstoyashchem Soveshchanii Ministrov Inostrannykh Del Chetyrekh Derzhav," 13 Jan. 1954, AVPRF, F.6, Op.13-g, Pap.65, D.26, Ll.90–116.
7. Ibid.
8. Filitov, "Germany as a European Problem," 328.
9. "Obsuzhdenie Voprosa na Berlinskom Soveshchanii ob Obshcheevropeiskom Dogovora o Kollektivnoi Bezopastnosti v Evrope," Jan. 1954, AVPRF, F.6, Op.13-g, Pap.65, D.25, Ll.10–11.
10. Roberts, *Molotov*, 146–47.
11. Ibid.
12. See, further, Roberts, "Molotov's Proposal."
13. On Soviet preparations for Geneva, see Obichkina, "SSSR v Uregulirovanii."
14. On Geneva see Gaiduk, *Confronting Vietnam*; and Olsen, *Soviet-Vietnam Relations*.
15. See Statler, "Alliance Politics."
16. Ibid.
17. "Priem Predsedatelya Soveta Ministrov Frantsii Mendes-Fransa," 21 Jul. 1954, AVPRF, F.6, Op.13a, Pap.25, D8, Ll.121–130. The French report is broadly similar. Mendès France later claimed he raised the Austrian question with Molotov, thus initiating the process leading to the Austrian State Treaty, but neither the Soviet nor the French reports mentions this. See further Angerer, "Re-launching East-West Negotiations."
18. Joxe, "Letter to P. Mendès France," 9 Nov. 1954, DDF 1954, vol. 2, 671–72.
19. *New Times*, no. 31 (1954): 4–8. *New Times* was a weekly Soviet magazine. Published in several languages, it was closely associated with the Soviet Foreign Ministry and carried official documents and statements and provided authoritative coverage of international affairs from Moscow's point of view.
20. *New Times*, no. 37 (1954): 2–5.
21. "Londonskie i Parizhskie Soglasheniya Zapadnykh Derzhav i Sopostavlenie Plana Sozdaniya 'Zapadnoevropeiskogo Souza's Planon Sozdania 'Evropeiskogo Oboronitel'nogo Soobshchestva,'" 29 Oct. 1954, RGANI, F.5, Op.30, D.69, Ll.147–66.
22. Joxe, "Letter to P. Mendès France," 17 Dec. 1954, DDF 1954, vol. 2, 932–33.
23. *New Times*, no. 50 (1954): 5–22.
24. *New Times*, no. 51(1954): 2–4.
25. Priem N.A. Bulganinym Frantsuzskogo Posla Lui Zhoksa," 5 May 1955, RGANI, F.5, Op.30, D.116, Ll.53–60.
26. "Spravka o Evropeiskom Ob'edinenii Uglya i Stali (Plan Shymana)," 20 Jan. 1955, RGANI, F.5, Op.30, D.114, Ll.1–38; "Spravka o Planakh 'Ob'edineniya Evropy,'" 20 Jan. 1955, RGANI, F.5, Op.30, D.114, Ll.47–65; "Spravka ob Organizatsii Evropeiskogo Ekonomicheskogo Sotrudnichestva," 7 Feb. 1955, RGANI, F.5, Op.30, D.114, Ll.115–137. See further Lipkin, *Sovetskii Souz*; Rey, "L'Europe occidentale"; and Rey, "Le retour à l'Europe?"
27. Eisenhower Library, Eisenhower Papers, A. Whitman File, International Meetings series, box 2, Geneva Conference 1955.
28. Roberts, "Averting Armageddon."
29. "O Vozmozhnykh Pozitsiyakh Zapadnykh Derzhav po Osnovnym Mezhdunarodnym Voprosam na Predstoyashchem Soveshchanii Glav Pravitel'stv Chetyrekh Derzhav," 7 Jul. 1955, Fond 89: The Soviet Communist Party on Trial, F.89, Op.7, D.7, Ll.79–84.

30. "Ob Itogakh Vsemirnoi Assamblei Mira (22–29 Iunya 1955g. Khel'sinki)," 11 Jul. 1955, RGANI, F.5, Op.28, D.356, LL.147-153, here 149–50.
31. "Direktivy dlya Delegatsii SSSR na Soveshchanii Glav Pravitel'stv Chetyrekh Derzhav," Jul. 1955, AVPRF, F.6, Op.14, Pap.3, D.43, Ll.155–156.
32. "Obostrenie Polozheniya vo Frantsuzskoi Severnoi Afrike i Vliyanie etogo Faktora na Vneshnepoliticheskii Kurs Frantsii pered Soveshchaniem Chetyrekh Derzhav," 28 Jun. 1955, RGANI, F.5, Op.20, D.337, Ll.68–90.
33. "O Vozmozhnykh Pozitsiyakh Trekh Zapadnykh Derzhav po Germanskomu Voprosu i Voprosu o Bezopasnosti v Evrope na Predstoyashchim Ministrov Inostrannykh Del SSSR, SShA, Anglii i Frantsii v Zheneve," 17 Oct. 1955, RGANI, F.5, Op.30, D.114, Ll.191–217.
34. "M. Pinay, Ministre des Affaires étrangères au ministère des Affaire étrangères," 5 Nov. 1955, DDF 1955, vol. 2, 779–781.
35. See Roberts, "A Chance for Peace?," 55–59.
36. "Vyskazyvaniya v Politicheskikh Krugakh Zapadnykh Stran o Putyakh Resheniya Problemy Evropeiskoi Bezopasnosti posle Zhenevskogo Soveshchaniya Ministrov Inostrannykh Del," 31 Jan. 1956, RGANI, F5, Op.20, D384, Ll.255–268.
37. Davieau-Pousset, "Maurice Dejean."
38. "Priem Frantsuzskogo Posla v Moskve M. Dezhana," 23 Jan. 1956, AVPRF, F.022, Op.9, Pap.40, D.2, LL.91–12.
39. Van Oudenaren, *Détente in Europe*, 67–70.
40. Lipkin, "Avril 1952."
41. Van Eerde, "The Comédie-Française."
42. "Spravka o Sovetsko-Frantsuzskikh Kul'turnykh Svyazykh 1957." RGALI, F.1204, D.3427, LL.1–4.
43. See the account of the socialist delegation's visit on the website "Voyages en URSS."
44. Narinsky, "La visite de la délégation française," 456–57.
45. The French record of the Franco-Soviet discussions may be found in DDF 1956, vol.1, 791–822. The Soviet record is cited and referenced in Narinsky, "La visite de la délégation française."
46. Reuters report in the file on French diplomatic relations, 1956-1964. Open Society Archive, Budapest, 300–80-1-1085.
47. "Memos of Franco-Soviet conversations, Moscow," 16–19 May 1956, 804.
48. AVPRF, F.0536, Op.1, Pap.2, D.27, Ll.1–13.
49. "Memos of Franco–Soviet conversations, Moscow, 16–19 May 1956," 802.
50. "Le communiqué final témoigne d'une bonne volonté mutuelle," *Le Monde*, 22 May 1956.
51. "Otkrytie Memorial'noi Dosku v Pamyat' Frantsuzskikhk Letchikov," *Pravda*, 19 May 1956.
52. "Pod Znamenem Mirnogo Sosushchestvovaniya," *Pravda*, 21 May 1956.
53. "Zapis Besedy Ministera Inostrannykh Del SSSR D.T. Shepilova s Poslom Frantsii v SSSR M. Dezhanom," 7 Aug. 1956, in *Blizhnevostochnyi Konflikt*, 470–472.
54. "Zapis Besedy Pervogo Zamestitelya Ministera Inostrannykh Del SSSR A.A. Gromyko s Vyvshim Prem'er-Ministrom Frantsii E. Forom," 21 Sept. 1956, in *Blizhnevostochnyi Konflikt*, 498–99.
55. Fursenko and Naftali, *Khrushchev's Cold War*, 132. Fursenko and Naftali cover the Suez crisis from the Soviet perspective. For the French point of view see Vaïsse, "Frantsiya, Sovetskii Souz."
56. Letter from Nikolai Bulganin to Guy Mollet on the Suez Crisis, 5 Nov. 1956, Centre Virtuel de la Connaissance sur l'Europe (CVCE; Virtual Centre for Knowledge on Europe), https://www.cvce.eu/content/publication/1999/1/1/55f243a1-de38-401d-9834-d279bf3874b3/publishable_fr.pdf (retrieved 28 Feb. 2019).
57. See Jansen, "Budapeshtskii Krizis."
58. Soutou, "Les Français et la question."

Bibliography

Angerer, T. 2005. "Re-launching East-West Negotiations While Deciding West German Rearmament: France, the Paris Treaties and the Austrian State Treaty." In *Der österreichische Staatsvertrag 1955. Internationale Strategie, rechtliche Relevanz, nationale Identität*, edited by G. Mueller, G. Stourzh, A. Suppan, 265–333. Vienna: Österreichische Akademie der Wissenschaften.

Bjornstad, S. 1998. *The Soviet Union and German Reunification during Stalin's Last Years*. Oslo: Norwegian Institute for Defence Studies.

Blizhnevostochnyi Konflikt 1947–1956. 2003. Moscow: Demokratiya.

Brogi, A. 2011. *Confronting America: The Cold War between the United States and the Communists in France and Italy*. Chapel Hill: University of North Carolina Press.

Buton, P. 2002. "Le Mouvement des partisans de la paix." In Dockrill, et al., *L'Europe de l'Est et de l'Ouest*, 227–39.

Davieau-Pousset, S. 2015. "Maurice Dejean, diplomatique atypique." *Relations internationales* 162, no. 2: 79–94.

Dockrill, S., et al. 2002. *L'Europe de l'Est et de l'Ouest dans la guerre froide 1948–1953*. Paris: PUPS.

Filitov, A. 2008. "Germany as a European Problem in Soviet and French Views." In Soutou and Robin-Hivert, *L'URSS et l'Europe*, 311–31.

———. 2010. *Germaniya v Sovetskom Vneshnepoliticheskom Planirovanii 1941–1990*. Moscow: Nauka.

Fursenko, A., and T. Naftali. 2006. *Khrushchev's Cold War*. New York: Norton.

Gaiduk, I. V. 2003. *Confronting Vietnam: Soviet Policy towards the Indochina Conflict, 1954–1963*. Washington, DC: Woodrow Wilson Center Press.

Jansen, S. 2005. "Budapeshtskii Krizis i Franko-Sovetskie Otnosheniya." In Vaïsse and Narinsky, *Sovetskii Souz, Frantsiya i Mezhdunarodnye Krizisy Pyatidesyatykh*, 106–34.

Lipkin, M. 2011. "Avril 1952, la conférence économique de Moscou. Changement de tactique ou innovation dans la politique extérieure stalinienne?." *Relations Internationales* 147, no. 3: 19–33. [English version of this article in *The Long Détente: Changing Concepts of Security and Cooperation in Europe, 1950s–1980s*, edited by O. Bange and P. Villaume, 53–76. Budapest, Hungary: Central European University Press, 2017.]

———. 2011. *Sovetskii Souz i Evropeiskaya Integratsiya*. Moscow: Rossiiskaya Akademiya Nauk/Institut Vseobshchei Istorii.

Loth, W. 2007. *Die Sowjetunion und die deutsche Frage. Studien zur sowjetischen Deutschlandpolitik von Stalin bis Chruschtschow*. Göttingen, Germany: Vandenhoek & Ruprecht.

Narinsky, M. 2008. "La visite de la délégation française en URSS en 1956." In Soutou and Robin-Hivert, *L'URSS et l'Europe*, 451–64.

Obichkina, E. 2005. "SSSR v Uregulirovanii Indokitaiskogo Konflikta 1954 god." In Vaïsse and Narinsky, *Sovetskii Souz, Frantsiya i Mezhdunarodnye Krizisy Pyatidesyatykh*, 4–22.

Olsen, M. 2006. *Soviet-Vietnam Relations and the Role of China 1949–1964*. London: Routledge.

Ot Atlantiki do Urala: Sovetsko-Frantsuzskie Otnosheniya 1956–1973. 2015. Moscow: Demokratiya.

Rey, M.-P. 2005. "Le retour à l'Europe? Les décideurs soviétiques face à l'intégration ouest-européenne 1957–1991." *Journal of European Integration History* 11, no. 1: 7–27.

———. 2008. "L'Europe occidentale et les décideurs soviétiques entre 1953 et 1955, perceptions et pratiques diplomatiques." In Soutou and Robin-Hivert, *L'URSS et l'Europe*, 411–25.

Roberts, G. 2008. "A Chance for Peace? The Soviet Campaign to End the Cold War 1953–1955." Cold War International History Project Working Paper 57. CWIHP, Washington DC (Dec.).

———. 2011. "Molotov's Proposal That the USSR Join NATO, March 1954." Cold War International History Project, e-Dossier 27. Available at http://www.wilsoncenter.org/publication/e-dossier-no-27-molotovs-proposal-the-ussr-join-nato-march-1954 (retrieved 6 Apr. 2017).

———. 2012. *Molotov: Stalin's Cold Warrior*. Dulles, VA: Potomac Books.

———. 2014. "Averting Armageddon: The Communist Peace Movement 1948–1956." In *The Oxford Handbook of the History of Communism*, edited by S. Smith, 322–38. Oxford: Oxford University Press.

Santamaria, Y. 2006. *Le parti de l'ennemi? Le parti communiste francais dans la lutte pour la paix 1947–1958*. Paris: Armand Colin.

Soutou, G.-H. 1988. "La France et les notes soviétiques de 1952 sur l'Allemagne." *Revue d'Allemagne* 20, no. 3: 261–73.

———. 2002. "La perception de la menace soviétique par les décideurs de l'Europe occidentale: Le cas de la France." In Dockrill, et al., *L'Europe de l'Est et de l'Ouest*, 21–43.

———. 2008. "Les Français et la question d'une éventuelle politique sovietique de "neutralité" en Europe 1954–1955." In Soutou and Robin-Hivert, *L'URSS et l'Europe*, 427–49.

Soutou, G.-H., and E. Robin-Hivert, eds. 2008. *L'URSS et l'Europe de 1941 à 1957*. Paris: PUPS.

Statler, K. C. 2006. "Alliance Politics after Stalin's Death: Franco-American Conflict in Europe and in Asia." In *The Cold War after Stalin's Death*, edited by K. Larres and K. Osgood, 157–75. Lanham, MD: Rowman & Littlefield.

Vaïsse, M. 2005. "Frantsiya, Sovetskii Souz i Suetskii Krizis." In Vaïsse and Narinsky, *Sovetskii Souz, Frantsiya i Mezhdunarodnye Krizisy Pyatidesyatykh*, 81–91.

Vaïsse, M., and M. Narinsky, eds. 2005. *Sovetskii Souz, Frantsiya i Mezhdunarodnye Krizisy Pyatidesyatykh*. Moscow: MGIMO.

Van Eerde, J. 1955. "The Comédie-Française in the USSR." *French Review* 29, no. 2: 131–39.

Van Oudenaren, J. 1991. *Détente in Europe: The Soviet Union and the West Since 1953*. Durham, NC: Duke University Press.

PART III

THE DE GAULLE FACTOR

CHAPTER 5

An Arbiter between the Superpowers

Charles de Gaulle and the German Question, 1958–1969

Garret J. Martin

"The German problem is the European problem par excellence," French President Charles de Gaulle famously declared during his press conference on 4 February 1965.[1] Throughout his eleven years in office (de Gaulle returned to power as prime minister in June 1958 and became president in January 1959), Germany remained a major preoccupation because it fundamentally intersected with his ambitions for France and Europe. Germany presented both a problem to be solved and a problem to be contained, as well as a vehicle to foster dramatic changes in Europe: this duality around Germany—both a challenge and an opportunity—was a constant of de Gaulle's foreign policy. De Gaulle actively pursued a new era of cooperation with West Germany because he believed that tying both countries closer together could serve his ambitious grand design, but a resurgent Bonn did not always prove so compliant.

De Gaulle regarded cooperation with the Federal Republic of Germany (FRG, or West Germany) as the cornerstone for a more independent Western Europe, one that could stand up to the superpowers; but that same partnership often caused great resentment with other allies on both sides of the Atlantic. In 1965, as well as in 1959, he described German reunification as a central component of a new European security order to overcome the division of Europe; such a reunification would have to be tightly controlled and regulated, though, to reassure and address the many concerns of other countries on the continent.

This chapter will focus on de Gaulle and the German question during his time in office from 1958 to 1969. It will outline the strategies that de Gaulle pursued to solve the German question, as well as how they changed over time according to circumstances—from a Franco-German rapprochement to a Franco-German partnership, to a pan-European approach with a close Franco-Soviet dialogue, and finally to an attempted Paris-Bonn-Moscow triangle.

De Gaulle and the German Question before 1958

De Gaulle was born in 1890 in a generation of people yearning for revenge for the loss of Alsace-Lorraine after the Franco-Prussian war of 1870–71.[2] Having served as an officer in World War I, he emerged as the leader of the Free French during World War II after his June 1940 appeal; in spring 1944, just before the liberation of France, a provisional government was created under his direction, and de Gaulle would remain in power as the country's head of government until January 1946. Germany, in other words, was continuously seen by de Gaulle as a threat to France until its surrender in May 1945. But with the emergence of the East-West conflict, the division of Germany into two states, and West Germany's integration into the Western alliance fundamentally changed its neighbors' perception of West Germany.

De Gaulle's stance toward Germany softened in the postwar era to reflect these new circumstances. Granted, his rhetoric after 1945 sometimes called for a punitive approach, preferring Germany to remain a weakened federation of states and opposing any moves toward the re-creation of a centralized Reich.[3] But, in practice, some of the directives de Gaulle put forward, as chairman of the Provisional Government of the French Republic (GPRF), for the French zone in Germany also emphasized the importance of cooperation, reconstruction, and democratization.[4] By late 1949 de Gaulle was committed to calling on the French and German people to overcome their troubled past, a position that he stuck to when he returned to power.[5]

De Gaulle's change of tone mirrored the change of atmosphere, as well as the improved relations between Paris and Bonn. During the 1950s, and despite the 1954 failure of the European Defence Community (EDC), many of the previous bones of contention between the two neighbors were resolved and both states cooperated closely within the framework of the European Coal and Steel Community (ECSC) and the European Economic Community (EEC), which had emerged in the wake of French Foreign Minister Robert Schuman's May 1950 declaration. In an era dominated by the superpowers and the beginning of the European construction project, France and (West) Germany had transcended their old quarrel.[6]

The German question—just like the European question—could not be separated from the international context of the Cold War. The general's embrace of reconciliation derived from his pragmatic understanding that he needed West Germany to fulfill his European objectives. Redemption for the continent could come through establishing a Western European organization, based on cooperation between states and not supranational integration, that could create a vital element of equilibrium between the superpowers.[7] In his memoirs de Gaulle argued that such a body might become "one of the three world powers, and if possible one day the arbiter between the Soviet Union and the Anglo-Saxon powers."[8] Yet there could be no meaningful Western European organization without a Franco-German entente as its foundation.[9]

De Gaulle's evolving views on the Cold War bipolar order, and its likely resiliency, shaped his approach toward the German question. Although de Gaulle was seriously worried about the danger posed by the Soviet Union at the start of the East-West conflict,[10] he increasingly resented France and Europe's relative marginalization in that conflict. In his eyes the February 1945 Yalta Conference (to which France had not been invited) had sealed the fate of Europe. That fate was now determined without the involvement of the European powers: the division of the continent into two blocs, de Gaulle deplored, had compromised the old European balance system.[11]

De Gaulle's opposition to the bipolar order sharpened in the years before his return to power. Despite initially welcoming the signing of the Atlantic Pact in 1949, he shifted to a more lukewarm stance during the 1950s, especially after the crises surrounding the EDC (1954) and the Suez Canal (1956). He resented the deterioration of France's position within the Atlantic alliance and the subordination of French leaders to their American counterparts.[12] At the same time, de Gaulle lambasted Paris's failure to reach out to the other side of the Iron Curtain.[13]

While de Gaulle deplored the detrimental impact of the Cold War on France's status, he also came to believe that the risks of war in Europe were declining. Besides his view that the chances of a Soviet invasion of Western Europe were receding in the 1950s because the Soviets faced internal challenges, he also came to the conclusion that the superpowers were not willing to start a nuclear war; if one did not resort to war, then one had to make peace sooner or later. This, according to de Gaulle, undermined the raison d'être of the existing military alliances in Europe.[14] It also offered an opportunity to eventually solve the German question.

1958–62: Rapprochement with Bonn

Thus, when de Gaulle returned to power in 1958, he did so with a long-term blueprint for overcoming the Cold War in Europe; this approach shaped his approach toward the German question. During his presidency, he would pursue a number of strategies that varied according to circumstances, but he never fundamentally deviated from his overarching goal and assumptions. France, through a partnership with West Germany, would establish a Western European grouping that could stand up to both superpowers. At the same time, he also believed that Russia would eventually discard communism, and accept to play a traditional balancing role in a modernized version of the Concert of Europe.[15]

Between 1958 and 1962 a number of domestic and international obstacles affected de Gaulle's stance toward the German question. At home the French president needed to deal, first and foremost, with economic recovery and the divisive Algerian War. Abroad, the renewed and enduring period of East-West tensions over Berlin (1958–61) and Cuba (1962) undermined any opportunity for a meaningful dialogue between both sides of the Iron Curtain.

These constraints contributed to de Gaulle focusing in this period on his Western European ambitions, and in particular on relations with Bonn. Starting with their first meeting in September 1958, the general went to great lengths to build close ties with the West German Chancellor Konrad Adenauer: in the following five years, the leaders would meet fifteen times, would have more than a hundred hours of discussion, and would correspond regularly.[16]

Two key factors played a vital role in cementing that strong partnership. First, the Soviet Union posed a common threat for both countries.[17] Soviet leader Nikita Khrushchev's speech on 10 November 1958, which called for the signature of a German peace treaty that would recognize the existence of two Germanys and establish West Berlin as a free city, unleashed a second Berlin crisis; the first had taken place in 1948–49 as a result of the Soviet blockade around West Berlin. For the next few years, Europe, the Soviet Union, and the United States remained in a state of extreme tension.[18] De Gaulle's intransigent attitude toward the Soviet Union, though, greatly pleased Adenauer, and created further common ground between the two leaders. The French president strongly opposed any negotiations with Moscow as long as it maintained its threatening attitude.[19]

Moreover, Adenauer and de Gaulle shared somewhat compatible ambitions when it came to Western Europe's place in the Cold War and its relationship with the superpowers. During their first meeting both men agreed on the need for greater European cooperation. When de Gaulle emphasized the need for Europe to become more independent of the United States, Adenauer concurred that it would be disastrous if Europeans allowed themselves to become mere instruments of the United States.[20]

That said, the Franco-German rapprochement was hardly plain sailing, and faced differences of opinions and perspectives. Unlike de Gaulle, Adenauer seemed more willing to accept the kind of federal Europe that derived from the Schuman Plan and was ingrained in the 1957 EEC Treaty, and he did not vigorously oppose integration in NATO. And while the general pushed for Franco-German reconciliation, he did not place both countries on an equal footing. France, for de Gaulle, was a Great Power with global reach, symbolized by its permanent seat in the United Nations Security Council, the presence of its troops in Germany and occupation rights in Berlin, and its nuclear status. Once in office, he immediately cancelled an agreement on tripartite cooperation between France, Italy, and West Germany on joint research and production of nuclear weapons.[21] Instead, he pushed for the development of a national *force de frappe*, and maintained an ambivalent attitude toward any German attempt to do likewise.[22]

Even the Franco-German convergence on the Soviet threat contained some differences of appreciation. While both leaders were wary of communism, they justified their rapprochement because they feared the risk of the other flirting with the Soviet Union.[23] Furthermore, de Gaulle showed greater optimism for the potential of détente in Europe. If the French president understood that there were no such prospects in the 1958–62 period, he still sent a number of signals to suggest that he anticipated future changes. Thus, in his press conference of 25 March 1959, the general stated that reunification was the destiny of the German people, as long as it occurred within a larger European organization that included the whole continent.[24]

De Gaulle also expressed greater faith that the Eastern bloc would one day evolve in a way favorable to détente.[25] As he outlined during a press conference in November 1959, the Soviet leaders understood the dangers created by nuclear weapons and the need for peace, the Russian people aspired to a better life and freedom, and Moscow could see the desire for independence of the peoples of Eastern Europe who craved emancipation. Moreover, de Gaulle believed that the communist camp would fragment because of the likely rivalry between Russia and communist China. Considering all these factors, he reached the conclusion that the communist world could not escape fundamental change.[26]

Additionally, de Gaulle took some steps to appease the Soviet Union. In his 25 March 1959 press conference the French president had made it clear that Germany should not be allowed to challenge the Oder-Neisse line in the future, a message that was well received in Moscow.[27] The following year, he told Khrushchev that only a European détente "from the Atlantic to the Urals" would solve the German question by "controlling the German body in a Europe of peace and progress," before suggesting that he was in "no hurry" when it came to German reunification; and in 1962, he publicly claimed that a close Franco-German cooperation would make possible the establishment of a new European equilibrium between East and West.[28]

But these differences and ambiguities notwithstanding, by 1963 de Gaulle and Adenauer had successfully laid the basis of a Franco-German partnership. In the summer of 1960, after the definitive failure of France's 1958 proposal for a tripartite directorate with the United States and Britain within NATO and against the backdrop of renewed East-West tensions, de Gaulle gave new momentum to European political cooperation.[29] Following the failure of the Fouchet Plan, a planned intergovernmental union in the economic, political, and military spheres between the EEC member states, Paris and Bonn agreed, in spring 1962, to conclude a bilateral political union. The resulting Franco-German Treaty of 22 January 1963 (which became known as the Elysée Treaty) marked a symbolic high point of Franco-German rapprochement.

1963–64: The Trials and Tribulations of the Franco-German Partnership

The Elysée Treaty signaled the start of a more ambitious phase in de Gaulle's approach toward the German question. De Gaulle felt he could take advantage of the more favorable domestic and international context to largely focus on foreign policy. The October 1962 Cuban Missile Crisis had further convinced de Gaulle that neither superpower wanted to fight a nuclear war.[30] At the same time, the Evian Accords in March had finally ended the war in Algeria, removing a major constraint on French diplomacy.[31]

The year 1963 signaled de Gaulle's shift to more-dramatic measures to fulfill his objective of reforming the Western world and bolstering his country's claim to Great Power status. The Franco-German Treaty served as an important cornerstone of this new ambitious phase of French foreign policy: it represented the solemn act of reconciliation between the French and German people; it promised bilateral cooperation in the fields of foreign policy, defense, and education;[32] and it hinted at a Europe that progressively emancipated itself from the United States.[33]

De Gaulle expected that the Elysée Treaty could strengthen Western Europe's ability to stand up to the Soviet Union. As he told his minister of Information, Alain Peyrefitte, "We did not sign the Franco-German treaty to please the Soviet Union."[34] Since Adenauer often lamented, "We are the victims of America's détente policy," the general also realized that he could maintain leverage over the West German chancellor by taking a tough line toward negotiations with Moscow.[35] This tactic was evident during the limited period of superpower détente following the Cuban Missile Crisis, which culminated with the Partial Test Ban Treaty of August 1963. De Gaulle opposed that treaty because it threatened to undermine their emerging independent nuclear arsenal, and because he viewed the superpower talks as an insufficient form of détente.[36]

De Gaulle believed he could capitalize on Bonn's uneasiness about the Partial Test Ban Treaty.[37] He seized the opportunity to warn Adenauer that both France and West Germany were threatened by the relations between the Anglo-Saxon powers and the Soviet Union.[38] The French decision makers further claimed that the talks between the Anglo-Saxon powers and the Soviet Union might lead to the neutralization of West Germany.[39]

For all de Gaulle's efforts, the Franco-German Treaty failed to live up to expectations. The 1963–64 period witnessed a sharp deterioration in relations between France and West Germany. Under pressure from Washington and from his own party,[40] Adenauer, as part of the ratification of the Franco-German Treaty by the Bundestag, had to accept the inclusion of a preamble that stated that the latter did not affect Bonn's loyalty to NATO, the Atlantic alliance, and the EEC. This effectively neutralized de Gaulle's ambition of creating a privileged partnership between France and West Germany, one that might act as a vehicle to solve the European question. As French Foreign Minister Maurice Couve de Murville had suggested in a speech in June 1963, the Franco-German axis could act as the foundation of a strong independent Western Europe that, after the Soviet Union had changed enough, could also balance the Soviet empire in the East and create the basis of a European settlement.[41]

In October 1963 Ludwig Erhard, minister of the economy, replaced Adenauer as chancellor. Erhard was less keen than his predecessor on a close partnership with France. Both states became estranged because of their differing attitudes toward the United States. Whereas Bonn wanted to avoid jeopardizing its ties with Washington, Paris did not hesitate to challenge American leadership within the Atlantic alliance. By the summer of 1964 de Gaulle was resigned that his objective of creating a Paris-Bonn axis was not feasible in the immediate future.[42]

The disappointing results of the Franco-German Treaty had significant consequences for de Gaulle's approach to the German question, though the consequences were not immediately apparent. Obsessed by the future of West Germany and its possible nuclear ambitions, the general had always kept on the lookout for "fall-back" allies.[43] Both privately and publicly, French leaders invoked a rapprochement with the Soviet Union as a possible tool to contain Germany.[44] Yet in summer 1964 closer ties with Moscow remained a pipe-dream because of Khrushchev's lack of interest.[45] This only started in earnest in the fall of 1964, following the multilateral force (MLF) affair.

In January 1963 the French president declared that his country would not integrate its *force de frappe* in the MLF, but he did not object to it going ahead since he privately believed it would never come to be. This assumption changed after Erhard publicly mentioned the possibility of a German-U.S. bilateral agreement over the MLF in October 1964.[46] The French government immediately launched a virulent crusade against the MLF, claiming it was not compatible with the Franco-German Treaty.[47] France opted for this fierce reaction precisely because it feared that the MLF would allow West Germany to indirectly possess nuclear weapons.[48] By adopting such a tough stance during the MLF crisis, France found itself defending similar positions to the Soviet ones.[49]

The MLF dispute created an important common ground between Paris and Moscow, and led both states, albeit for different reasons, to consider future cooperation as potentially beneficial. Moscow became more sensitive to the opportunities offered by de Gaulle's policies to undermine American influence in Europe and isolate West Germany.[50] For France, the tensions over the MLF contributed to a further deterioration of relations with West Germany: "We [France] are getting closer to the Russians to the extent that the Germans are moving away from us," de Gaulle confided to one of his ministers.[51]

Common opposition to Bonn's seeming nuclear ambitions was not the sole factor bringing Moscow and Paris together. Despite Khrushchev's downfall on 14 October 1964, the French president remained initially wary of Soviet intentions.[52] While de Gaulle believed both countries had a lot in common and he observed that Russia was taking into account France's growing prestige in the world, he feared that the Soviets' courtship could be just another way for Moscow to gain an edge over the United States.[53]

Yet the general overcame his doubts because of his belief in early 1965 that Europe was undergoing a fundamental transformation. As he told Peyrefitte, "There has been a change lately. We can feel it everywhere. The Cold War is out of date. . . . The Soviet bloc is crumbling. . . . As to the Western bloc, it is also crumbling. France has recovered its freedom."[54] With the changing international context, de Gaulle saw a unique opportunity to overcome Europe's division and to pursue a more ambitious approach toward the German question. The press conference of 4 February 1965, built on the ideas he exposed in previous conferences in 1959, gave him a chance to outline in greater details how he envisaged the reunification of Germany and of the continent.

During his speech, de Gaulle proposed a European solution to the central problem of Germany's division.[55] Arguing that the German question could not "be solved by the confrontation of the ideologies and the forces of the two camps opposed to each other," he suggested instead that it needed to be considered from a different perspective: "The entente and conjugated action of the peoples that are and will remain most interested in the fate of Germany, the European nations."[56] But he carefully added that such a solution could occur only in the long term and depended on many conditions: The Eastern bloc would have to evolve in order to allow Russia to move away from totalitarianism and let the satellite states play a more significant role in Europe. The states of Western Europe would have to extend their organization to cover political and defense matters. West Germany would have to accept that any reunification would involve a settlement on its borders and weapons that was accepted by all its neighbors. And finally, a solution to the German question would only become possible once a general "détente, entente and cooperation" had developed between all the European states.[57]

1965–66: Switching to a Pan-European Strategy

Through the triptych détente, entente, and cooperation, the general emphasized that the end of the Cold War would result from an incremental process of détente, thereby reversing the previous orthodoxy that détente would follow German reunification. This press conference signaled an important turning point in the evolution of French foreign policy.[58] De Gaulle's overarching aim—overcoming the Cold War in Europe and creating a new continental security system to solve the German question—remained unchanged, but he was adopting a different strategy to achieve that goal.[59]

By early 1965, instead of his privileged focus on Franco-German cooperation, de Gaulle had switched to a pan-European approach. This new approach resulted, in part, from his reading of major international developments over the previous two years: the realization that the Franco-German Treaty could not meet his expectations in the foreseeable future; the internal and external weaknesses of the Soviet Union; and the growing assertiveness of Eastern Europe. Taken together, these changes convinced de Gaulle that Europe was ripe for East-West détente and overcoming its division inherited from the Cold War. If Europe could restore its unity and peacefully end the division of Germany, the other states of Western Europe might be less reticent to take their distances from the United States and establish a political union to balance the Soviet Union.[60] After 1965 de Gaulle effectively subordinated his Western European aims to the larger objective of achieving overall European reconciliation.[61]

The crises that drove France and its Western Allies apart in 1965–66—the crisis over the international monetary system, the empty chair crisis in the EEC, and France's withdrawal from NATO—encouraged de Gaulle's switch to a pan-European strategy. At odds with its Allies in the West, with no prospect of establishing a more independent Western Europe in the immediate future, France saw greater opportunities through cooperation with the East.[62]

De Gaulle's détente policy did not always please Bonn. Reactions in West Germany to de Gaulle's February 1965 press conference showed a mix of palpable fascination and ambivalence.[63] The West German government in part feared the rapprochement between France and the Soviet Union, and opposed the general's way of solving the German question within a European framework.[64] Bonn worried even more about the fact that France's shift to the East was happening in parallel to its policy of challenging the foundations of the Western alliance. But Erhard would eventually praise de Gaulle's support for German reunification, and his refusal to recognize the German Democratic Republic (GDR, or East Germany) during his trip to the Soviet Union in June 1966.[65]

Bonn's refusal to abandon the MLF project in 1965 created additional resentment in Paris. West Germany's alleged nuclear ambitions, as perceived by de Gaulle, risked impeding any real peace between Western and Eastern Europe.[66] By late 1965 de Gaulle's disillusionment seemed complete: "The Germans have taken a dissident position towards our treaty of cooperation and friendship. We cannot stop them. Germany follows its way, it is not ours. They look for reunification at all costs and without delay; they will not get it as long as the Soviets resist."[67] French leaders remained committed on paper to regular consultations with West Germany, albeit with limited expectations; but some, like Couve de Murville, played on German fears by threatening to look toward the Soviet Union.[68]

In 1965–66 the rapprochement with the Soviet Union–and its satellite states– became the primary focus of de Gaulle's foreign policy, and was symbolized by a growing number of high-profile visits. Soviet Foreign Minister Andrei Gromyko went to Paris in April 1965, and his French counterpart Maurice Couve de Murville returned the favor that fall.

A shared opposition to the American intervention in Vietnam brought Paris and Moscow together, which de Gaulle used to his advantage to seek common ground on the German question and the future of Europe during his visit in June 1966. On the one hand, he appeased his Soviet counterparts when he argued that although he viewed the partition of Germany as abnormal and not permanent, he accepted that partition was an accomplished fact for the time being. On the other hand, he confronted his interlocutors about whether they perceived the situation in Europe as definitive, or whether they accepted the possibility of change, in particular over Germany.[69] De Gaulle wanted to know whether the Soviet Union could go along with his vision of a new European system. While the Soviet leaders did not believe a reunification to be feasible in the short term and pushed for the recognition of the East German state, they also implied that they did not oppose reunification per se. There was at least a growing overlap—beyond their shared acceptance of the Oder-Neisse frontier—between the French and Soviet positions.[70]

Despite the general giving priority to relations with the Soviet Union in this period, he sought to avoid extending the gap with his Western Allies. French leaders went to great lengths to reassure their allies and public opinion about the aims of de Gaulle's visit to the Soviet leaders.[71] Paris downplayed the possible impact of de Gaulle's trip. During a meeting with Adenauer, de Gaulle made it clear that he was not naive and that he did not plan any far-reaching agreement with Moscow.[72] De Gaulle told Peyrefitte that his trip to Moscow could actually help the cause of German reunification: "It is not at the moment when the two blocs are cracking up that I am going to think of leaving one bloc for the other. . . . I will speak for Western Europe."[73] At the same time, however, the general believed that his Soviet visit could be vital for his long-term goal of transforming the European order and addressing the German question.[74] As Couve de Murville said in an interview with a Soviet radio station on 4 June 1966, Franco-Soviet cooperation on European matters could act as a role model for their respective allies, and encourage them to follow the path leading to peace on the continent.[75]

1967–69: The Limits of the Grand Design

Franco-Soviet cooperation was a vital part of de Gaulle's approach, but it was not sufficient in itself. Achieving success for his pan-European strategy for solving the German question depended on mediating between West Germany and the Soviet Union so as to create a positive Paris-Moscow-Bonn triangle: "It is essential to push [West] Germany towards a rapprochement with Russia. We have to disarm their reciprocal aggression. It is our game, it is the only one."[76] If France could change the reciprocal perceptions of the German and Soviet threat, there would be no justification for keeping both NATO and the Warsaw Pact. The regimes in Eastern Europe would no longer be able to use the threat of Germany as they had in the past to justify the Cold War against the Free World.[77]

French leaders needed to convince first and foremost the FRG and the Soviet Union that such a rapprochement was in their interests. They wooed their Soviet counterparts because they believed that the Soviet Union could act as a role model and encourage the other Eastern European states to normalize relations with West Germany.[78] As for the West Germans, the French president wanted them to understand that the Soviet Union, and not the United States, held the key to a German reunification.[79] By offering the prospect of German unity, albeit with some limits on borders and access to nuclear weapons, de Gaulle would entice Bonn to gravitate away from Washington and toward Paris.

De Gaulle anticipated that a German-Soviet détente, mediated by France, could eventually convince Moscow to allow German reunification. And he expected that the eventual departure of the U.S. troops from Europe could be bought in exchange for the Soviet Union making these concessions on Germany.[80] The end result of this process of change and détente would be a modernized version of the Concert of Europe of the nineteenth century.

The two main pillars of the system would be France and the Soviet Union, as nuclear powers, but the system would be guaranteed by an interlocking set of checks and balances. Paris and Moscow could contain Bonn if the Germans were ever tempted to pursue an independent path that disrupted European security, while a closer union between the states of Western Europe—including a reunified Germany tied to France— would be theoretically strong enough to contain a declining Soviet power.[81] Finally, the nuclear balance of terror between both superpowers would provide an additional element of equilibrium, allowing Western Europe to act as the arbiter between the Soviet Union and the Anglo-Saxon powers, as de Gaulle indicated in his memoirs.[82]

Events at the end of 1966 gave de Gaulle an opportunity to further consolidate that vital Paris-Bonn-Moscow triangle, which could help to solve the German question. After the fall of Erhard's government in September 1966, the new Grand Coalition government in West Germany, headed by the Christian Democrat Chancellor Kurt Georg Kiesinger and the socialist Foreign Minister Willy Brandt, was determined to mend relations with both France and the Eastern bloc.

The first meetings in January 1967 between the Grand Coalition and the French government appeared promising.[83] Kiesinger announced that West Germany had given up on the Hallstein Doctrine and the MLF, and accepted de Gaulle's analysis that German reunification could happen only through a rapprochement with the Eastern bloc. Bonn was now ready to establish diplomatic relations with some of the satellite states, though not with East Germany.[84] Moreover, Brandt and Kiesinger repeatedly asked France to champion their Ostpolitik.[85] The January meetings largely convinced de Gaulle that "they [the Germans] are going through key changes. They realize that détente is the most promising path for them. They are getting closer to us."[86] And by supporting Bonn's Ostpolitik, we can speculate that French leaders were hoping that they might ensure German solidarity in other Western matters, including monetary questions and the imminent British application to the EEC.

However, de Gaulle's expectations for a German-Soviet rapprochement quickly gave way to disillusion, because the Soviet Union was not prepared to treat West Germany less harshly.[87] In 1967–68 neither Bonn nor Moscow was really in a position to do business with the other; and that was particularly the case for Moscow.[88] Under pressure from the more conservative elements of the Warsaw Pact, the Kremlin leaders felt deep-rooted anxiety about the controllability of a sweeping European détente, and this only worsened when unrest developed in Czechoslovakia in 1968.[89] Moreover, the core of Bonn's Ostpolitik implied that it would now take greater control over its own fate, rather than let others speak on its behalf.[90] Even if West German leaders, especially Willy Brandt, followed France's détente policy with great interest, they expected only minimal gains from cooperation with Paris. The possibilities of common actions toward Eastern Europe were seen as very limited and could not be overstated. Instead, Brandt considered that Germany could take decisive steps toward the Eastern bloc only at a bilateral level.[91]

Paris's ability to play the mediator between Bonn and Moscow quickly deteriorated in this period. After the initial bout of optimism, relations between France and West Germany soured quickly, in large part because of de Gaulle's stance during the Six Day War and his second veto of the British application to join the EEC. Similarly, Soviet doubts about détente meant that they were still not receptive to the general's plea for a more open attitude toward Germany's Ostpolitik.[92] Additionally, de Gaulle's ambition to create a new European order suffered two major blows in 1968. The May events in France largely damaged the general's prestige, and reminded him that he could no longer ignore domestic problems, while the Soviet decision to crush in August the reform movement in Czechoslovakia highlighted the fact that the leaders in the Kremlin were not ready to accept a loosening of their control in Eastern Europe.

Conclusion

The events of 1968 constituted a serious setback to de Gaulle's ambitious grand design for overcoming the Cold War order in Europe. As Hervé Alphand, the Quai d'Orsay's general secretary, stated in his diary soon after the Soviet invasion of Czechoslovakia, "It is maybe indeed the end of a grand effort to reunite two worlds beyond ideology. . . . So the General's disappointment must be very profound, after the unrest of May and June, and the blows to the country's economy and finance, as well as to his morale."[93] The French president would resign soon after in April 1969. In September of that year Brandt became West German chancellor and would soon initiate a more ambitious Ostpolitik. In time, West Germany would establish itself as the leading force in the European process of East-West détente.

Despite the setbacks, de Gaulle's presidency remains significant because it outlined an ambitious path to address and solve the German question. At the heart of it stood the process of Franco-German reconciliation and close cooperation, which survived the many disputes and drama of the period. The general never considered that reconciliation as an end in itself, but rather believed it could become the foundation of a more independent Western Europe, which could in turn create a new equilibrium to help the continent overcome the divisions inherited from the Cold War.

In that respect, the French president expected that the Soviet Union would naturally have a vital role to play in solving the German question. On one level, ever wary of Soviet military power in particular and German potential to a lesser degree, de Gaulle's strategic aims depended on containing—albeit in a different fashion— Moscow and Bonn.[94] At the same time, however, his vision went beyond simply playing one power against the other. Ultimately, the French president realized that his country's long-term security objectives would be better served by tying both competitors, the Soviet Union and West Germany, to a European structure of cooperation.[95] Only in that framework, according to the general, could Europe finally solve the German question.

Garret J. Martin is term faculty in the School of International Service at American University. He has written widely on transatlantic relations in the fields of history and contemporary affairs, and focuses in particular on security, U.S. foreign policy, NATO, European foreign policy and defense, Europe, the European Union, France, and the United Kingdom.

Notes

Parts of this chapter have been previously published in Martin, *General de Gaulle's Cold War*.

 1. De Gaulle, *Discours et messages*, vol. 4, 338. The expressions "German problem" and "German question" are essentially interchangeable.
 2. See the text of an imaginary military campaign against Germany written by fifteen-year-old Charles de Gaulle in de Gaulle, *Lettres, notes et carnets*, vol. 1, 7–23.
 3. See radio speech, 5 Feb. 1945, and press conference, 12 Oct. 1945 (de Gaulle, *Discours et messages*, vol. 1, 518, 634); see declaration, 9 Jun. 1948 (de Gaulle, *Discours et messages*, vol. 2, 188–93).
 4. See Rainer Hudemann's contribution in this volume for more details.
 5. See speech in Bordeaux, 25 Sept. 1949 (de Gaulle, *Discours et messages*, vol. 2, 304–10).
 6. Vaïsse, "La réconciliation Franco-allemande," 963, 971.
 7. See, e.g., the speech in Bar-Le-Duc, 28 Jul. 1946 (de Gaulle, *Discours et messages*, vol. 2, 12–17).
 8. Quoted in Schreiber, *Les actions de la France*, 75.
 9. See the press conference at the Palais d'Orsay, 21 Dec. 1951 (de Gaulle, *Discours et messages*, vol. 2, 482).
10. Speech in Rennes, 27 Jul. 1947 (de Gaulle, *Discours et messages*, vol. 2, 102).
11. See the speech in Rennes, 27 Jul. 1947 (de Gaulle, *Discours et messages*, vol. 2, 102); and meeting Charles de Gaulle–Harold Wilson, 3 Apr. 1965, AMAE, Cabinet du ministre, Couve de Murville, box 379.
12. Bozo, *Two Strategies for Europe*, 7–8. This frustration with the Atlantic Alliance was widely shared by the French political class of the Fourth Republic; see Bozo, "France, 'Gaullism,' and the Cold War," 62–64.
13. Rey, *La tentation du rapprochement*, 17.
14. De Gaulle, *Memoirs of Hope*, 201.
15. Soutou, "La décision française," 194–96.
16. Vaïsse, "La réconciliation Franco-allemande," 964.
17. See Martin, "The Soviet Factor," 199–209.
18. Zubok and Pleshakov, *Inside the Kremlin's Cold War*, 194–95.
19. Rey, "De Gaulle, l'URSS," n21, 220.
20. Granieri, "More than a Geriatric Romance," 192.
21. Ibid., 193.
22. Vaïsse, "La réconciliation Franco-allemande," 969–971.
23. McGhee, *At the Creation*, 30; Vaïsse, "La réconciliation Franco-allemande," 965.
24. De Gaulle, *Discours et messages*, vol. 3, 82–87.
25. De Gaulle, *Memoirs of Hope*, 201.
26. See press conference, 10 Nov. 1959 (de Gaulle, *Discours et messages*, vol. 3, 129–44) ; La Gorce, *La France contre les empires*, 209.
27. Rey, "De Gaulle, l'URSS et la sécurité européenne," 216.
28. Soutou, "The Linkage between European Integration and Détente," 15, 17. See also Benedikt Schoenborn's contribution in this volume.
29. Soutou, " The Linkage between European Integration and Détente," 16.
30. Vaïsse, "Une hirondelle ne fait pas le printemps," 104–5.
31. See Connelly, *Diplomatic Revolution*.

32. Maillard, *De Gaulle et le problème allemand*, 187; meeting de Gaulle–Adenauer, 21 Jan. 1963, AMAE, Cabinet du Ministre, Couve de Murville, box 375.

33. Schoenborn, *La mésentente apprivoisée*, 59.

34. Meeting 13 Feb. 1963, described in Peyrefitte, *C'était de Gaulle*, vol. 2, 226.

35. Mahan, *Kennedy, De Gaulle*, 145.

36. De Gaulle–Chang-Huan meeting, 2 Sept. 1963, AMAE, Cabinet du Ministre, Couve de Murville, box 376.

37. Gray, *Germany's Cold War*, 143; Locher and Nuenlist, "What Role for NATO?," 189. Bonn signed the Partial Test Ban Treaty, but was upset by the upgrading of East Germany as a signatory.

38. De Gaulle to Adenauer, 23 Aug. 1963 (de Gaulle, *Lettres, Notes et Carnets*, vol. 9, 364).

39. De Gaulle–Dixon meeting, 17 Sept. 1963, AMAE, Cabinet du Ministre, Couve de Murville, box 376; Paris to Foreign Office, telegram 217, 10 Sept. 63, TNA, FO 371/172077.

40. See Geiger, *Atlantiker gegen Gaullisten*.

41. Couve de Murville's speech to the Assemblée Nationale, 12 Jun. 1963, FNSP, Fonds Maurice Couve de Murville, box 1.

42. See Martin, *General de Gaulle's Cold War*, chap. 1.

43. Vaïsse, *La grandeur*, 566.

44. Meeting 7 Jul. 1964 (Peyrefitte, *C'était de Gaulle*, vol. 2, 261); Couve de Murville–Schroeder meeting, 4 Jul. 1964, AMAE, Secrétariat général, Entretiens et messages, box 22.

45. Zubok and Pleshakov, *Inside the Kremlin's Cold War*, 181; Sodaro, *Moscow, Germany and the West*, 51.

46. Haftendorn, *NATO and the Nuclear Revolution*, 132.

47. Vaïsse, *La Grandeur*, 575.

48. Meeting Couve de Murville–Hasluck, 4 Nov. 1964 ; meeting de Gaulle–Adenauer, 9 Nov. 1964, AMAE, Secrétariat général, Entretiens et messages, box 23.

49. Telegram Laboulaye to Couve de Murville, number 5513, 7 Nov. 64, AMAE, Europe, URSS 1961–65, box 1931.

50. Wolfe, *Soviet Power and Europe*, 288; note by the political director to Couve de Murville, 19 Nov. 1964, AMAE, Europe, URSS 1961–65, box 1931.

51. Meeting 18 Nov. 1964 (Peyrefitte, *C'était de Gaulle*, vol. 2, 62).

52. Alphand, *L'étonnement d'être*, 445.

53. Meetings 3, 6, and 12 Jan. 1965 (Peyrefitte, *C'était de Gaulle*, vol.2, 314–17).

54. Meeting 4 Jan. 1965 (ibid., vol. 2, 313).

55. Soutou, "De Gaulle's France," 180.

56. Press conference 4 Feb. 1965 (de Gaulle, *Discours et messages*, vol. 4, 341).

57. Ibid.

58. Telegram Bohlen to Rusk, 4451, 5 Feb. 1965, NARA, RG 59, Central Foreign Policy Files, 1964–66, box 2178.

59. See Soutou, "De Gaulle's France," 173–75.

60. Diary entry 3 Jan. 1965 (Alphand, *L'étonnement*, 445).

61. Compare Couve de Murville's speech to the French Parliament, 12 Jun. 1963. FNSP, Fonds Maurice Couve de Murville, box 1, to the press conference, 28 Oct. 1966 (de Gaulle, *Discours et messages*, vol. 5, 101–4).

62. Kolodziej, *French International Policy*, 344.

63. See Benedikt Schoenborn's contribution in this volume.

64. Vaïsse, *La grandeur*, 578; Seydoux, *Dans l'intimité Franco-allemande*, 50.

65. See Benedikt Schoenborn's contribution in this volume.

66. Meeting de Gaulle–Mansfield, 15 Nov. 1965, AMAE, Cabinet du Ministre, Couve de Murville, box 381.

67. Meeting 13 Oct. 1965 (Peyrefitte, *C'était de Gaulle*, vol. 2, 303).

68. CIA Intelligence Info Cable, 25 Aug. 1965, Lyndon Baines Johnson Library, Presidential Papers, National Security Files, Country Files, box 172. Couve de Murville allegedly made that point during a conversation with Jean-Marie Soutou, the Quai d'Orsay's director of the Africa–Levant department.

69. Meeting de Gaulle–Brezhnev–Kosygin–Podgorny, 21 Jun. 1966, AMAE, Secrétariat général, Entretiens et messages, box 27.
70. Soutou, "De Gaulle's France," 181; meeting de Gaulle-Brezhnev–Kosygin–Podgorny, 21 Jun. 1966, AMAE, Secrétariat général, Entretiens et messages, 27.
71. Vaïsse, *La grandeur*, 425.
72. Meeting de Gaulle–Adenauer, 10 Mar. 1966, AMAE, Cabinet du Ministre, Couve de Murville, box 382; Letter, de Gaulle to Erhard, 16 Jun. 1966 (de Gaulle, *Lettres, Notes et Carnets*, vol. 10, 306).
73. Lefort, *Souvenirs et secrets*, 149.
74. De Gaulle, *Lettres, notes et carnets*, vol. 10, 246–249.
75. Airgram Charles Bohlen to Dean Rusk, number 2425, 24 Jun. 66, NARA, RG59, Central Foreign Policy Files, 1964–66, box 2180.
76. Meeting 5 Dec. 1966 (Peyrefitte, *C'était de Gaulle*, vol. 3, 206).
77. Kolodziej, *French International Policy*, 350–51.
78. Airgram Charles Bohlen to Dean Rusk, number 2425, 24 Jun. 1966, NARA, RG 59, Central Foreign Policy Files, 1964–66, box 2180; reproducing an interview given by Couve de Murville to Soviet radio on 4 Jun. 1966, see CIA Intelligence Info Cable, 25 Aug. 1965, Lyndon Baines Johnson Library, Presidential Papers, National Security Files, Country Files, box 172.
79. Meeting de Gaulle–Kiesinger meeting, 14 Jan. 1967, AMAE, Secrétariat général, Entretiens et messages, box 29.
80. Maillard, *De Gaulle et le problème allemand*, 226.
81. Soutou, "La décision française," 194–196.
82. See Schreiber, *Les actions de la France à l'Est*, 75.
83. See the series of meetings in AMAE, Secrétariat général, Entretiens et messages, box 29.
84. Meeting de Gaulle–Kiesinger, 13 Jan. 1967, AMAE, Secrétariat général, Entretiens et messages, box 29.
85. See Maurice Couve de Murville–Willy Brandt meeting, 13 Jan. 1967, AMAE, Secrétariat général, Entretiens et messages, box 29.
86. Meeting 18 Jan. 1967 (Peyrefitte, *C'était de Gaulle*, vol. 3, 194).
87. Seydoux, *Dans l'intimité Franco-allemande*, 85.
88. Ash, *In Europe's Name*, 56.
89. Newton, *Russia, France*, 79–80.
90. Brandt, *People and Politics*, 168–69.
91. Wilkens, "L'Europe en suspens," 331.
92. See meeting de Gaulle–Zorin, 20 Feb. 1968, AMAE, Secrétariat général, Entretiens et messages, 32; meeting de Gaulle–Zorin, 4 Oct. 1967, AMAE, Cabinet du Ministre, Couve de Murville, box 391.
93. Alphand, *L'étonnement*, 25 Aug. 68, 513.
94. Mahan, *Kennedy, De Gaulle*, 22.
95. Kolodziej, *French International Policy*, 324.

Bibliography

Alphand, H. 1977. *L'étonnement d'être. Journal, 1939–1973*. Paris: Fayard.
Ash, T. G. 1993. *In Europe's Name: Germany and the Divided Continent*. New York: Random House.
Bozo, F. 2001. *Two Strategies for Europe: de Gaulle, the United States, and the Atlantic Alliance 1958–1969*. Lanham, MD: Rowman & Littlefield.
———. 2010. "France, 'Gaullism,' and the Cold War." In *The Cambridge History of the Cold War*, Vol. 2, edited by M. P. Leffler, 158–78. Cambridge: Cambridge University Press.
Brandt, W. 1978. *People and Politics: The Years 1960–1975*. London: Collins.
Connelly, M. 2002. *Diplomatic Revolution: Algeria's fight for independence and the origins of the post–Cold War Era*. Oxford: Oxford University Press.
De Gaulle, C. 1970. *Discours et messages*. Vol. 1, *Pendant la guerre*. Paris: Plon.

———. 1970. *Discours et messages*. Vol. 2, *Dans l'attente*. Paris: Plon.

———. 1970. *Discours et messages*. Vol. 3, *Avec le renouveau*. Paris: Plon.

———. 1970. *Discours et messages*. Vol. 4, *Pour l'effort*. Paris: Plon.

———. 1970. *Discours et messages*. Vol. 5, *Vers le terme*. Paris: Plon.

———. 1971. *Memoirs of Hope: Renewal and Endeavor*. New York: Simon and Schuster.

———. 1980–87. *Lettres, notes et carnets*, 10 vols. Paris: Plon.

Geiger, T. 2008. *Atlantiker gegen Gaullisten. Außenpolitischer Konflikt und innerparteilicher Machtkampf in der CDU/CSU 1958–1969*. Munich, Germany: Oldenbourg.

Germond, C., and H. Türk, eds. 2008. *A History of Franco-German Relations in Europe: From "Hereditary Enemies" to Partners*. New York: Palgrave Macmillan.

Granieri, R. 2008. "More Than a Geriatric Romance: Adenauer, de Gaulle and the Atlantic Alliance." In Germond and Turk, *A History of Franco-German Relations*, 189–98.

Gray, W. G. 2003. *Germany's Cold War: The Global Campaign to Isolate East Germany, 1949–1969*. Chapel Hill: University of North Carolina Press.

Haftendorn, H. 1991. *NATO and the Nuclear Revolution: A Crisis of Credibility, 1966–1967*. Oxford: Clarendon Press.

Kolodziej, E. 1974. *French International Policy under de Gaulle and Pompidou: The Politics of Grandeur*. Ithaca, NY: Cornell University Press.

La Gorce, P. M. 1969. *La France contre les empires*. Paris: Grasset.

Lefort, B. 1999. *Souvenirs et secrets des années gaulliennes*. 1958–1969, Paris: A. Michel.

Locher, A., and C. Nuenlist. 2004. "What Role for NATO? Conflicting Western Perceptions of Détente, 1963–65." *Journal of Transatlantic Studies* 2, 185–208.

Loth, W., ed. *Crises and Compromises: The European Project 1963–1969*. Brussels, Belgium: Bruylant.

Mahan, E. 2002. *Kennedy, de Gaulle, and Western Europe*. New York: Palgrave Macmillan.

Maillard, P. 2001. *De Gaulle et le problème allemand. Les leçons d'un grand dessein*. Paris: Guibert.

Martin, G. 2008. "The Soviet Factor in Franco-German Relations, 1958–1969." In Germond and Turk, *A History of Franco-German Relations*, 199–209.

———. 2013. *General de Gaulle's Cold War: Challenging American Hegemony, 1963–1968*. New York: Berghahn Books.

McGhee, G. 1989. *At the Creation of a New Germany: From Adenauer to Brandt—An Ambassador's Account*. New Haven, CT: Yale University Press.

Newton, J. 2003. *Russia, France and the Idea of Europe*. New York: Palgrave Macmillan.

Peyrefitte, A. 1994–2000. *C'était de Gaulle*, 3 vols. Paris: Fayard.

Rey, M.-P. 1991. *La tentation du rapprochement. France et URSS à l'heure de la détente 1964–1974*. Paris: Publications de la Sorbonne.

———. 2006. "De Gaulle, l'URSS et la sécurité européenne, 1958–1969." In Vaïsse, *De Gaulle et la Russie*, 213–27.

Schoenborn, B. 2007. *La mésentente apprivoisée. De Gaulle et les Allemands, 1963–1969*. Paris: Presses Universitaires de France.

Schreiber, T. 2000. *Les actions de la France à l'Est, ou les absences de Marianne*. Paris: L'Harmattan.

Seydoux, F. 1977. *Dans l'intimité Franco-allemande. Une mission diplomatique*. Paris: Albatros.

Sodaro, M. 1991. *Moscow, Germany and the West from Khrushchev to Gorbachev*. London: I. B. Tauris.

Soutou, G.-H. 2000. "La décision française de quitter le commandement intégré de l'OTAN 1966." In *Von Truman bis Harmel. Die Bundesrepublik Deutschland im Spannungsfeld von NATO und europäischer Integration*, edited by H.-J. Harder, 185–208. Munich, Germany: Oldenbourg.

———. 2003. "De Gaulle's France and the Soviet Union from Conflict to Détente." In *Europe, Cold War and Coexistence, 1963–1965*, edited by W. Loth, 173–89. London: Frank Cass.

———. 2007. "The Linkage between European Integration and Détente: The Contrasting Approaches of de Gaulle and Pompidou, 1965 to 1974." In *European Integration and the Cold War: Ostpolitik-Westpolitik, 1965–1973*, edited by N. P. Ludlow, 11–35. London: Routledge.

Vaïsse, M., 1993. "La réconciliation Franco-allemande: le dialogue de Gaulle–Adenauer." *Politique étrangère* 58, no. 4: 963–72.

———. 1993. "'Une hirondelle ne fait pas le printemps.' La France et la crise de Cuba." In *L'Europe et la crise de Cuba*, edited by M. Vaïsse, 89–107. Paris: Colin.

———. 1998. *La grandeur. Politique étrangère du général de Gaulle 1958–1969*. Paris: Fayard.

———, ed. 2006. *De Gaulle et la Russie*. Paris: CNRS Éditions.

Wilkens, A. 2001. "L'Europe en suspens. Willy Brandt et l'orientation de la politique européenne de l'Allemagne fédérale 1966–1969." In Loth, *Crises and Compromises*, 323–43.

Wolfe, T. 1970. *Soviet Power and Europe: 1945–1970*. Baltimore: Johns Hopkins Press.

Zubok, V., and C. Pleshakov. 1996. *Inside the Kremlin's Cold War: From Stalin to Khrushchev*. Cambridge: Harvard University Press.

CHAPTER 6

The German Question in the Eastern Policies of France and Germany in the 1960s

Benedikt Schoenborn

In June 1966 the Soviet leaders discussed the omnipresent "core" issue, the German question, with French President Charles de Gaulle, while the Germans rather suspiciously watched from a distance.[1] Yet most of the German elites applauded the results of de Gaulle's bold trip to Moscow and deemed it favorable to their cause.[2] At the time some influential German politicians, like Franz Josef Strauß, even advocated assigning the French diplomacy to represent vital German interests on the other side of the Iron Curtain. Others, like Willy Brandt, perceived in de Gaulle's policy welcome support for ideas they themselves wished to implement.[3]

De Gaulle had indeed been the first European leader to take advantage of the leeway created by the apparent détente between the superpowers. The construction of the Berlin Wall in August 1961, and the Cuban Missile Crisis of October 1962, had consolidated the status quo in Europe and demonstrated the reluctance of both the United States and the Union of Soviet Socialist Republics (USSR, or Soviet Union) to go to war with each other. From the French perspective, Warsaw Pact aggression against Western Europe had become unlikely, and by 1964 Paris deemed that the time was right to initiate bilateral talks with Moscow and other Eastern European capitals. The German question represented a vital element in the ensuing, regular discussions. In 1967 de Gaulle still endeavored to lead European détente and to "help" the Germans, "notably in Moscow."[4] But Franco-Soviet discussions were becoming increasingly formal and eventually Paris had to concede that the Soviets preferred to hold the decisive talks with the Americans and—after 1969—with the Germans.

While the role of France in Eastern affairs was relatively significant in the mid-1960s and lost some of its importance toward the end of the decade, Bonn's momentous Ostpolitik of the early 1970s was conversely preceded in Germany by a decade of less consummate skill to shape relations with the East. In 1961 the Western powers' tacit acquiescence to the construction of the Berlin Wall painfully exposed the limits of previous beliefs that Western force could bring about German reunification. Yet until 1969 the West German government remained unable to propose a viable alternative concept. Bonn's attempts to relaunch the German question within the four-power framework failed to achieve any result, and in the latter half of the 1960s the Federal Republic of Germany's (FRG, or West Germany) hesitant efforts to engage in a dialogue with the East were rebuffed. Only with the launch of Willy Brandt's Neue Ostpolitik in October 1969, and Moscow's warming to West German initiatives, did Bonn's Eastern policy finally gain momentum.

This chapter argues that two key characteristics distinguished the German and the French handling of the German question in their respective Eastern policies of the 1960s. First, Paris pursued a sustained dialogue with the decision makers in the Kremlin, while Bonn was unable to do so. Second, the West German government of the 1960s lacked any viable reunification concept to guide their Eastern policy. By contrast, de Gaulle in his press conference of 4 February 1965 famously presented a French roadmap toward the ultimate objective of German reunification that also served as point of reference for the French contacts with the East. This chapter further argues that the German leaders were intrigued by de Gaulle's approach, yet for most of the decade their suspicions and diverse assessments impeded a common Franco-German Eastern policy. According to the analysis presented here, the French position on the German question included significant elements of continuity throughout de Gaulle's presidency (1959–69). Indeed, he had proclaimed the key points of the 1965 press conference already in March 1959, shortly after gaining the French presidency.

Awaiting the Time to Discuss the German Question with Moscow

De Gaulle gave the press conference of 25 March 1959 at a moment of particular East-West tension. He vehemently rejected Nikita Khrushchev's ultimatum of 27 November 1958 and the veiled Soviet threat to terminate Western access rights to West Berlin. Yet even in this time of intense East-West confrontation, in his press conference de Gaulle portrayed a political vision of longer-term détente and of eventually solving the German question within a pan-European framework. The French president emphasized that the reunification of the two factions into one Germany was "the normal destiny of the German people," and that it could happen only "dans une organisation contractuelle de toute l'Europe pour la cooperation, la liberté et la paix" (within a contractual organization encompassing the entire European continent and aiming at cooperation, liberty, and peace). Moreover, de Gaulle resolutely denounced Soviet attempts at solving the German question by means of force and threats against the West, or by pushing the German territories into neutrality. Thus he made clear that he would not approach the issue of German reunification until the Soviet stance transformed from menacing to nonaggressive. "Awaiting the possibility" to achieve these preconditions, for the time being de Gaulle encouraged the proliferation of concrete contacts between the two separate populations of German people.[5]

The key conditions for German reunification put forward in this press conference were remarkably similar to de Gaulle's later (albeit more-encompassing) statements. On 4 February 1965 he again insisted that a unified Germany needed to be integrated into a pan-European, peace-oriented structure, and that Germany must recognize its postwar borders. Likewise, de Gaulle's 1959 claim that the Germans' hope for eventual reunification deserved encouragement was later repeated in confidential talks with Soviet officials.[6] And de Gaulle's utter refusal to recognize the German Democratic Republic (GDR, or East Germany) was confirmed during his Moscow visit in summer 1966.

When discussing the German question with Khrushchev in March 1960, de Gaulle reiterated his position as outlined in the 1959 press conference, but with certain additions. Notably, the French president told Khrushchev that German armament must be restricted and that he foresaw reunification as a "German confederation," possibly composed of "two or three German States." Finally, de Gaulle pointed out that he was "in no hurry" regarding German reunification.[7] This last element, which indicates some ambiguity in de Gaulle's position on the German question (in the sense that reunification could be adjourned sine die), also appeared in some of his later, confidential statements.

As is well known, de Gaulle adopted a tough attitude against Soviet threats during the Berlin crisis of 1958–61, and sided firmly with the Western Allies during the Cuban Missile Crisis of October 1962. Yet these confrontations did not alter his longer-term view. As he said to American Secretary of State Dean Rusk in June 1962, the German question could be resolved only "in an atmosphere of peace and détente."[8] This approach also corresponded to de Gaulle's public references to a "Europe from the Atlantic to the Urals," which he eventually aimed to achieve.[9]

Until 1963 the Franco-Soviet dialogue did not progress very far, and relations between Paris and Moscow were characterized by confrontation rather than cooperation. Thus, from the French perspective the preconditions for addressing the German question with the Eastern leaders had not yet emerged. In a speech in July 1963, de Gaulle rejected the totalitarianism prevailing in the Soviet bloc and augured that a real détente would eventually come about in the future. At that time, de Gaulle said, France would advance constructive proposals.[10]

German Chancellor Konrad Adenauer clearly welcomed this absence of close Franco-Soviet contacts. Ever since gaining the chancellorship in 1949, he had prioritized Germany's Westbindung over reunification, which for the time being he deemed illusionary. The concept of the Hallstein Doctrine and nonrecognition of the GDR implied the belief of the Adenauer government that the artificial, nonelected

East German regime would ultimately crumble under the pressure of Western superiority and democratic values. This line of thought followed the logic that German
reunification was eventually to happen under Western terms, but the construction
of the Berlin Wall greatly depleted the credibility of traditional Western thinking.[11]
Indeed the West German Ministry of Foreign Affairs (Auswärtiges Amt) stopped
drafting any operative unification plans after 1960.[12]

Chancellor Adenauer's Moscow visit of 1955 had resulted in the establishment of
diplomatic relations between Bonn and Moscow, but was to remain the only German-
Soviet meeting on the highest level until 1970. In the late 1950s Adenauer established
some secret contacts with the Soviets in order to sound them out on the German
question. His attempts deviated quite radically from Bonn's official policy line, but
remained tentative and never went very far. Addressing Soviet Ambassador Andrey
Smirnov in March 1958, Adenauer had first envisaged an Austrian solution with two
neutral German states. His subsequent suggestions (Globke-Plan, Burgfriedensplan,
and Stillhalteplan) rather aimed at freezing the German question for five or ten years
to break out of the rhetorical antagonism between Bonn and Moscow.[13] However,
when in June 1963 the Kremlin finally expressed interest in discussing the German
question directly with Bonn, Adenauer doubted the sincerity of Khrushchev's motives and declined to meet with him. Discussing this issue with de Gaulle, Adenauer
agreed that the time was not yet ripe for an in-depth dialogue with Moscow.[14]

More than any other German leader of the time, Konrad Adenauer pushed for
closer cooperation with Paris and embraced the French ideal of a common Franco-
German foreign policy as inscribed in the Elysée Treaty of January 1963. Nevertheless, it remains doubtful whether Adenauer and de Gaulle would have been able
to lead a common Eastern policy if the old chancellor had remained in office beyond 1963. From his perspective, an essential purpose of the Franco-German treaty
was specifically to forestall any arrangement between Paris and Moscow.[15] When the
French initiative toward the East started to unfold in 1964, Adenauer was the first to
sound alarm bells in Germany. He was highly suspicious of Moscow's intentions and
even feared a reversal of alliances by the French.[16]

The Social Democratic Party's (SPD) (unsuccessful) candidate for the chancellery
in 1961 and 1965, Willy Brandt, had started to develop ideas on peaceful coexistence
and dialogue with the East as early as in the mid-1950s.[17] Yet Brandt declined to
meet with Khrushchev in March 1959 and again in January 1963, much to his own
subsequent regret.[18] In July 1963 Brandt and his adviser Egon Bahr declared that
German reunification could result only from a long process and Soviet consent, but
so far their agenda was limited to rather modest contacts with East Berlin in view of a
Passierscheinabkommen (border pass agreement). Still, Brandt appreciated de Gaulle's
encouragement to further these contacts.[19] Subsequently the French side followed
Brandt's parallel reasoning with interest but not enthusiasm, remaining skeptical as to
whether Brandt would be able to make an impact on the German question.[20]

Eastward Ambitions and Franco-German Suspicions

Ludwig Erhard gained the German chancellorship in October 1963 with the mind-set of keeping friendly relations with Paris, but without really trusting de Gaulle. This was notably the case with regard to Eastern policies and the German question. In the following three years, Erhard and his foreign minister, Gerhard Schröder, repeatedly disagreed with de Gaulle over these issues.

Erhard had developed his own economy-driven approach to the German question during the fourteen years he had been the German minister of economic affairs. When he finally was elected chancellor, he was eager to pursue his personal idea of reunification—although it never became the official German policy. This confusing situation in Bonn, brought about by general perplexity regarding the German question, contrasted with the situation in Paris, where President de Gaulle autocratically determined the French approach. Hence, during the first year of Erhard's chancellorship, Bonn pursued two different lines of action regarding the German question: there was first, the official line. Already in March 1963 Schröder had initiated a policy of movement in Eastern affairs by establishing a West German trade mission in Warsaw. Equivalent offices in Hungary, Romania, and Bulgaria were set up within the following twelve months, while Czechoslovakia installed a semiofficial trade mission in Frankfurt.[21] Schröder's policy was designed to improve relations and promote contacts with Eastern Europe without renouncing the Hallstein Doctrine, but did not follow any master plan regarding the German question. To address this issue, in December 1963 Schröder launched a peace plan calling for the creation of a four-power committee on the German question. From the outset the three Western Allies (including Paris) considered the idea passé and a waste of time but to accommodate the Germans they engaged in discussions, which led nowhere.[22]

The second, unofficial German policy was Erhard's idea to "buy reunification" from Moscow. His reasoning was that the "[West] Germans would contribute industrial installations for the development of Siberia over a period of 10–20 years," and in return "Khrushchev could promise a complementary phased program involving the wall, reunification, self-determination, and freedom for Germany." Erhard also envisaged offering the Soviet Union massive loans—up to DM100 billion according to a Moscow rumor—in exchange for greater political liberty in the GDR.[23] From September 1963 until June 1964 Erhard only discussed this idea with the Americans, gave hints to the Soviets, and deliberately kept it from the French. Erhard explained that de Gaulle was "adamantly opposed to any discussions with the Soviets on a possible modus vivendi" and described him as "totally inflexible on political questions."[24] Interestingly, at the time Erhard perceived himself as innovative and de Gaulle as backward-looking with regard to Eastern policy. By contrast, today's literature tends to measure the outcome of their respective policies and to emphasize Erhard's failure.

Since U.S. President Lyndon B. Johnson had declined to convey Erhard's offer to Moscow, on 13 June 1964 the German chancellor made a bold move and extended an invitation to Khrushchev to visit Bonn. The French learned of this invitation only because the West German ambassador in Moscow, Horst Groepper, exceeded his mandate and informed his American, British, and French colleagues.[25] Despite criticism from the Western Allies and opposition from his own advisers, the idea of buying German reunification clearly remained on the chancellor's agenda. In early September 1964, Khrushchev quite sensationally agreed to visit Bonn and to engage in an unrestricted discussion with the German chancellor. Subsequently, Erhard declared to the Bundestag that his major motivation in seeking a dialogue with Moscow was to reunite Germany.[26] While nothing in Khrushchev's 1964 statements indicates that he was ready to make political concessions on the German question in exchange for economic benefits, it is quite possible that the Soviet leader had started to consider the idea of improving relations with Bonn.[27]

Much to Erhard's chagrin, Khrushchev was ousted from office in mid-October 1964 and replaced by Leonid Brezhnev, Nikolai Podgorny, and Alexei Kosygin. They justified Khrushchev's removal—among several other reasons—with his alleged closeness to Bonn.[28] Arguably, by adopting this position the new Soviet leadership precluded closer relations with the West Germans, and indeed Bonn's direct access to the Kremlin remained barred until the end of the decade. Erhard's government, unable to develop a significant new approach to the German question, fell back on the positions previously maintained by Adenauer, and for the next two years rather passively surrendered the initiative to the Western Allies.

The French president observed the Erhard–Khrushchev episode reflectively but critically. Back in 1963 de Gaulle had assured Adenauer that there was "nothing impossible or bad about the idea of West Germany conversing with Khrushchev," and in summer 1964 he maintained this position. According to the notes taken by a French official, de Gaulle was not disconcerted by an Erhard–Khrushchev meeting, also because the Germans had no liberty of action with Moscow.[29] However, de Gaulle was clearly offended about not being consulted on the progress of German-Soviet relations. This is understandable, because Erhard had insisted just a few months earlier on the need to establish Franco-German cooperation in Eastern policies, in line with the objectives of the Elysée Treaty.[30]

In contrast to Bonn's assessment, the French considered Khrushchev's downfall as rather positive for détente and direct contacts with Moscow.[31] Franco-Soviet relations had already started to warm a few months earlier. The French minister of Finance and Economic Affairs, Valéry Giscard d'Estaing, had met with Khrushchev in Kiev in January 1964, and Nikolai Podgorny, a member of the Soviet Politburo, was received by de Gaulle in March 1964. Likewise delegations from Eastern European governments came to visit Paris, with increasing frequency.

De Gaulle's opening up to the East in 1964 also heralded a change regarding the German question, since the French government now regularly discussed it with Soviet and Eastern European leaders. This begs the questions: What actually changed in 1964, and why? The evidence examined in this chapter suggests that de Gaulle hardly altered his fundamental approach to the German question, but rather that his perception of the international context evolved over time. In other words, the change was not in what he said, but rather to whom he said it.

According to François Puaux, at the time in charge of Eastern affairs at the Quai d'Orsay, the signing of a Friendship Treaty between the Soviet Union and East Germany on 12 June 1964 was a key element in explaining de Gaulle's opening up to Moscow. In de Gaulle's reading, this treaty signified the end of Moscow's aggression against West Berlin and more generally the Soviet acceptance of the status quo in Europe.[32] Interestingly, Willy Brandt reached exactly the same conclusion.[33] Puaux further emphasizes that the Paris visit of an outspoken Romanian delegation in July 1964 impressed the French hosts to the point that de Gaulle detected "a new dimension of détente" in direct contacts with Eastern European leaders, thereby encouraging their national interests.[34] Indeed, on 31 July the Quai d'Orsay informed the French embassies of "interesting perspectives" in Eastern Europe and a possible "thaw of a situation that had been frozen for 20 years."[35] De Gaulle himself explained his opening to the East by the observation that both the Soviet regime and ideology had begun to evolve in a positive direction.[36] In this sense, de Gaulle was now living up to his promise to make constructive proposals and address the German question once the Soviet Union abandoned their belligerent stance. De Gaulle's press conference of 4 February 1965 can be seen as such a constructive proposal.

The evolving international constellation also favored de Gaulle assuming a more prominent role in East-West relations. As mentioned, the solution of previous crises (Berlin, Algeria, Cuba) created room to maneuver for the West Europeans, and their alignment behind Washington's leadership became less of an imperative. Moreover, the French initiatives to actively influence East-West affairs coincided with the escalation of U.S. involvement in the Vietnam War and de Gaulle's insistent promotion of a European Europe, in which the European leaders would be less dependent on American decisions and gradually shoulder their own responsibilities.[37] The French move was consistent with de Gaulle's objective of re-establishing France's grandeur and international rank, but likewise corresponded to his fundamental ambition to transcend the international bloc system headed by Washington and Moscow. According to de Gaulle's conviction, a world in equilibrium needed a strong European pillar.[38] As president of the leading country within the expanding framework of the European Economic Community (EEC), de Gaulle was also in a position to claim more European influence on East-West affairs.

Whereas Franco-Soviet contacts were thawing, by July 1964 Franco-German relations had cooled. De Gaulle was clearly alienated by Erhard's complete alignment with American policy and blamed him for neglecting the objectives of the Elysée Treaty.[39] Arguably, Erhard's lack of communication and bold invitation to Khrushchev further caused de Gaulle to pursue a more active Eastern policy in order to secure a mediating role for Paris and not to lose the reins to Bonn. According to French explanations, the task of animating the discussions with the East appertained to Paris and not to Bonn, because Germany was one of the subjects under discussion, and because of war-related anti-German feeling in the East.[40]

The representatives from Eastern European nations, whose independence of mind de Gaulle hoped to encourage, regarding the German question remained strictly in line with official Soviet policy. In the conversations with Paris starting in 1964, they demanded that the West Germans abandon their bellicose attitude and discuss the German question directly with the East German regime (thereby recognizing the GDR as a state). The Eastern officials also suggested disarming both German states to end the stalemate situation. The French side firmly and frankly opposed all these proposals. First, de Gaulle and Foreign Minister Maurice Couve de Murville argued that West Germany was "not a threat to international peace." Second, they dismissed the idea of letting the two German states settle their disputes as "out of touch with reality," because the important decisions regarding East Germany were taken in Moscow. And third, the French insisted that any plan for disarming the German states had "no future," since it would inevitably lead to a neutral Germany under Soviet influence.[41]

Over the following years, similar discussions between French and Eastern officials continued, and contradicting each other on the German question became part of the meeting routine. What seems remarkable are the perseverance of the French in discussing the German question with the Soviets and other Eastern European leaders, and de Gaulle's insistence that "the division of Germany into two states does not correspond to a lasting reality."[42] Another important fact is that the French president remained loyal to his allies and repeatedly refused to sign any Franco-Soviet agreement that could have been used against Germany. Khrushchev, Gromyko, and Kosygin in vain attempted to sign such a pact with de Gaulle, in June 1964, April 1965, and December 1966, respectively.[43] Despite these fundamental differences between Paris and Moscow, the discussions on the German question continued. From the French perspective, improving the atmosphere was an essential motivation and therefore considered a contribution to solving the German question.[44]

Overlooked by most scholars, de Gaulle's famous press conference of 4 February 1965 was actually preceded by Chancellor Erhard's request that the general "take the lead" in matters of German reunification, the French approach being "realistic and the only promising one."[45] And take the lead he did. In a masterfully crafted speech (these so-called press conferences were anything but spontaneous) de Gaulle laid out his view of the road toward reunification, emphasizing that the German question or problem was the European problem par excellence, and needed to be settled by an agreement among the peoples of Europe. For this to happen, the Soviet Union and the countries of Eastern Europe would have to abandon their totalitarian regimes, while the successful organization of Western Europe would bring about a new equilibrium on the continent. De Gaulle demanded that Germany's armament and borders be settled—meaning that Germany officially recognize the postwar borders and definitively renounce any nuclear weaponry.[46]

In West Germany the reactions to de Gaulle's press conference manifested not only a palpable fascination with and ambivalence toward de Gaulle, but also Bonn's own incertitude on the German question. On 10 February a special session of the Bundestag debating de Gaulle's speech was broadcast directly on German television. On this occasion Erhard applauded the importance attached to German reunification by de Gaulle's public statement. But the chancellor lacked a clear line on the issue and in late March complained at a Christian Democratic Union (CDU) congress: "In the long run, there may be realistic elements in de Gaulle's concept. But this is useless to me! I cannot address the German people and say that the long-desired day might come in 20 or 30 years."[47] The Franco-German disagreement increased by May 1965, now focusing on de Gaulle's demand that the German question be settled by an agreement among the peoples of Europe. Instead, Bonn insisted that the German question remained the responsibility of the Four Powers—France, the Soviet Union, the United Kingdom, and the United States. Schröder argued that Bonn's initially positive reactions to de Gaulle's press conference had been an error and that any "Europeanization" of the German question should be avoided.[48]

The strained relations between Paris and Bonn reached a nadir during the EEC's empty chair crisis, in the second half of 1965. In response to the European Commission's plan to gain higher authority, and following a dispute over the financing of agriculture, France abandoned the EEC negotiations and on 1 July 1965 withdrew its representative from Brussels. Although the European Commission's ambitious plan was substantially curtailed by late July, Paris did not return to the negotiation table (the French chair in Brussels was to remain empty until the Luxembourg compromise of January 1966). Instead, de Gaulle used the crisis as a means to impose French views regarding the EEC's future and deliberately "intimidated" his partners with a possible end of the Common Market.[49] From the German perspective, at the outset all issues disputed by Paris appeared resolvable (agriculture, the European Commission's role, voting procedures), yet the hectoring style of de Gaulle's policy alienated the German elite entirely, for the time being alienating even Adenauer. Willy Brandt declared that it had become impossible to follow de Gaulle's lead. Schröder complained bitterly that the French lacked any sense of teamwork or equality, and as spokesman of the other five member states of the EEC he acted as the French president's direct opponent during the crisis.[50]

Eastern policy was not part of the EEC crisis itself, yet indirectly suffered the consequences. While in March 1965 the Auswärtiges Amt had emphasized that the French initiatives contributed positively to mitigate anti-German feeling in the East, a few months later this favorable aspect was stifled by the acrimonious atmosphere. In a rather hostile confrontation in November 1965, Couve de Murville urged Schröder to improve relations with Moscow and to open the road toward reunification by officially renouncing any kind of German access to nuclear weapons[51] and any territorial claim in the East. In response, Schröder claimed equality for his country and accused the French of giving in to Soviet pressure and undermining Atlantic solidarity.[52] According to the analyses made in Bonn, at this point the Germans rejected de Gaulle's approach to the German question for various reasons: (1) West Germany could not afford and did not want to loosen its close ties with Washington. (2) The risk of depending on Paris in the dialogue with Moscow was considered too high. (3) The French pressure regarding the borders and German armament was not appreciated. (4) De Gaulle overestimated French importance and underestimated the Soviet threat. (5) France was too inconsistent to be a reliable partner for the Germans. And (6) the French might have ulterior motives for keeping Germany powerless.[53]

The French government expressed similarly negative judgments on Bonn's approach, accusing the Erhard government of seeking reunification through force instead of détente. At the heart of the French critique was Bonn's refusal to officially recognize the Oder-Neisse border and to forever renounce any access to nuclear weapons.[54] But, significantly, these French complaints were voiced internally and, according to the records of conversations, were not conveyed into the many meetings with Soviet or Eastern European officials in 1965–66. On these occasions the French instead argued that the West Germans had no evil intent and would eventually come around to embrace détente.[55] Moreover, and in contrast to German suspicions, de Gaulle's confidential statements did not display any attempt to exclude the United States from the German question. On 4 February 1966 de Gaulle informed his officials that German reunification ought to be envisaged in the long run, "by agreement with all those who have defeated Germany."[56] De Gaulle affirmed this position even more clearly during his landmark visit to Moscow in June 1966. He insisted that because of America's participation in World War II, the United States were rightfully involved in the German question.[57] On the same occasion, the French president reiterated his long-term political vision of German reunification in a context of détente, on condition that Germany renounce nuclear weapons and the postwar borders remained unchanged. Beyond these conditions—well-known and appreciated by the Soviet leadership—de Gaulle mentioned that a unified Germany could take the form of a confederation, but preferably not of a centralized Reich.[58]

De Gaulle's Moscow visit of June 1966 was a major media event in Germany and around the world. The comments by German personalities anticipating the visit varied greatly. While business circles and officials of the SPD and the small liberal party (Free Democratic Party, or FDP) talked quite optimistically of de Gaulle's forthcoming visit, statements from Erhard's CDU were mixed. Schröder argued that France had no real power and nothing important could happen. Erhard confidentially explained his own assessment of de Gaulle's hidden objective: a neutral, unified Germany under Franco-Soviet control on the basis of the Rapacki Plan.[59] Erhard's assessment bears witness to how poorly he understood the objectives of de Gaulle, who throughout his presidency consistently and firmly rejected the neutralization of Germany.

Erhard's judgment was quite different after June 1966. He applauded de Gaulle's support for German reunification in Moscow and the French refusal to recognize the GDR.[60] He even started to consider an Eastern policy in close cooperation with

France, and subsequently the Auswärtiges Amt began looking into the possibilities of developing a common, Franco-German Eastern policy.[61] However, this endeavor was to be pursued by a new German government. Under attack by his own party and abandoned by his FDP coalition partner, Erhard stepped down as chancellor in November 1966.

Parallel to de Gaulle's successful Moscow visit in 1966, the Germans also acknowledged the absence of their own results. Official invitations—for example, to Kosygin—had remained unanswered and unofficial Moscow visits had proved to be fruitless. Bonn's Peace Note of March 1966 had not included any significant concession and was rebuffed by Warsaw and Prague. At least some secret negotiations between Bonn and Moscow on the renunciation of force resulted, but did not go very far at this point (these negotiations were eventually resumed more successfully after 1969). As a result of the stalemate, individual initiatives in favor of reunification were launched outside the German government. Finally, as senior official Karl Carstens put it, since the 1950s Bonn's Eastern policy had brought about no advancement toward German reunification, had caused strained relations with the Soviet Union and Eastern Europe, and increasingly clashed with the objectives of the Western Allies.[62] It was indeed time for a new approach to the German question.

Halted Attempts at Common Eastern Policy

In December 1966 the new German government—with Chancellor Kurt Georg Kiesinger (of CDU) and Foreign Minister Willy Brandt (of SPD)—took office with the declared objective of cooperating closely with the French, notably with regard to Eastern policy. Despite some initial results in this endeavor, obstacles quickly arose. Until de Gaulle stepped down as president of France in April 1969, substantial discussions on the longer-term solution of the German question were actually rather scarce. Instead, Franco-German talks often focused on practical aspects of Eastern policy and Franco-Soviet discussions on international crises (e.g., in the Middle East and in Vietnam), while the Germans struggled to establish any fruitful contact with the East at all.

De Gaulle's initial reaction to the new German leadership was largely positive. From his perspective, a crucial change had taken place since Bonn no longer aspired to reunification through force but through détente with the East.[63] In January 1967 Chancellor Kiesinger did indeed tell de Gaulle that he accepted the French concept of détente and that he aimed to create a new atmosphere of trust with the East, being aware that German reunification could be the result only of a long evolution.[64] Foreign Minister Brandt was eager on a national level to pursue the policy of small steps he had initiated as mayor of West Berlin. He pledged to develop contacts across the Iron Curtain and acknowledged that Paris had "progressed farther" than Bonn in this respect.[65] In a private conversation with Brandt, de Gaulle assured him of French support: "We will help you if you want, especially in Moscow. We have started already. . . . We are your friends, but only as long as you are not imperialists." De Gaulle also suggested the practical steps leading toward German reunification: recognition of the German borders, contacts with the "people of the GDR," and autonomy from the United States. As to the last point, de Gaulle explained that American hegemony "prevents us from being ourselves and from getting along with the East." Brandt, who did not share de Gaulle's attitude toward the United States, preferred not to comment on this issue.[66]

The Kiesinger government not only talked about détente but also took action. In January 1967 West Germany and Romania established diplomatic relations. In June that year Kiesinger sent a letter to GDR Prime Minister Willi Stoph proposing official talks with the GDR. By taking these steps, Bonn turned away from the core idea of the Hallstein Doctrine and from the attempted isolation of the GDR that had been pursued since the 1950s. Bonn intended to establish diplomatic relations with other Eastern European states, but only Yugoslavia eventually accepted and followed the Romanian example.

Indeed, the Eastern leaders decided to reject Bonn's overture toward Eastern Europe as a new version of German expansionism and *"Drang nach Osten"* (eastward expansion).[67] The East Germans succeeded in their promotion of the Ulbricht Doctrine (this was named after GDR leader Walter Ulbricht, and was an Eastern counterpart to the Hallstein Doctrine), stipulating that the member states of the Warsaw Pact would not establish diplomatic relations with Bonn unless the GDR was fully recognized as a state. Furthermore, in April 1967 a conference of the European Communist Parties in Karlovy Vary ended with the declaration that normalization of relations with Bonn also required a radical change of West German foreign policy. The long catalogue of demands included the recognition of the GDR and postwar borders, renunciation of any nuclear armament, and an independent status for West Berlin.[68]

To a large extent the reaction of the Warsaw Pact achieved its purpose of blocking the Eastern policy of Bonn's Grand Coalition government. The West Germans were confronted with a choice between sticking to old principles and adopting a fundamentally new policy by offering substantial concessions to the East. There did not seem to be a middle way, and as a result the Grand Coalition's whole Eastern policy faltered. While Brandt's SPD was inclined to move ahead and accept further changes, Kiesinger and the CDU refused to make any more concessions, and in the face of the harsh Soviet propaganda even hardened their initial positions.[69]

Meanwhile, in their contacts with Soviet and Eastern European officials the French defended the good intentions of the Grand Coalition government. Meeting with Ambassador Valerian Zorin in January 1967, de Gaulle exhorted the Soviet government to make an effort and not to leave the Germans "adrift." After Moscow's intransigent attitude was confirmed in the following months, de Gaulle's parlance became more direct. In October 1967, he told Zorin that Moscow should "encourage and not discourage the good intentions of the Germans" and sternly rebuffed the ambassador's renewed proposal to sign an agreement against Germany.[70]

The exchange of delegations between France and Eastern European countries had increased in number since de Gaulle's Moscow visit (more than thirty in 1967 alone). The French president also made official visits to Poland in September 1967 and to

Romania in May 1968. But the German question now played a less substantial role and the French mostly restated their known position. For example, when de Gaulle exclaimed during the Poland visit that Zabrze was "the most Polish of all Polish cities," essentially he reconfirmed the statement that the postwar borders were irreversible.[71]

In this context one aspect of the French position merits attention. In talks with Kosygin and with the Polish Foreign Minister Adam Rapacki, de Gaulle insisted that a unified Germany could only be a confederation and not a centralized Reich. Hence in the French talks with the East this element was added to the other preconditions (no nuclear weapons, recognition of borders). But when meeting with U.S. Vice President Hubert Humphrey shortly thereafter, de Gaulle brought up the same topic and explained that a confederation would only be a step toward reunification, the ultimate result being a single German state.[72] Arguably, de Gaulle's mentioning of the confederation element may be interpreted as an effort to make the reunification idea more palatable to the Eastern leaders, rather than a French attempt at deceiving the Germans. At some point the Soviets had themselves floated the idea of a confederation between East and West Germany (in 1955 and again in 1959), and de Gaulle may have picked up on it to facilitate the discussion.[73]

In November 1967 Bonn's efforts to cooperate with Paris were once again hampered by de Gaulle's European policy. The French president's public declaration that "the British Isles" still needed to undergo a "very vast and very profound transformation" before they could join the EEC, was subscribed to in Germany neither by public opinion nor the political or economic elite.[74] Bonn had acted as mediator between Paris and the European partners in view of the EEC's enlargement, and now endeavored to pursue this role although clearly disagreeing with de Gaulle. Privately, Chancellor Kiesinger described the French president as "rigid and inflexible" and incapable of heeding the voice of European public opinion.[75] Foreign Minister Brandt, whose SPD was campaigning massively for the EEC's enlargement, strictly instructed his diplomatic personnel to express dissent with de Gaulle on this issue. Yet, Brandt also advised them to keep the Franco-German contacts friendly, being aware that there could be no EEC without France.[76]

Hence, by early 1968 Paris and Bonn were still pursuing the objective of a common Eastern policy, but the overall atmosphere had become more fraught. Differences with regard to Eastern policy itself also started to manifest themselves. While de Gaulle encouraged Kiesinger to officially recognize the Oder-Neisse border and predicted an "enormously" positive effect on détente, the chancellor firmly refused.[77] He feared that Germany would otherwise be "sucked into the undercurrent of Soviet policy."[78] The fissures gradually appearing between de Gaulle and Brandt were of a different nature. In December 1967 the Quai d'Orsay transmitted an unofficial warning to Brandt not to avoid Moscow and seek détente with the satellites only.[79] And, in early February 1968, a German news agency caused considerable uproar when reporting that Brandt had made disparaging remarks about de Gaulle during an SPD gathering. In response to these alleged remarks, the French president cancelled his meeting with two German ministers and privately stated that Brandt was not a real leader.[80] Maybe most importantly, Brandt was "bitterly shocked" to see how readily the French believed the allegations and how little trust he enjoyed in Paris. His subsequent, somewhat insufficient communication with the French may be seen in this context.[81]

Already before this incident, the planning papers of Brandt's office contained an important element of dissatisfaction with de Gaulle's Eastern policy. On the one hand, the French were perceived as genuinely aiming at détente and as having a positive effect on some Eastern leaders' attitudes toward Germany. For example, Brandt observed that a Polish minister's mind-set had become more amenable and considerate after meeting with de Gaulle.[82] On the other hand, Brandt's advisers pointed out that de Gaulle claimed for himself the role of East-West mediator and denied it to Bonn. Since France did not have the same interests as Germany, and aimed at increasing its room to maneuver rather than tying itself to Bonn, from the outset Brandt's staff had reservations as to the comprehensiveness of the common Eastern policy. Notably, Brandt's office emphasized that the Germans needed to take the decisive steps themselves, through their own bilateral contacts with the East.[83]

According to the argument presented here, Brandt's intention to pursue his own Eastern policy became manifest to the French during the Prague Spring of 1968. Three elements deserve to be mentioned in this context. First, the French discovered that Brandt was engaging in regular contacts with the reformist Dubček government without informing Paris and despite his promise to abstain from any involvement with Prague during this particular time. One of Brandt's staff shared the (correct) news of the Bonn-Prague contacts with a French diplomat on 25 June 1968.[84] Second, during a visit to Belgrade in the same month, Brandt followed the suggestion of his adviser Egon Bahr and tried to ascertain whether the Yugoslavs would participate in a potential new security system that could eventually replace NATO and the Warsaw Pact. At the time, Bahr's planning group prepared a novel political concept that aspired to overcome the bloc system by creating a vast denuclearized zone in Central Europe (including East and West Germany, Belgium, Holland, Luxemburg, Poland, and Czechoslovakia). Bahr was well aware that his concept ran contrary to de Gaulle's, and for the time intended to keep it secret. Yet the Yugoslavs, who expressed little enthusiasm for the abolition of the two military blocs, were also in regular contact with the French.[85]

Third, Paris received two contradictory accounts of Brandt's meeting with the influential Soviet Ambassador Piotr Abrassimov in East Berlin on 18 June 1968. While Brandt's own report expressed disappointment at the meeting's unproductiveness, two days later the French heard a different story from Brandt's aide, Gerhard Ritzel. He had assisted at the meeting and reported that large-scale cooperation between Moscow and Bonn had been envisaged, and that Brandt had referred to the Elysée Treaty as a model for German-Soviet reconciliation.[86] In an interview with the author, Egon Bahr insisted that Ritzel must have misunderstood the Brandt–Abrassimov conversation. Yet Bahr also admitted that Paris must have been alarmed by this report.

Indeed, in summer 1968 the French were concerned that Bonn and Moscow may have concluded an agreement to divide Central Europe into two zones of influence.[87]

The invasion of Czechoslovakia by the troops of the Warsaw Pact on 21 August 1968 represents a turning point in the overall context. A rather serious Franco-German clash ensued. During a Bonn visit in late September, de Gaulle vigorously accused the Germans of having conducted an Eastern policy beyond their mandate, and of having succumbed to a fatal *Drang nach Osten*. To some extent he even blamed Bonn for the invasion of Czechoslovakia.[88] De Gaulle's outburst was certainly excessive and has been explained by various reasons. His frustration stemming from the May–June uprisings in France may have played a role, as well as some rancor against the economic rise of Germany.[89] The evidence mentioned above also suggests that Brandt and his office bore some responsibility for provoking the general's wrath (but not the invasion of Czechoslovakia). Two former French officials have indeed supported the interpretation that de Gaulle's accusations in September 1968 aimed at Brandt rather than Kiesinger.[90]

In reality, the Franco-German effort to pursue a common Eastern policy ended here. Kiesinger bitterly observed that de Gaulle ceased to notify Bonn of his contacts with Eastern leaders. From the chancellor's perspective, the events of August 1968 had exposed de Gaulle's inability to influence Soviet behavior, and thus the failure of French Eastern policy. Brandt had become more skeptical of French policy and even suspected a Franco-Soviet collusion to prevent EEC enlargement. Moreover, after the Warsaw Pact's aggression against Czechoslovakia Brandt decided to put any major Eastern initiative on hold until the Bundestag elections of September 1969.[91]

The French ambition to discuss the German question with the East stopped quite abruptly after 21 August 1968. The dialogue with Moscow soon resumed, but no further substantial discussion on Germany took place. Significantly, in these talks the French totally blamed the Soviets for the invasion of Czechoslovakia and according to the records did not mention any German coresponsibility. De Gaulle instead emphasized, "Not Germany but the USSR has marched in, this time."[92]

Until de Gaulle stepped down as French president in April 1969, in terms of Eastern policy he "reflected and hesitated."[93] When he did discuss the German question, it was with the Americans. He still depicted German reunification as a long-term objective resulting from a contractual agreement between Eastern and Western countries, yet now also "with the United States to guarantee the situation." Arguably, this additional element implies a possible American role in Europe beyond German reunification. But overall, from the Prague experience de Gaulle concluded that German reunification would not happen "as long as Soviet Russia remains standing."[94]

Conclusion

The reciprocal influence between Paris and Bonn on their Eastern policies and respective approaches to the German question is difficult to fathom and ultimately remains a matter of interpretation. Nevertheless, it seems coherent to argue that Bonn's influence on Paris was less than the other way around. De Gaulle publicly outlined his long-term approach to the German question in March 1959 and—in more detail but very similarly—in February 1965. Overall, French Eastern policy remained faithful to the declared concept throughout de Gaulle's presidency, with only minor adaptations to political circumstances. Even the British Foreign Office, which was on less-than cordial terms with Paris at the time, (regretfully) informed a suspicious German official that the French position on the German question was the same irrespective of the situation, and that all evidence pointed to the fact that de Gaulle was "genuinely trying to help German relations with Eastern European countries."[95]

Indeed, de Gaulle consistently argued in favor of German reunification in the long run and under certain conditions. On several occasions he also emphasized that he was not in a hurry to see reunification happen. This ambivalence in de Gaulle's position became especially manifest when he was annoyed over German policy, as in spring 1963 (preamble to the Elysée Treaty), in 1965 (Bonn's apparent rejection of détente), and in fall 1968 (perceived German *Drang nach Osten*). Moreover, de Gaulle readily used the German question to promote other aspects of his policy. For example, he argued that the road to reunification would be blocked by any kind of German access to nuclear weapons, likewise by Bonn's political closeness to the United States. Not least did he attempt to use the German question to enhance his own international role as mediator and spokesman on behalf of Germany.

From Bonn's perspective, a common Eastern policy with the French was also impeded by almost permanent disagreements on European and transatlantic policies. These divergences and de Gaulle's hectoring political style made it difficult for the Germans to accept him as a spokesman for the German cause, especially during the EEC crisis of 1965 and again toward the end of the decade. Taking a different approach, Marc Trachtenberg has argued that ultimately de Gaulle had nothing to offer to the Germans to justify his taking the lead, and that Bonn necessarily would not agree to a secondary position.[96] Yet with regard to Eastern policy, at least in the mid-1960s the idea of following the French lead was considered an option. Strauß openly promoted this idea in 1965, Erhard seriously considered it after de Gaulle's successful trip to Moscow in 1966, and in early 1967 Brandt readily accepted that Paris had progressed farther in Eastern affairs. At that time, what de Gaulle had to offer were regular contacts with Eastern decision makers (in contrast to Bonn) and a programmatic approach toward German reunification, whereas in the Auswärtiges Amt "the cupboard was bare."[97]

Even though the Germans had decidedly mixed relations with de Gaulle, his political statements always received considerable attention in Bonn. Notably his press conference on the German question in February 1965, and his high-profile trip to Moscow in June 1966, provoked far-reaching debates among the German elite, media, and public opinion. While the exact effect on Bonn's policy cannot be measured, several German sources suggest that de Gaulle's sustained and promising dialogue through the Iron Curtain was one of the influences leading to a change of course in 1966, when the CDU leaders opted for a more conciliatory attitude toward the East.[98] De Gaulle's importance for the political program gradually elaborated by Brandt's group is more obvious. Already in 1964 Brandt publicly applauded de Gaulle's groundbreaking effort "to think the unthinkable" and to set the frozen East-West fronts in motion.[99] In his planning papers, Bahr evaluated French Eastern policy as a positive initiative, and at one point used an adapted version of de Gaulle's triptych (détente, entente, cooperation) to explain the basis of German Eastern policy.[100] In hindsight, Bahr has said he was "convinced" that de Gaulle sincerely advocated the cause of German reunification in the East, and has argued that this was "a good background" for Brandt's later Ostpolitik.[101]

Benedikt Schoenborn is senior research fellow at the Institute for Advanced Social Research, Tampere University, Finland. He researches European history since World War II with a special interest in peace-related aspects. In the context of this book, relevant publications include *La mésentente apprivoisée: de Gaulle et les Allemands* (Geneva, 2014) and "Bargaining with the Bear: Chancellor Erhard's Bid to Buy German Reunification" (*Cold War History*, 2008). Schoenborn's next book analyzes Willy Brandt's Ostpolitik from the viewpoint of reconciliation.

Notes

1. "Franco-Soviet meeting," 21 Jun. 1966, CADN, Bonn 216.
2. Meeting Erhard–de Gaulle, 21 Jul. 1966, Institut für Zeitgeschichte, AAPD 1966, 955–60.
3. See the Bundestag debate of 10 Feb. 1965, in "Bundesrepublik Deutschland," *Bulletin des Presseamtes*, 12 Feb. 1965, 209–12.
4. Conversation de Gaulle–Brandt, 15 Dec. 1966, AMAE, EM, 29.
5. De Gaulle, *Discours et messages*, vol. 3, 82–87.
6. De Gaulle's conversations with Brezhnev and Kosygin, 21 Jun. 1966; and Zorin, 23 Jan. 1967 and 4 Oct. 1967, AMAE, EM 29–32.
7. MAE, DDF 1960, vol. 1, 358–61, 382–84.
8. Conversation de Gaulle–Rusk, 19 Jun. 1962, quoted in Vaïsse, *La grandeur*, 282.
9. Starting in March 1950, de Gaulle publicly used the formula sixteen times; Larcan, "L'Europe de l'Atlantique à l'Oural," 181–84.
10. De Gaulle, *Discours et messages*, vol. 4, 123 ; Rey, "De Gaulle," 218–21.
11. According to some interpretations, Adenauer's policy line ultimately proved successful; Buchstab, "Adenauer."
12. Spohr, "German Unification," 887.
13. Against the background of Khrushchev's ultimatum of Nov. 1958, Adenauer asked his adviser Hans Globke to draft a plan for easing tensions and eventually for German reunification. This Globke-Plan recommended spectacular Western concessions (the recognition of the GDR as a state, the transformation of Berlin into an independent city) and proposed a five-year moratorium between East and West to open the road toward free elections in the GDR. Following an exchange between Khrushchev and the West German ambassador in Moscow, Hans Kroll, from Jan. 1960 onward the moratorium idea of the Globke-Plan was internally referred to as the Burgfriedensplan. Between 1959 and 1962,

in conversations with Western and Soviet officials Adenauer also used the term "Stillhalteplan" in the sense of a *Waffenstillstand* (an East-West truce) for ten years. See Kühlem, "Burgfrieden." For more detail, see Erhard, *Adenauers deutschlandpolitische*.

14. Conversation Adenauer–de Gaulle, 5 Jul. 1963, AnF, 5AG1, 161. See also AAPD 1963, 502–5, 682–83, 692–98, 1187–92.

15. Memorandum Konrad Adenauer, 10 Sept. 1963, BKAH, Nachlass Adenauer, III 12.

16. Tape recording of Adenauer: "Mein Aufenthalt in Paris," 8–11 Nov. 1964, BKAH, Nachlass Adenauer II 106.

17. Schmidt, *Kalter Krieg*, 168–78.

18. According to Brandt's notes, he had yielded to pressure exerted by the U.S. representative in Berlin (in 1959) and by his local coalition partners (in 1963). Brandt, *Begegnungen und Einsichten*, 110–13; Grebing et al., *Willy Brandt*, 48–49, 258–65.

19. Meeting de Gaulle–Brandt, 24 Apr. 1963, CADN, Bonn 179. Brandt expressed his appreciation on 15 Dec. 1966, AMAE, EM 29.

20. Meeting de Gaulle–Brandt, 3 Jun. 1965, CADN, Bonn 179. Conversation Bahr–Winckler, 25 May 1965, AdsD, Bonn, Depositum Egon Bahr. At the time, from the French perspective Brandt's position on German borders and armament did not differ substantially from Erhard's.

21. Eibl, *Politik der Bewegung*, 257–73.

22. Memo for the prime minister, 27 Dec. 1963, TNA, Prem, 11/4818. For the Allied discussions of the German peace plan, see Miller, FRUS, 2–107.

23. Conversation Erhard–McGhee, 3 Oct. 1963, FRUS 1961–63, vol. 15, 586 (quotes). For more detail, see Schoenborn, "Bargaining with the Bear," published in 2008 and accessible from the "Ludwig Erhard" entry in Wikipedia. Three years later, in 2011, with no reference to the aforementioned article, Erhard's plan and discussions with U.S. officials were revealed to a wider German audience. See "Der Preis der Freiheit," *Der Spiegel* 40/2011, 1 October 2011.

24. Conversation Erhard–Johnson, 28 Dec. 1963, National Archives at College Park, MD, Central Foreign Policy Files 1963, box 3915.

25. Telegram Laboulaye (Moscow), 15 Jun. 1964, CADN, Bonn 220. For Groepper's extensive exchange with the Auswärtiges Amt, see, B150, 1964, 4–14 Jun. 1964, PA/AA, Berlin.

26. Conversation Erhard–Smirnov, 27 Jul. 1964, AAPD 1964, 879–83. Deutscher Bundestag, 4. Wahlperiode, Plenarprotokoll 04/137, 137. Sitzung am 15. Oktober 1964, 6786–87. See also Kosthorst, "Sowjetische Geheimpolitik in Deutschland?," 289–90.

27. On this last point, see Selvage, "The Warsaw Pact," 7.

28. "Stenographic Protocol," 20–21 Nov. 1964.

29. Meeting de Gaulle–Adenauer, 5 Jul. 1963, AnF, 5AG1, 161. Alphand, *L'étonnement d'être*, 435–40.

30. Franco-German meeting, 15 Feb. 1964, AAPD 1964, 249–55. Conversation Erhard–de Margerie, 10 Sept. 1964, AAPD 1964, 1004–6. Conversely, de Gaulle was not at pains to consult with the Germans before announcing political decisions.

31. Memorandum, "Rapports Franco-soviétiques," 5 Jan. 1965, AMAE, Europe 1961–70, URSS 1931.

32. Interview Puaux, 24 Oct. 1989, AMAE, Archives orales, 34.

33. Meeting Brandt–Winckler, 20 Jun. 1964, AMAE, Europe 1961–70, RFA, 1603.

34. Puaux, "La conception gaullienne," 67.

35. Telegram Puaux, 31 Jul. 1964, AMAE, EM 22.

36. Meeting de Gaulle–Podgorny, 2 Mar. 1964, AMAE, EM 20.

37. "Conférence de presse du 23 juillet 1964," quoted in de Gaulle, *Discours et messages*, vol. 4, 225–31.

38. Vaïsse, *La grandeur*, 34–40, 413–25.

39. Franco-German meeting, 3–4 Jul. 1964, AMAE, EM 22.

40. Conversation Wehner–Couve de Murville, 5 Feb. 1968, ACDP, St Augustin, Nachlass Kiesinger A288. Meeting de Gaulle–Fock, 29 Mar. 1968, AMAE, EM 33.

41. First quote: Couve de Murville–Naszkowski, 11 Feb. 1964; second quote: Couve de Murville–David, 26 Nov. 1964; third quote: Couve de Murville–Koça, 25 Nov. 1964, AMAE, EM 20–23.

42. Meeting de Gaulle–Gromyko, 27 Apr. 1965, AMAE, EM 24.

43. Message of Khrushchev, 18 Jun. 1964, CADN, Bonn 216. Meeting de Gaulle–Gromyko, 27 Apr. 1965 and meeting de Gaulle–Kosygin, 2 Dec. 1966, AMAE, EM 24 and 29.
44. Meeting Couve de Murville–Gromyko, 29 Oct. 1965, CADN, Bonn 216.
45. Meeting de Gaulle–Erhard, 19 Jan. 1965, AMAE, EM 23.
46. De Gaulle, *Discours et messages*, vol. 4, 337–40.
47. Erhard, "Öffentliche Kundgebung," 37. For more detail on the German reactions, see Schoenborn, *La mésentente apprivoisée*, 285–88.
48. AAPD 1965, 782–95, 822–33, 941–47. Quote from p. 822, meeting Schröder–Rusk, 13 May 1965.
49. Interview Couve de Murville, 16 Jan. 1984, Fondation Jean Monnet, Lausanne, Archives orales (quote); draft telegram, 6 Jul. 1965, Fondation Nationale des Sciences Politiques, Paris, CM8 ; Peyrefitte, *C'était de Gaulle*, vol. 2, 292.
50. Telegram Lahr, 9 Jul. 1965, PA/AA, B150 ; Brandt speech, 13 Sept. 1965, AMAE, Europe 1961–70, RFA 1606; meeting Schröder–McGhee, 13 Sept. 1965, AAPD 1965, 1427–35.
51. At the time, Bonn still hoped for the creation of a nuclear multilateral force within NATO.
52. Meeting Couve de Murville–Schröder, 12 Nov. 1965, AMAE, EM 26. For the German version see AAPD 1965, 1699–703.
53. French Eastern policy, 25 Nov. 1965, ACDP, Nachlass Schröder 286/2. Memorandum Carstens, 27 Jan. 1966, Bundesarchiv, Nachlass Carstens 639.
54. De Gaulle, *Lettres, notes et carnets*, vol. 10, 247; Memorandum by the political director, 12 Nov. 1965, AMAE, EM 26.
55. The records of conversation are consistent in this respect: meeting Couve de Murville–Kosygin, 31 Oct. 1965; meeting Couve de Murville-Brezhnev, 1 Nov. 1965; meeting Couve de Murville–Maurer, 27 Apr. 1966; meeting Couve de Murville–Ceausescu, 28 Apr. 1966; meeting Couve de Murville–Bachev, 29 Apr. 1966; meeting Couve de Murville–Gomulka, 20 May 1966; meeting de Gaulle–Kliszko, 13 May 1966; meetings de Gaulle-Brezhnev and Kosygin, 21–29 Jun. 1966, AMAE, EM 25–27.
56. De Gaulle, *Lettres, notes et carnets*, vol. 10, 246.
57. "L'Amérique a fait la guerre, elle a des droits en ce qui concerne l'Allemagne dans son ensemble": Franco-Soviet meeting, 21 Jun. 1966, CADN, Bonn 216.
58. Franco-Soviet meeting, 21 Jun. 1966, CADN, Bonn 216.
59. Meeting Erhard–Wilson, 23 May 1966, AAPD 1966, 657.
60. Meeting Erhard–de Gaulle, 21 Jul. 1966, AAPD 1966, 955.
61. Osterheld, *Außenpolitik*, 332; PA/AA, B24/567, France and German Ostpolitik,17 Oct. 1966; PA/AA, B41/755, Memorandum, 24 Oct. 1966.
62. Memorandum, 17 Oct. 1966, AAPD 1966, 1378–81. See also memorandum on German foreign policy, 14 Nov. 1966, AAPD 1966, 1502–15.
63. Peyrefitte, *C'était de Gaulle*, vol. 3, 194–95.
64. Meeting Kiesinger–de Gaulle, 14 Jan. 1967, ACDP, Nachlass Kiesinger A292.
65. Meeting Couve de Murville–Brandt, 27 Apr. 1967, AMAE, EM 30.
66. Conversation de Gaulle–Brandt, 15 Dec. 1966, AMAE, EM 29. AAPD 1966, 1641.
67. Meeting de Gaulle–Ochab, 7 Sept. 1967, AMAE, EM 32.
68. Haftendorn, *Deutsche Außenpolitik*, 176; Soutou, *La guerre de Cinquante Ans*, 474–75.
69. Kielmansegg, *Nach der Katastrophe*, 195–96.
70. Meetings de Gaulle–Zorin, 21 Jan. and 4 Oct. 1967, AMAE, EM 29, EM 32.
71. Despite the controversial claim in Zabrze, the Auswärtiges Amt considered de Gaulle's trip to Poland as a "good service to the German cause"; "Analyse von de Gaulle's Staatsbesuch," memorandum, 14 Sept. 1967, PA/AA, B2/132.
72. Meeting de Gaulle–Kosygin, 2 Dec. 1966; meeting de Gaulle–Rapacki, 27 Jan. 1967; meeting de Gaulle–Humphrey, 7 Apr. 1967, AMAE, EM 29–30.
73. Roberts, "A Chance for Peace?," 51–52.
74. De Gaulle, *Discours et messages*, vol. 5, 243; memoranda Lahr, 14 and 18 Dec. 1967, PA/AA, B2, 130.
75. Meeting Kiesinger–Monnet, 11 Oct. 1967, AAPD 1967, 1357.

76. Telegram Brandt to Klaiber, 7 Dec. 1967, PA/AA, B2, 130; memorandum Bahr, 30 Nov. 1967, AdsD, Depositum Bahr 396.
77. Meeting de Gaulle–Kiesinger, 12 Jul. 1967, AMAE, EM 31; AAPD 1967, 1041–45.
78. Memorandum Osterheld, 31 Mar. 1967, ACDP, Nachlass Osterheld, Kiesinger 1.
79. Memorandum Thomas, 20 Dec. 1967, WBA, Bonn, Nachlass Brandt, Außenminister 10.
80. Memorandum "Propos du général de Gaulle," secrétariat général, 5 Feb. 1968, AMAE, EM 33.
81. Quoted by Thomas: meeting Thomas–d'Aumale, 9 Feb. 1968, WBA, Nachlass Brandt, Außenminister 10. See also Brandt, *Erinnerungen*, 240–43.
82. Meeting Brandt–Couve de Murville, 27 Apr. 1967, AMAE, EM 30.
83. Memoranda Bahr, 11 Jan. and 7 Jul. 1967, AdsD, Depositum Bahr 441; memorandum "Französische Außenpolitik," 8 Jan. 1968, PA/AA, B150.
84. Telegram Seydoux, 25 Jun. 1968, AMAE, Europe 1961–70, RFA 1576.
85. Memorandum Bahr for Brandt, 11 Jun. 1968, AdsD, Depositum Bahr 399; meeting Brandt–Nikezic, 14 Jun. 1968, AAPD 1968, 715; memorandum Bahr, "Europäische Sicherheit," 27 Jun. 1968, AAPD 1968, 796–814. See also Brandt, *Erinnerungen*, 220.
86. Telegrams Seydoux, 19 and 25 Jun. 1968, AMAE, Europe 1961–70, RFA 1576. See also meeting Brandt–Abrassimov, 21 Jun. 1968, AAPD 1968, 752–61.
87. Debré, *Mémoires*, vol. 4, 257–58 ; author's interview with Egon Bahr on 14 Apr. 2004. For more detail, see Schoenborn, "Willy Brandt infidèle?"
88. Franco-German meetings, 27–28 Sept. 1968, AMAE, EM 34; AAPD 1968, 1205–9, 1251–53.
89. Schwarz,"Die Regierung Kiesinger," 180–82.
90. Author's interviews with Pierre Messmer (25 Sept. 2003) and Bruno de Leusse (21 Jul. 2004).
91. "Koalitions-Gespräch," 1 Oct. 1968, Bundesarchiv, Nachlass Guttenberg 95; "Informationsgespräch," 12 Dec. 1968, ACDP, Nachlass Kiesinger 008-1.
92. Meeting de Gaulle–Zorin, 19 Nov. 1968, AMAE, EM 35; meeting Debré-Zorin, 2 Sept. 1968, AMAE, Europe 1961–70, Czechoslovakia 244.
93. AnF, 5AG1, 164, meeting Debré–Brandt, 10 Mar. 1969 (quote by Debré).
94. Meeting de Gaulle–Mansfield, 19 Nov. 1968, AMAE, EM 35. See also meetings de Gaulle–Nixon, 28 Feb. and 31 Mar. 1969, AMAE, EM 36.
95. Memorandum Lush, 2 Feb. 1968, National Archives, Kew, FCO 33/119.
96. Trachtenberg, "The de Gaulle Problem," 83.
97. Cramer, *Gefragt*, 50–51. The Bahr quote refers to 1967.
98. Memorandum Carstens, 27 Aug. 1966, PA/AA, B2/143; "Analyse," 7 Oct. 1966, B38/80 (see also B41/755, various documents); Osterheld, *Außenpolitik*, 332.
99. For Brandt's speech of 15 May 1964 in New York, see Brandt, *Erinnerungen*, 247–48.
100. Memorandum Bahr, 1 Jun. 1965, AdsD, Dep. Bahr 441 (quote). See also "Thesen zur Osteuropapolitik," 1967, AdsD, Dep. Bahr 400. In his version, Bahr replaced "détente" with "rapprochement."
101. Interview with the author, on 14 Apr. 2004.

Bibliography

Alphand, H. 1977. *L'étonnement d'être. Journal 1939–1973*. Paris: Fayard.
Brandt, W. 1976. *Begegnungen und Einsichten. Die Jahre 1960–1975*. Hamburg, Germany: Hoffmann und Campe.
———. 1989. *Erinnerungen*. Berlin: Propyläen.
Buchstab, G. 2000. "Adenauer und die Wiedervereinigung." *Die Politische Meinung* 45, no. 373: 47–54.
Bundesrepublik Deutschland, ed. 1965. *Bulletin des Presse- und Informationsamtes der Bundesregierung*. Bonn, Germany: Deutscher Bundes-Verlag.
Cramer, D. 1975. *Gefragt: Egon Bahr*. Bornheim, Germany: Zirngibl.
De Gaulle, C. 1970. *Discours et messages*. Vol. 3. *Avec le renouveau*. Paris: Plon.
———. 1970. *Discours et messages*. Vol. 4. *Pour l'effort*. Paris: Plon.

————. 1980–1987. *Lettres, notes et carnets*, 10 vols. Paris: Plon.

Debré, M. 1993. *Mémoires*, 4 vols. Paris: Albin Michel.

Eibl, F. 2001. *Politik der Bewegung. Gerhard Schröder als Außenminister 1961–1966*. Munich, Germany: Oldenbourg.

Erhard, L. 1965. "Öffentliche Kundgebung," Speech, 28 Mar. 1965. In *Bundesparteitag 1965 in Düsseldorf*, edited by Presse- und Informationsdienste der CDU, 28–39. Bonn, Germany: Deutschlands Verlagsgesellschaft.

Erhard, V. 2003. *Adenauers deutschlandpolitische Geheimkonzepte während der zweiten Berlin-Krise 1958–1962*. Hamburg, Germany: Kovac.

Grebing, H., G. Schöllgen, and H. A. Winkler, eds. 2004. *Willy Brandt: Berliner Ausgabe*, Vol. 3. Berlin: Dietz.

Haftendorn, H. 2001. *Deutsche Außenpolitik zwischen Selbstbeschränkung und Selbstbehauptung 1945–2000*. Stuttgart, Germany: Deutsche Verlags-Anstalt.

Kielmansegg, P. G. 2000. *Nach der Katastrophe. Eine Geschichte des geteilten Deutschland*. Berlin: Siedler.

Kosthorst, D. 1996. "Sowjetische Geheimpolitik in Deutschland? Chruschtschow und die Adschubej-Mission 1964." *Vierteljahrshefte für Zeitgeschichte* 44, no. 2: 257–93.

Kühlem, K. 2009. "'Burgfrieden': Die Bedeutung und Verwendung des Begriffs zwischen Bonn und Moskau 1958–1963." *Historisch-Politische Mitteilungen* 16: 37–55.

Larcan, A. 2006. "L'Europe de l'Atlantique à l'Oural." In Vaïsse, *De Gaulle et la Russie*, 181–98.

Miller, J. E., ed. 1999. *Foreign Relations of the United States, 1964–1968*, Vol. 15. Washington, DC: U.S. Government Printing Office.

Osterheld, H. 1992. *Außenpolitik unter Bundeskanzler Ludwig Erhard 1963–1966: ein dokumentarischer Bericht aus dem Kanzleramt*. Bonn, Germany: Droste.

Peyrefitte, A. 1994–2000. *C'était de Gaulle*, 3 vols. Paris: Fayard.

Puaux, F. 1996. "La conception gaullienne de la détente 1964–1968." *Espoir* 109: 66–71.

Rey, M.-P. 2006. "De Gaulle, l'URSS et la sécurité européenne, 1958–1969." In Vaïsse, *De Gaulle et la Russie*, 213–27.

Roberts, G. 2008. "A Chance for Peace? The Soviet Campaign to End the Cold War, 1953–1955." Cold War International History Project, Working Paper 57. Wilson Center, Woodrow Wilson International Center for Scholars, Washington, DC.

Schmidt, W. 2001. *Kalter Krieg, Koexistenz und kleine Schritte: Willy Brandt und die Deutschlandpolitik 1948–1963*. Wiesbaden, Germany: Westdeutscher Verlag.

Schoenborn, B. 2007. *La mésentente apprivoisée. De Gaulle et les Allemands, 1963–1969*. Paris: Presses Universitaires de France.

————. 2008a. "Bargaining with the Bear. Chancellor Erhard's Bid to Buy German Reunification, 1963–64." *Cold War History* 8, no. 1: 23–53.

————. 2008b. "Willy Brandt infidèle? Les incertitudes françaises durant le Printemps de Prague, 1968." *Relations Internationales* 134, 69–81.

Schwarz, H.-P. 1999. "Die Regierung Kiesinger und die Krise in der CSSR 1968." *Vierteljahrshefte für Zeitgeschichte* 47, no. 2: 159–86.

Selvage, D. 2001. "The Warsaw Pact and Nuclear Nonproliferation 1963–1965." Cold War International History Project, Working Paper 32. Wilson Center, Woodrow Wilson International Center for Scholars, Washington, DC.

Soutou, G.-H. 2001. *La guerre de Cinquante Ans. Les relations Est-Ouest 1943–1990*. Paris: Fayard.

Spohr, K. 2000. "German Unification: Between Official History, Academic Scholarship, and Political Memoirs." *Historical Journal* 43, no. 3: 869–88.

"Stenographic Protocol of the II Plenary Session of the Central Committee of the Polish United Workers' Party (excerpts), 20–21 November 1964." Wilson Center, Woodrow Wilson International Center for Scholars, Washington, DC. Available at http://digitalarchive.wilsoncenter.org/document/112670

Trachtenberg, M. 2012. "The de Gaulle Problem." *Journal of Cold War Studies* 14, no. 1: 81–92.

Vaïsse, M. 1998. *La grandeur. Politique étrangère du général de Gaulle 1958–1969*. Paris: Fayard.

————, ed. 2006. *De Gaulle et la Russie*. Paris: CNRS Éditions.

PART IV
THE ERA OF
OSTPOLITIK

CHAPTER 7

PERCEPTIONS OF *OSTPOLITIK*

FRENCH–WEST GERMAN RELATIONS AND THE EVOLVING GERMAN QUESTION UNDER WILLY BRANDT AND GEORGES POMPIDOU

GOTTFRIED NIEDHART

The coming to power in October 1969 of a social-liberal government with the Social-Democrat Willy Brandt as chancellor and the Liberal Walter Scheel as foreign minister marked a distinct caesura. The main feature of the new Bonn government was its bold new approach to relations with Eastern Europe. The German word *Ostpolitik* became a term widely used and internationally understood in the politics of East-West relations.[1] At the same time there was a strong element of continuity, comparable to France's Eastern policy launched by President Charles de Gaulle (it was a French term that gave the name to a whole period in East-West relations: the era of détente). Brandt had been foreign minister in the previous Grand Coalition government headed by the Christian Democrat Kurt Georg Kiesinger. When Georges Pompidou, de Gaulle's successor, received Brandt in June 1969 his diplomatic adviser put him in the picture about the "West German policy of opening to the East."[2] In a French perspective it was of utmost importance that Bonn regarded any solution of the German question no longer as a precondition for détente in Europe. Such a stance fell in with positions uttered before by Presidents de Gaulle and Lyndon B. Johnson: according to them any development toward a unified Germany was conceivable only in the context of overcoming the division of Europe. The message was crystal clear: if the Germans wished to uphold the idea of a reunification they had to strive for détente in Europe. It was in this context that the Kiesinger–Brandt government had started a first phase of a new Ostpolitik (Neue Ostpolitik) in 1966.

This chapter is concerned with perceptions of Ostpolitik—mainly with French perceptions but also, though to a lesser extent, with the question of how the Federal

Republic of Germany (FRG, or West Germany) believed its Ostpolitik was perceived by the French government. In the French perspective three main questions arose: First, would Brandt's Ostpolitik, by aiming at a rapprochement with the German Democratic Republic (GDR, or East Germany), affect the rights of the Four Powers regarding Germany as a whole and the status of Berlin? In other words, was Ostpolitik an attempt to solve the German question through a direct understanding with the Union of Soviet Socialist Republics (USSR, or Soviet Union) outside the legal framework that existed since 1954? Second, would Ostpolitik have an impact on the unequivocal Western orientation of West Germany? Since its foundation the FRG was firmly integrated within the international and transnational Western world; given the new Ostpolitik, was there a danger of emancipation of the FRG from its Western Allies, ending in a possible neutralization of Central Europe? Last but not least, and intertwined with the second question, did Brandt's Ostpolitik signal that the FRG had moved on to an enhanced status in international affairs?

On the one hand the FRG was ready to tie itself to the multilateral structures of Western institutions; on the other, it tended increasingly to pursue individual national interests. Since the Adenauer era the dialectics of integration and regaining power by integration had been a pattern of West German foreign policy; step by step, this had led to an increased freedom of action, eventually questioning France's status as the unchallenged leading power in Western Europe. When in late 1968 the FRG was confronted with French, British, and American calls for a revaluation of the deutschmark and refused to do so it provoked its allies' resentments. In retrospect the French ambassador in Bonn complained bitterly that West Germany, striving for leadership in Europe, had decided egoistically in favor of its national interest.[3]

France and the FRG in the Era of Détente

Compared to France, which had been a pioneer in improving relations with the Soviet Union and the other Warsaw Pact states, the FRG was a latecomer in the policy of détente. By 1970, however, the FRG was in a pole position. Brandt emerged as a new personification of détente. This development has to be seen in the context of change within the international system. Broadly speaking, the bipolarity of the Cold War was supplemented by a trend toward multipolarity with Europe and China as new centers of power, which increasingly appeared as international actors in their own right. Moreover, the superpowers were confronted by the danger of imperial overstretch. The Tet offensive that started in January 1968 was a turning point in the war in Vietnam. The Soviet empire was challenged by Romania's wish for a less dependent position within the Warsaw Pact and, in particular, by the Prague Spring.

In other respects too, the year 1968 was a year of crisis and reorientation. It became a symbol for the process of transformation, both domestically and internationally.[4] French as well as West German politics were severely affected. Apart from the domestic impact of the so-called spirit of '68,[5] both France and the FRG realized that any successful Ostpolitik had to start in Moscow or, to put it more precisely, had to accept the Soviet hegemony in Eastern Europe for the time being. President de Gaulle's détente concept suffered from a setback when the Soviet Union upheld its empire by force and tried to forestall any signs of disintegration of the Eastern bloc—a possible disintegration that de Gaulle had had in mind at the onset of his policy toward the East. Clearly, his grand design was called into question. But it was not only de Gaulle's aspiration that ended in disillusionment: in the wake of the Czechoslovakian crisis, West German Ostpolitik was also forced to lower its expectations concerning a rapid and smooth "change through rapprochement," Egon Bahr's celebrated catch-phrase from 1963. For the FRG the situation was difficult because it was challenged on two fronts. On the one hand, the Warsaw Pact launched a fierce propaganda campaign: allegedly, Bonn's aim had been to enstrange Czechoslovakia from its allies. On the other hand, conveying a milder but nevertheless painful variant of the same accusation, de Gaulle also reproached the FRG for having provoked the Soviet Union by irresponsibly encouraging the reform movement in Czechoslovakia.[6] Yet de Gaulle's criticism was somewhat misplaced because France and the FRG were on common ground with respect to the dynamic version of détente. Contrary to the détente concept of the superpowers with their preference for a détente that should help to stabilize the international status quo, both de Gaulle's three-phase approach ("détente, entente, et coopération") and Brandt's transformation strategy aimed not only at a lessening of tensions but also at overcoming the division of Europe.[7]

Given the shocking experiences during the summer of 1968, the turn of 1968 to 1969 proved to be a crucial phase of adaptation to international realities. After the occupation of Czechoslovakia, France kept "somewhat aloof" in political relations with the Soviet Union.[8] But this was mainly meant as a symbolic act and by no means as a break in the policy of détente.[9] The same holds true for West Germany: in spite of a controversial debate in Bonn about the significance of the Soviet intervention in Prague and the ensuing Brezhnev Doctrine, the federal government was determined to continue with its rapprochement toward the East. The continuation of Ostpolitik was made easier when the Soviet Union was also willing to accept a fundamental West German position: in March 1969, the Budapest Appeal of the Warsaw Pact abstained for the first time from demanding the full recognition of the GDR as a precondition for a European Security Conference (ESC) and for a lessening of tensions in Europe in general. Contrary to East Berlin's position, Moscow was satisfied with a de facto recognition of the GDR. For the Soviet leadership it was of utmost importance to have solid relations with the FRG, which was regarded not only as an economic power house but also as a rising major actor in international politics.[10]

In fact, the overall impression was that, a quarter century after the end of World War II and the total defeat of Germany, the FRG was back in the international arena.[11] According to the British ambassador in Bonn, Roger William Jackling, one could detect "a new consciousness of national interest and power" and a "new trend" in West German policy: "Among its features are a greater self-reliance, a feeling that the period of atonement for the war is over, impatience with restraints on German liberty of action."[12] Obviously, the immediate postwar period had come to a close; after the Adenauer era, the FRG went through its second foundation phase with repercussions on domestic and foreign affairs. Unsurprisingly, a new term turned up in the language of the political elite: "national interest." Chancellor Kiesinger wished to preserve West German "national interests" when it came to the enlargement of the European Economic Community (EEC).[13] Foreign Minister Brandt maintained, "There is a German policy because there are German interests."[14]

Initial Reactions to Brandt's Ostpolitik

In late August 1969 Egon Bahr, at that time still in charge of the planning staff at the West German Ministry of Foreign Affairs (Auswärtiges Amt) before becoming responsible for the implementation of Ostpolitik, and Léo Hamon, press spokesman for Chaban-Delmas's government, met for an informal exchange of views. Without knowing the results of the elections in the FRG due four weeks later, they reached a fundamental Franco–West German consensus about the future political course toward the East. They considered the hitherto much-neglected Elysée Treaty as a platform for close cooperation in the fields of political and economic relations with Eastern Europe.[15] Shortly after the elections in which the Social Democratic Party (SPD) and the Free Democratic Party (FDP; the liberal party) had won a narrow majority and were able as a result to form a new government, Bahr went to see François Seydoux, the French ambassador in Bonn. Bahr stressed the importance of West German–French cooperation within the EEC and informed Seydoux about the imminent steps in Ostpolitik.[16] Brandt himself, after having been elected chancellor by the Bundestag, wished to exchange views on the experiences that both sides had in dealing with the East. Ambassador Seydoux foresaw a historical chance for a common approach toward the Warsaw Pact countries.[17]

In his first government declaration on October 28, 1969, Brandt underscored West Germany's commitment to the North Atlantic Treaty Organization (NATO) and the West in general, but he also announced "a more independent German policy."[18] While remaining in close touch with his partners in the West, he wanted the FRG to be "more equal" than before.[19] Striving for equality had been the FRG's goal since Adenauer; it was now confirmed by Brandt. Adenauer had never been an entirely easy partner within the Western alliance, but, unlike Brandt, he had not pursued an active Ostpolitik. Although the Western Allies did not directly oppose or even block Brandt's policy, they did not conceal some uneasiness with respect to its possibly implications and consequences. Foreign Minister Scheel was well aware of this uneasiness and was "running from country to country" in order to get sufficient backing for the Ostpolitik.[20] Brandt recalls in his memoirs that Washington would have liked a clear prerogative in the policy of détente. London had the fewest reservations and Paris fluctuated between understanding and "wild speculations."[21]

Brandt and Scheel tried to keep a balance between their own determination to explore new avenues in matters of Ostpolitik on the one hand, and the necessity to show signs of empathy for the French worries on the other. Bahr recommended an initiative to start a regular correspondence with Pompidou and occasional expressions of modesty; this, he hoped, would help, given the fact that the influence of the FRG in Europe had increased.[22] Accordingly, four days prior to the EEC summit in December 1969 Brandt conveyed to Pompidou his wish that he would like to elucidate his "thoughts on the Eastern component of the German policy in Europe." Brandt chose this formulation deliberately, altering an earlier draft where it was simply stated that he wanted to explain his "thoughts on German Ostpolitik."[23] The message was clear: Ostpolitik was no German Sonderweg—rather it sought to expand the already existing West European zone of peace, which Brandt regarded as a first step toward a pan-European peace order.[24]

Brandt's assessment of the French mood was not entirely incorrect. Pompidou's diplomatic adviser foresaw problems and did not hide his reservations toward the new government in Bonn, which was independently taking initiatives in its Eastern policy, including the GDR, while at the same time demanding the full support by the Western Allies—"a posture that was somewhat problematic".[25] In this vein, Pompidou welcomed the Ostpolitik and the Western policy of détente in general, provided the responsibility of the Three Powers was not questioned. With respect to Berlin and the European Security Conference (ESC) he insisted on remaining in step.[26] The reference to the ESC made sense because the conference could take place only if both German states were participants in it—which, in turn, required an accord between Bonn and East Berlin. Given the responsibility of the Four Powers, what was the significance of Brandt's recognition of the statehood of the GDR and his suggestion of direct negotiations on the relationship between both German states? Was this unilateral move compatible with the rights of the Allies? France was basically in favor of having an ESC but wished to preserve its rights and responsibilities in the context of the German question. Would the Three Powers have any say in the rapprochement between the FRG and the GDR? What would be the effect of a German-German rapprochement on the status of Berlin? These questions were also raised by the Americans and the British and were immediately brought up in the so-called Bonn Group, a forum for regular consultations between the Three Powers and West Germany. Calling it the business of the German government ("vraiment votre affaire") the French representative gave his German colleague to understand that Paris did not want to stand in the way of Brandt's policy.[27]

Both at the Elysée and the Quai d'Orsay numerous memoranda were produced regarding the German question in the light of the Neue Ostpolitik. As to the grand design, Jean-Bernard Raimond, the diplomatic adviser of President Pompidou, realized at once that the FRG expected to absorb the GDR "peacefully" in the long run by launching a policy of contacts. How this would work, how the Soviet Union would react, and what the outcome would be were open questions. What in his view mattered most at the moment was safeguarding Allied rights over Berlin.[28] Yves Pagniez, head of the foreign ministry's Central European department, stressed that France had "special responsibilities and fully intended to exercise them." He complained that one "had not had a chance to discuss adequately with the new German government the implications of their latest policy statement." Unfortunately, there was a "tendency on the part of the Germans these days to act in parallel to or even separately from the allies instead of in concert on matters of common concern."[29] At the end of November 1969 Pagniez was puzzled at being left in the dark with respect to Bonn's ultimate goals. For sure, the GDR will not be recognized according to international law. But how far was Brandt really prepared to make concessions? The fact that Bonn did not consult with France prior to the decision to acknowledge the statehood of the GDR and the Oder-Neisse line as the de facto Polish Western border was a "substantial problem."[30] French diplomats complained repeatedly about the lack of information given by the German side.[31] Having a premonition of the French discontentment, Bahr encouraged Seydoux to raise any questions that might exist. Seydoux, however, would have preferred not to ask questions but rather to be informed beforehand. Bahr stressed that Brandt's policy was shaped by "prudence."[32]

Right from the outset the internal French views were conveyed to the West German government. On the occasion of their first meeting, Foreign Ministers Maurice Schumann and Walter Scheel touched only shortly on Ostpolitik and talked mainly about West European issues and the upcoming summit at The Hague.[33] Early in December 1969 Schumann endorsed the West German détente initiatives but warned also of their risks and demanded more-precise information as to its objectives.[34] During their next bilateral encounter Scheel and Schumann focused again on West European issues. Regarding East-West relations Schumann mentioned the problem of Berlin, which for him was the nodal issue in the ongoing East-West discussions ("le nœud de toutes les conversations actuelles entre l'Est et l'Ouest"). If the GDR is recognized and participates in an ESC, sooner or later the Soviet Union will declare the GDR is responsible for Berlin. Not immediately but in the long run Schumann saw Berlin in the danger of suffocation. There was only one way to prevent such a development: the Four Power status of the city must be preserved at all costs.[35] Implicitly, mention of the Berlin issue could also be understood as a warning: given the rights of the Four Powers, Bonn should not forget that the FRG was not a fully sovereign state and was by no means entitled to make any deal with the Soviet Union or the GDR that would substitute the Four Power status of Berlin. Yet, in the perspective of the Quai d'Orsay this was exactly the worst possible consequence, considering that the rapprochement toward the East could not avoid unsettling "the legal construct" resulting from the 1954 Paris agreements.[36]

This topic was also touched on during the first bilateral top-level talks on 30 January 1970, the same day that Bahr had the first encounter with Andrei Gromyko in Moscow. Pompidou and Brandt knew each other since they had met while the former was French prime minister and the latter mayor of West Berlin and later foreign minister in Bonn.[37] In December 1969 they worked together at the Hague summit of the EEC.[38] Now they met within the framework of the regular twice-yearly French–West German consultations. It goes without saying that they talked in great detail about East-West relations and West German Ostpolitik. Pompidou mixed his support for Brandt's policy with several warnings: (1) One has to be realistic. The Soviet Union is afraid of overly intensive communication and too many contacts with the West. The example of Czechoslovakia has proved this well enough. A transformation of the Soviet bloc is conceivable only as a slow process. First and foremost, a transformation depends on change of the political regime in the Soviet Union itself. There are no signs whatsoever in this direction. (2) Patience is needed, in particular with respect to the relations between the two German states. The Soviet Union is afraid of a German reunification and will not tolerate any excessive amount of East German contacts with West Germany. (3) Of utmost importance will be the mutual and sufficient information among the Western Allies. A successful policy toward the Soviet Union depends on a prior Western accord. One has to move in step. There should be no solo policy. (4) Any troop reductions in Europe must not lead to an American-Soviet condominium with a subsequent demilitarization or neutralization of Western Europe.[39]

When asked about the former German capital Brandt referred to French Foreign Minister Maurice Schumann's statement and repeated the answer Scheel had already given to his French counterpart: any fear the FRG might overlook the legal framework of the status of Berlin was unfounded. At the same time the links between West Berlin and the FRG must be secured. Pompidou's answer indicated that he wanted both an improvement for West Berlin and the maintenance of the Four Power status, which represented the only guarantee for preserving the ties between the FRG and West Berlin.[40]

Pompidou did not voice these issues as point-blank warnings. Rather he raised them in a very diplomatic way, always saying in advance that he happily agreed with Brandt on these points. In fact, Brandt did not differ from Pompidou on any of these issues. Hence, Brandt understood Pompidou's encouragement to proceed with Ostpolitik and his best wishes for success as endorsement without any reservations; he was grateful for the "full support."[41] Of course, Pompidou could have been more outspoken. But he did not express his worry that the FRG might be drawn in to the Soviet orbit. Neither did he insist on proper consultations. His concern, rather, was that France could be faced with a fait accompli. Pompidou was willing to respect Bonn's stance vis-à-vis the GDR, but he wanted a better Franco-German coordination ("Mais il faut marcher du même pas"). In particular, he did not wish to learn from the press that Bonn had recognized the GDR according to international law.[42] Obviously, Pompidou found his admonition reasonable although he must have known that Brandt had always strictly excluded such a step. Perhaps he was not sure whether Brandt's position was really fixed. At the Quai d'Orsay, Claude Arnaud, head of the European Department, did not rule out that Brandt might change his view: "If the FRG was going to recognize the GDR, a new situation would result in which the two German states might gradually work toward German unity. . . . After recognition of the GDR, there would be little possibility for the West to 'orient or to control' German evolution. Perhaps the immediate result would be a great improvement of atmosphere in Europe. But what will the situation look like in the future?" Arnaud posed this question to an American diplomat on the very day when Brandt and the East German head of government Willi Stoph met in Erfurt for the first German-German summit ever.[43]

French-American relations were improving since Richard Nixon had been elected president.[44] In late February 1970 Pompidou visited the United States for the first and only time.[45] When Nixon asked about his "views on the German problem," Pompidou felt insecure as to both Brandt's short-term and ultimate goals. He wished to be consulted and wanted to know in advance what Brandt's Ostpolitik was up to. With the upcoming summit between Brandt and Stoph in mind, Pompidou complained once again that he did not want "to learn from the press that the FRG had recognized East Germany." Turning to longer-term anxieties he foresaw "some dangers" because the Germans, contrary to other Western Allies, "were largely dependent on the Soviets for the hopes of reunification of their country." Pompidou "trusted" Brandt. "But there is a need for vigilance." Nixon did not share Pompidou's confidence in Brandt, and he declared that the answer to the danger of a drift of West Germany toward the East was to anchor West Germany in NATO. The Western alliance had been set up for three reasons. Two of them, the threat from the East and the economic and military weakness of Western Europe, had receded or had been overcome respectively. "But one thing had not changed and this was the German problem and the Soviets in 20 years have always kept their eye on the German problem." Consequently, NATO was still an instrument to contain the Soviet Union and keep a watch on West Germany. Essentially, Pompidou did not differ with Nixon over this assessment. He, too, was convinced that the Soviet Union wished to "neutralize Germany and perpetuate its division."[46] The Western postwar concept of containing not only the Soviet Union but also Germany had lost its urgency but it had not become totally obsolete.[47]

When the first phase of Bahr's negotiations with Gromyko came to a close in May 1970, the foreign ministers of the Three Powers agreed with their West German colleague that the Bahr mission could be regarded as a substantial success.[48] At the Quai d'Orsay the assessment was ambivalent, though. On the one hand one could be satisfied. The recognition of the territorial status quo complied with French interests: "We can only congratulate ourselves." On the other hand, the room of maneuver for West Germany had dramatically increased, as France did not play any role in this process of rapprochement between West Germany and the Soviet Union. France was confined to an "inferior position".[49] It could not be ignored that West Germany and the Soviet Union, "the other two powers on the continent," had reached an accord that to a large extent was equivalent to a peace treaty in Europe. Meanwhile, the German question was not settled once and for all. On the contrary, the present state of affairs could well prove to be a point of departure in a less static international constellation.[50] Given this ultimately volatile situation the most important task was to secure the responsibilities of the Four Powers.[51]

During the second half of 1970 the negotiations for the treaties of Moscow and Warsaw were brought to a conclusion. The quadripartite talks on Berlin proceeded slowly but steadily, and the German-German negotiations on the normalization of relations between Bonn and East Berlin began in November 1970. In January 1970 Pagniez assumed this would be "a long-term enterprise."[52] But within a relatively short period of time the first cornerstones of Brandt's Ostpolitik became visible. Taking stock in December 1970, the main impression at the Quai d'Orsay was that Ostpolitik so far deserved French support. As to future developments, what mattered most was strengthening the economic, cultural, and military links of the West with West Germany in order to counterbalance the position of the Soviet Union in Central Europe, which was enhanced as a consequence of Ostpolitik.[53]

Summarizing the French perceptions of Ostpolitik so far, we can distinguish five main points that proved durable for the whole Pompidou presidency, revealing an amalgam of sober assessments, diffuse sentiments and deep-rooted unease: First, Bonn was finally prepared to come to terms with the postwar realities in Europe, including the existence of two German states. Second, at the same time, Bonn re-opened the German question by attempting to overcome the country's division with new means. Third, Brandt's strategy of transformation must not unravel the postwar order regarding Germany as a whole with the special rights of the Four Powers. Fourth, when taking initiatives in its Eastern policy, West Germany proceeded self-confidently and established itself, side by side with France, as a major power in European affairs. Fifth, Brandt's Ostpolitik, although West Germany's adherence to the West was absolutely confirmed, might trigger a dynamic that could have a negative impact on West Germany's allegiance to the West.

The Continuity of Backing Ostpolitik and Harboring Anxieties

Throughout Brandt's chancellorship France clearly endorsed Ostpolitik inasmuch as it contributed to defusing the German question by confirming the postwar borders in Europe. In fact, the acceptance of the territorial status quo by West Germany was an indispensable first step in the attempt to deescalate not only the intra-German antagonism but also the East-West conflict in Europe. However, right from the start when the concept of a "new" Ostpolitik was formulated in West Berlin in the early 1960s,[54] the acknowledgment of the status quo was regarded as a precondition for its final overcoming. The dialectics of stability and change was a guiding principle. Unsurprisingly, French politicians and diplomats wished West Germany to emphasize stability rather than change. Pompidou's assessment of Brandt's approach as a double strategy of both confirming and questioning the status quo was totally realistic. Any change implied risks and dangers such as the erosion of the rights of the Four Powers, the increasing influence of the Soviet Union in Europe, or the neutralization of

Germany. The French president did not hide his worries in his conversations with Brandt. The West German chancellor, on his part, never really succeeded in alleviating French reservations.

To be sure, Ostpolitik did not endanger Western positions; rather, it was an attempt to adapt them to the process of European détente. But even so, it could not be overlooked that West Germany's negotiations with the Soviet Union, notwithstanding the confirmation of the rights and responsibilities of the Four Powers, affected the political framework of Central Europe. That is why Pompidou strictly insisted on the preservation of the status of Berlin when it came to the quadripartite negotiations. In fact, he was quite reluctant.[55] He did not question the necessity to improve the situation in and around Berlin, but any infringements on Allied rights had to be prevented. Berlin was a lever for the ongoing French presence in Germany. Furthermore, Berlin was the key point in the East-West balance.[56] Consultations among the Western Allies about the Berlin talks took place on various levels. One important forum for tuning the Western strategy was the Bonn Group.[57] That group also served to bind West Germany to a common course. Formally, Bonn had no rights whatsoever to deal with the problem of Berlin. But France and the other Western allies could not hinder Bahr from talking about Berlin during his negotiations with Gromyko in Moscow. Neither could Bonn be hindered to insist on an agreeable solution for West Berlin and to put some pressure on the Three Powers to proceed vigorously in the Berlin talks with the Soviet Union.

If he had been aware of it, Pompidou would have objected to the way progress was made during the negotiations on the quadripartite agreement. Although the issue fell within the exclusive authority of the Four Powers, Henry Kissinger and Anatoly Dobrynin agreed in January 1971 on a special back-channel system with the participation of Bahr in Bonn.[58] This mechanism was to operate parallel to the negotiations which were pursued on the ambassadorial level and left the French and the British completely in the dark. Bahr was admitted to the inner circle of super-power diplomacy.[59]

From the French point of view, though, direct German-Soviet contacts exposed West Germany to the sinister goals of Soviet power politics. Hence, Paris was agitated when Brandt accepted an invitation to see Leonid Brezhnev in Oreanda, the summer resort of the Soviet leadership near Yalta in the Crimea. The West German–Soviet summit took place from 16 to 18 September 1971 on very short notice. The Soviet invitation was delivered on 1 September and was made public six days later. According to international standards, this schedule was extremely unusual. French observers found it was hard to believe that this was not a spectacular sign of a growing special West German–Soviet relationship.[60] The Western Allies were told that Brandt wanted to enquire about the Soviet intentions regarding, first, Berlin and the not constructive East German stance and, second, the ESC and the problem of troop reductions.[61] After his talks with the Soviet leader, Brandt drew the conclusion that both states had entered a phase of "natural and normal" relations, including both cooperation and conflict: "Both sides know where they agree, where rapprochement is conceivable, and where they have differences."[62] As to the atmosphere of the meeting, there was something completely new compared to previous East-West summits. There was no formal agenda and there was ample time for nonpolitical conversations in a relaxed mood and to go for a swim in and a boat trip on the Black Sea.

During a press conference some days later Pompidou commented not only on Oreanda but also on remarks in the French press alluding to a competitive race to Moscow. Pompidou, who himself was expecting Brezhnev's visit to Paris in October, rejected this view as absurd. Interestingly, the president spoke at some length about the economic dimension of East-West relations, an issue that had played only a marginal role during the summit in the Crimea. While acknowledging the West German economic superiority, he maintained that there was room for everybody on the Soviet market. As to the political implications, Pompidou recognized that West Germany—notwithstanding Brandt's wish for emancipation and for having "free hands" in his relations with the East—operated in full accordance with French positions, apart from the disagreement on troop reductions. So, why should he be disquieted about Oreanda? Of course, Brandt could have given more information in advance. But nothing, Pompidou added with a hint of slight resignation, would have been different if Brandt had done so.[63] In fact, Brandt's tête-à-tête with Brezhnev expressed nothing that was really new. According to *Le Monde*, West Germany behaved like a "major nation" and an "adult nation."[64] Similar expressions were used by the Quai d'Orsay. Completely taken by surprise and indignant about the secrecy that had been kept in Bonn during the preparations of Brandt's trip, Quai officials realized that West Germany, while emphasizing its "Western solidarity," claimed to be a major, emancipated country ("État majeur," "émancipé").[65] The French ambassador to the Soviet Union, after a talk with Brezhnev, came to the partly comforting conclusion that West Germany was regarded as "a major power" but, contrary to France, not as "a world power."[66]

These points of procedure and imagery apart, French interests were not fully safeguarded. When Brandt agreed with Brezhnev that a ESC could now be prepared, he met French expectations. Much earlier than West Germany, France had welcomed Brezhnev's favorite foreign policy project in Europe. An important effect of a pan-European conference would be the multilateralization and thereby channeling of German Ostpolitik.[67] The Soviet Union consented to negotiate on a multilateral and balanced reduction of troops in Europe. The whole issue was the main topic of Bahr's conversations with Andrei Alexandrov-Agentov, Brezhnev's adviser in matters of foreign policy and security. They found the interim formula that troops should be reduced "without any disadvantages for either side."[68] In the French perspective this was too vague and even a dangerous phrase. Any reduction of troops in Central Europe at that time appeared as an opener for unforeseeable changes in the balance of power. In the last instance the United States would possibly retreat from Europe. And there was a worst case scenario: West Germany would sink into neutrality, being at the mercy of the Soviet Union.[69] Fortunately, the present reality was much brighter. The Quai d'Orsay was pleased that Brandt had stressed West Germany's NATO membership. He did not deviate from the general Western course of détente. Displaying a characteristic measure of self-esteem, French diplomats considered that this course had first been pursued by France.[70]

The next Franco-German exchange of views at the highest level did not produce any new arguments or insights. When Pompidou and Brandt met in Paris in early December 1971 for an unscheduled summit they assured each other of their cooperative attitude. In the wake of Washington's decision to unravel the Bretton Woods system, economic and monetary problems were more urgent than East-West relations.[71] As to the latter Brandt found it appropriate to underscore that West Germany was firmly attached to Western Europe. There was no tendency whatsoever of a neutralization of West Germany. Pompidou stated that there were no such anxieties and that he was in perfect agreement with Brandt's policy. After all, Ostpolitik followed the French example.[72] Since the days of de Gaulle the quest for détente in Europe had been a vital French interest. In this context Brandt's resolution to achieve an interim settlement of the German question was appreciated as an essential contribution to détente. Accordingly, Pompidou pleaded for a ratification of the Eastern treaties by the Bundestag without much delay.[73] Otherwise the whole train of détente would be in danger of derailment.[74]

Furthermore, the ratification of the treaties of Moscow and Warsaw and the coming into effect of the Berlin Agreement depended on each other. In turn, the ensuing search for a modus vivendi between Bonn and East Berlin finalized in November 1972 with the Basic Treaty (*Grundlagenvertrag*) was a precondition for, first, the establishment of diplomatic relations between France and the GDR[75] and, second, the start of the multilateral preparatory talks of the Conference on Security and Cooperation in Europe (CSCE) with both German states as participants. As mentioned before, Pompidou's attitude to this conference was positive throughout. He did not expect spectacular results. But provided a common strategy was pursued and West Germany was firmly anchored in Western Europe, the conference could change the atmospherics ("créer une autre atmosphère en Europe"). A gradual rapprochement between all Eastern and Western peoples, including the two German states, might contribute to a slight loosening of the blocs. Without having any illusions, Pompidou envisaged small steps toward a liberalization of the states in the East. Improved East-West relations of this kind would be an antidote to the ongoing Soviet aspirations to solve the German question by a neutralization of Germany.[76] Taking this ultimate and threatening Soviet quest into account, Pompidou did not rule out that Moscow calculated on taking advantage of any Mutual and Balanced Force Reductions (MBFR) negotiations. But one should not "lead the Soviet Union into temptation"![77] From Pompidou's point of view the time was not ripe for a military détente.

In early 1973, when the Ostpolitik had just been confirmed by Brandt's electoral triumph in November 1972, Pompidou hoped for a better coordination of Western trade with the East. France had increased its trade with the Soviet Union[78] but it was West Germany that had become the outstanding Western partner for the Soviets. Fundamentally, however, Pompidou saw no problems between Paris and Bonn in the field of East-West relations. They should be further developed, but in a way that no risks for Western Europe might evolve as a result.[79] Pompidou never forgot to point out possible risks. Was he notoriously pessimistic or was he not quite sure regarding Brandt's grand design? A highlight of the West German–Soviet rapprochement was Brezhnev's visit to West Germany in May 1973. In the assessment of the Quai d'Orsay the summit was "a spectacular success" for Brandt. More importantly, however, it proved West Germany's strong allegiance to NATO and to Western Europe. Beyond all doubt, Brandt did not waver in his determination to proceed with the construction of the EEC.[80]

One could not ignore the active West German role in the process of West European integration that, since the European summit in October 1972, was destined for ending up in a European Union. But when Pompidou met Brandt in June 1973 he bombarded him with a "hopefully not too indiscreet" question of "fundamental" importance. Considering the overall changes in world politics and "in view of the German Ostpolitik and West Germany's relations with the Eastern countries," how did Brandt envisage the "German future"?[81] In his far-reaching reply the chancellor both spoke about the key components of his political thinking and did his best to calm down French uneasiness that he sensed was at the heart of Pompidou's question. He emphasized that two issues were crucial, even more crucial than the national question: first, securing peace in Europe, and second, embedding West Germany in Western Europe, which might be regarded by the Germans as a sort of substitute Fatherland ("eine Art Ersatz-Vaterland"). Whatever might be the outcome of any historical process in the future, including a solution of the German question, Pompidou need not fear a German "seesaw policy." Pompidou was grateful for this "remarkable explanation" and underscored his full understanding for the "exigency of Ostpolitik." He also admitted certain moments of agitation on the French side. But Brandt had been successful in establishing a mood of confidence.[82] This was absolutely vital because in Pompidou's perspective the familiar framework of international politics had disappeared. The overwhelming superiority of the United States, the Cold War, the internationally common fear of a Germany that had resisted the whole world—all this had gone. Living in a period of transition Pompidou agreed with Brandt that one could not know what the future would bring.[83] Hence, one has to be on guard: the Soviet Union was ready to neutralize Central Europe. Contrary to Brandt, Pompidou was convinced that the MBFR was a "dangerous affair."[84] On top of that there was the danger of a tacit or even open American-Soviet condominium that could leave Western Europe at the mercy of the Soviet superpower and West Germany in a floating position.[85]

Although Pompidou felt haunted by his deep-rooted lack of confidence in the motives of Soviet policy he remained determined to pursue a policy of détente. In agreement with Brandt he did not think that Europe had already entered a phase of stable peace. At the same time, however, he believed Europe might be on the threshold of a new era. The CSCE might end "this kind of Cold War" with its dangerous clashes.[86] When he thought the Cold War had come to an end,[87] he had the "Cold War conflict in its 1940s and 1950s form" in mind.[88] Notwithstanding the still stressful antagonism between East and West, détente constituted a new and less dangerous form of the East-West conflict.[89]

Conclusion

In Pompidou's mental map of European politics Germany was an area that aroused contradictory impressions. The era of détente consisted of both progress and insecurities with West Germany playing an ambivalent role. Respecting the postwar borders helped to remove dangerous tensions that rooted in the Cold War during the long 1950s. But in the last instance one could not know where West Germany, confronted by a mix of Soviet pressure and accommodation, was finally going to. The Elysée remained suspicious of alleged tendencies in Bonn that might alienate West Germany from the West. Regarding the actual state of West German–Soviet relations, such fears were hardly justified. Pompidou himself said so repeatedly. Furthermore, French diplomats realized that, in 1973, the honeymoon of Ostpolitik was over.[90] In fact, there was no causal nexus between the stagnation of Ostpolitik and Bonn's various efforts to proceed with the West European integration. But the French ambassador in Bonn seemed to be pleased that he could report on a turn to the West.[91]

During the Pompidou–Brandt era French and West German concepts of détente were essentially compatible. Both Bonn and Paris were opposed to an exclusive superpower détente leading to a hardening of the status quo. France as well as West Germany argued in favor of a détente that was to combine conflict management and peaceful coexistence on the one hand and the quest for peaceful change and overcoming the status quo on the other hand. Contrary to "the static attitude" that prevailed in Washington and Moscow, "the European dynamic attitude" aimed at a profound transformation of international relations.[92] However, the question tormenting Pompidou was, what would be the final result of this transformation? He was not sure about its ultimate repercussions.

Gottfried Niedhart is professor emeritus of modern history at the University of Mannheim. He has published on English and German history and on the history of international relations, recently in particular on East-West relations during the era of détente: *Entspannung in Europa. Die Bundesrepublik Deutschland und der Warschauer Pakt 1966 bis 1975* (2014), "Ostpolitik: Transformation through Communication and the Quest for Peaceful Change," in *Journal of Cold War Studies* 18, no. 3: 14–59. Together with Oliver Bange he edited *Helsinki 1975 and the Transformation of Europe* (2008).

Notes

1. Fink and Schaefer, *Ostpolitik*.
2. Memorandum by Jean-Bernard Raimond, 3 Jul. 1969, Schirmann and Mohamed-Gaillard, *Georges Pompidou*, 252–53.
3. "Les Germains bombaient le torse. . . . La République fédérale se substituait à la France et s'emparait en Europe occidentale de la direction!" (Seydoux, *Dans l'intimité franco–allemande*, 130–31). For an overview of the Franco-West German relationship in the context of the European integration, see Miard-Delacroix, *Im Zeichen*; Krotz and Schild, *Shaping Europe*.
4. Fink, Gassert, and Junker, *1968: The World Transformed*.
5. Horn, *The Spirit of '68*.
6. For details, see the chapter by Benedikt Schoenborn in this volume.
7. This is the overarching theme in Badalassi, *En finir avec la guerre froide*. See also Niedhart, "Revisionistische Elemente"; Niedhart, "The Transformation of the Other Side"; Juneau, *Egon Bahr*.
8. Foreign Minister Michel Debré in a circular to the French missions abroad, 31 Aug. 1968, MAE, 2010, DDF 1968, vol. 2.
9. Vaïsse, *La puissance ou l'influence?*, 250.
10. Zubok, *A Failed Empire*, 210–12.
11. For a succinct contemporary analysis Kaiser, *German Foreign Policy*. For French attitudes, see Raus, "Willy Brandt et l'Allemagne fédérale." See also the contribution by Guido Thiemeyer to this volume.
12. Jackling to Foreign and Commonwealth Office, 9 Apr. 1969, TNA, FCO 33/566.
13. Kiesinger during a workshop on foreign policy issues, 2–3 May 1968 (AAPD 1968, 551, n27).
14. Willy Brandt during a meeting of the Social Democratic Party executive, 2 Nov. 1968 (Brandt, *Ein Volk der guten Nachbarn*, 210).
15. Conversation between Bahr and Hamon, 25 Aug. 1969, AdsD, Bahr Papers, 441.
16. Seydoux reporting on Bahr's statements of 8 Oct. 1969, DDF 1969, vol. 2, 540–41.
17. Conversation between Brandt and Seydoux, 30 Oct. 1969, PAAA, B 150/163.
18. Speech by Brandt in the Bundestag, 28 Oct. 1969 (Verhandlungen des Deutschen Bundestags, 6. Wahlperiode, 31).
19. Brandt, *Erinnerungen*, 189.
20. Scheel during a meeting of the FDP executive, 25 Apr. 1970, Archiv des Deutschen Liberalismus, Gummersbach, Bestand Bundesvorstand, 160.
21. Brandt, *Erinnerungen*, 189.
22. Notes by Bahr for Brandt, 6 and 13 Nov. 1969, AdsD, Bahr papers 436, 441.
23. Brandt to Georges Pompidou, 27 Nov. 1969, AAPD 1969, 1347. For the draft of the letter, see AdsD, Bahr papers 441.
24. During a cabinet meeting on 7 Jun. 1970 Brandt spoke about the primacy of peace and called the West European integration a "Bauelement einer gesamteuropäischen Friedensordnung" (WBA, A8/91).
25. Note by Raimond, 6 Nov. 1969, AnF, Pierrefitte-sur-Seine, 5 AG 2, 1010.
26. Pompidou in a conversation with Carlo Schmid, coordinator for the West German-French relationship in Bonn, 7 Novembre 1969. Ibid.
27. Meetings of the Bonn Group 5 and 7 Nov. 1969, AAPD 1969, 1251–53.
28. Note by Raimond for Pompidou 8 Dec. 1969 (Schirmann and Mohamed-Gaillard, *Georges Pompidou*, 306, 309).
29. British embassy Paris on a conversation with Pagniez of 13 Nov. 1969, 17 Nov. 1969, TNA, FCO 33/567.
30. Draft of a memorandum by Pagniez, "Politique de M. Brandt à l'égard des pays de l'Est," 24 Nov. 1969. The final version is dated 1 Dec. 1969, AMAE, Série Europe 1961–70, sous-série RFA, 1546.
31. See, e.g., Seydoux to Paris 17 and 29 Nov. 1969, (AMAE, RFA, 1539); memorandum by the Central European Department 25 Feb. 1970 (ibid., 1540).
32. Seydoux to Paris 27 Nov. 1969 on a conversation with Bahr (ibid., 1539).
33. Meeting in Paris 9 Nov. 1969, AAPD 1969, 1238.

34. Schumann during a meeting with his American, British and West German colleagues on the evening before the conference of the NATO Council of Ministers in Brussels, 3 Dec. 1969. AAPD 1969, 1362.

35. Conversation between Scheel and Schumann in Bonn, 16 Jan. 1970 (AMAE, Europe 1961–70, RFA, 1547). The French wording "nœud de la question" is quoted in the German record (AAPD 1970, 30).

36. Memorandum by Direction des affaires juridiques at the Quai d'Orsay, 30 Jan. 1970, AMAE, Europe 1961–70, RFA 1547.

37. Brandt, *Begegnungen und Einsichten*, 135, 158. The first meeting between Pompidou in his capacity as president and Brandt took place in July 1969. On this occasion they talked only briefly on East-West relations and agreed on the necessity to make progress with the policy of détente (AAPD 1969, 779–80).

38. Hiepel, *Willy Brandt und Georges Pompidou*, 37–72.

39. For the German record, see AAPD 1970, 119–26. The French version can be found in Schirmann and Mohamed-Gaillard, *Georges Pompidou*, 255–59, 333–36.

40. Schirmann and Mohamed-Gaillard, *Georges Pompidou*, 311–13.

41. Note by Brandt, "Deutsche Ostpolitik erklärt. Dankbar für volle Unterstützung," 31 Jan. 1970, WBA, A8/91.

42. Schirmann and Mohamed-Gaillard, *Georges Pompidou*, 259. On French attitudes and the policy toward the GDR, see Wenkel, *Auf der Suche*, 400–72.

43. U.S. embassy Paris to Washington on a conversation with Arnaud on 19 Mar. 1970. Participants were also the heads of the Central European Departement, Pagniez, and of the Eastern European Department, Andréani (NA, College Park, RG 59/2265).

44. Trachtenberg, "The French Factor," 4–9. See also Niedhart, "Frankreich und die USA," 70–73.

45. Soutou, "Le président Pompidou," 116–18.

46. Conversations between Pompidou and Richard Nixon in Washington, 24 and 26 Feb. 1970 (Richard Nixon Presidential Library and Museum, Yorba Linda, CA, National Security Council, Presidential-HAK Memcons 1024). According to the French record, Nixon said, "la question allemande reste inchangée. . . . Les Soviétiques sont restés vigilants devant ce problème, qui est un très gros morceau. Nous devons agir en consequence." Pompidou replied, "Il l'est pour nous aussi." And Nixon concluded, "Certes, et peut-être même plus que nous-mêmes" (preceding quotes in DDF 1970, vol. 1, 238–39).

47. Soutou, "Willy Brandt, Georges Pompidou et l'Ostpolitik," 132.

48. Scheel in a conversation with his American, British, and French colleagues in Rome on the evening before the meeting of the North Atlantic Council, 25 May 1970, AAPD 1970, 868–69.

49. Memorandum by the Department for Central Europe, 29 May 1970, AMAE, Europe 1961–70, RFA, 1540.

50. Memorandum by J. D. Jurgensen, deputy head of the Political Department, 8 Jun. 1970 (ibid., 1541). One danger from Jurgensen's point of view was the Soviet ambition to neutralize the FRG. At the same time Paris and Moscow had a mutual interest insofar as they wanted to "surveiller l'évolution à la long terme des rapports entre les deux Allemagnes" (Memorandum by Jurgensen for Schumann, 16 Jul. 1970, ibid.).

51. See, e.g., Memoranda by the Central European Department, 10, 11, 22 Jun. 1970 (ibid.).

52. Memorandum 22 Jan. 1970, DDF 1970, vol. 1, 89–92.

53. "Position de la France vis-à-vis de l'Ostpolitik du gouvernement fédéral," memorandum by Gérard Montassier of the Central European Department, 4 Dec. 1970, DDF 1970, vol. 2, 724–28.

54. Hofmann, *The Emergence of Détente in Europe*.

55. Note by Pompidou, 26 Mar. 1970 (Schirmann and Mohamed-Gaillard, *Georges Pompidou*, 317).

56. Pompidou in conversation with Rainer Barzel, the leader of the opposition in Bonn, 3 Jun. 1971 (ibid., 325).

57. Osmont, "La négociation de l'accord, quadripartite sur Berlin (1969–1971): le rôle du groupe de Bonn," *Relations internationales* 135, 37–52.

58. Geyer and Selvage, *Soviet-American Relations*, 266.

59. For an appreciation of Bahr's role, see Kissinger, *Years of Upheaval*, 146.
60. On French resentments see a telex by Hans Ruete, West German ambassador to France, 13 Sept. 1971. Ruete reported on various indignant reactions, among them a comment by Jurgensen, AAPD 1971, 1369–72. On French reactions to Oreanda, see Wilkens, *Der unstete Nachbar*, 105–11; and Rey, "France and the German Question," 61.
61. State Secretary von Braun to the German ambassadors in Paris, London, and Washington, 10 Sept. 1971, AAPD 1971, 1354–56.
62. Notes taken by Brandt for a press communication, 18 Sept. 1971, WBA, A8/92. See also Brandt, *Begegnungen*, 471.
63. Pompidou's press conference 23 Sept. 1971 (Pompidou, *Entretiens et discours 1968–1974*, vol. 2, 161–64).
64. *Le Monde*, 21 Sept. 1971. See also Schmitz, *Zwischen Mythos und Aufklärung*, 170–71.
65. Memorandum by the Central European Department, "Rencontre germano-soviétique d'Oreanda," 28 Sept. 1971, AMAE, Europe 1971–76, RFA, 2988.
66. Roger Seydoux to Quai d'Orsay, 22 Sept. 1971. The French ambassador was received by Brezhnev on 21 Sept. 1971 in order to be informed about Oreanda (ibid.).
67. See the contribution by Nicolas Badalassi to this volume.
68. Bahr, *Zu meiner Zeit*, 499.
69. Badalassi, *En finir avec la guerre froide*, 157–62.
70. Memorandum by the Central European Department, "Rencontre germano-soviétique d'Oreanda," 28 Sept. 1971, AMAE, Europe 1971–76, RFA, 2988.
71. Hiepel, *Willy Brandt und Georges Pompidou*, 147–56.
72. Conversations between Pompidou and Brandt, 3 and 4 Dec. 1971, AAPD 1971, 1871–87 and 1893–11, in particular 1877, 1894, 1899, 1903–4. See also their next meeting on 10 Feb. 1972 (Schirmann and Mohamed-Gaillard, *Georges Pompidou*, 350–51; AAPD 1972, 113 and 115).
73. Pompidou in conversation with Brandt, 10 Feb. 1972, AAPD 1972, 115.
74. See Pompidou's warning to Barzel, the leader of the opposition in the *Bundestag*, 22 Mar. 1972 (Schirmann and Mohamed-Gaillard, *Georges Pompidou*, 287).
75. On French considerations for West German interests in this matter, see Wenkel, *Suche*, 409, 414.
76. Conversation between Pompidou and Brandt, 10 Feb. 1972 (Schirmann and Mohamed-Gaillard, *Georges Pompidou*, 350–52). See also AAPD 1972, 118–19, 123.
77. Pompidou in conversation with Brandt, 3 Jul. 1972, AAPD 1972, 898. See also Schirmann and Mohamed-Gaillard, *Georges Pompidou*, 356.
78. For the figures, see Rey, *La tentation du rapprochement*, 130.
79. Pompidou in conversation with Brandt, 22 and 23 Jan. 1973, AAPD 1973, 66, 100. See also Pompidou during his meetings with Brandt, 27 Nov. 1973, AAPD 1973, 1936 (Schirmann and Mohamed-Gaillard, *Georges Pompidou*, 389) and Helmut Kohl, Barzel's successor as leader of the opposition, 15 Oct. 1973 (Schirmann and Mohamed-Gaillard, *Georges Pompidou*, 294).
80. Memorandum by the Department for Central Europe, 1 Jun. 1973, AMAE, Europe 1971–76, RFA, 2989.
81. Pompidou right at the beginning of the French–German consultations, 21 Jun. 1973, AAPD 1973, 1018–19. Interestingly enough, this paragraph is missing in Schirmann and Mohamed-Gaillard, *Georges Pompidou*.
82. AAPD 1973, 1019–21.
83. Ibid., 1021. For the French version see Schirmann and Mohamed-Gaillard, *Georges Pompidou*, 367: "La supériorité écrasante de l'Amérique par rapport à la Russie, la guerre froide, la crainte que tous ressentaient d'une Allemagne qui avait résisté pratiquement au monde entier, tout cela est fini. Les rapports sont différents, les rapports de force sont différents, les rapports politiques sont différents; cet univers d'alors est donc mort et vous avez raison de dire aussi que nous ne savons pas ce que l'avenir nous réserve."
84. AAPD 1973, 1021; Schirmann and Mohamed-Gaillard, *Georges Pompidou*, 368. See also a memorandum by the Central European Department "Hésitations de l'Allemagne entre l'Ostpolitik et l'unifica-

tion européenne," 28 Jan. 1974, quoting a warning by François Puaux, political director at the Quai d'Orsay, for his West German colleague Günther van Well, that MBFR might lead to a finlandization of Europe, AMAE, Europe 1971–76, RFA, 2980. For a succinct account see Loth, "Willy Brandt, Georges Pompidou."

85. Trachtenberg, "The French Factor," 36–41.
86. Pompidou in conversation with Brandt, 10 Feb. 1972 (Schirmann and Mohamed, *Georges Pompidou*, 351).
87. In the conversation with Brandt mentioned above, 21 Jun. 1973 (ibid., 367).
88. This is a formulation by Westad, "The New International History," 563.
89. On the problem of terminology and chronology, see Bange and Villaume, *The Long Détente*.
90. Memoranda by the Central European Department, 17 Dec. 1973 and 20 Mar. 1974, AMAE, Europe 1971–76, RFA, 2989, 3019. See also Niedhart, *Entspannung in Europa*, 106–22.
91. "Comme par un mouvement de balancier de l'Est vers l'Ouest, le gouvernement fédéral s'est tourné progressivement vers une politique axée sur la sécurité et l'unification européenne, donc sur l'intensification de la coopération occidentale." Ambassador Sauvagnargues to Foreign Minister Jobert, "Politique étrangère du gouvernement fédéral. Bilan et perspectives fin 1973," 15 Nov. 1973, AMAE, Europe 1971–76, RFA, 2980.
92. "Conception française de la détente," memorandum by the East European Department at the Quai d'Orsay, 17 Dec. 1973, AMAE, Europe 1971–76, RFA, 3019. For the differentiation between détente statique and détente dynamique, see also Andréani, *Le piège*, 41.

Bibliography

Andréani, J. 2005. *Le piège. Helsinki et la chute du communisme*. Paris: Odile Jacob.

Badalassi, N. 2014. *En finir avec la guerre froide. La France, l'Europe et le processus d'Helsinki, 1965–1975*. Rennes, France: Presses universitaires de Rennes.

Bahr, E. 1996. *Zu meiner Zeit*. Munich, Germany: Blessing Verlag.

Bange, O., and P. Villaume, eds. 2016. *The Long Détente: Changing Concepts of Security and Cooperation in Europe from the 1950s to the 1980s*. Budapest: Central European University Press.

Brandt, W. 1976. *Begegnungen und Einsichten. Die Jahre 1960–1975*. Hamburg, Germany: Hoffmann und Campe.

———. 1989. *Erinnerungen*. Frankfurt/Main, Germany: Propyläen Verlag.

———. 2005. *Ein Volk der guten Nachbarn. Außen- und Deutschlandpolitik 1966–1974*. Bonn, Germany: Dietz Verlag.

Fink, C., P. Gassert, and D. Junker, eds. 1998. *1968: The World Transformed*. Cambridge: Cambridge University Press.

Fink, C., and B. Schaefer, eds. 2009. *Ostpolitik, 1969–1974. European and Global Responses*. New York: Cambridge University Press.

Geyer, D. C., and D. E. Selvage, eds. 2007. *Soviet-American Relations: The Détente Years, 1969–1972*. Washington, DC: U.S. Government Printing Office.

Hiepel, C. 2012. *Willy Brandt und Georges Pompidou. Deutsch-französische Europapolitik zwischen Aufbruch und Krise*. Munich, Germany: Oldenbourg Verlag.

Hofmann, A. 2007. *The Emergence of Détente in Europe: Brandt, Kennedy and the Formation of Ostpolitik*. London and New York: Routledge.

Horn, G.-R. 2007. *The Spirit of '68. Rebellion in Western Europe and North America, 1956–1976*. Oxford: Oxford University Press.

Juneau, J.-F. 2014. *Egon Bahr, l'Ostpolitik de la République fédérale d'Allemagne et la transformation de l'ordre européen 1945–1975*. Pessac, France: Presses universitaires de Bordeaux.

Kaiser, K. 1968. *German Foreign Policy in Transition: Bonn Between East and West*. London: Oxford University Press.

Kissinger, H. 1982. *Years of Upheaval*. Boston and Toronto: Little, Brown and Company.

Krotz, U., and J. Schild. 2013. *Shaping Europe: France, Germany, and Embedded Bilateralism from the Élysée Treaty to Twenty-First Century Politics.* Oxford: Oxford University Press.

Loth, W. 2005. "Willy Brandt, Georges Pompidou und die Entspannungspolitik." In Möller and Vaïsse, *Willy Brandt und Frankreich,* 167–80.

Miard-Delacroix, H. 2001. *Im Zeichen der europäischen Einigung 1963 bis in die Gegenwart.* Darmstadt, Germany: Wissenschaftliche Buchgesellschaft.

Möller, H., and M. Vaïsse, eds. 2005. *Willy Brandt und Frankreich.* Munich, Germany: Oldenbourg Verlag.

Niedhart, G. 2002. "Revisionistische Elemente und die Initiierung friedlichen Wandels in der neuen Ostpolitik 1967–1974." *Geschichte und Gesellschaft* 28, 233–66.

———. 2004. "Frankreich und die USA im Dialog über Détente und Ostpolitik 1969–1970." *Francia. Forschungen zur westeuropäischen Geschichte* 31, no. 3: 65–85.

———. 2012. "The Transformation of the Other Side. Willy Brandt's Ostpolitik and the Liberal Peace Concept." In *Visions of the End of the Cold War in Europe, 1945–1990,* edited by F. Bozo, M.-P. Rey, and P. Ludlow, 149–62. New York and Oxford: Berghahn Books.

———. 2014. *Entspannung in Europa. Die Bundesrepublik Deutschland und der Warschauer Pakt 1966–1975.* Munich, Germany: Oldenbourg Verlag.

Osmont, M. 2008. "La négotiation de l'accord quadripartite sur Berlin (1969–1971). Le rôle du groupe de Bonn." *Relations internationales* 135: 37–52.

Pompidou, G. 1975. *Entretiens et discours 1968–1974,* 2 vols. Paris: Librairie Plon.

Raus, R. 2011. "Willy Brandt et l'Allemagne fédérale dans l'opinion publique française, 1966–1974." In *Willy Brandt et l'unité de l'Europe. De l'objectif de la paix aux solidarités nécessaires,* edited by A. Wilkens, 187–210. Brussels, Belgium: Peter Lang.

Rey, M.-P. 1991. *La tentation du rapprochement. France et URSS à l'heure de la détente 1964–1974.* Paris: Publications de la Sorbonne.

———. 2008. "France and the German Question in the Context of Ostpolitik and the CSCE, 1969–1974." In *Helsinki 1975 and the Transformation of Europe,* edited by O. Bange and G. Niedhart, 53–66. New York: Berghahn Books.

Schirmann, S., and S. Mohamed-Gaillard. 2012. *Georges Pompidou et l'Allemagne.* Brussels, Belgium: Peter Lang.

Schmitz, C. M. 1990. *Zwischen Mythos und Aufklärung: Deutschland in der außenpolitischen Berichterstattung der Zeitung "Le Monde" 1963–1983* . . . Frankfurt, Germany: Peter Lang.

Seydoux, F. 1977. *Dans l'intimité franco-allemande. Une mission diplomatique.* Paris: Editions Albatros.

Soutou, G.-H. 2000. "Le président Pompidou et les relations entre les Etats-Unis et l'Europe." *Journal of European Integration History* 6, no. 2: 116–46.

———. 2005. "Willy Brandt, Georges Pompidou et l'Ostpolitik." In Möller and Vaïsse, *Willy Brandt und Frankreich,* 121–54.

Trachtenberg, M. 2011. "The French Factor in U.S. Foreign Policy during the Nixon-Pompidou Period, 1969–1974." *Journal of Cold War Studies* 13, no. 1: 4–59.

Vaïsse, M. 2007. *La puissance ou l'influence? La France dans le monde depuis 1958.* Paris: Fayard.

Wenkel, C. 2014. *Auf der Suche nach einem "anderen Deutschland." Das Verhältnis Frankreichs zur DDR im Spannungsfeld von Perzeption und Diplomatie.* Munich, Germany: Oldenbourg Verlag.

Westad, O. A. 2000. "The New International History of the Cold War: Three (Possible) Paradigms." *Diplomatic History* 24, no. 4: 551–65.

Wilkens, A. 1990. *Der unstete Nachbar. Frankreich, die deutsche Ostpolitik und die Berliner Vier-Mächte-Verhandlungen 1969–1974.* Munich, Germany: Oldenbourg.

Zubok, V. M. 2007. *A Failed Empire: The Soviet Union in the Cold War from Stalin to Gorbachev.* Chapel Hill: University of North Carolina Press.

CHAPTER 8

France, the Conference on Security and Cooperation in Europe, and the German Question

Nicolas Badalassi

Because Germany was at the epicenter of the East-West conflict in Europe, the German question was naturally at the heart of the negotiations of the Helsinki process. Ever since the early proposals for a pan-European conference on security (ECS) in the 1950s, the main goal of the Soviets and their Polish allies had been to obtain Western acknowledgment of the realities of 1945, and first of all the division of Germany.[1] In the minds of the Soviet leaders, peace in Europe essentially relied on the guarantee that Germany would not be tempted to return to its old demons.[2] As a result, Moscow, through the Conference on Security and Cooperation in Europe (CSCE), in essence sought an ersatz peace treaty. Thus between the fall of 1972 and the summer of 1975 the discussions in Helsinki and Geneva never lost sight of the German situation when the various issues on the conference's agenda were tackled—be they the political and territorial status quo, the situation in Berlin, human contacts, economic and cultural exchanges, and so on. Under Willy Brandt, the leaders of the Federal Republic of Germany (FRG, or West Germany) wanted the West German people to see that the CSCE was not only a legal and abstract affair on the agenda, but also a process which could produce concrete effects on Germany.[3] Brandt and his adviser Egon Bahr understood at an early stage the impact the Helsinki process could have on Germany and the Germans. Even though they knew that it would not produce immediate geopolitical changes, they were convinced that it could contribute to one of the goals Brandt had assigned to Ostpolitik: preventing the political division between the two Germanys from leading to a lasting cultural and psychological division between the East Germans and the West Germans.[4]

Because of the defining importance of the German question for France, Paris, unsurprisingly, wanted to make its voice heard when the question was discussed within the CSCE. The rights and responsibilities over Berlin and Germany as a whole, obtained in Potsdam in 1945, gave the French a great political ascendancy over the West German partner. Thanks to these rights and responsibilities, France could justify its status as a victorious power in World War II and keep a leverage over the future of Germany. Hence the considerable interest Paris showed in the aspects of the CSCE that involved the German question; as a result, France's approach to the CSCE was an integral part of France's German policy.[5]

As a matter of fact, the German question explains why the French were among the last Westerners to accept the conference. In 1965, when the Soviets started campaigning for the Western countries' acceptance of their project of an ECS, Moscow was convinced that France and the Union of Soviet Socialist Republics (USSR, or Soviet Union) shared a common goal: to make the division of Germany definitive.[6] General Charles de Gaulle's repeated calls for West Germany to definitively recognize its borders, France's withdrawal from the North Atlantic Treaty Organization's (NATO) military integration, and the French policy of détente based on the entente of all countries from the Atlantic to the Urals, strengthened the Kremlin's conviction that France would accept a project whose goals were to freeze the European status quo and to create a collective security system replacing the Atlantic alliance and the Warsaw Pact. Yet, from the outset, the misunderstanding between Paris and Moscow was clear: de Gaulle promoted the concept of pan-Europeanism in order to overcome the status quo, and not the other way around. When he wanted the Germans to recognize their borders, he had in mind the Oder–Neisse line, not the intra-German border. Furthermore, the general was opposed to any collective security system, and he believed the Atlantic alliance was necessary for Western Europe's security. When the Soviets brought up the pan-European conference in 1965–68, de Gaulle replied that while he was not against the principle of such a conference, he could not agree to it yet. One condition had to be fulfilled first: détente had to be sufficiently strengthened—in other words, the ECS could only be the outcome of the détente process, not its starting point. And, for de Gaulle, this was possible only if (1) the Soviet Union relaxed its grip over Eastern countries, (2) Bonn improved its relations with the communist bloc while recognizing the Oder–Neisse line and definitively renouncing nuclear arms, (3) the United States put an end to the war in Vietnam, and (4) the two German states became closer.[7] In essence, de Gaulle was telling the Soviets that the ECS could not take place for the time being in large part because of the Germans.[8]

From then on, the French position with regard to the CSCE remained, until 1975 at least, closely related to the German question. This chapter will demonstrate why this issue was one of the main factors that led France to reject and then to accept the CSCE, and why the issue became the central theme of French diplomacy during the 1972–75 negotiations. Between 1969 and 1975, Paris' attitude toward the Helsinki process combined three objectives concerning the German question: channeling the Ostpolitik, keeping the German question open, and preserving the quadripartite rights over Berlin and Germany. For French diplomats the CSCE was, first and foremost, a way to deal with the German question.[9]

Channeling the Ostpolitik

From 1964 onward one of the objectives of de Gaulle's policy of détente was to make France the major Western interlocutor of the Soviets. In his view, the Soviet retreat during the 1962 Cuban Missile Crisis had proved that the Soviet Union was no longer a pressing threat and that the time had come for Paris to engage in a rapprochement with the Eastern countries for the sake of overcoming the bipolar order.[10] For de Gaulle, this was all the more urgent because, after the partial failure of the 1963 Elysée Treaty on Franco-German cooperation, Chancellor Ludwig Erhard, who had succeeded Konrad Adenauer in October 1963, wanted to give priority to the U.S.-German partnership. De Gaulle believed that a collusion between Bonn and Washington could only strengthen bipolarity and contradict his concept—expressed eloquently during his press conference of 4 February 1965—according to which European and especially German political and territorial issues had to be settled by the Europeans themselves.[11] The coming to power of the Grand Coalition government in West Germany in December 1966 allowed de Gaulle to conciliate entente with Bonn and détente with Moscow, the latter being, in the Gaullist logic of détente, entente, coopération, the first stage of the rapprochement with a country of the socialist bloc. When Brandt, the new minister of foreign affairs, informed the Elysée that he wanted to improve German-Soviet relations (evoking a non-use of force agreement, Germany's recognition of the Oder-Neisse border, nullification of the Munich agreements, renunciation of nuclear arms, and improvement of inter-German relations[12]), de Gaulle supported Brandt's effort and sought to act as an intermediary between West Germany and the Soviet Union.

By 1967, however, disillusion prevailed: the Poles and the East Germans had managed to convince their allies that relations between the socialist countries and the FRG could not be improved as long as Bonn did not fully recognize the Oder-Neisse line and the German Democratic Republic (GDR, or East Germany); in addition, the principle of non-use of force had to be multilateralized.[13] Simultaneously, Chancellor Kurt-Georg Kiesinger slowed Brandt's attempts to establish a constructive dialogue with Moscow and demanded that the Soviets make the first move.[14] Although he was disappointed, de Gaulle continued his policy of détente toward the East, but he refused to embrace both the West German and the Soviet conceptions of European security, the former because it was based on attaining reunification first (although the West German government's declaration of December 1966 seemed to nuance this)[15] and the latter because it involved acknowledging the European status quo. De Gaulle was convinced that his conception remained the best option: it was necessary to lay the foundations of a genuine European rapprochement in order to promote, in the long term, the reunification of the whole continent, including Germany.[16] The suppression of the Prague Spring by Warsaw Pact troops in August 1968 reinforced de Gaulle's opinion: according to him, West German activism in Czechoslovakia during the previous months had been seen in Moscow as an expression of the German propensity to challenge existing borders.[17] In response, the Kremlin decided to intervene in Czechoslovakia, which showed that the territorial and political status quo remained the top priority, particularly at a time when the Soviet Union was facing a growing Chinese threat.

Still, by 1968 the French were aware that they no longer were Moscow's privileged interlocutors. For political and economic reasons, the Soviets were now giving priority to Bonn and Washington. The year 1969 did not change the situation: the election of Richard Nixon in the United States and of Brandt in West Germany led Soviet leader Leonid Brezhnev to intensify relations with both countries. Once he became chancellor, Brandt launched his Ostpolitik, marking a turning point in West German foreign policy. As seen from Paris, the man who symbolized this policy was of course Egon Bahr, who led wide-ranging negotiations with the Soviets about the non-use of force, the inviolability of borders, intra-German relations, the nullity of the Munich agreements, and, of course, the ECS project (the talks led to the Bahr paper of 22 May 1970 and to the Moscow Treaty of 12 August 1970).

The frequency and intensity of German-Soviet meetings reinforced the French feeling of being relegated to a secondary role. Granted, Brezhnev and his ministers were keen to reassure the French about the vital importance of Franco-Soviet relations in order for détente to proceed smoothly; but at the Quai d'Orsay as well as the Elysée, nobody was fooled.[18] Hence the ESC project, which the Soviets, starting in 1968, frequently proposed—in particular in the Warsaw Pact's March 1969 Budapest appeal—was seen by French diplomacy as an opportunity to be seized, as shown by Pompidou's January 1970 remarks: "I have in fact little to say to the Russians during my trip to Moscow. Therefore, I ought to give them a more formal agreement about the Conference on Security."[19]

Pompidou was thus keener to accept an ESC than his predecessor; first, this allowed him to maintain a dialogue with the Soviets; second, contrary to de Gaulle, he was not fundamentally opposed to multilateral meetings; and, third, the ESC was an excellent way of challenging the exclusivity of the relationship between Bonn and Moscow. The new French president was indeed wary of Brandt's long-term intentions and feared that the chancellor would be led to make excessive concessions to the Soviets, including by accepting German neutralization in exchange for its reunification. Such a German-Soviet arrangement would destabilize the West and have disastrous consequences for French security: West Germany would be detached from NATO, from the European Economic Community (EEC), and, consequently, from France.[20]

For the same reason, France refused to take part in the Mutual and Balanced Force Reductions (MBFR) negotiations, proposed by the NATO countries in June 1968.

The MBFR were supported by West Germany, mostly because that country wanted to prevent a unilateral withdrawal of U.S. forces from Germany.[21] But for Georges Pompidou, implementing force reductions in Central Europe before establishing political détente would create a demilitarized and neutralized zone that, in the case of renewed East-West tension, would become the center of a new race for land with the potential to degenerate into World War III.[22] Pompidou confided to Brandt that he believed the Soviets were trying to finlandize Germany by neutralizing it through the MBFR. What the French feared, it should be underlined, was the neutralization of Germany rather than its reunification, which they did not consider possible in the short term anyway. In addition, France was opposed to the military situation in Europe serving as a safety valve to the Soviet Union: any buffer zone created in the center of the continent by reducing the forces would have allowed the Russians to concentrate on Asia and the Middle East.[23]

Ostpolitik, the MBFR, and the desire to resume their dialogue with Moscow thus led the French to become the main supporters of the Soviet project of a pan-European conference in the West. By expanding its agenda to include issues such as the free movement of people, ideas, and information, as well as principles such as respect for human rights, self-determination, and free cooperation between Europeans,[24] Paris wanted to make the CSCE the multilateral transposition of the Gaullist model of détente based on the overcoming of the bipolar order, an instrument to prevent any further intervention similar to what happened in Prague in 1968,[25] and a way to channel the Ostpolitik. Likewise, because every European country would participate on an equal footing, for France the CSCE was the antithesis of the MBFR, which was based on bloc-to-bloc relations.[26] Since the 1970 Moscow Treaty, by proclaiming the inviolability of borders, territorial integrity, and non-use of force, already seemed to sanction the European status quo, the French believed that they had nothing to lose from committing to the CSCE.[27]

In 1971 Paris began bilateral talks with the Eastern European countries in order to prepare the conference's agenda. Issues relating to security proper—the future first basket—were among the top priorities of French diplomacy, hence its intense involvement in the drafting of the ten principles designed to govern relations between states. To be sure, despite the Elysée's worries about Brandt's Eastern policy, Paris supported Ostpolitik: first, because failure to do so would affect the Franco-German friendship and, second, because it would go against one of the fundamental principles of the French policy of détente which, since the 1960s, had called for improved relations between West Germany and the Eastern countries. Yet France's involvement in the drafting of the ten principles reflected the French desire to channel the Ostpolitik; through the Decalogue, France indeed managed to get involved in the Soviet–German debate on non-use of force, inviolability of borders, and territorial integrity. Paris not only intervened in the definition of these principles, but also proposed other principles. In fact, the French succeeded in channeling the Ostpolitik because in Helsinki and Geneva they promoted principles that were not included in the Moscow Treaty and gave a dynamic nature to détente: the states' freedom of choice with regard to military alliances, individual freedom, nonintervention in internal affairs, and, not least, peaceful change of borders. The latter represents the second objective that French diplomacy sought to achieve at the CSCE—in other words, keeping the German question open.

Keeping the German Question Open

On 4 February 1965 President Charles de Gaulle spelled out his approach to the German question: "It is clear that a real peace, and consequently fruitful relations between the East and the West, will not be established as long as German anomalies, worries they provoke and ordeals they create will persist."[28] De Gaulle clearly understood that robbing the West Germans of all hope of reunification would have probably led them to dissociate themselves from the Western camp, with catastrophic consequences for European and French security. If de Gaulle's acceptance of German unification ("The normal destiny of the German people," he famously declared in 1959)[29] is well documented, Georges Pompidou's attitude still sparks off debates. Yet analyzing his approach to the CSCE shows that Pompidou's stance was entirely in line with that of his predecessor. In fact, any other attitude would have constituted a flagrant violation of the existing treaties and strongly harmed Franco-German relations, particularly at a time when Pompidou and Brandt wanted to rekindle the European political cooperation process. At any rate, during the early 1970s the reunification of Germany was conceivable only in the long term: the French, as a result, did not take risks by supporting, even passively, the idea of a possible reunification. Above all, they did not want to put themselves in an awkward position toward the Germans and wished to remain coherent with the goals set by de Gaulle with regard to the German question and détente: the possibility of German reunification had to be preserved at least for the indefinite future.

As mentioned above, when the Warsaw Pact countries reiterated their ESC project in the mid-1960s, one of their major goals was to obtain a multilateral recognition of the intangibility of borders. For West Germany, this was clearly unacceptable because it would consecrate Germany's division. During the negotiation of the Moscow Treaty, Bahr played a key role in obtaining the replacement of the Soviet preferred formula on the intangibility of borders by a formula mentioning their inviolability, which did not rule out a change of borders by negotiation. The treaty established, "The High Contracting Parties . . . regard, today and in the future, the borders of all countries in Europe as inviolable in the form that they exist on the day of the signing of this Treaty, including the Oder-Neisse line, which forms the Western border of the People's Republic of Poland, and the border between the Federal Republic of Germany and the German Democratic Republic."[30] From then on, the term "inviolability" became the reference, and Bonn wished, quite naturally, to include it in the agenda of the CSCE.

In Paris, meanwhile, the watchword was to avoid anything that could appear as an acknowledgment of the existing borders or make "the conference . . . a substitute for a German peace settlement"[31] which would sanction existing borders, including the inner-German border. French diplomacy believed it was possible to accept a mention of borders in Europe, provided that the limit on which the Germans themselves had settled during the signing of the Moscow and Warsaw Treaties was not exceeded. It was thus necessary to speak of respect of the borders, not of recognition, and it was especially important to preserve the possibility of a peaceful change of borders. As previously stated, it was essential for the French to avoid putting themselves in an awkward position toward West Germany concerning this issue; moreover, Paris had to remain coherent with the Gaullist idea that part of France's security depended on the West German continued belief in a future reunification.

However, during the Helsinki multilateral preparatory talks (from November 1972 to June 1973), Moscow rejected the Western proposal to couple inviolability of borders to non-use of force, which for Western countries would have clearly left open the option of a change of borders by peaceful means; for them, inviolability involved only prohibiting any unilateral reassessment of frontiers through the use of force. Despite renouncing intangibility of borders in favor of inviolability in 1970, the Soviets continued to interpret the latter as a synonym of the former: for the Kremlin, proclaiming the inviolability of borders meant prohibiting *any* modification of borders, whether or not through the use of force.[32] Yet, in order to obtain an early start of the conference, Andrei Gromyko finally admitted that the inviolability of borders did not preclude their modification by agreement between the governments concerned. Content with this formula, Bonn gave up the idea of coupling this principle with the non-use of force.[33]

Nevertheless, when the CSCE began, the Soviets retreated. In its "General declaration on the basis of European security and the principles aiming to govern the relations between the states in Europe," which it submitted to the other delegations in July 1973, Moscow defined inviolability of frontiers as "the principle whereby the participating states consider the existing frontiers in Europe as inviolable today and in the future, will desist from any territorial claims, and will recognize that peace in this region can be saved only if nobody makes an attempt on the current frontiers."[34] This statement amounted to an unequivocal recognition of the European territorial status quo, ignoring Western objections raised during the multilateral preparatory talks while severely restricting principles such as self-determination and non-use of force. The Soviets reinforced this by giving a highly restrictive definition of territorial integrity, the fourth principle of the Decalogue.

But while the West Germans were determined to prevent the Helsinki Final Act from confirming the status quo, they were also aware that their active involvement in the negotiation on this issue could irritate the Soviets and legitimize the Kremlin's propaganda about German revanchism. So Bonn asked its allies to park themselves on the first line during the combat for peaceful change.[35] Yet West Germany felt isolated: hence for Secretary of State Henry Kissinger the idea of peaceful change was no less than delirious and absurd.[36] Convinced that German reunification was not possible for the time being, Kissinger did not want to sacrifice the U.S.-Soviet détente for the sake of the Germans. He said as much to his Western counterparts—indirectly at least—during the June 1974 NATO ministerial meeting in Ottawa.[37]

France, in that context, rapidly appeared as one of the few Western countries most willing to defend German positions. Once again, Pompidou ruled out taking a stance that could appear ambiguous to the Germans; at the same time, the French had to show the Germans that, despite Kissinger's skepticism, belonging to the Western world was the best guarantee for one day resolving the German question in line with Bonn's interests. In other words, Gaullist conceptions had to remain firmly on the agenda. When they proposed a formula that linked inviolability to peaceful change while rejecting the Soviet definition of the principle of respect for territorial integrity, the French delegation faced immediate criticism from the Eastern countries, who emphasized the need for "crystal purity"[38] in stating the principle of inviolability of borders; the latter, in their view, should not to be marred by that of peaceful change.

As a result of this issue, the CSCE negotiations were paralyzed for several months. In January 1974, however, Brezhnev decided to bypass the delegations in Geneva and attempt to unlock the situation by speaking directly to Pompidou. In a long letter, he asked the French president to ensure that inviolability of borders would not be associated with any other concept and would be kept "in its absolute purity."[39] Yet Pompidou's response (the French president was very ill at the time and prone to bluntness) was forthright: France could not accept a text that would not allow a peaceful change of borders.[40] Two months later, Brezhnev tried his luck again when he received Pompidou in Pitsunda, but in vain.[41] Until the very end of his life in April 1974, Pompidou provided unwavering support to the Germans on this issue at the CSCE. For him, it was natural that Germany should aspire to be reunified someday.[42] France, above all, had to remain consistent with the Gaullist Doctrine concerning the German question. Ironically, during the first months of the conference the representatives of West Germany, not wanting to attack the Soviets head-on, did not speak in defense of the French proposals on inviolability of borders and territorial integrity, leaving the French alone in defending their positions.[43] Pompidou's attitude suffices to dispel the legend of his alleged hostility toward German reunification: on the contrary, after Pitsunda he explicitly urged his diplomats in Geneva to resist any Soviet attempt to undermine a fundamental tenet of Gaullist policy, namely to enable the establishment of a Europe from the Atlantic to the Urals within which a reunification of Germany could eventually take place.

This did not prevent the French from trying to find solutions in order to unlock the negotiations. The Quai d'Orsay's secretary general, Geoffroy de Courcel, told the head of the Soviet delegation, Anatoly Kovalev, that although France was prepared to remove some qualifications limiting the impact of inviolability of borders, it could not accept proclaiming the principle of inviolability without the possibility of peacefully changing borders being mentioned somewhere in the final document. What the French could offer the Soviets was to move the formula on peaceful change to another principle of the Decalogue.[44] Kovalev accepted the transfer, but only to the paragraph concerning sovereignty because, he said, "the USSR considers changes of borders as an expression of the state's sovereignty."[45] Understanding that inviolability and peaceful change had little chance of ending up in the same paragraph, French diplomacy, at that point, used a roundabout way of placing the two concepts on the same level: France was willing to include peaceful change in the section on sovereign equality, as demanded by the Soviets, but only if the Final Act contained a clause on the unity and interdependence of all principles.[46] Although it took several more months for everyone to agree on the wording of peaceful change, this solution eventually prevailed.

There is more: the French prevailed when it came to territorial integrity and non-use of force. While the Soviet Union wanted to rely on the former principle to outlaw land claims and lay the foundations for an understanding that the CSCE recognized territorial realities resulting from World War II,[47] for France—and for its European political cooperation partners—respect for territorial integrity was a concrete obligation that derived from the general principle of non-use of force. According to the nine countries of the EEC (EEC Nine), though, the reaffirmation of this principle did not prevent the participating states from consensually making "a modification of their territorial heritage or political and territorial status of a territory, without using force, by taking full account of the right of peoples to self-determination or the will of the population of the territory in question."[48] Thanks to France's insistence on equality and interdependence of principles, the Soviet Union thus obtained a less-satisfactory result than was the case with the German-Soviet Treaty which, in contrast with the Decalogue, contained little if any link between inviolability of borders and non-use of force. In addition, the idea of peaceful change was included in the declaration of principles, whereas Germany, upon signing the Moscow Treaty in 1970, had managed only to "issue a unilateral declaration in the form of a letter to the Soviet government stressing that [the treaty] did not affect the possibility of a unification of the German people."[49]

In the Helsinki Final Act, as a result of the clause on equality and interdependence of principles, inviolability of borders thus appeared as a corollary of non-use of force and therefore was seen as a prohibition to impair or change frontiers by force. In addition, the language on peaceful change of borders, included in the definition of the principle of sovereignty, was a further confirmation that the declaration did not imply in any way immutability of borders.[50] France played a central role in this outcome, thereby demonstrating its support for the German stance: until the end, the French held on to both inviolability and peaceful change of borders, a dual concept held since de Gaulle. In that sense, the Decalogue can be seen as a form of consecration of certain principles dear to French diplomacy.

However, while the French congratulated themselves for playing an active part in establishing the principles that did not freeze the European status quo in any way, Bonn did not seem particularly grateful to Paris for its help during the negotiations. Despite the efforts of the French in Geneva, the Germans felt isolated in the combat for peaceful change. According to Gottfried Niedhart, "During the period of drafting the third principle the German delegation had to realize that neither the EEC Nine nor the NATO Fifteen [countries] were prepared to press the Soviet Union too hard. Given the strict Soviet attitude toward the issue of inviolability of borders, it seemed pointless to insist on the West German position. Jacques Andréani of the French delegation recommended more flexibility on the part of the West Germans."[51]

Indeed, in April 1974 the French decision to accept the separation of the inviolability of the borders and peaceful change had given rise to some unease between the French and German delegations. The West German Ministry of Foreign Affairs feared that the Soviet Union might succeed in imposing its own interpretation of the Decalogue that would have frozen the European status quo once and for all.[52] The first version of the floating sentence about peaceful change, partly drafted by Jacques Andréani and François Plaisant—in charge of the negotiations of the Decalogue within the French delegation[53]—was phrased as follows: the borders "can be changed only in accordance with international law, by peaceful means and by way of agreement."[54] Bonn regarded this formulation as dangerous because it implied that any territorial changes had to be in compliance with international law, which did not always offer relevant solutions in this area. Therefore, even after the French had accepted the necessity of looking for a more precise formula and were engaged in the negotiations about the equality and interdependence of principles, the Germans could suspect them of not categorically rejecting Soviet arguments on the status quo, especially because the countries of the EEC discovered a few months later that the French delegation was covertly negotiating some issues of the third basket with the Soviets but without the backing of its partners.[55] Consequently, the German vision of France's attitude concerning the issue of borders was not always consistent with the perception the French had of their own approach, even though Paris did not stop claiming that it gave priority to the first basket at the CSCE.

The deep interest of the French in the Decalogue was largely due to the men then in charge of its negotiation. Among them, François Plaisant was a specialist on the German question: he had directly participated in the discussions that had led to the Quadripartite Agreement on Berlin on 3 September 1971, along with Jean Sauvagnargues who at that time was ambassador to Bonn. As Giscard d'Estaing's minister of foreign affairs from June 1974 onward, Sauvagnargues was keenly interested in the substance of the Decalogue and became quite involved in CSCE dealings. Thus when Gromyko tried to squeeze concessions out of Sauvagnargues, the Soviet minister realized that his French counterpart was fully aware of the lexical subtleties of the CSCE.[56] Sauvagnargues was famously skeptical of the results that could be expected from the Helsinki process. So his involvement reflected, first and foremost, his desire to make sure that the CSCE would not jeopardize what was for him an essential asset of France's foreign policy: the quadripartite rights and responsibilities over Berlin and Germany.

Preserving the Quadripartite Rights

From 1965 to 1975 the issue of the preservation of the quadripartite rights was, in the minds of French leaders and diplomats, a major stake of the CSCE. When the Soviets tried to persuade de Gaulle to organize a conference that would lead to the creation of a pan-European security system, the protection of the quadripartite rights figured prominently among Paris' causes for refusal.[57] Since 1945 France's rights and responsibilities over Germany and Berlin have given France leverage over the German question and East-West relations: the rights guaranteed France's status as a victorious power of World War II, legitimized its claim to maintaining a dialogue with Moscow, and justified a certain political ascendancy over West Germany by allowing France to have a droit *de regard* over Germany's future. Finally, last but not least, the rights were a key part of the legal arsenal devised in 1945; based on that arsenal Germany's division could be described by the West as temporary.[58]

In fact, these rights and responsibilities were considered in Paris as untouchable, almost sacred. Yet the CSCE presented a risk in that regard: the fact that the GDR would sit at the conference on an equal footing with the other participating states could lead to its de facto recognition and lead the Soviet Union to relinquish its rights, which would mean giving up quadripartism. In addition, as Maurice Schumann explained to his Italian counterpart Aldo Moro in May 1970, East Berlin would be tempted to settle the Berlin matter by using force, and the serious crisis that would result could be resolved only through a negotiation between the United States and the Soviet Union, confirming the U.S.-Soviet condominium over Europe, France's perennial nightmare.[59] The inter-German rapprochement initiated by Brandt reinforced this risk, especially because the chancellor intended to make the Soviets admit realities in West Berlin—in other words, belonging to the legal and economic system of the *Bund* (federal state), which could limit the sovereignty of the Allies in Berlin.[60] In sum, while from 1968–69 onward the CSCE was gradually seen as a useful instrument to contribute to overcoming the European status quo, it could also prove to be dangerous for France's status. While the French were happy to start a pan-European discussion over security, to do what it took to put an end to the division of the continent, and to struggle against a bloc-to-bloc approach, calling into question the rights and responsibilities over Germany and Berlin was a nonstarter.

Concern was so strong in Paris that by 1969 France, followed by its EEC and NATO partners, made a quadripartite agreement on Berlin as a sine qua non condition for the normalization of relations between the West and the GDR and for the final acceptance of an ECS.[61] The Quai d'Orsay waged this approach despite Pompidou's personal fears: the French president thought that, on the contrary, opening negotiations on Berlin could lead the Westerners to erode their position in Berlin—which had been gained in Potsdam—and to establish "quasi-diplomatic relations with the GDR."[62] Yet Western powers had to improve the situation in West Berlin, especially concerning its access routes: Brandt considered this question as a primordial condition for the normalization of relations between West Germany and the Eastern countries. Paris, London, and Washington were aware of that, which is why Pompidou yielded on this issue to Schumann, who thought that the initiation of quadripartite discussions was vital. Nevertheless, Pompidou insisted on close consultations between the four Western countries to avoid excessive concessions from West Germany toward the Soviet Union, even if it meant creating the impression of a new bloc. Moreover, Pompidou believed it was necessary, in compensation, to start the preparation of the conference with the Soviets before the signing of the quadripartite agreement, much to West Germany's displeasure.

Although the agreement of 3 September 1971 reaffirmed the quadripartite rights and responsibilities over Berlin and therefore provided a shield against the potentially negative effects of Ostpolitik, some French diplomats remained worried about the consequences of the Decalogue concerning these rights.[63] Admittedly, in the eyes of the French, British, and American governments, the Declaration of Principles was not legally binding and could not affect the nature of relations between the Four Powers and the two German states; but, for the Quai d'Orsay, this text would inevitably have considerable political weight, whatever form it would take and however it would be passed. The French were convinced that it would be considered—at least by the Soviet Union and its allies—to be an essential document, defining the basis of European order, and particularly German order. As a result, these countries could use it to challenge aspects of the situation in Germany that were favorable to the three Allies and West Germany.

Because of the substance of some of the principles in the Decalogue, particularly the principle of inviolability of borders and those related to sovereign equality and territorial integrity, there was concern in France that the Warsaw Pact countries could be tempted to claim that the German borders were permanently fixed and to challenge the rights and responsibilities of the three.[64] Similarly, since the CSCE would produce a text signed by all European states, it was important to avoid giving the whole of Europe a reason to interfere in German affairs. This risk would be increased if the CSCE had a follow-up.[65] Finally, Sauvagnargues worried that the reference in the tenth principle (on "the execution in good faith of obligations under international law") to "all the rights inherent in sovereignty" could be used for subsequent claims of the GDR on particular rights of sovereignty that it did not have at that time, for example regarding air traffic. Sauvagnargues therefore considered it necessary to add a clause concerning the respect for previous international obligations that covered the quadripartite rights. The Germans, he argued, had to understand that the existence of the quadripartite rights was the only way they could preserve the German option and a chance of an eventual reunification.[66]

At first, the idea of adding a clause reserving previous agreements was badly received by Bonn: because the future declaration was not supposed to carry the same weight as a treaty, they argued, the declaration could not be a threat for existing treaties. Consequently, it was not necessary to insert such a clause since it would carry the risk of creating a doubt about its noncompulsory character.[67] When he became minister in June 1974, Sauvagnargues took the matter in hand and urged the CSCE participants to add in the tenth principle of the Decalogue a sentence according to which the document "cannot infringe on the treaties and bilateral and multilateral agreements previously subscribed by the participating states or concerning them."[68] The expression "concerning them" was intended to cover the quadripartite rights and all the arrangements made by the three Western Allies—France, the United Kingdom, and the United States—from 1952 onward. The Germans were somewhat averse to such a formulation because they saw in it a reference to Articles 53 and 107 of the United Nations Charter relating to former enemies.[69] As to the neutral and non-aligned countries, they were outright hostile: Yugoslavia, Malta, and Cyprus, on account of the agreements they had previously subscribed, feared being seen as second-class states or protectorates as a result.[70] Because of its generality, they argued, the phrase "concerning them" could be interpreted in a way that was favorable to the Brezhnev Doctrine. In addition, by highlighting the prominent role of the Four Powers among the participants at the CSCE, the French proposal created a discrimination between great and medium powers.[71] France, in other words, was suspected of an attitude it had always denounced—discarding the interests of small and medium-size European states. As a compromise, Paris accepted a sentence—without the expression concerning them—which was harmless to Yugoslavia and the other neutral and non-aligned countries.[72] However, as a preventive measure, it reached agreement with Washington and London to the effect that, upon signing the Final Act in 1975, Giscard, Gerald Ford, and Harold Wilson would declare that the CSCE does not alter the quadripartite rights.

Throughout the Helsinki process the French were obsessed with preserving their rights over Germany and Berlin. This obsession crops up even during the negotiations of the second and third baskets when Paris rejected the West German proposals aiming to create a scientific forum and an economic and industrial center for East-West cooperation in West Berlin. France considered it unwise to establish a European body in West Berlin: although this proposal aimed to promote the role of Berlin as a bridge between both parts of Europe, it could be at the expense of the ties between West Germany and the Western sectors, whose strengthening was a permanent objective for Bonn. It would thus have justified the Soviet theory according to which the dislocation of the Reich had led to the emergence of three entities in Germany (FRG, GDR, and West Berlin), thereby infringing on the quadripartite rights.[73]

Conclusion

By imposing many of its viewpoints in the Decalogue, France managed to achieve one of the main objectives set by Pompidou for the CSCE when he accepted it at the Conference in 1969—in other words, multilateralizing the Ostpolitik without internationalizing the German question. Thanks to the debates on the principles for governing relations between states, the French were able to interfere as early as 1969 in the German-Soviet negotiations on several key concepts with direct relevance for Moscow and Bonn such as the non-use of force, the inviolability of borders, and the possibility of a peaceful change of these borders. Through its involvement in the CSCE, France demonstrated to its West German partner that it was a faithful ally and that, despite the suspicions raised by some aspects of Ostpolitik, Paris was supportive of it. In fact, the French attitude at the CSCE reflected France's policy toward the German question in general. The French were keen to preserve their political ascendancy over Bonn and did everything to prevent West Germany from drifting toward the East. But, at the same time, if only as a result of the Franco-German partnership, they wanted to preserve at least the possibility of reunification—which in any way seemed to be conceivable only in a remote future—in line with General de Gaulle's conceptions.

Nicolas Badalassi is associate professor of contemporary history at the Institut d'études politiques d'Aix-en-Provence (Sciences-po Aix). He is the author of *En finir avec la guerre froide: La France, l'Europe et le processus d'Helsinki, 1965–1975* (2014). He has published various articles concerning French foreign policy in the Cold War era, the Helsinki Process, and security in the Mediterranean. He has also coedited with Sarah B. Snyder *The CSCE and the End of the Cold War: Diplomacy, Societies and Human Rights, 1972–1990* (2018), and with Houda Ben Hamouda, *Les pays d'Europe orientale et la Méditerranée, 1967–1989* (2013).

Notes

1. Mastny, "The Soviet Union."
2. Trachtenberg, *A Constructed Peace*, 3–33.
3. Conversation Puaux/van Well, 18 Dec. 1973, AMAE, Europe 1971–76, FRG, 3019.
4. That was explained by Brandt in his inaugural speech on 28 Oct. 1969.
5. Badalassi, *En finir avec la guerre froide*.
6. Doubinine, *Moscou–Paris*, 214–16; note from the Office for Eastern Europe, 30 Aug. 1965, AMAE, Europe 1944– . . . , Poland, 369.
7. Press conference, 4 Feb. 1965 (de Gaulle, *Discours et messages*, vol. 4, 325).
8. Conversation de Gaulle/U-Thant in Paris, 30 Apr. 1966, AnF, Paris, 5 AG 1 179, UN, 1959–58; conversation de Gaulle/Brezhnev in Moscow, 21 Jun. 1966, AnF, 5 AG 1 187, USSR, 1966.
9. Andréani, *Le Piège*, 48.
10. Conversation de Gaulle/Peyrefitte in Paris, 28 Oct. 1964 (Peyrefitte, *C'était de Gaulle*, 648).

11. Conversation de Gaulle/U-Thant in Paris, 30 Apr. 1966, AnF, 5 AG 1 179, UN, 1959–68.
12. Conversations de Gaulle/Brandt in Paris, 15 and 16 Dec. 1966, AnF, 5 AG 1 163, FRG, 1966–67.
13. Selvage, "The Warsaw Pact," 86–87.
14. Schoenborn, *La mésentente apprivoisée*, 308.
15. In the government declaration of December 1966, Kurt Kiesinger expressed his desire to eliminate tensions with Moscow and to establish diplomatic relations with the Eastern countries. Schoenborn, *La mésentente apprivoisée*, 300.
16. Conversation de Gaulle/Kiesinger in Bonn, 27 Sept. 1968, AMAE, General Secretariat, EM, 34; Cable no. 4544/52, Wormser, 6 Nov. 1968, AMAE, Europe 1966–70, USSR, 2666.
17. Conversation de Gaulle/Sargent Shriver in Paris, 23 Sept. 1968, AnF, 5 AG 1 202, United States: diplomatic conversations, 1966–69.
18. Cables 6962/78 and 6979/94, Seydoux, 27 Dec. 1969, AMAE, Europe 1966–70, USSR, 2667.
19. Pompidou to the Secretary of State Jean de Lipkowski, 6 Jan. 1970, AnF, 5 AG 2 1041, NATO, East-West relations, 1969–74. Translation by the author.
20. Conversation Pompidou/Brandt in Paris, 30 Jan. 1970, AnF, 5 AG 2 104, FRG, 1969–70.
21. Bange, "An Intricate Web."
22. Conversation Pompidou/Nixon in Reykjavik, 31 May 1973, AnF, 5 AG 2 1023, United States.
23. Conversation Pompidou/Brandt in Paris, 10 Feb. 1972, AnF, 5 AG 2 106, FRG, 1972–73.
24. Notes from the Office for Eastern Europe, 13 Sept. and 20 Nov. 1969, AMAE, Europe 1966–70, International organizations and international issues, 2014; Note, 22 Nov. 1969, AMAE, Europe 1966–70, Quadripartite meetings, 1727.
25. Conversation Jurgensen/Drndic in Belgrade, 24 Nov. 1969, AnF, 5 AG 2 114, Yugoslavia, 1969–74; conversation Schumann/Sharp in Ottawa, 23 Sept. 1971, AnF, 5 AG 115, Canada, 1969–74.
26. Conversation Pompidou/Brezhnev in Paris, 29 Oct. 1971, AnF, 5 AG 2 1018, USSR. 1969–74.
27. Note from the Office for Eastern Europe, 23 Oct. 1970, AMAE, Europe 1966–70, International organizations and international issues, 2032.
28. Press conference, 4 Feb. 1965 (de Gaulle, *Discours et messages*, vol. 4, 325). Translation by the author.
29. Press conference, 25 Mar. 1959 (de Gaulle, *Discours et messages*, vol. 3, 84–5). Translation by the author.
30. The Moscow Treaty, 12 Aug. 1970, http://ghdi.ghi-dc.org/sub_document.cfm?document_id=919 (accessed 19 Apr. 2019).
31. Dispatch no. 175, de Rose, 23 Feb. 1972, AMAE, Europe 1971–76, International organizations and international issues, 2923. Translation by the author.
32. Cable no. 1001/04, Charles Lucet, 24 Mar. 1973, AMAE, CSCE, 31.
33. Cable no. 173, Puaux, 17 Mar. 1973, AMAE, CSCE, 28.
34. Document CSCE/I/3, 4 Jul. 1973, URSS, CSCE Archives, Prague, Helsinki 1972–75, Book 1. Translation by the author.
35. Cable no. 1870/74, Fernand-Laurent, 9 Nov. 1973, AMAE, Europe 1971–76, Romania, 3535.
36. Niedhart, "Peaceful Change of Frontiers," 45.
37. Ibid., 48.
38. Words of Anatoly Kovalev to Geoffroy de Courcel, 11 Jan. 1974, Paris, AnF, 5 AG 2 113, USSR, 1972–74.
39. Message from Leonid Brezhnev to Georges Pompidou, 8 Jan. 1974, AnF, 5 AG 2 111, USSR, 1969–74. Translation by the author.
40. Message from Georges Pompidou to Leonid Brezhnev, 31 Jan. 1974, AnF, 5 AG 2 111, USSR, 1969–74.
41. Conversation Pompidou/Brezhnev in Pitsounda, 13 Mar. 1974, AnF, 5 AG 2 113, USSR. 1972–74.
42. In 1970 Pompidou asked Brezhnev "not to take hope of reunification away from Germany." (translation by the author). Conversation Pompidou/Brezhnev in Moscow, 7 Oct. 1970, AnF, 5 AG 2 1018, USSR, 1969–74.
43. Note CSCE no. 395, 14 Nov. 1973, AMAE, Europe 1971–76, FRG, 2982.
44. Conversation Courcel/Kovalev in Paris, 11 Jan. 1974, AnF, 5 AG 2 113, USSR, 1972–74.

45. Cable no. 2554/62, Morizet, 13 Jun. 1974, AMAE, Europe 1971–76, FRG, 3040. Translation by the author.
46. Conversation Sauvagnargues/Gromyko in Moscow, 11 Jul. 1974, AMAE, Europe 1971–76, USSR, 3726.
47. Document CSCE/I/3, 4 Jul. 1973, from the delegation of the Soviet Union (Archives CSCE, Helsinki 1972–75, Book 1).
48. Report CPE, CSCE (73)57D, 22 Aug. 1973, AMAE, CSCE, 22. Translation by the author.
49. Ghebali, "La CSCE et le mythe de l'immutabilité des frontières en Europe," 26. Translation by the author.
50. Report from the Political Committee, CP(75)23 P, 8 Jul. 1975, AMAE, Europe 1971–76, EEC, 3820.
51. Niedhart, "Peaceful Change of Frontiers," 46.
52. Ibid., 47.
53. Note CSCE, 21 Jan. 1975, AMAE, Europe 1971–76, FRG, 2982.
54. Note CSCE, no. 170, 6 Jun. 1973, AMAE, Europe 1971–76, FRG, 2982.
55. Badalassi, *En finir avec la guerre froide*, 245.
56. Conversation Sauvagnargues/Gromyko in Moscow, 20 Mar. 1975, AMAE, Europe 1971–76, USSR, 3727.
57. Note from the Office for Political Affairs, 10 Jun. 1966, AMAE, Europe 1966–70, International organizations and international issues, 2034.
58. The provisions of the Potsdam Conference (17 Jul.–2 Aug. 1945), juridically available until the German reunification, established that the destiny of the whole of Germany falls under the final responsibility of the United States, the Soviet Union, the United Kingdom, and France. The agreements had to maintain the administrative, political, and economical unity of a demilitarized, denazified, democratized, and decentralized country.
59. Conversation Schumann/Moro in Paris, 20 May 1970, AnF, 5 AG 2 109, Italy, 1969–73.
60. Wilkens, "Accords et désaccords," 371.
61. Conversation Schumann/Rogers/Stewart/Scheel at the embassy of the FRG in Brussels, 3 Dec. 1969, MAE, Europe 1966–70, Quadripartite meetings, 1727.
62. Quadripartite meeting of the political directors in Bonn, 8–9 May 1970, AMAE, Europe 1966–70, Quadripartite meetings, 1726; and note from Georges Pompidou, "Négociation sur Berlin," 26 Mar. 1970, AnF, 5 AG 2 1009, FRG, 1969–74. Translation by the author.
63. The quadripartite agreement guaranteed civil access to Berlin by road, rail, and waterways, and stated that the ties between Berlin and the FRG would be maintained and developed, given that Berlin was not a constituent element of the FRG and was not governed by it.
64. Cable no. 2548/53, Morizet, 13 Jun. 1974, AMAE, Europe 1971–76, FRG, 3040.
65. Cable no. 1844/58, Sauvagnargues, 28 Apr. 1974, AMAE, Europe 1971–76, FRG, 3040.
66. Cable no. 564/70, Sauvagnargues, 11 Feb. 1974, AMAE, CSCE, 33.
67. Note CSCE no. 126, 28 Jun. 1974, AMAE, Europe 1971–76, FRG, 2982.
68. Cable no. 2563/69, Morizet, 13 Jun. 1974, AMAE, Europe 1971–76, FRG, 3040.
69. The risk to Germany was that the formulation of the tenth principle as proposed by France would confirm Germany's status as ex-enemy while the Ostpolitik treaties had sought to quash Soviet interpretation of the articles in question.
70. Malta made reference to the agreements it had signed during the colonial period, with Britain and other countries. Cyprus wanted to prevent the CSCE from confirming the treaties of Zurich and London of February 1959 by which it acceded to an independence limited by the so-called patronage of Turkey, Greece, and the United Kingdom.
71. Cables no. 756 to 767, Fernand-Laurent, 3 Mar. 1975, AMAE, Europe 1971–76, International organizations and international issues, 2927.
72. In the Final Act, the participating states "note that the present Declaration does not affect their rights and obligations, nor the corresponding treaties and other agreements and arrangements."
73. Note CSCE no. 395, 14 Nov. 1973, AMAE, Europe 1971–76, FRG, 2982.

Bibliography

Andréani, J. 2005. *Le Piège. Helsinki et la chute du communisme*. Paris: Odile Jacob.

Badalassi, N. 2014. *En finir avec la guerre froide. La France, l'Europe et le processus d'Helsinki, 1965–1975*. Rennes, France: Presses universitaires de Rennes.

Bange, O. 2008. "An Intricate Web. Ostpolitik, the European Security System and German Unification." In Bange and Niedhart, *Helsinki 1975*, 30–35.

Bange, O., and G. Niedhart. 2008. *Helsinki 1975 and the Transformation of Europe*. New York: Berghahn Books.

De Gaulle, C. 1970. *Discours et messages*. Vol. 3, *Avec le renouveau*. Paris: Plon.

De Gaulle, C. 1970. *Discours et messages*. Vol. 4, *Pour l'effort*. Paris: Plon.

Doubinine, Y. 2001. *Moscou–Paris dans un tourbillon diplomatique. Témoignage d'ambassadeur*. Paris: Imaginaria.

Ghebali, V. Y. 1991. "La CSCE et le mythe de l'immutabilité des frontières en Europe." *Nouvelle Europe* 5, 24–27.

Mastny, V. 2000. "The Soviet Union and the Origins of the Warsaw Pact in 1955." In *Mechanisms of Power in the Soviet Union*, edited by N. E. Rosenfeldt, J. Bent, and E. Kulavig, 241–66. New York: St. Martin's Press.

Niedhart, G. 2008. "Peaceful Change of Frontiers as a Crucial Element in the West German Strategy of Transformation." In Bange and Niedhart, *Helsinki 1975*, 39–52. New York: Berghahn Books.

Peyrefitte, A. 2002. *C'était de Gaulle*. Paris: Gallimard.

Schoenborn, B. 2007. *La mésentente apprivoisée. De Gaulle et les Allemands, 1963–1969*. Paris: Presses universitaires de France.

Selvage, D. 2008. "The Warsaw Pact and the European Security Conference, 1964–1969. Sovereignty, hegemony, and the German question." In *Origins of the European Security System: The Helsinki Process revisited, 1965–1975*, edited by A. Wenger, V. Mastny, and C. Nuenlist, 86–87. London: Routledge.

Trachtenberg, M. 1999. *A Constructed Peace: The Making of the European Settlement. 1945–1963*. Princeton, NJ: Princeton University Press.

Wilkens, A. 2000. "Accords et désaccords. La France, l'*Ostpolitik* et la question allemande. 1969–1974." In *La RDA et l'Occident. 1949–1990*, edited by U. Pfeil, 357–378. Paris: Publications de l'Institut d'allemand d'Asnières.

CHAPTER 9

The Economic and Monetary Dimensions of the German Question
A French Perspective, 1969–1979

Guido Thiemeyer

From a French perspective, the German question in the 1970s had two key dimensions. The first related to a possible reunification: it seemed clear that the architects of the Neue Ostpolitik aimed at the dissolution of the Cold War in Europe with German reunification as the final objective. This political dimension of the French perception of the German question in the 1970s has already been explored.[1] There was, however, a second dimension of the German question in the 1970s: due to its remarkable economic success, the Federal Republic of Germany (FRG, or West Germany) was about to become the most influential economic power in Western Europe and within the European Economic Community (EEC). The industrial structure of West Germany, in particular, was much stronger than the corresponding structure was in France. This gave the FRG an important and growing influence, in particular when it came to monetary issues.

This chapter focuses on this second dimension of the German question. The period under discussion covers the presidencies of Georges Pompidou (1969–74) and Valéry Giscard d'Estaing (1974–81). This long decade is of particular interest because the international system changed considerably during these years, affecting Franco-German relations and, to some extent, driving them forward. This chapter will not offer a detailed narrative of Franco-German relations, which has already been done.[2] Rather, it will discuss the three main French approaches that were used in this period to deal with this aspect of the German question: the European integration approach, the bilateral approach, and the approach to strengthen the French economy.

Structural Changes in the European State System in the 1970s

Three main structural factors influenced the French perception of the German question. The first was the East-West conflict that, since the mid-1960s, had been dominated by détente. After the confrontation between the superpowers over Berlin and Cuba in the early 1960s, the Western alliance had changed its strategy: instead of containing or rolling back the influence of the Soviet Union, the principal objective was now to cooperate with the Eastern bloc, reduce armaments, establish predictability, and increase security in order to prevent a nuclear war. In this context, French President Charles de Gaulle developed his own concept of détente aiming at a European security system from the Atlantic to the Urals. The West German government, by contrast, initially only reluctantly accepted the new Western strategy because the acceptance of the status quo in Europe implied recognizing the existence of two German states and the division of the German nation. From 1969 on, however, the new government, under Chancellor Willy Brandt and Vice-Chancellor Walter Scheel, embarked on a new Ostpolitik—the German version of détente—whose long-term consequences aroused some unease in Paris.

The second structural factor influencing Franco-German relations was the EEC. Since the mid-1960s the EEC had undergone important changes. Following the empty chair crisis in 1965–66, national governments had gained considerable influence in EEC policy at the expense of the European Commission. At The Hague Summit in December 1969, the heads of states and governments of the EEC ended the period of European crisis that de Gaulle's policies had provoked. The EEC member states agreed to open negotiations with Britain, Ireland, Norway, and Denmark on joining the EEC. They also accepted the proposal made by Brandt and Pompidou on a closer monetary cooperation that should lead to a monetary union within ten years. And, finally, they reached an agreement on the financing of the Common Agricultural Policy (CAP), which had played a major role during the crisis. Even though contemporaries considered the EEC to be in crisis during most of the 1970s, recent research has emphasized its considerable dynamic in that period. Even though monetary union could not be achieved within the planned ten-year period and a common external policy turned out to be an illusion, direct elections for the European Parliament and the foundation of the European monetary system in 1979 changed the institutional structure of Western Europe. From a French perspective, European integration in the framework of the EEC provided a response to the German question and to the question of German economic and monetary power in Europe.

A third important structural factor at play was the global economic crisis, which had two key aspects. The first was the breakdown of the Bretton Woods international monetary system. After having provided monetary stability in the transatlantic framework, with the U.S. dollar as the anchor currency, the system fell into crisis when the United States was no longer able to lead in monetary questions. For both internal and external reasons, the American currency lost value compared with the other currencies and the whole system entered into a swirl of inflation. While in 1972 a European monetary arrangement called the "snake" had emerged, in March 1973 the Bretton Woods system in effect ceased to exist. That same year, the first oil price shock drew the Western countries into a recession, causing inflation and unemployment. The shock led to the first deep recession since World War II. Many contemporaries still remembered the world economic crisis at the end of the 1930s and its consequences. The early 1970s were a turning point in postwar European history.

All three structural factors were of course interrelated, and all of them influenced the French perspective on the German question and Germany as a whole. In the middle of the 1960s it was still clear for President de Gaulle that France, as one of the Allied victors of World War II, was the leading power in continental Europe. In his eyes the FRG was not a fully sovereign state, as he explained in a conversation with President Richard Nixon in March 1969: "And then, there is Germany, the source of all misfortunes, especially during the first and the second world wars. Its situation is quite special: it is divided . . . and under the surveillance of the Soviet Union and its satellites, starting with Poland. It has been kept down, not economically, but politically. It is no longer an independent country. In fact, it is forced to ask for, and to accept your protection, without which it would not be able to survive."[3] In de Gaulle's eyes, German's sovereignty was limited for two reasons: it was divided in three (the FRG, the German Democratic Republic [GDR, or East Germany], and Berlin) and its Western part was, in his view, an American protectorate. Under de Gaulle, there was therefore a feeling of superiority toward Germany combined with a claim for French leadership in bilateral relations. Of course, de Gaulle was well aware of the fact that France was too weak to play a decisive role on the global scene, which was dominated by the United States and the Soviet Union. Yet with the FRG as its junior partner, France's influence in world politics could be significantly strengthened.[4]

The Gaullist attitude dominated French policy toward Germany throughout the 1960s. In the second half of that decade however, officials within the French administration and the Quai d'Orsay as well as public intellectuals became more and more skeptical concerning French leadership in continental Europe and the EEC. As a result of its economic success, the FRG was indeed emerging as the leading industrial power in Western Europe. From a French perspective, this rise was mostly felt through the growing influence of the deutschmark and the Bundesbank, which became the leading central bank, whose monetary policy affected all other central banks in Europe. In addition to the unease caused by the economic performance of Western Germany, the new German Ostpolitik had an impact on bilateral relations between Bonn and Paris. Whereas de Gaulle had accused the Germans of being too reticent concerning détente, his successor Georges Pompidou was anxious that Bonn might go too far in its Ostpolitik. Despite trusting Brandt, he was skeptical about the growing German political influence in Europe.[5]

When in May 1974 Helmut Schmidt and Valéry Giscard d'Estaing became chancellor and president, respectively, they had to find a new balance in bilateral relations.[6] While de Gaulle had been convinced of the natural leadership of France, West Germany was now considered an equal partner. France as a nuclear power and a permanent member of the United Nations Security Council was more influential in world politics, whereas Germany assumed leadership in economic affairs. Helmut Schmidt's ascent to power was considered in Paris to mark a fundamental change in Franco-German relations. Schmidt was seen as representing the new Germany, as Raymond Aron put it in an article for *Le Figaro*: "Thirty years after the Third Reich's unconditional surrender, more than forty years after Adolf Hitler's coming to power, Mr. Schmidt, who is too young to have taken part in the events of the 1930's, incarnates . . . today's Germany."[7] According to Aron, who represented an important part of the French intellectual elite, Schmidt and the "new" Germany claimed equality between France and Germany. France had stopped considering itself the leading power in continental Europe. President Giscard d'Estaing agreed with this vision though, at the same time, he realized that the policy of détente would eventually reopen the German question.[8] Giscard was therefore in a complex situation. On the one hand, he supported the policy of détente in order to strengthen the French position in European policy; on the other, he wanted to avoid German unification, at least in the short or medium term.

So how did the French government and officials try to cope with the German question in this new context? Three approaches can be identified between 1969 and 1979: a first approach was a strengthening of European integration in the framework of the EEC; a second approach tried to bind Germany bilaterally with France; and a third aimed at strengthening the French economy along the line of the German economic model.

Three Approaches to the German Question in the 1970s

The European Integration Approach

From a French perspective, European integration since the 1950s was closely connected to the German question. When Robert Schuman proposed a supranational community for the organization of the coal and steel markets in May 1950, his primary objective was to integrate the emerging German coal and steel industry in order to enhance French security. The German armament industry was now under European control. The same pattern played a role for the Common Market founded in 1958 in the framework of the European Economic Community.

This argument—integrating West Germany into supranational European organizations—also played a major role in French debates on the German question during the 1970s. Already under the presidency of Charles de Gaulle, Georges Pompidou (then prime minister) had advanced new approaches to the integration of Europe.[9] French initiatives for the deepening and widening of the EEC, however, were ruled out as long as de Gaulle was in power. After his election in June 1969, Georges Pompidou immediately made clear that he was about to change French policy toward European integration. A few weeks later, in December, he took the initiative at the meeting of the heads of states and governments in The Hague in order to relaunch European integration.

The motives of the French president for his new European policy are still being debated. Some scholars stress the economic motives. Pompidou, the argument goes, wanted to foster European economic integration because, in his eyes, this was a precondition for the economic reform and recovery of France.[10] Another interpretation stresses the political aspects of Pompidou's initiative.[11] Seen from this angle, the new French president wanted to overcome the political isolation of France within the EEC, which had resulted from de Gaulle's European policies in the second half of the 1960s.[12] With Pompidou's European initiative, France regained its freedom of action in Europe.

A last interpretation, however, refers to the role of the German question in two ways. The first side of the argument has been formulated by Schmidt in his memoirs. Schmidt argued that Pompidou took the initiative to integrate Britain into the EEC in order to counterbalance the growing German economic and political power within the EEC.[13] It was also stressed by Brandt in his speech in The Hague, when he argued that the integration of the FRG into the EEC is in the national interests of all other members: "Whoever is concerned that the economic weight of the FRG might work against the internal balance of the Community," Brandt declared, "should be in favor of enlargement."[14]

Yet although this argument seems to have played a role in German perceptions of French policy in the late 1960s, there is no empirical evidence in the files of the French administration that it effectively influenced Pompidou's thinking—hence the second side of the argument. In December 1970 Pompidou declared in a conversation with the French journalist Pierre Viansson-Ponté, "Europe must be used to bind Germany irreversibly."[15] One year later, he mentioned the same idea in a conversation with President Richard Nixon: "Europe must be unified so as to deal effectively with the East. It is above all necessary with regard to Germany which, I believe, is now firmly anchored to the West, but whose evolution is always unpredictable. It is clear that eventually its reunification can be granted only by the Soviet Union. Will Germany one day give its priority to this project?"[16] In a conversation with the British Prime Minister Edward Heath on 21 May 1973, Pompidou reaffirmed his confidence in Brandt but still followed the same line of reasoning: "We have time, but the [German] question will be brought up one day or another. It is a supplementary reason to try and move the Community forward, even though all ties are broken when the essential is at stake: no legal commitment can prevent political upheaval."[17] These statements show that the German question still played an important role for Pompidou and that the EEC was considered as a tool to solve it. The EEC offered a framework that kept the FRG in the West while preventing uncontrolled German reunification or German neutralism.

Pompidou's arguments relate to the geopolitical dimension: German Ostpolitik was, in his view, about to change the position of the Bonn government in the international system. There was, however, also an economic aspect. From a French point of view the EEC—and the CAP in particular—had always been an instrument to counterbalance the industrial power of Western Germany. The FRG had accepted paying by far the largest share in financing the CAP whereas France took the greatest advantage of this policy. This argument had played a role for Pompidou, hence his demand for a completion of the EEC, which was first and foremost geared toward establishing a final mode for financing the CAP.

In the French public debate this argument seemed all the more important because there was, in the French perception, a strong tendency in Germany to free itself of its European commitments. The media coverage of European integration in West Germany, in particular that of the influential news magazine *Der Spiegel*, aroused suspicion in Paris concerning the German support for European integration. In the second half of 1973 *Der Spiegel* published a series of articles criticizing German payments for the EEC and the CAP in particular. The parliamentary secretary of state in the West German Ministry of Foreign Affairs, Hans Apel, was quoted: "We must finally behave as a normal European country—after all, the others also defend their interests."[18] In late 1969 the journalist Pierre Drouin had already published an article entitled "L'épouvantail allemand" (the German scarecrow) in *Le Monde*. Drouin mainly focused on the economic development of Germany, which was, in his eyes, about to take the leadership in Europe again and compared this with the German aggression during the wars: "What we are afraid of is not so much U.S. investments as the glaring health of our neighbor across the Rhine. Is the German economic machine about to achieve what weapons had not accomplished? Since 'the flag always follows the goods,' will German might dominate continental Europe?"[19] This was a frequently used argument in the French public debate at the time: the German economic strength was interpreted as a substitute for military strength combined with the idea that West Germany would again try to submit Europe under German leadership. Even though in Drouin's opinion this was first of all a French problem, it could only be solved through a European solution: "By strengthening ties among the Six and by enlarging the circle so that German influence might be offset by that of others, the French economy, in effect, will be able to stimulate its energies."[20] Again, the integration of Europe was seen as a response to the German question—first of all by preventing Germany from taking up the leadership in Western Europe.

When Valéry Giscard d'Estaing succeeded Pompidou in 1974, European integration still played a major role in French foreign policy. Giscard developed a double approach to the EEC. In contrast to de Gaulle and in line with Pompidou, the French administration on the one hand was cooperative in the framework of the EEC. This was due first of all to the economic benefit the country took from the CAP but also to the existence of a regional policy project. Giscard was the first French president to accept direct elections to the European Parliament; in close cooperation with Helmut

Schmidt he initiated the European Council and gave the impetus for the European monetary system. On the other hand, the French government under Giscard still did not favor the supranational approach. The establishment of the European Council reinforced the role of the governments and the foundation of the European monetary system outside the EEC as well as the strengthening of the European Parliament went along with a weakening of the European Commission, which stopped being the most influential European institution. The Quai d'Orsay officials therefore spoke of a two-pillar strategy toward European integration.[21]

In Giscard's perception it was not the EEC but the nation-states that played the decisive role concerning the German question. Even though Giscard developed an excellent relationship with Schmidt and was anything but anti-German, he was anxious to maintain French political interests in Europe. In reaction to German Ostpolitik, Giscard frequently pleaded for a close Franco-Soviet cooperation. "An independent Europe is in the interest of the Soviet Union," he explained to Leonid Brezhnev on 21 June 1977, "because it binds the FRG with countries of comparable size. Otherwise the FRG would intensify its relationship with the United States also in the military sector which would threaten the peace in Europe."[22] This thought was very similar to what Pompidou had said to Edward Heath in May 1973: a strong European alliance was needed to control Germany and to keep the international postwar system in Europe. The German question also explained Giscard d'Estaing's engagement for the European monetary system. While European nations had established the snake in order to cope with the consequences of the breakdown of the Bretton Woods monetary system, Paris quickly realized that its monetary policy was now dependent on the deutschmark instead of the dollar. In January 1974 the French franc had to be withdrawn from the "snake" because of the constant revaluation of the deutschmark. After it returned in July 1975, it became a victim of large-scale speculative attacks from monetary markets in January 1976; two months later the French government had to accept a 3 percent devaluation. What monetary experts had already foreseen in the late 1960s now became apparent: the FRG was the monetary hegemon in Western Europe.[23]

So it came as no surprise that France's new approach to European integration concentrated on the monetary dimension. The German question—in this particular case the problem of how to assuage German monetary dominance in Europe—was a key motive behind European monetary integration in the 1970s.[24] On 18 March 1976 the minister of economic affairs and finance, Jean-Pierre Fourcade, presented his proposals for a reform of the "Snake" System, which had turned into a deutschmark bloc. Other proposals for European monetary integration were made, among others, by the Dutch Wim Duisenberg and the Belgian Gaston Geens. But the initiatives failed mainly because of two reasons. First, the Rambouillet meeting, the first world economic and monetary summit gathering the leaders of the six most industrialized countries under French leadership, received priority attention. Second, the West German government at this time showed no interest in European monetary integration. Yet the debate went on within the framework of the influential Committee of Governors of the European Central Banks.[25] The decisive impetus came from Giscard d'Estaing and Schmidt. The French motives were openly discussed: "Why do I speak a lot about Federal Germany, and why it is my objective that France should have a comparable economic power? Because it would not be good if Europe were dominated by a single country. Right now, if there were only one [economic] power, it would be Germany. But we can't have a confederation that would be dominated by one country only. It would break up."[26] From a French perspective, the European monetary system was not only an instrument to counter German hegemony in monetary questions, but also a first step toward the establishment of a European currency on a global level. The key instrument was the establishment of the European currency unit, a currency basket based on the weighted value of the currencies of the member states. Even if it turned out as a failure in the 1980s, the European currency unit was meant to respond to the German question on the economic level by replacing the deutschmark as the key currency in Europe and as the point of reference for all other currencies.

All in all, the acceleration of European construction was an important part of the French answer to the German question in the 1970s. The meaning of European integration, however, changed throughout that period. In Pompidou's perspective, the German question was first of all a geopolitical problem. This was due to the fact that he was confronted with the emergence of the new German Ostpolitik; as a consequence, he had accepted the widening and deepening of the EEC even though he remained skeptical concerning supranationality. But for Valéry Giscard d'Estaing, the economic and monetary hegemony of Germany was the principal problem. He, too, tried to solve the problem by integrating West Germany into a European framework; but in contrast to Pompidou and in the tradition of de Gaulle, he advocated a European confederation instead of supranational integration. The European monetary system was constructed outside the legal framework of the EEC and was politically based on the close cooperation of national governments and central banks.

The Bilateral Approach

The EEC solution for the German question had proved to be highly efficient since the early 1950s, but there were, from a French point of view, some disadvantages. While supranationality was an instrument to bind the FRG politically, France, too, was obliged to delegate parts of its national sovereignty to an independent organization. De Gaulle had always rejected European supranational integration, advocating intergovernmental cooperation instead. Bilateral cooperation had been the principal motive behind the Elysée Treaty between France and Germany, but an important segment of the German political and economic elite of the 1960s was not interested in an exclusive Franco-German cooperation, mainly for two reasons. First, Franco-German bilateralism in Germany was considered a menace for German-American relations; the FRG relied on American nuclear protection and a Franco-German defense alliance was no real alternative to the North Atlantic Treaty Organization (NATO). Second, Franco-German bilateralism was not considered an alternative but rather a threat for the supranational EEC, for both political and economic reasons. The French efforts to bind the FRG bilaterally therefore depended on the German willingness for cooperation.

There were different levels of bilateral relations. The personal relationship between the French president and the German chancellor was especially important. De Gaulle and Adenauer had staged their political friendship and understanding in highly symbolical encounters.[27] Even though Georges Pompidou did not follow up on this practice of Franco-German relations, he put emphasis on a personal relationship with Chancellor Brandt: "I give much importance to relations between France and the FRG and in particular to my personal relations with the chancellor. I see only advantages in direct and confidential exchanges of views."[28] Recent research has shown that the personal relationship between Pompidou and Brandt was better than generally assumed by contemporaries. They frequently met and openly discussed matters of common interest.[29] Even though they were very different personalities, Brandt and Pompidou trusted one another. Both were anxious to reanimate the Elysée Treaty. As Sylvain Schirmann puts it, "When one re-reads the correspondence and the minutes of conversations between [Brandt and Pompidou], one sees that taboo subjects are rare. Each letter is an opportunity for a tour d'horizon of international questions, a reminder of one's own position, and sometimes a presentation of the modalities of a forthcoming political action. The quality of exchanged information is striking. So is the frankness of the exchanges."[30]

Things changed, however, when Schmidt and Giscard both took office in 1974. They had known each other quite well for a couple of years. They were both members of Jean Monnet's Action Committee for the United States of Europe.[31] Both had been ministers of finance of their respective countries, sharing interest and expertise in monetary questions. Whereas Brandt and Pompidou were dependent on interpreters, Schmidt and Giscard had their conversations in English and therefore developed a more personal relationship.[32]

There can be no doubt that Schmidt and Giscard both trusted one another even though they were fully aware of their disagreements. Hence, Schmidt knew that Giscard was skeptical concerning German reunification whereas he, Schmidt, was obliged to stand for it, at least formally. Yet there were at least three levels of understanding between the two leaders. First, both Schmidt and Giscard frequently underlined the significance of personal trust. As Giscard said in retrospect, "I am fully aware that diplomats do not like non rational notions such as trust. . . . But trust exists. . . . Having known Helmut Schmidt for several years, having gone together with him through very strong monetary turbulences, I had total trust in him."[33] Second, Schmidt and Giscard shared the same view on the economic and political problems of the mid-1970s—and their solution: "the need for a more stable international structure for consultation, the need for improvements of the snake . . . , and finally, the need for taking measures to support economic activity."[34] And, finally, in contrast to Brandt and Pompidou, Schmidt and Giscard were prone to displaying their good relationship in public.

Franco-German relations on the ministerial level were much less smooth, however. Since the early 1970s the economic directorate of the Ministry of Foreign Affairs in Paris was wary of the new role of the FRG. In a memorandum drafted for Giscard in preparation for the Franco-German talks in Hamburg on 5 and 6 July 1976, the directorate expressed its conviction that West Germany would no longer accept the limitations that were put on its international status after World War II: "[Our] previous notes have highlighted the increasing German power and its political repercussions. This German power has not been checked, quite on the contrary." The memorandum noted that the West German federal government now openly challenged the financing of the CAP. Germany had become more active in Africa and increased its development aid significantly in order to gain more influence on the continent. West German self-confidence seemed to have increased as a result of West Germany's membership in the United Nations Security Council. "In spite of the quasi-automatic character of this designation, the press gave it a considerable profile. . . . The FRG now feels it has the wherewithal to pursue on the international scene a role that reflects its power and to reach out to the Third World."[35] This concerned perception of Germany as a resurgent power was not shared by Giscard, who later declared, "In contrast to the Quai d'Orsay . . . I was never preoccupied by the rise or the growing role of Germany"[36] Giscard was ready to accept dealing with the FRG on equal terms. The FRG took the lead in economic and monetary affairs, but France was predominant on the political and military sector. Together with the personal factor, this equilibrium was the basis of political bilateralism between France and Western Germany during the Giscard years.

Since the middle of the 1950s there was also close cooperation between the administrations and civil societies of both countries. Some scholars even argue that the effective functioning of the Elysée Treaty would not have been possible without the civil societies.[37] Partly as a result of the existing cooperation at the political level and partly on their own initiative, the business associations in both countries—the National Council of French Employers (Conseil national du patronat français; CNPF) and the Federation of German Industries (Bundesverband der Deutschen Industrie; BDI)—relaunched their cooperation in October 1970 in the wake of The Hague summit, achieving immediate results.[38] To be sure, there were sectors where the French wish for close cooperation with the German economy had its limits, for instance in space industries. Whereas the German industry in this sector was interested in fundamental research and sought close relations with the leading U.S. industry, French enterprises supported research in satellite-based communication in order to facilitate communication among the francophone countries.[39] But in spite of these limits, the spirit of cooperation prevailed in both countries. Bilateral cooperation was therefore another approach for France in solving the German question as it would bind and control its neighbor to the east. In contrast to the supranational framework of the EEC however, there was no instrument for the French government to force Germany into cooperation.

Strengthening the French Economy Approach

Besides the EEC and the bilateral approach to the German problem in the 1970s, a third, related approach was pursued: strengthening the French economy, in particular in fields in which it was inferior to its German counterpart—in other words, industry and services. When Pompidou took office, one of his key aims was to modernize France by reducing subsidies, giving incentives for private investment and the merging of enterprises of strategic value.[40] In his inaugural address, he declared his intention to make France one of the leading industrial nations.[41] This, as mentioned above, was also an important argument for the enlargement and deepening of the EEC.[42] The French economy, in his view, should be exposed to the competition of the European, and, in particular, the German, economy. But for Pompidou, the modernization of the French economy was not an end in itself. The French elite were well aware of the fact that Franco-German relations had profoundly changed since the 1960s, first of all because of the economic success of Germany. The German decision in May 1971 to float the deutschmark, a decision that was not coordinated with the European partners, was a shock for the French president.[43] It became a symbol of the growing German self-assertiveness and of a new nationalism based on economic strength, as illustrated by press coverage and reports from the economic directorate in the French Ministry of Foreign Affairs quoted above. Economic recovery was the answer: only if France were able to keep up with German industry would it be able to control its neighbor to the east in a bilateral or multilateral framework.

Pompidou's efforts, however, were affected by the world economic crisis of the early 1970s.[44] When Giscard succeeded Pompidou in 1974, the situation was the same. After Jacques Chirac's resignation as prime minister in summer 1976, the minister of trade, Raymond Barre, replaced him. He was a trained economist advocating an anti-inflationist policy. This was not in line with the traditional French economic model, which combined the search for high employment and political control over monetary policy, as opposed to the German model and its key objective of monetary stability.[45] Only if France was able to match German stability would it be able to influence German decisions in the bilateral and European framework.[46] This was all the more important because the U.S. dollar, up to this point the leading world currency, was now weakened; a strong Franco-German alliance in monetary questions could increase European influence in this domain. The French president justified his internally contested economic program in the German weekly magazine *Der Spiegel*: "I think it would not be a good thing for Europe if one economic power were clearly dominant. The nature of the confederal system that we want to build requires that we have relations among partners with roughly equal power."[47] Economic recovery and reorientation toward monetary and budgetary stability was therefore an instrument to reestablish an economic and political equilibrium in Western Europe and to avoid German economic hegemony.

Conclusion

In the late 1960s and in the decade of the 1970s, the German problem from a French perspective was not limited to the consequences of Ostpolitik. German economic superiority and leadership in Western Europe were central. From the late 1960s onward the FRG became in French perception the leading industrial power of Western Europe. This German economic rise mirrored the relative economic decline of the United States. The U.S. dollar was, at least in Western Europe, challenged by the deutschmark. Seen from Paris, these fundamental changes caused serious problems because French monetary and economic policies depended more and more on German decisions. The Bundesbank in particular became an important actor in European and French monetary policy.

The French government had to find a new strategy to cope with these developments. As we have seen, three major approaches can be identified for the period between 1969 and 1979. The first could be called the community approach. Even though it had been discussed since the early 1950s, it had lost influence during the de Gaulle era. The European Coal and Steel Community had been devised to bind and control the leading German industry, and the Common Market obliged Germany to pay a large part of French agricultural subsidies. The community approach, however, had a major disadvantage that made it controversial in Paris: France was obliged to delegate important parts of its national sovereignty to a supranational European institution.

Hence a second instrument to cope with the German problem: the bilateral approach. Launched in the mid-1950s, bilateral political cooperation had culminated in the Elysée Treaty. After de Gaulle's departure from power, Pompidou had established a close political relationship with Brandt. For Schmidt and Giscard d'Estaing, things were easier because of their close personal relationship and their mutual trust. Cooperation at the highest political level was supplemented by close contacts between French and German economic actors. The bilateral approach to the German question from a French point of view had the advantage of binding Germany without restricting French national sovereignty—yet it rested on German willingness for cooperation, which was a given on the political level but less so in the economic sector.

Both approaches played an important role in French debates on policy toward Germany during the 1970s. The French Ministry of Foreign Affairs spoke in the middle of the 1970s of a two pillar concept, combining the community and the intergovernmental approaches.[48] Both approaches, however, rested on a precondition: French economic recovery, which was therefore also a way to deal with the German problem. Both Pompidou and Giscard insisted on the economic modernization of

France in order not to let Germany take the leadership in economic and monetary affairs in Western Europe. The French perception of Germany as a potentially hegemonic power, in particular in the economic sector, was therefore an important element of French policy in the 1970s.

The evolution of the international economic and monetary system starting in the late 1960s led to a redefinition of Franco-German relations. The origins of this reorientation can be found in the economic decline of the United States–led Bretton Woods monetary system and the rise of a new monetary organization in Europe under German leadership. The main objective of French policy in this context was to restore an economic and through this a political balance between the two states. This was the main driving force behind the establishment of the European monetary system in the late 1970s, much as it had been with the European Coal and Steel Community in the early 1950s when the German dominant position in the coal and steel sector had been a key motivation for the French government to embark on supranational integration.[49] This again shows another important factor that had shaped the international system in the second half of the twentieth century: the rise of economic power as a component of Great Power politics. Since World War II political power was no longer defined only in military and political categories, but also in economic ones, which led in the 1970s to a close interaction between the political and the economic aspects of the German question.

Guido Thiemeyer holds the chair for contemporary history at the Heinrich-Heine-Universität Düsseldorf. From 2010 to 2013 he was adjunct professor at the Université de Cergy-Pontoise. His main research interest refers to European integration history in the nineteenth and twentieth centuries and Franco-German relations in particular. His most recent publications are "European Liberal Parties and the Challenge of Populism," in *Populism, Populists and the Crisis of Political Parties: A Comparison of Italy, Austria, and Germany 1990–2015* (edited by G. Pallaver, M. Gehler, and M. Cau, 2018) and *Der Rhein / Le Rhin. Eine politische Landschaft zwischen Deutschland und Frankreich 1815 bis heute / Un espace partagé entre la France et l'Allemagne* (edited with Hélène Miard-Delacroix, 2018).

Notes

1. See, e.g., Soutou, "L'anneau et les deux triangles."
2. Miard-Delacroix, *Deutsch-französische Geschichte.*
3. De Gaulle–Nixon meeting, 1 Mar. 1969, DDF 1969, vol. 1, 410.
4. The German administration of the foreign office was well aware of this aspect. Note on the Franco-German relations at the beginning of 1969 (PA/AA, B24 82.00.0, box 629 "Frankreich 1966–1969").
5. See, e.g., his remarks in a conversation with Edward Heath (first Pompidou–Heath meeting, 21 May 1973, printed in Roussel, *Georges Pompidou 1911–1974*, 652–656; Hiepel, *Willy Brandt und Georges Pompidou*).
6. Miard-Delacroix, *Deutsch-französische Geschichte*, 55.

7. Aron, "L'Allemagne d'aujourd'hui," 1411. On the perception of Germany in the French press, *Le Monde* in particular, see Schmitz, *Zwischen Mythos*.

8. Soutou, "L'anneau et les deux triangles"; Soutou, "Staatspräsident Valéry Giscard d'Estaing," 373.

9. Schirmann, "Georges Pompidou et l'Allemagne," 12.

10. This argument is stressed by Hiepel, *Willy Brandt und Georges Pompidou*, 42.

11. Bitsch, "Le Sommet de La Haye." See also Roussel, *Georges Pompidou 1911–1974*, 309–32.

12. Warlouzet, *Le choix de la CEE*; Bajon, *Europapolitik "am Abgrund."*

13. Schmidt, *Menschen und Mächte*, vol. 2, 300.

14. Willy Brandt, Declaration at the summit meeting of Heads of State or Government of the European Economic Community in The Hague, 1–2 Dec. 1969 (Wilkens, *Wir sind auf dem richtigen Weg*, 453).

15. Quoted in Fontaine, *Un seul lit pour deux rêves*, 248.

16. Pompidou–Nixon meeting, 13 Dec. 1971 (quoted in Roussel, *Georges Pompidou 1911–1974*, 469).

17. First Pompidou–Heath meeting, 21 May 1973 (quoted in ibid., 653).

18. "Dusselige Deutsche," *Der Spiegel* 53, 33.

19. Drouin, "L'épouvantail allemand."

20. Ibid.

21. Meeting of the heads of the Political Divisions of the West German and the French Foreign Ministry, 20 Feb. 1979, AMAE, Europe, Allemagne, Rencontres franco-allemands, box 4006.

22. Giscard d'Estaing–Leonid Brezhnev meeting, 21 Jun. 1977 (quoted in Soutou, "Staatspräsident Valéry Giscard d'Estaing," 380).

23. Sutton, *France and the Construction of Europe 1944–2007*, 221.

24. For a detailed analysis, see Mourlon-Druol, *A Europe Made of Money*.

25. James, *Making the European Monetary Union*, 146–80.

26. Valéry Giscard d'Estaing in French TV "Questionnaire" TF1, 16 Oct. 1978 (quoted in Weinachter, *Valéry Giscard d'Estaing*, 79). See also Weinachter, "Valéry Giscard d'Estaing."

27. Thiemeyer, "Eine symbolische Inszenierung."

28. Note by President Giscard d'Estaing, 28 Nov. 1969 (quoted in Schirmann and Mohamed-Gaillard, *Georges Pompidou et l'Allemagne*, 41).

29. Hiepel, *Willy Brandt und Georges Pompidou*.

30. Schirmann and Mohamed-Gaillard, *Georges Pompidou et l'Allemagne*, 39.

31. Thiemeyer, "Helmut Schmidt."

32. Waechter, *Helmut Schmidt und Valéry Giscard d'Estaing*, 81.

33. Witness of Valéry Giscard d'Estaing (Berstein and Sirinelli, *Les années Giscard*, 101–2).

34. Mourlon-Druol, *A Europe Made of Money*, 70.

35. Note "La RFA et sa politique extérieure au début de 1977" for the Franco-German summit, 3–4 Feb. 1977, AMAE, Europe 1976–80, Communautés européennes, box 4001.

36. Comments by Valéry Giscard d'Estaing (Berstein and Sirinelli, *Les années Giscard*, 102–3).

37. See for this argument, inter alia, Defrance and Pfeil, *Deutsch-französische*, 160–77.

38. Note by the Economic Division on the Franco-German cooperation, 14 Jan. 1971, AMAE, Europe, Allemagne, box 3000.

39. Note by the cultural division on the Franco-German cooperation in space industries, 20 Jan. 1971, AMAE, Europe, Allemagne, box 3000; Defrance and Pfeil, *La construction d'un espace*.

40. Berstein and Milza, *Histoire de la France*, 158–60.

41. Esambert, *Pompidou*, 21.

42. Hiepel, *Willy Brandt und Georges Pompidou*.

43. Schirmann and Mohamed-Gaillard, *Georges Pompidou*, 29.

44. Frank, "Les problèmes monétaires," 16.

45. On economic models see, Müller-Armack, "Stil und Ordnung."

46. Aron, "De Rueff à Barre," 118.

47. Valéry Giscard d'Estaing, *Der Spiegel* interview, 18 Dec. 1978 (quoted in Weinachter, *Valéry Giscard d'Estaing*, 79).

48. Note "La RFA et sa politique extérieure au début de 1977" for the Franco-German summit, 3–4 Feb. 1977, AMAE, Europe 1976–80, Communautés européennes, box 4001.
49. See, for this aspect, Thiemeyer, "Supranationalität als Novum."

Bibliography

Aron, R. 1974. "L'Allemagne d'aujourd'hui et son chancelier." *Le Figaro*, 27 Sept. 1974. Reprinted in R. Aron. 1997. *Les articles de politique internationale dans Le Figaro de 1949 à 1977. Les crises (février 1965 à avril 1977)*, Vol. 3. Paris: Editions de Fallois.

———. 2005. "De Rueff à Barre." In *De Giscard à Mitterrand 1977–1983*, edited by R. Aron, 117–123. Paris: Editions de Fallois.

Bajon, P. 2012. *Europapolitik "am Abgrund." Die Krise des "leeren Stuhls" 1965–66*. Stuttgart, Germany: Steiner.

Berstein, S., and P. Milza, eds. 1992. *Histoire de la France au XXe siècle 1958–1974*. Vol. 4. Brussels, Belgium: Complexe.

Berstein, S., and J.-F. Sirinelli. 2006. *Les années Giscard. Valéry Giscard d'Estaing et l'Europe 1974–1981*. Paris: Colin.

Bitsch, M.-T. 2003. "Le Sommet de La Haye. L'initiative française, ses finalités et ses limites." *Journal of European Integration History* 9: 83–99.

Defrance, C., and U. Pfeil. 2011. *Deutsch-französische Geschichte 1945–1963*. Darmstadt, Germany: Wissenschaftliche Buchgesellschaft.

———, eds. 2012. *La construction d'un espace scientifique commun? La France, la RFA et l'Europe après le "choc du Spoutnik."* Brussels, Belgium: Peter Lang.

Drouin, P. "L'épouvantail allemand." *Le Monde*, 20 Nov. 1969.

Esambert, B. 1994. *Pompidou. Capitaine d'industries*. Paris: Odile Jacob.

Fontaine, A. 1981. *Un seul lit pour deux rêves. Histoire de la détente 1962–1981*. Paris: Fayard.

Frank, R. 2006. "Les problèmes monétaires et la création du SME." In Berstein and Sirinelli, *Les années Giscard*, 18–19.

Hiepel, C. 2012. *Willy Brandt und Georges Pompidou. Deutsch-französische Europapolitik zwischen Aufbruch und Krise*. Munich, Germany: Oldenbourg.

James, H. 2012. *Making the European Monetary Union: The Role of the Committee of Central Bank Governors and the Origins of the European Central Bank*. Cambridge: Harvard University Press.

Miard-Delacroix, H. 2011. *Deutsch-französische Geschichte. 1963 bis in die Gegenwart*. Darmstadt, Germany: Wissenschaftliche Buchgesellschaft.

Mourlon-Druol, E. 2012. *A Europe Made of Money: The Emergence of the European Monetary System*. Ithaca, NY: Cornell University Press.

Müller-Armack, A. 1966. "Stil und Ordnung der Sozialen Marktwirtschaft." In *Wirtschaftsordnung und Wirtschaftspolitik. Studien und Konzepte zur sozialen Marktwirtschaft und zur Europäischen Integration*, edited by A. Müller-Armack, 231–42. Freiburg, Germany: Rombach.

Roussel, E. 1994. *Georges Pompidou 1911–1974*. Paris: Lattès.

Schirmann, S. 2012. "Georges Pompidou et l'Allemagne." In Schirmann and Mohamed-Gaillard, *Georges Pompidou et l'Allemagne*, 11–37.

Schirmann, S., and S. Mohamed-Gaillard, eds. 2012. *Georges Pompidou et l'Allemagne*. Brussels, Belgium: Peter Lang.

Schmidt, H. 1990. *Menschen und Mächte*, Vol. 2: *Die Deutschen und ihre Nachbarn*. Munich, Germany: Beck.

Schmitz, C. M. 1990. *Zwischen Mythos und Aufklärung. Deutschland in der außenpolitischen Berichterstattung der Zeitung "Le Monde" 1963 bis 1983*, Frankfurt, Germany: Peter Lang.

Soutou, G.-H. 2006. "L'anneau et les deux triangles. Les rapports franco-allemands dans la politique européenne et mondiale de 1974–1981." In Berstein and Sirinelli, *Les années Giscard*, 45–80.

———. 2008. "Staatspräsident Valéry Giscard d'Estaing und die deutsche Frage." In *Geschichtswissenschaft und Zeiterkenntnis. Von der Aufklärung bis zur Gegenwart*, edited by K. Hildebrand, 373–82. Munich, Germany: Oldenbourg.

Sutton, M. 2007. *France and the Construction of Europe 1944–2007. The Geopolitical Imperative*. New York, Oxford: Berghahn Books.

Thiemeyer, G. 1998. "Supranationalität als Novum in der Geschichte der internationalen Politik der fünfziger Jahre." *Journal of European Integration History* 4, no. 2: 5–21.

———. 2011. "Helmut Schmidt, le Comité d'action pour les Etats-Unis d'Europe et l'intégration monétaire européenne." In *Une dynamique européenne. Le Comité d'action pour les Etats-Unis d'Europe*, edited by Fondation Jean Monnet pour l'Europe, 117–30. Paris: Economica.

———. 2012. "Eine symbolische Inszenierung. Die bilaterale Freundschaft im Rahmen des Elysée-Vertrages." *Dokumente* 4: 58–62.

Waechter, M. 2011. *Helmut Schmidt und Valéry Giscard d'Estaing. Auf der Suche nach Stabilität in der Krise der 70er Jahre*, Bremen, Germany: Ed. Temmen.

Warlouzet, L. 2011. *Le choix de la CEE par la France. L'Europe économique en débat de Mendès France à de Gaulle 1955–1969*. Paris: Comité pour l'histoire économique et financière de la France.

Weinachter, M. 2004. *Valéry Giscard d'Estaing et l'Allemagne. Le double rêve inachevé*. Paris: Harmattan.

———. 2011. "Valéry Giscard d'Estaing, l'Europe et l'Allemagne. Visions et conceptions de la construction européenne." In *Quelles architectures pour quelle Europe? Des projets d'une Europe unie à l'Union européenne 1945–1992*, edited by S. Schirmann, 229–50. Brussels, Belgium: Peter Lang.

Wilkens, A., ed. 2010. *Wir sind auf dem richtigen Weg. Willy Brandt und die europäische Einigung*. Bonn, Germany: Dietz.

Part V
The End Game

CHAPTER 10

The French "Obsession" with the German Question

Willy Brandt, François Mitterrand, the German Question, and German Unification, 1981–1990

Bernd Rother

Why do Willy Brandt's talks with François Mitterrand about the German question during the 1980s matter? Brandt, who was the chairman of the Social Democratic Party (SPD) of Germany from 1964 until 1987, was at that time no more than a party leader—a party that, in addition, was in power only until 1982. What is more, Brandt and his political line were not unchallenged in his own party; and in the late 1970s and the early 1980s opinion polls showed him to be at the lowest level ever of popular appreciation, ranking not far from Franz Josef Strauß, who had long been the most controversial West German politician.[1] Granted, he was also president of the Socialist International, but this organization depended more on him than the reverse. All in all, Brandt was far from directly exercising political power. His moral power as founder of the Ostpolitik, Nobel Peace Prize laureate, proven anti-Fascist, and anti-communist did not balance this deficit. Nevertheless, even after being elected as French president, Mitterrand met Brandt on a regular basis for political discussions, and this did not end when Brandt resigned as party chairman. Mitterrand's cultivation of Brandt needs to be explained, especially because both had to go a rather long way until they developed some kind of mutual respect.

In the first years after the refounding of the French Socialist Party and its take-over by Mitterrand in 1971, relations with the SPD were strained. The SPD was suspicious of Mitterrand's Union of the Left with the communists, which the German

Right labeled a popular front. The Parti Socialiste (PS) for its part was not amused that the Social Democrats held regular meetings with the Gaullist party, the Union des démocrates pour la République.[2] Brandt and Mitterrand met for the first time in 1972. Both had some features in common, but they also had important differences. As Hélène Miard-Delacroix rightly notes, Brandt as well as Mitterrand modernized their parties, were for a long time the undisputed party leader (and today are seen as two of the most important twentieth-century political leaders), possessed charisma, but at the same time had a pragmatic understanding of how to exercise power.[3] Brandt was quite Francophile; Mitterrand kept romantic sentiments for Germany.

On the other hand, there were obvious differences: Brandt had a proletarian family background; Mitterrand's family belonged to the petite bourgeoisie. Brandt started as Social Democrat, switched in 1931 to the radical Left, and rejoined the SPD in 1944. He had an undoubted record of anti-Fascism (and also of anti-communism), had accumulated an impressive array of international experiences since the 1930s, was multilingual, and despite his political pragmatism he was recognized as a political leader with high moral standards, best demonstrated by his kneeling down in Warsaw 1970 and his resignation in 1974. Most of this was quite different from Mitterrand who could be described as a liberal non-Marxist socialist.

Clearly, Mitterrand was keen to benefit from Brandt's experience and from his insider's knowledge, not only with regard to politics in Germany but also with a view to Brandt's contacts to the communist leaders in Eastern Europe and the Soviet Union. Brandt, on the other hand, could receive first-hand information and analyses from Mitterrand. Whereas Mitterrand during their numerous talks put himself in a receptive position, Brandt tried to convince Mitterrand of his political views or, if this was not possible, to prevent Mitterrand from publicly contradicting him. Brandt's enduring international prominence was clear even after he resigned as chancellor, and Mitterrand's proximity to Brandt, both as founder of the Ostpolitik and Nobel Peace Prize laureate, could serve to augment his stature nationally and internationally. But, like Mitterrand, Brandt never made public use of what the other had told him behind closed doors, except for some diplomatically molded press releases. Even in their memoirs published years later both men kept a polite tone. Fortunately for historians, Brandt did keep some notes containing his unadorned views on Mitterrand. But to read their exchanges as a master–disciple relation would miss the reality. Brandt also needed Mitterrand, if only to preserve the unity of the democratic socialist movement he presided over from 1976 onward.

From 1972 on meetings became regular, reflecting a complicated process of mutual rapprochement. Mitterrand's public reproaches against the so-called Berufsverbote (decree prohibiting members of extremist organizations from becoming civil servants or teachers that was introduced during Brandt's term as chancellor), and against the SPD's reformism did not contribute to a relaxed climate between both party presidents. Helmut Schmidt for his part added fuel to the fire by openly attacking Mitterrand's cooperation with the communists. Brandt, who as SPD chairman was under pressure from the Christian Democratic Union/Christian Social Union (CDU/CSU) to denounce the fact that his French friends sided with communists, tried to downplay the Union of the Left's importance, and tried to convince Mitterrand of the virtues of Social Democracy. Among SPD leaders, Brandt's strategy to strengthen the bonds with the PS was not an undisputed choice. Helmut Schmidt openly showed his preferences for Valéry Giscard d'Estaing, including carefully crafted statements during the 1974 French presidential election campaign. Mitterrand would never forget, as Brandt jotted down years later.[4] Still, in the second half of the 1970s the PS and the SPD as well as Brandt and Mitterrand started to get closer and succeeded in establishing a working relationship based on mutual respect more than on friendship.

Until 1981 these were normal transnational contacts between two parties and their leaders who shared a certain common ideological ground. No one would have asked why the chairmen of two important Socialist/Social Democratic Parties met. When Mitterrand was elected president of the Republic on 10 May 1981, the relation became asymmetric: it was a relation between a foreign party chairman who held no governmental office and the president of the Republic, who now represented his entire nation. At the same time the relation became even more intensive. Brandt was the one who, on 21 May 1981, spoke on behalf of the foreign guests who had been invited to participate in the inauguration of Mitterrand.[5] After another Brandt visit to the Elysée a German TV reporter remarked, "It is quite unusual to have the president of the Republic say goodbye to a party leader on the stairs of the Palace, just as well as it is unusual to have a guard of honor present at such an occasion."[6] Even if this constituted an exception, Mitterrand, now the powerful statesman, was the one who usually took the initiative to propose a meeting with Brandt, the man without formal power.

Hence, in May 1985, Mitterrand wrote to Brandt, "Dear friend, I just learned that you are currently staying in Paris. I would have been happy to meet you, [but] my schedule for today doesn't allow it. Could you come back soon (in June) to have the conversation I propose and for which I again would like to welcome you? Time goes by. One event follows the other. I would greatly profit from your advice and your experience."[7] And during the early months of 1990, when the German question caused a busy, tight agenda for all European leaders, Mitterrand again asked to meet with Brandt. Mitterrand was not the only foreign leader treating Brandt as if he were still in charge of governing Germany: on 10 November 1989 Mikhail Gorbachev voiced his concerns about the unstable situation in the German Democratic Republic (GDR, or East Germany) in telegrams to two West German political leaders. One of these, of course, went to Chancellor Helmut Kohl, and the other to Brandt, who at this time held neither an official nor a party position. But Mitterrand as well as Gorbachev still considered Brandt to be one of the most influential voices—and here this word "voice" should be taken literally—among German politicians.

The Euromissile Crisis, Peace Movement, and Neutralism

For the PS, the SPD was by far the most important international partner. The huge amount of documents on Germany stored at the PS archives proves this. Both parties knew that they had to find at least a modus vivendi. Mitterrand's 1983 economic U-turn (including a major financial adjustment program) made it easier to build bridges. But at the same time the gap between both parties and their most prominent figures widened over armament issues and relations with the East. The French non-communist left attacked the SPD on grounds of its alleged proximity to communist governments, its weakness vis-à-vis Soviet rearmament, and its aloofness from East European dissidents. The SPD responded that the French comrades were playing Reagan's play. Thus, Mitterrand's first presidential mandate coincided with a profound estrangement between the SPD and the PS over the North Atlantic Treaty Organization (NATO) double-track decision. In many ways, this was a dialogue of the deaf.[8] This issue was not directly linked with the German question but many who participated in the discussions were aware that it was important for the future of détente and thereby also for the possible evolution of the German question.

In their enthusiasm for the first socialist president of the Fifth French Republic and the first Popular Front–style government in Europe since the outbreak of the Cold War (except for Portugal in 1974–75), the German Left—and not only the Social Democrats—expected "comrade" Mitterrand to side with them in every political aspect. Of course, Mitterrand had announced he would fight for disarmament. But after NATO had adopted the double-track decision, Mitterrand had defined his position in a speech at the Assemblée Nationale on 20 December 1979: the Soviets had gained military superiority in Europe. He preferred a negotiated solution for this problem but his words made clear that a Western reaction would be necessary if the super-powers' talks were to fail.[9] Mitterrand repeated his concerns about the deployment of the Soviet SS 20 missiles in a book published in 1980 and in a TV interview in March 1981.[10] Accordingly, the 110 proposals the French PS made for the upcoming presidential election not only called for the Soviet Union to stop the deployment of the SS 20 missiles but also demanded the withdrawal of missiles already deployed. In exchange, NATO should abandon plans to deploy U.S. Pershing II missiles.[11] In sum, the PS's main concern was with the Soviet Union. By contrast, the SPD, including its chairman Willy Brandt, gave clear signs that it was unhappy with the double-track decision. Out of respect for Chancellor Helmut Schmidt and in order to save the social-liberal coalition, the party did not cross the Rubicon for the time being. But since 1979 it had become clearer and clearer that many German Social Democrats did not see a Soviet superiority and did not fear a Soviet threat. Ronald Reagan's election as president of the United States in November 1980 further fueled fears of Western rearmament and growing confrontation with the Soviet Union. The United States became the main target for the German Left.

Shortly after his election, the French president shocked his German admirers from the political Left who seemingly had overlooked his previous statements. In early July 1981, in a *Stern* magazine interview, he explained that the SS 20s and the Backfire bombers had destroyed the balance of power in Europe. The West, he argued, needed even more arms before negotiations were possible.[12] Even Schmidt, who of all people portrayed himself as having engineered the double-track decision, disagreed with Mitterrand. In an encounter three days after the publication of the interview he explained to Mitterrand that saying negotiations could only start after further arms build-up clearly transcended Schmidt's point of view.[13] The PS saw Schmidt's point and considered publishing a disclaimer arguing that to read Mitterrand's words like this would be an oversimplification, but in the end it decided to refrain from it because it could be misinterpreted.[14]

The next day Brandt met Mitterrand. The *Spiegel* reported that Mitterrand stuck to his bold position that first the West needed to reach the Soviet level of armaments as a prerequisite.[15] Among Brandt's own short (and unpublished) notes about what Mitterrand told him we find, "Pershing (fear) good for negotiations."[16] Mitterrand focused on Soviet concern of Pershing deployment to accelerate the negotiations. A strategy of fear: this was definitely not what Brandt had in mind.[17] He emphasized that Germany neither pursued neutralization nor had anti-American sentiments.

Only five weeks later Brandt and Mitterrand met for the third time in three months. In Nogaro in southwest France, the SPD leader tried to change the president's stance on the dual-track decision— in vain.[18] Yet Brandt did not give up. One month later, in September 1981, the next encounter with Mitterrand took place. This time the president proved to be more conciliatory. He admitted the existence of an overall strategic balance between the United States and the Soviet Union; this would change, though, and in 1985 the Soviets would reach superiority, followed by American superiority around 1992. He admitted that the Soviets could take the French missiles into account, but he refused that the French forces be actually included in the Geneva negotiations. He added that he wished that the Pershing deployment would prove unnecessary. Finally, Mitterrand promised to stop using the term "neutralism" to describe political trends in Germany.[19] These were signs of a possible understanding, but Mitterrand himself did not opt for caution with regard to his German comrades. Despite his promise not to interfere in the German electoral campaign that started after Kohl had replaced Schmidt as chancellor in October 1982, he openly sided with Helmut Kohl in his famous Bundestag speech in January 1983. Brandt was upset.

In 1983 relations between German and French socialists hit rock bottom. Behind closed doors Brandt told his associates that Mitterrand's defense and foreign policy was "totally Gaullist. De Gaulle was always of the view that the Americans should get out of Europe, but not necessarily out of Germany. Similarly Mitterrand takes the view that the Americans should station nuclear missiles in West Germany." And Brandt continued: "The type of thinking on defense and security matters of the French Socialists seems to be formed by what Mitterrand learned as a cabinet minister in the 1950s."[20] It is not quite clear what Brandt—who previously had admired de Gaulle's foreign policy and its independence from both superpowers—meant when he compared in such a derogatory way Mitterrand with the founder of the Fifth French Republic. Brandt may have had the impression that Mitterrand wanted Germany to serve as a launching base for U.S. missiles and as theatre for a limited nuclear conflict. This was exactly what Brandt tried to avoid under all circumstances.

But Brandt and Mitterrand knew that an enduring German-French conflict, be it between the SPD and the PS or between the two governments (and the SPD was hopeful to win the 1987 Bundestag election) would heavily damage the socialist movement as well as European unity. While unable to compromise on hard policy issues, they tried to understand, at least, their respective motives. History and geopolitics were the key factors both sides highlighted. In private talks Mitterrand told Brandt that he understood the stance of the SPD. In September 1981 he said to his guest that he perfectly grasped the special German situation.[21] In 1982 he repeated that, if he were in Brandt's place, he would probably think the same, but he now sat in another chair.[22] For Brandt, Mitterrand's privileged interlocutor among the German Social Democrats, this was barely more than lip service. When Kohl told him in late 1989 that Mitterrand had shown some kind of understanding for his policy once again saying "if I was German," Brandt smiled.[23]

Nevertheless, the Germans took notice that their French comrades tried to calm them down. Talking to Brandt, the PS's first secretary Lionel Jospin admitted that the French side must show more understanding with the German motives, because Germany had a different history and a different geographical situation.[24] But only two weeks after Jospin's mediation attempt, his comrade Jacques Huntzinger, a minor political figure nationally but, as international secretary of the PS, an important interlocutor for the SPD, added fuel to the flames. According to the *Spiegel* he reportedly said, "It may be that the Pershing II and Cruise missiles make little sense, but at least they help deepen the division of Germany and thus keep the German problem for at least 20 years at arm's length."[25] Even if we admit that the *Spiegel* might not be a reliable source, this quote was never denied and made its way in Germany as a perfect description of how the PS saw the situation.

The French seesaw with respect to Germany continued in another issue. Since 1982 PS and SPD security experts had discussed the possibility of extending the French nuclear umbrella to Germany and even to the whole of Western Europe, in addition to the NATO umbrella. Egon Bahr, Brandt's longtime key adviser on security issues, and Huntzinger were the main protagonists. With such a redefinition of the force de frappe's role the German Social Democrats would possibly be ready to accept the French missiles, and it could help to bring about what Brandt called the Europeanization of Europe—its emancipation from the hegemony of the superpowers· The idea was backed by Laurent Fabius and Jean-Pierre Chevènement, but it was rejected by Michel Rocard. But it had no chance of becoming reality because Mitterrand early on had made clear that he did not share it.[26]

Against this background it comes as little surprise that in September 1987 Brandt told Erich Honecker, "For us the French remain a big problem. They keep being suspicious of everything German that happens. Even his last talks with Mitterrand in June had confirmed this impression. Perhaps it might make sense that delegates from both sides discuss how to calm down the French."[27]

Reunification?

This remark, had Mitterrand been aware of it, would no doubt have confirmed his suspicions: Was this not another piece of evidence that the two German states came closer and closer—to the point of considering a joint initiative toward France? Five years earlier, Brandt himself had sensed that this might be the French reaction. In an article for the *Spiegel* published in February 1982, he wrote that when Germans use the argument of defending "national interests" U.S. newspapers react writing about "German nationalism," and French papers speculate about "German patriotism" that might be ready to work together with the Russians to bring about the feared reunification. And he warned his compatriots that efforts to preserve peace, détente, and disarmament did not become easier when they were amalgamated with the German question.[28] Brandt understood the French concerns. On the occasion of the tenth anniversary of Mitterrand's victory he wrote in an article that in the end was not published, "Certainly it was not always easy for the president to understand the neighbor on the other side of the Rhine. . . . Did not the German peace movement take a steep path towards an unrealistic pacifism?"[29]

On several occasions Mitterrand asked Brandt about a possible German reunification. In August 1981 it was the most important issue for Mitterrand. Brandt was taken by surprise and answered, "At the moment, this is only a French question—the Germans don't discuss it."[30] According to the *Akten zur Auswärtigen Politik* Mitterrand was in 1981 the only leader worldwide to mention German reunification in a conversation—apart from one other leader: Deng Xiaoping. Six years later, in June 1987, when Brandt once again came to the Elysée, nothing had changed in this regard. Mitterrand asked him about the most important political issues in Western Germany, but he did not wait for Brandt's answer, instead drawing up his own list: first reunification, followed by disarmament and East-West relations. Brandt's list differed totally: first environment, then unemployment, and third international security. According to Brandt, Mitterrand replied, "Did I really mean, he said, that ecological concerns and not the national question were our prime concern? That was typical of German *romantisme*."[31] Brandt's widow, Brigitte Seebacher, even suggests that Mitterrand year in and year out used to ask Brandt whether the Germans still kept reunification in mind. Her husband, she continues, was astonished by what he saw as a French lack of understanding for the German situation.[32] In a note jotted down in early 1989 when Brandt was preparing his memoirs, he summarized his view on Mitterrand's interest for German reunification with one word: "Obsession" (in German, "*Tick*").[33] But he did not dare to publish it in the book.

Here we have in a nutshell the mutual misunderstandings and misperceptions between the SPD and Brandt on the one hand and the PS and Mitterrand on the other. Despite the media coverage and despite his own 1982 warning, Brandt obviously had not fully realized the French fears of a resurrecting German nationalism. And despite all the possibilities a French president had to obtain published and confidential information about the biggest neighbor, Mitterrand had not grasped the importance of social and ecological problems for the German political debate. The regular personal meetings gave the chance to receive additional information, but the short description above shows that reiterated clarifications did not really change long-standing opinions or prejudices, and this applies to both sides.

What was Brandt's own position on the German question between 1981 and 1989? Brandt always had been a democratic patriot but until 1989 he did not expect German unity to happen in the foreseeable future, not to speak of seeing it in his lifetime. He even went so far as to declare reunification to be postwar Germany's *Lebenslüge* (grand delusion). Faced with strong criticism he explained that this referred to all dreams of reconstructing Germany in its prewar (i.e., pre-1938) boundaries. According to Brandt, the unity of the German nation could only be achieved as part of a European peace order. He doubted that a newly unified German state ever would be possible. But when directly asked in 1985 whether the SPD still pursued German unity, he replied, provided that the German people still wants it and provided that the European neighbors accept it, the SPD would be in favor. And Brandt never ceased to deny any allegations of being a neutralist or a pacifist.[34] Compared with other German Social Democrats this was a clear position in favor of German unity. Many of his comrades argued that the division of Germany was the just punishment for Auschwitz.

Mitterrand was convinced that the Soviet empire would end before the turn of the century and he wanted to be prepared for a possible German unification that might be the result of the Soviet Union's weakening.[35] Early in his presidency he ordered the Quai d'Orsay to work out scenarios for such a situation. As to the time horizon this was not totally different from Brandt's expectations. The main difference lay–it seems—in the institutional framework in which such evolutions were likely to take place. Brandt believed frontiers could be overcome as a part of the construction of a new, pan-European entity that would substitute the nation-states and replace the antagonistic blocs. In contrast, Mitterrand's vision presupposed the continuity of the nation-states.

Mitterrand was not the only French socialist leader who believed it was necessary to be prepared for the moment when reunification could become a pressing question. At the very same time when Brandt criticized all hopes for German reunification as a grand delusion, Lionel Jospin declared in the French socialists' "Commission des propositions" on 23 June 1987, "The Socialists must be for German reunification but without fighting [*militer*] for it." And the minutes continue: "Jean-Pierre Chevènement agrees."[36] Chevènement feared, as he revealed in two sessions of the Steering Committee (Comité Directeur) of the PS in July and September 1987, that with the approval of the Soviet Union, Germany could reunify and become neutral in a not-too-distant future. The Soviet Union, he declared, had started the struggle for Germany's future, and the West, especially France, was in need of its own new strategy with regard to its neighbor. He pleaded for deeper European integration, for a Europe that would not depend on the superpowers.[37] But these were discussions behind closed doors that went unnoticed by the German comrades and were speculative preparations for a theoretical situation. No one could know that within two years reunification would be a real issue.

Bad Chemistry

Before turning to 1989–90, when Germany reunified but did not become neutral, it is interesting to emphasize another kind of German perception of French policy toward Germany. Until now we have quoted German and French positions that fit in the conventional pattern of mutual perceptions, most often showing a degree of misunderstanding of the other side but remaining in the realm of politics. But Brandt, looking back in early 1989 and explaining Mitterrand's behavior, added a psychological touch. In a note he wrote when he prepared his autobiography, Brandt described Mitterrand's German policy as president as an act of revenge, as an act of vengeance. Brandt portrayed Mitterrand in the following way: "[How] he had been annoyed that Giscard in 74 could rely on Helmut Schmidt; sensation he [Mitterrand] would take revenge." And then Brandt listed three occasions that had made him feel angry about Mitterrand and that he perceived as such acts of revenge. Not surprisingly, Mitterrand's Bundestag speech ranked first. The second occasion was a visit Mitterrand had paid together with Kohl to Friedrich Ebert's birthplace in Heidelberg at the exact time when a national SPD party convention was held, and the third was when Mitterrand had come to Baden-Württemberg, once again with Kohl, and met the CDU Minister-President Lothar Späth few days before the regional elections took place, thus in effect backing the CDU against the SPD.[38]

With the exception of the Bundestag speech, these so-called revenges nearly went unnoticed by the broad German public. Of course, to meet a regional CDU leader during his campaign against the SPD was not a friendly act, but to understand it as part of a long-reaching plan seems to be an exaggeration. Brandt, too, had a kind of obsession with Mitterrand. He did not publish these notes and left them in a soft version in his memoirs, arguing that Mitterrand had a certain disposition to pay the SPD back for his defeat against Giscard caused by Schmidt.[39] As Brandt's notes indicate, his opinion about Mitterrand was not overly positive. But both men were in no need of finding a common strategy. They had the privilege that they could agree to disagree without provoking a diplomatic crisis.

Reunification!

In 1989 Mitterrand once again talked much more about German reunification than Brandt dared to do. Even in a private letter written in January 1989, Brandt warned against defining the unity of Germany as a precondition for an all-European security system. On the contrary: Germany would only have the chance for unification when the fundamental European security problems was solved.[40] Mitterrand was more proactive. In July 1989 he gave a press conference and an interview in which he declared that the longing of the German people for reunification was legitimate.[41] SPD chairman Hans-Jochen Vogel praised the president's well-balanced position, which embedded, in Vogel's view, the right of the Germans to self-determination in a European context.[42]

In the middle of 1989 Brandt, too, started to sense that Eastern Europe was on the brink of a major transformation. He still declined to speak of reunification; *Neuvereinigung* (new or fresh unification) was the term he preferred for a possibility he expected for the end of the century. Soon things speeded up, however. In September 1989 he wrote an article for *Bild* in which he spoke about national self-determination. And on 10 November 1989, he declared that the unity was imposing itself from below. For Brandt, with the fall of the Berlin Wall the German question was decided on: national unity now was only a question of time, no more a question of principle. It is well known that many of Brandt's comrades did not share his view. The party was split between supporters of national self-determination and unity, and those who only very reluctantly accepted unification.[43]

By chance, Horst Ehmke, the SPD's deputy parliamentary leader at this time, was paying a visit to the French socialists when the wall fell. Two days later, back in Bonn, he reported to the SPD leadership that he had experienced understanding and sympathy, particularly because in France the symbiosis between democracy and nation goes without saying. Ehmke welcomed Mitterrand's reaction to intensify efforts in favor of the European integration.[44] Apart from the president, the first French reactions differed wildly, ranging from sympathy to fears. Pierre Mauroy summarized the French reaction to the German reunification as not having shown much enthusiasm, "to say the least," he added.[45] One week after the fall of the wall, Brandt warned in an article for *Die Zeit* the "esteemed French neighbor" not to dispute the German right to self-determination. But Brandt agreed with Mitterrand that both processes, that of German unification and that of European integration, must run parallel.[46] This had been his position since the end of World War II, and his talks with Mitterrand during the 1980s had reassured him that only a European Germany, not a German hegemon of Europe, would receive the international agreement to the reunification.[47]

In his speech to the national party convention on 18 December 1989, Brandt recommended to take Mitterrand's advice seriously.[48] The French president had declared that theoretically Germany could reunify without the consent of the Allied Powers, but in reality it must take into consideration the European postwar constellations. But Mitterrand's visit to the GDR some days after caused new irritations. In a handwritten note probably from 1991,[49] Brandt described the visit as "Mitterrand straying [*umherirren*] through the GDR," by Brandt's standards a very harsh comment. In the same note we read that Gorbachev had warned him in October 1989 against Mitterrand and Margaret Thatcher's double-dealing: "They talk to me differently than to you."[50] Paris, Brandt believed in retrospect, would have preferred to keep two German states. He continued his note saying that the French had not expected how rapidly Gorbachev showed flexibility. But Brandt did not only have a low opinion of France (since de Gaulle's times he was in the habit of calling it an honorary winner of World War II),[51] but also of the Allies as a whole. Until 1989, they had only supported German unity in the firm conviction that this would never happen, he wrote in the same context.

In late 1989 and early 1990, Willy Brandt gave a couple of interviews for French newspapers explaining his position, not only because he owned a summer cottage in the South of France but also—at least one may speculate—because he believed that the French public opinion was crucial for the ongoing process of German unification. One of his main arguments was, those who fear the German economic power have to strengthen Europe. This was an important bridge between German Social Democrats and French socialists. The other bridge was his reiterated assurance that Germany would not leave the Atlantic alliance and seek neutralization. But to deny the German people their national unity, contrary to all promises since 1949, would produce fatal consequences. This was less aimed at Mitterrand than at Thatcher. Brandt did not lump together Mitterrand and Thatcher. He celebrated the fact that Mitterrand had been the first foreign leader to speak about reunification, in July 1989.[52]

This did not go unnoticed by Mitterrand. Brandt ranked for him among the few sage politicians in Germany, and his opinion mattered. On 8 March 1990 Brandt met Mitterrand in Paris to discuss East-West relations in general and the state of the German question in particular. Brandt and Mitterrand both criticized Kohl's refusal to recognize the Oder-Neisse border. As to the future status of Germany in NATO and the European Economic Community (EEC), Mitterrand told Brandt, "C'est votre affaire" (That's your business), but with the qualification that NATO troops should not advance to the East. The president added that he intended to withdraw the French troops from Germany. Brandt replied that they were welcome. But Mitterrand held that stationing foreign troops was not healthy.[53] The meeting in the Elysée was an attempt by two extremely experienced political leaders who both liked to think in historical perspectives to classify and interpret the revolutionary changes and to find a European solution to it. But neither Mitterrand nor, of course, Brandt had the power to direct the events. Only Bush and Gorbachev, together with Kohl, held the key to the future.

Conclusion

The basic differences between Brandt and Mitterrand, between Bahr and Huntzinger, and between the SPD and the PS reflected the differing national interests. In the realm of diplomacy this is a platitude, though the media and public opinion tend to forget it. But there is another factor that might help to explain the controversy. During the 1980s the SPD understood the world through purely German lenses and forgot to reflect about the consequences of their policies on Germany's integration into the Western bloc. Some inside the SPD like Lafontaine played with that ambiguous situation. Others, like Bahr and Brandt, overestimated Germany's leeway and underestimated their Western neighbor's fears of a reunified Germany. They did not really understand that talking about a common German responsibility for peace set off the alarm bells, especially in London and Paris.

One question remains open: Had Mitterrand and other French socialists before 1989 rightly sensed and predicted the importance of reunification for the Germans in general and especially the SPD (against what the Social Democrats themselves publicly claimed), or had they hit the mark only by chance? Be that as it may, they had at least prepared themselves for this eventuality—but with the side effect that the constant preoccupation with the German question raised some incomprehension on the German side. That this did not result in a real split was basically due to the fact that there was another issue that both sides agreed on during all these years: that to deepen European integration was decisive.

Bernd Rother is research fellow at the Federal Chancellor Willy Brandt Foundation in Berlin. He wrote his thesis about Portugal's Socialist Party. His fields of research include German and European labor movements, contemporary history, Social Democracy, and Jewish history. He is the editor of *Willy Brandts Außenpolitik* (2014) and coeditor of *Berliner Ausgabe—Willy Brandt*, vol. 8: *Über Europa hinaus. Dritte Welt und Sozialistische Internationale* (2006), vol. 10: *Gemeinsame Sicherheit. Internationale Beziehungen und deutsche Frage 1982–1992* (2009), and *The Euromissile Crisis and the End of the Cold War* (2015).

Notes

1. Noelle-Neumann and Piel, *Allensbacher Jahrbuch*, 272, 276.
2. AdsD, SPD-Parteivorstand, 11986: Vermerk: Parteibeziehungen zu den Parteien des westlichen Europas und der USA.
3. Miard-Delacroix, *Willy Brandt*, 211.

4. For Brandt's impression, see WBA, B 25, 174, Bl. 22.
5. WBA, A 3, 847.
6. Transcript of ZDF, Heute, 12 Jul. 1985, 17.00, WBA, A 3, 998.
7. WBA, A 19, 173.
8. Luc Rosenzweig (*Libération*, 5 Jun. 1984).
9. *Journal officiel de la République française*, Assemblée nationale, 20 Dec. 1979, 2e séance, 12427.
10. Maury, "La politique de défense," 148.
11. Complete text of the 110 proposals available at "Programme électoral du Parti socialiste (PS) pour l'élection présidentielle de 1981, intitulé: 110 propositions pour la France, avril–mai 1981," Vie-publique.fr, http://discours.vie-publique.fr/notices/083001601.html (accessed 18 Feb. 2019).
12. *Stern*, 9 Jul. 1981.
13. Gespräch Schmidt-Mitterrand, 12 Jul. 1981 (Möller, Schöllgen, and Wirsching, *Akten zur Auswärtigen Politik*).
14. CAS, Paris, 60 RI (WB) 229: SI: désarmement: SIDAC, 1981–83: "Note SPD—PS Helsinki, À propos Interview F. Mitterrand au *Stern*," probably written by Louis Le Pensec.
15. *Spiegel*, 35/1981, 24 Aug. 1981, 23.
16. WBA, A 11.14, 16, Bl. 160. In German, "Pershing [peur] gut für Verhandlungen."
17. E.g., Brandt, *Berliner Ausgabe*, vol. 10, 132.
18. WBA, A 11.15, 7, "Begegnung mit FM Nogaro," 20 Aug. 1981; *Spiegel*, 35/1981, 24 Aug. 1981, 22–24; Lappenküper, *Mitterrand und Deutschland*, 160.
19. Brandt, *Berliner Ausgabe*, vol. 9, 345–47.
20. IISH, Amsterdam, Bernt Carlsson papers, 34: Some private notes on the meetings in Bonn, 21 Oct. 1982. A similar view in Lappenküper, *Mitterrand und Deutschland*, 161.
21. Brandt, *Berliner Ausgabe*, vol. 9, 345–47.
22. Some private notes on the meetings in Bonn, 21 Oct. 1982, IISH, Bernt Carlsson papers, 34.
23. Seebacher-Brandt, *Willy Brandt*, 303.
24. Meeting on 14 Nov. 1983, AdsD, SPD-Parteivorstand, 10911.
25. Brandt, *Berliner Ausgabe*, vol. 10, 28.
26. CAS, 2 PS (Premier Secrétariat Lionel Jospin, 1981–88), 311: Defense: Désarmement nucléaire en Europe, 1983–87: P. Guelman, note à L. Jospin, 23. Juin 1987: France—RFA: Rappel des récentes prises de position de responsables du PS; for Rocard: Meeting between Hans-Jochen Vogel and Michel Rocard, 17 Dec. 1987. WBA, A 13, 165.
27. Stiftung Archiv der Parteien und Massenorganisation der DDR, Berlin, DY 30/ IV 2/1/671.
28. Brandt, *Berliner Ausgabe*, vol. 9, Doc. 72 (*Spiegel*, 1 Feb. 1982).
29. Handwritten draft for the article (WBA, A 3, 1096). Brandt deleted both sentences, and in the end the whole article—thought to be published in May 1991 in the socialist weekly *Vendredi*—did not appear.
30. Begegnung mit FM Nogaro, 20 Aug. 1981 (WBA, A 11.15, 7); *Spiegel* 35/1981, 22–24; Lappenküper, *Mitterrand und Deutschland*, 160.
31. Notes on the meeting (WBA, A 13, 191, WBA, B 25, 174, Bl. 23); quotation from Brandt, *A Life in Politics*, 455.
32. Seebacher-Brandt, *Willy Brandt*, 39.
33. WBA, B 25, 174, fol. 23.
34. Brandt, *Berliner Ausgabe*, vol. 10, 35–38.
35. Mitterrand, Über Deutschland, 10.
36. CAS, 70 RI 10.
37. Socialist Party, Executive Committee, Summary, 4 Jul. and 12/13 Sept. 1987, http://62.210.214.184/cg-ps/documents/pdf/codir-1987-07-04.pdf (accessed 18 Feb. 2019).
38. WBA, B 25, 174, Bl. 22.
39. Brandt, *Erinnerungen*, 491.
40. Brandt, *Berliner Ausgabe*, vol. 10, 353.

41. Schabert, *Wie Weltgeschichte*, 292–93; Bozo, *Mitterrand*, 92–93.
42. SPD press release 522/89, 27 Jul. 1989, http://library.fes.de/cgi-bin/digibert.pl?id=021227&dok=41/ 021227 (accessed 11 Jul. 2016).
43. Sturm, *Uneinig in die Einheit.*
44. Fischer, *Die Einheit sozial gestalten*, 146.
45. Mauroy, *Mémoires*, 435.
46. *Zeit*, 17 Nov. 1989.
47. Hiepel, "Europakonzeptionen."
48. I do not share Ulrich Lappenküper's opinion that Brandt in his speech to the national party convention on 18 December 1989 showed indignation about the French policy. Lappenküper, *Mitterrand und Deutschland*, 272–73.
49. WBA, B 25, 196.
50. This statement does not appear in the minutes of the Brandt-Gorbachev meeting.
51. B. Seebacher-Brandt, *Willy Brandt*, 15: "Siegermacht honoris causa."
52. Brandt, *Berliner Ausgabe*, vol. 10, 406–16, 424–31, 435–42.
53. AnF, Paris, AG 4/CD 73. We have only the French notes taken by Hubert Védrine; it seems Brandt did not take notes.

Bibliography

Bozo, F. 2005. *Mitterrand, la fin de la guerre froide et l'unification allemande.* Paris: Odile Jacob.
Brandt, W. 1989. *Erinnerungen.* Frankfurt, Germany: Propyläen.
———. 1993. *A Life in Politics.* London: Penguin.
———. 2003. *Berliner Ausgabe*, Vol. 9. Bonn, Germany: Dietz.
———. 2009. *Berliner Ausgabe*, Vol. 10. Bonn, Germany: Dietz.
Fischer, I. 2009. *Die Einheit sozial gestalten. Dokumente aus den Akten der SPD-Führung 1989/90.* Bonn, Germany: Dietz.
Hiepel, C. 2014. "Europakonzeptionen und Europapolitik." In *Willy Brandts Außenpolitik*, edited by B. Rother, 21–91. Wiesbaden, Germany: Springer.
Lappenküper, U. 2011. *Mitterrand und Deutschland.* Munich, Germany: Oldenbourg.
Mauroy, P. 2003. *Mémoires. Vous mettrez du bleu au ciel.* Paris: Plon.
Maury, J.P. 1985. "La politique de défense conduite par un président socialiste—France 1981–84." In *Social-Démocratie et défense en Europe*, edited by H. Portelli and D. Hanley, 145–64. Nanterre, France: Université Paris X.
Miard-Delacroix, H. 2013. *Willy Brandt.* Paris: Fayard.
Mitterrand, F. 1998. *Über Deutschland.* Frankfurt, Germany: Insel Verlag.
Möller, H., G. Schöllgen, and A. Wirsching, eds. 2012. *Akten zur Auswärtigen Politik der Bundesrepublik Deutschland 1981.* Munich, Germany: Oldenbourg.
Noelle-Neumann, E., and E. Piel. 1983. *Allensbacher Jahrbuch der Demoskopie 1978–1983*, Vol. 8. Munich, Germany: Saur.
Schabert, T. 2002. *Wie Weltgeschichte gemacht wird. Frankreich und die deutsche Einheit.* Stuttgart, Germany: Klett-Cotta.
Seebacher-Brandt, B. 2004. *Willy Brandt.* Munich, Germany: Piper.
Sturm, D. F. 2006. *Uneinig in die Einheit. Die Sozialdemokratie und die Vereinigung Deutschlands 1989/90.* Bonn, Germany: Dietz.

CHAPTER 11

ALL ABOUT EUROPE?
FRANCE, GREAT BRITAIN, AND THE QUESTION OF GERMAN UNIFICATION, 1989–1990

Ilaria Poggiolini

Reunification was a momentous event in the long history of the German question. The role of the three main, non-superpower European actors—the Federal Republic of Germany (FRG, or West Germany), France, and Britain—have been the subject of wide discussion. In earlier historiography, the roles of France and Britain were seen as marginal and problematic, playing insignificant parts in the process that led to the end of the Cold War.

In the 2000s, however, French policies at the time of German unification underwent a significant reassessment.[1] Britain, by contrast, seen as firmly tied to Thatcher's deeply felt opposition to a united Germany, remained the villain of the piece. Now a further reassessment is called for, and with the publication of a volume of British documents on German unification in 2010,[2] academic and media interest in the role played by Downing Street and Whitehall has been revived.[3] The release of these documents show, for the first time with great clarity, the growth of a marked division of view, about both German unification and the future of Germany in the European Economic Community (EEC), between the prime minister in No.10 Downing Street and the Foreign Office a few meters away.

This chapter builds on available primary sources on the reunification of Germany,[4] either published or accessible on-line via French,[5] British and American archives or at the Cold War International History Project and the National Security Archives.[6] On Thatcher's policies, the Margaret Thatcher Foundation's website is an extraordinary source of interviews, speeches, and documents.[7] As for the debate on the process of change in Europe that led to the unification of Germany, the release of primary sources in record time has spurred research in this area since the 1990s.[8]

New releases of sources do not change what we know of Thatcher's mistrust of the Germans and the EEC, and her fears of the role that a unified Germany could play in Europe. Yet the sources show how starkly the attitude of the Foreign and

Commonwealth Office differed from that of the prime minister[9] and add important elements to the complexity of the interaction between the United Kingdom and its European partners.

Two main questions are at the core of this chapter: First, did Britain have an unfavorable hand of cards in the game of German unification compared to France? And second, was it the Europeanization of German unification that ultimately made the difference between the two countries' attitudes, and revealed the widely differing approaches to alternative ideas of Europe?

Patrick Salmon, the main editor of the volume on *German Unification 1989–1990* and chief historian of the Foreign and Commonwealth Office, draws the conclusion that, "at a practical level, Great Britain made a vital contribution to German unity."[10] This chapter aims at assessing this claim and setting it against what we now know of Britain and the German question in the 1980s—notably in light of the French case.

British Views of the German Question and of Franco-German Relations in the 1980s

Britain felt marginalized by the Franco-German partnership in the 1980s. This perception was not unfounded and originated from two main causes: London's lack of empathy for the cause of European integration and the intrinsic limits this set to the development of Anglo-German relations. "Britain did not matter to Germans in the way that France did, and British diplomacy still lacked the leverage to convince them that British policies must be taken seriously."[11] In a scenario of close and intense Franco-German relations, Britain either resisted or opposed European political integration; this situation represented a major obstacle in its relations with Germany[12] and France.[13]

A case in point is the 1985 European debate on the Treaty of the European Union, following the Stuttgart Declaration of June 1983. British diplomacy envisaged closer intergovernmental cooperation in foreign policy while the goal of its partners was the relaunch of an ever-closer union.[14] The case of the single market was quite different. It represented a shared objective in Europe—though one pursued with different degrees of enthusiasm by the European partners. Britain stood apart, mainly pursuing liberalization at home and abroad. By contrast, France and Germany, enjoying a large consensus on the future direction of the EEC, pursued the goal of more Europe. The UK government continued to oppose treaty change, including at the Milan European Council, in June 1985, when Thatcher found herself isolated. The founding members aimed at creating the single market as an integral component of the revival of institution building, eventually leading to a new European treaty. The clash at Milan meant that the atmosphere thereafter remained bitter.

One can argue that, apart from the European question, Britain, France and Germany could draw on other sources of strength in their relations. The Anglo-German relationship rested on the alliance that had developed during the long military involvement of the United Kingdom in Germany, within the North Atlantic Treaty Organization (NATO) framework.[15] Britain deployed 55,000 army and about 11,000 Royal Air Force personnel in West Germany and was a guarantor of Berlin, with 3,000 troops there. Joint training and activities in military and intelligence initiatives were indicative of high levels of cooperation.[16] Relations with Germany as part of a defense strategy for Europe had strong elements of continuity in the British post–World War II foreign policy. However, potentially troubling was the British opposition to ideas of common defense and security under the umbrella of European institutions as a potential alternative to NATO.[17]

The British government took a conservative approach to the German question that centered on the preservation of NATO and the nuclear balance of power in Europe.[18] By the early 1980s Thatcher's defense views roused fierce opposition from the antinuclear movement, which regained strength in reaction to the deployment of U.S. Cruise and Pershing missiles in Britain and continental Europe and Soviet deployment of SS-20 missiles in the Eastern bloc. Thatcher did not regard Euromissiles as a threat to security and emphasized this point to Pope John Paul II, assuring him, "The strategy of deterrence has remained effective."[19] In the United States Thatcher was expected to prevail over the British peace movement,[20] while in France this victory was not at all taken for granted and rumors of a *dérive anglaise* (British drift) away from support for the missiles were spreading.[21]

The October 1986 Reagan-Gorbachev Reykjavik summit, in which the U.S. and Soviet leaders found themselves in agreement on the need to abolish nuclear weapons, brought about an unprecedented movement in favor of nuclear abolitionism. It met strong opposition from Margaret Thatcher and was never a practical outcome: but it did quicken the pace of the process of radical arms reduction.[22] The zero nuclear option produced strong criticism in France—though not from Mitterrand, who played down the risk of denuclearization and its effect on French and British weapons.[23] Thatcher's refusal to countenance abolition led her to be even more concerned than before with strengthening Anglo-German relations as a guarantee of exercising influence on Bonn's future strategic decisions.[24]

Starting in 1985 (which, during the visit of West German President Richard von Weizsäcker, was marked by a formal postwar reconciliation between London and Bonn)[25] the impact of the process of change in the Union of Soviet Socialist Republics (USSR, or Soviet Union) and Eastern Europe on bilateral and triangular relations among London, Paris, and Bonn grew exponentially. A major, positive turning point in Franco-British relations was prompted by the experience of getting to know Mikhail Gorbachev, and the potential for change he appeared to promise. The importance of this discovery was felt equally by Thatcher and Mitterrand, and created a strong understanding between the two leaders. In a similar way, at the end of the decade, the decline of Gorbachev contributed to distance Paris and London even farther in relation to the German question and in dealing with its links with European integration.

Discovering Gorbachev and creating a strong relationship with him could not have been predicted. The years immediately before his accession to supreme power were those of the leaderships of two ailing men, who died after brief periods in office—Yuri Andropov, (November 1982–February 1984) and Konstantin Chernenko (February 1984–March 1985). Neither were reformers, nor had shown reformist ideas if they had them. Nevertheless, the evident decay of the Soviet system was dramatized by their short period of rule, while at the same time the French, British, and Germans were exploring their own brands of Ostpolitik toward the communist bloc.[26] The possibility of reformism was in the air and finding an interlocutor in the Soviet Union also depended on searching for one: as Thatcher proudly claimed, "I spotted him because I was searching for someone like him. And I was confident that such a person could exist, even within that totalitarian structure."[27]

The Gorbachev factor not only created a solid understanding between Mitterrand and Thatcher, but also made possible a fresh start in bilateral British-Soviet relations, as well as French-Soviet relations, prompted by Gorbachev's use of the Common European Home metaphor[28] in London in 1984. Mitterrand, who invited Gorbachev to Paris in October 1985 as leader of the Soviet Union also felt the promising novelty of receiving a man who "incarnated a transformation of the nature of Soviet power."[29] Mitterrand and Thatcher became convinced that Gorbachev could deliver change in the Soviet Union, in the Eastern bloc and in East-West relations. Later on, Mitterrand and Kohl also saw a potential partner to engage in negotiations on the reunification of Germany within a European framework.

Gorbachev's commitment to reformism at home and self-determination within the Eastern bloc matched Thatcher's and Mitterrand's visions of progressive change in Europe[30] and—particularly on Thatcher's side—a strong wish to control the intensity and time frame of the expected transformations.[31] Thatcher never anticipated the dramatic acceleration of history[32] that took place at the end of the decade and the dismantling of the Cold War system.[33] Gorbachev agreed with her, seeing the division of Germany as central to Soviet national interest in 1988, as it had been in 1948.[34]

Before this extraordinary acceleration, Thatcher had believed that German unity represented only an aspiration—one she said she shared—on the part of the federal government. At a meeting in Oxford in May 1984 between Prime Minister Thatcher and Chancellor Kohl, both leaders proclaimed their conviction that stability in Europe could be better achieved by putting an end to the division of Germany. For Thatcher, however, it was a distant ideal; for Kohl, it was an increasingly active possibility.

Gorbachev's leadership in the Soviet Union was reviving the debate on reunification in the FRG. A certain degree of alarm in London led to the submission by the Foreign and Commonwealth Office's planners to the Foreign secretary in September 1987, of a paper on "The German Question and Europe."[35] The planners foresaw no significant change in the medium term. They did not expect Gorbachev to repeat Stalin's 1952 offer of establishing a neutral Germany,[36] at least while Soviet control on Eastern Europe remained strong. However, in the longer term the break-up of the existing division of Europe was perceived as inevitable and the emergence of a united Germany seen as very likely.[37] Under these circumstances, it was becoming very important for the United Kingdom to keep the dialogue with West Germany open on bilateral cooperation on defense issues and responsibilities in Berlin, as well as working on possible convergence on issues related to European integration.[38]

In the area of institutionalized security cooperation, Britain had a poor record, particularly when set against Franco-German political and strategic cooperation, which had led to the creation of the Franco-German Council on defense and security at the twenty-fifth anniversary of the Elysée Treaty in January 1988.[39] Lacking leverage with West Germany, particularly in comparison to France, represented a serious problem for British policy over the years 1987–89. At the Foreign and Commonwealth Office this lack was largely ascribed to the government refusal to engage constructively in Europe.[40]

Events in the the German Democratic Republic (GDR, or East Germany) in October 1989 exerted extraordinary pressure on all actors on the European scene, including Britain and France, who reacted in quite different ways. Paris could share "responsibility for the German future" but feared "dilution" of the EEC before institutional deepening would be achieved.[41] Thatcher believed she could prevent the unification of Germany and by doing so prevent also Franco-German convergence toward European Monetary Union.[42]

Dealing with the end of the European division while bringing about monetary union in the EEC was France's aspiration, but the French met a rejection of deeper integration by the British government.[43] Thatcher had always harbored anti-German feelings that originated in her memories of the days of appeasement in the interwar period. Her anti-German unification beliefs derived from her lack of trust in the German people and determination to contain the territorial, strategic, and economic expansion of West Germany and its merging with the GDR. Furthermore, the potential convergence of the German question and further European integration represented a scenario that Thatcher wanted to prevent at all costs. The contrasting French attitude of constant engagement in Europe would soon distance Paris and London in their dealing with the question of German reunification.[44]

In September 1989, during her visit to Moscow, Thatcher shared with Gorbachev her concerns regarding stability in Europe[45] and in doing so made a notoriously controversial point. She attributed her own position—of no present interest in the unification of Germany—to all European partners.[46] This exchange is at the core of the controversy over Thatcher's hard-line anti-German views.

On 8 November 1989, when German reunification ceased to be "a distant, hypothetical aspiration,"[47] views of the German question at the *deux maisons*—as the French embassy in London had labeled the Foreign Office and Downing Street—more obviously collided than in 1987 when the Foreign and Commonwealth Office planners had advised the government to accept the inevitable path toward German reunification and the link between European integration and the future role of Germany. Thatcher's prolonged silence on German self-determination became dramatically deafening, particularly after Bush (on 24 October) and Mitterrand (on 3 November) granted their support to Kohl.[48] On 10 November Thatcher finally spoke of the extraordinary events taking place in Germany and celebrated a "great day for freedom," while making no mention of German self-determination. She reiterated her belief that the "borders of the Warsaw Pact" would remain "intact"[49] and existing alliances (NATO and the Warsaw pact) in place,[50] reassured by Kohl that things would not "get out of hand."[51] The difference in feeling the acceleration of events in Downing Street and at British embassies in Central Eastern Europe at this stage was dramatic.[52]

In Moscow, Ambassador Rodric Braithwaite feared Gorbachev could be overrun by events at a time of fast change sweeping through Central Eastern Europe.[53] Douglas Hurd visited Bonn and Berlin on 15 November and gathered the impression that "the German analysis of developments in the GDR is very close to our own. They want to encourage free elections, avoid talk of reunification and reassure the Soviet Union."[54] Two weeks later, Thatcher was in agreement with Ambassador Broomfield in East Berlin reacting to the announcement of Helmut Kohl's Ten-Point Plan for German Unity.[55] It was a short cut,[56] and she could not accept that Kohl had seated himself in the driving seat.[57] British diplomacy was alarmed—in particular Ambassador Braithwaite, who shared with his French counterpart concerns regarding the future boundaries of Germany.[58] Mitterrand, equally concerned with this fundamental issue, also saw the elephant in the room: the missing link between the Ten-Point Plan and further European integration.[59] The plan itself took center stage at the Malta Bush-Gorbachev summit on 2 December.[60] Thatcher was resentful and unprepared in facing the unexpected consequences of change. Together with Gorbachev, she had firmly believed that democratic reforms could be granted without activating a radical process of self-determination in the Eastern bloc.[61]

Was It All about Europe?

The acceleration of history in 1989 took not just Thatcher, but also everyone else by surprise. In a matter of weeks, at the EEC summit in Strasbourg in early December 1989 German unification received a general blessing on condition that its pursuit would blend into the process of European integration and abide by all previous international commitments. Indeed, Kohl acknowledged the "manifest link existing between the European and German dossiers."[62] Margaret Thatcher, on the contrary, openly rejected the connection between German unification and European integration and joined forces with Giulio Andreotti and Rudd Lubbers, prime ministers of Italy and the Netherlands, attacking Kohl on 8 December.[63] Very aggressively indeed Thatcher gave full rein to her conviction that Germany should not be allowed to come back once again to a dominant position in Europe in an extreme attempt at slowing down the quickening pace of German reunification.[64] Mitterrand instead looked at German unification as inevitable now that the European Monetary Union and intergovernmental conference paths were back on track, but did not ignore the negative reactions of his partners, particularly Thatcher's.[65] He met Thatcher twice on the margins of the Strasbourg European Council, and again on 20 January 1990, at the Elysée palace. Reported by Charles Powell to Stephen Wall,[66] passages of the meeting are also recalled in Thatcher's memoirs. According to Powell, Thatcher and Mitterrand would have put aside their differences and agreed that they were all that was left in resisting Germany.[67] The meeting between the two leaders at the Elysée Palace in Paris is surrounded by even more controversy, particularly when they allegedly spoke of the German as "bad Germans." Literally reported or not, this exchange could have been an attempt by Mitterrand to make Thatcher believe that he shared her views.[68] However, the episode gets even more intriguing if one considers that both Mitterrand and Thatcher seemed to agree on the never-changing nature of the Germans but also openly differed on how the story of German unification may end. The French president stood by his conviction that nothing could stop German unification and Thatcher by her own opposite view that it could be prevented. Thatcher made equally clear that she would do her best to delay the process, either confronting Kohl—as she did[69]—regarding the need to preserve the Oder-Neisse border of Germany with Poland, or by promoting East German membership of the EEC, thus activating a long transition period before accession.[70] Thatcher's unwillingness to acknowledge German self-determination was at the core of her talks with Mitterrand.[71] This attitude had a major impact and often clashed with the experience of British diplomats operating on the ground, and reporting signals of change back to London in real time. Foreign Secretary Douglas Hurd engaged in a difficult act of balancing himself between government and diplomacy, being unable to follow his French counterpart, Roland Dumas, in prioritizing the goal of "locking the Germans into deepening European integration."[72] Thatcher persisted in rejecting deepening, and demanding a slow process of unification, marked by progressive steps, compliance with guarantees, and harmonization of German self-determination within the NATO framework.[73]

The British foreign secretary and Chancellor Kohl met on 7 February, when British-German relations were poor and Thatcher's interview to the *Wall Street Journal* on 24 January had caused further damage.[74] Visiting Churchill's grave, Kohl used a brilliant metaphor describing Thatcher and himself: "The difference between you and me, Margaret, is that you are Churchill before the Zurich speech and I am Churchill after it."[75]

Thatcher and Charles Powell, after a conversation with Teltschik,[76] remained unconvinced by German plans,[77] and advanced the proposal of a slow process of transitional agreements, favored also by Moscow. However, the process could not be slowed down. On the contrary, the acceleration continued at Ottawa in mid-February 1990. The choice of a Two Plus Four mechanism engaged the two Germanys and the guarantor powers in negotiations regarding the external dimension of German unification, mainly the security of the neighboring states, causing strong resentment in all other NATO member states.[78] Kohl briefed Mitterrand, not Thatcher, on 15 February,[79] their dialogue being already deeply embedded in the parallel European projects.[80] Borders, however, particularly the German-Polish border, still concerned both Mitterrand and Thatcher, but the French president had no intention to stall the process of unification on this account. On the other hand, Thatcher's approach lacked flexibility because her deeply rooted anti-German feelings dictated her views of the recognition of the Oder-Neisse border.[81]

Dining at the French embassy in mid-March, the British prime minister appealed again to France for a common action against the domination of Europe by 80 million Germans.[82] By this time, Thatcher's lack of flexibility and use of language, particularly in relations to the Germans, had become deeply unpopular. Within her government, Douglas Hurd came out openly against Britain acting as a brake on everything and came forward with some positive ideas such as expanding the Conference on Security and Cooperation in Europe framework, granting support for the democratic process and monitoring arms control agreements. This new post–Cold War order included opening a dialogue with the president of the European Commission, Jacques Delors. But Thatcher remained totally aloof from such a plan.[83] At that time, even in Moscow German unification had come to be seen favorably, provided the Soviet Union played a part in shaping the process. Moscow approached the question of a new European security system as one that would build on conventional arms negotiations, the Conference on Security and Cooperation in Europe process, and the creation of a common European home.

By March 1990 both Mitterrand and Gorbachev had distanced themselves from Thatcher's efforts at slowing down German unification. Mitterrand and Thatcher only shared concerns regarding Gorbachev's political fragility.[84] Thatcher's anti-German attitudes were evident once again following a seminar on the past, present, and future of the German question at Chequers. According to Timothy Garton-Ash, who was one of the six historians attending the seminar, "The overwhelming message of all the historians present was that the FRG, as it had proved itself over 40 years, must be trusted and supported in carrying through the unification of Germany in freedom."[85] However, in mid-July the resignation of Nicholas Ridley as secretary of State for Trade and Industry after an interview to *The Spectator*, famously describing monetary union as a "German racket,"[86] reinforcing the perception of very strong anti-German feelings harbored by the government in London. The next day—on 15 July—the *Independent on Sunday* published the leaked record by Powell of the seminar on Germany at Chequers in March, doubling the effect of the Ridley affair.[87] Apparently, even the credibility of the German commitment to European integration was questioned: "Just a tactic to reassure others?"[88] Such views blended dangerously with the *Spectator* interview with Ridley, with the headline: "Saying the Unsayable about the Germans," and illustrated by a cartoon of Kohl's face sporting a Hitler's type mustache.[89] As this story and its aftermath was running in Britain the European summit approving of German unification under a European umbrella was taking place in the neighboring capital of Dublin. The two events seemed to be taking place on different planets.[90]

With the process of German unification well under way, Gorbachev met Thatcher on 8 June and argued, "We should change the nature of our respective alliances," suggesting "that the two alliances might sign a declaration or agreement signaling a rapprochement between them."[91] Thatcher had now accepted the inevitability of German unification and the advantage—from her viewpoint—of how Germany would reunite, namely by reentering both the EEC and NATO, as one country. Thatcher told Gorbachev that she had no intention of jeopardizing the security of the Soviet Union "but we had to be realistic. Certain consequences flowed from German unification, and membership of NATO was one of them."[92] From preventing or slowing the unification of Germany, Thatcher had shifted her full attention to the concept of binding—another word full of meaning—Germany to the existing international structure of the West.[93] The prime minister's view was that "a united Germany should remain part of NATO; that American and other stationed forces should remain in Germany, although we hope in reduced numbers; and that NATO should continue to have nuclear weapons based in Germany."[94] The continental European way of binding Germany to the West by merging the unification process with that of an ever-closer union was Mitterrand's and Kohl's way but definitely not Thatcher's.

Going for the Europeanization of German reunification meant that—borrowing from Sarotte—Gorbachev's "heroic model" of a common European home from the Atlantic to the Urals, would lose to the "prefabricated model," extending Western institutions to the new, undivided post–Cold War scenario.[95] Thatcher's previous interest in Gorbachev's pan-European vision was linked to her policy of keeping both Moscow and Paris on board and the reunification of Germany in check.

Was this a missed opportunity?[96] It certainly can be argued that it was. Thatcher—in contrast with her European partners—saw the Common European home in 1989 as an alternative to the EEC. Mitterrand instead had advanced the idea of a European Confederation, launched in December 1989, and aimed at the creation of a European Europe with the EEC as the pivotal center for the post–Cold War transformation and stabilization of Central Eastern Europe.[97] Thatcher believed that the two halves of Europe should be brought back together but not via the consolidation of the EEC; she felt the need to keep the Soviet leader solidly in charge of a democratic transition of Eastern Europe toward reformism, democratization, and eventually a new international order. This approach had originally the support of Gorbachev. However, the economic situation of the Soviet Union was deteriorating rapidly and required financial support. Indeed, aid for an increasingly harried Gorbachev was on the agenda of the forthcoming Dublin European Council. Short-term credit from German banks, for which the federal German government would act as guarantor, had been requested by Moscow. It seemed that acquiescence by the Soviet Union to politico-military issues in the New Europe could be bought—though it was no longer certain that this would necessarily imply the preservation in power of Gorbachev.[98]

This was not a trend in the Soviet Union that Thatcher would have wanted to witness. She had aimed at limiting the damage of a process of reunification in Germany that she had for some time tried very hard to prevent and then delay. However, her late and reluctant acceptance of German unity had consequences in limiting the impact of British policy and diplomacy in the final phase of her leadership. Patrick Salmon—prefacing the volume on documents on German unification—takes the view that, "considering the options open to British diplomacy in the winter of 1989–90, one has the impression of a missed opportunity." He also argues, "The most rational approach would have been an early acknowledgment on the part of the prime minister that German unity was going to happen."[99]

Conclusion

As emphasized in this chapter, Thatcher's German policy was at the core of the rift between the *deux maisons*, and between Britain and her European partners. This meant that, as argued by Mallaby, Britain received only a bronze medal in the unification race mainly because Downing Street remained deaf to the appeals of the Foreign and Commonwealth Office to take a rational approach to the German question and rejected French policies of German Europeanization at a very crucial time.[100] Differences between the approaches of Mitterrand and Thatcher were fundamental: France's priorities included both restructuring NATO and bringing to completion the two intergovernmental conferences on economic and political union. The British government led by Thatcher fought to the end against federalism, thereby opposing German reunification in Europe as well as a deepening of the EEC. Sir Rodric Braithwaite, commenting on the theme of this chapter, is adamant in passing a severe judgement: "There is little or nothing positive to say of Thatcher's policy of trying to slow down or prevent reunification. It was doomed to failure. . . . British officials did play a positive role at various stages, but that was on the whole despite Thatcher."[101] Indeed, Thatcher's inability to come to terms with German unification until the very end is consolidated and linked to three main factors: her own long-lasting experience of growing up harboring very strong anti-German feelings; her pan-European anti-Europeanism; and, finally, her vision of Western security, which aimed at keeping the Soviet Union in a dialogue with the West within a reformed Cold War scenario.

Thatcher did not pass the test of the unexpected acceleration of change in Europe and failed to play a decisive role in the very last chapter of the end of the Cold War, notwithstanding a history of significant involvement of both British government and diplomacy in support of the return of Central Eastern Europe to the West and a significant international negotiating effort that eventually made German unification possible.

Historiography is beginning to address the question of how Thatcher's Britain missed the opportunity of playing a coherently constructive role in the process leading to German unification.[102] This chapter argues that Thatcher chose reformism in the Soviet bloc over transformation as long as she could and this included opposing German unification.[103] She maintained this position until it was too late to obtain any benefit from joining the diplomatic process leading to unification. Mitterrand's hand of cards won over Thatcher's because it included the Europeanization of the German question. It was indeed all about Europe in the end because Mitterrand envisaged the future of the German question and the process of unification within the European framework,[104] while Thatcher did not.

Gorbachev's rise to power united France and Britain while his decline separated them. The Soviet leader became progressively more and more instrumental to Mitterrand's plans of monetary union and German unification. Kohl had foreseen since the beginning of 1990 the need of negotiating terms for German unification acceptable to Gorbachev: a combination of strategic reassurances—particularly regarding the future of NATO—coupled with a considerable offer of financial aid. Mitterrand very much like Thatcher remained convinced that German unification and its repercussions in the Soviet Union could seal Gorbachev's fate, as actually happened in August 1991 when the Soviet leader was the victim of a coup. However, once the financial package was offered to Gorbachev the previous summer and his consent obtained, Mitterrand felt free of prioritizing his European grand design.[105] Thatcher had no European solution to her German question and this contributed to her own political epilogue in November 1990. She was forced out of power while Gorbachev failed to stabilize his reformist project at home and to see a European home welcoming the Soviet Union in it.[106] These events had long-term repercussions, as Gorbachev put it to Douglas Hurd in September 1991.[107] By not prioritizing the integration of the Soviet Union in the new world order, the process leading to the unification of Germany produced long-term unexpected consequences in European relations with the Soviet Union (Russia).

Ilaria Poggiolini is professor of international history and pro-vice-chancellor for international relations, member of the teaching staff of the doctorate program in history at the University of Pavia, and of the committee on publication of Italian diplomatic documents (MAECI, Rome). Previously she was visiting Fulbright Scholar (United States), NATO Fellow, visiting Fellow at the Center of International Studies and Woodrow Wilson School, Princeton (United States), at the London School of Economics (LSE London) and European Study Centre, St. Antony's College, Oxford. Her present research and publications focus on British membership of the EEC/ EU since accession, on British Ostpolitik in the 1970s, and on Thatcher's European and East-West policy (1985–90).

Notes

1. See Bozo, "Mitterrand's France"; Bozo, *Mitterrand*; and Schabert, *How World Politics Is Made*.
2. Salmon, Hamilton, and Twigge, *German Unification 1989–1990*.
3. Witness Seminar, Berlin in the Cold War, 1948–1990, German Unification, 1989–1990, Lancaster House, 16 Oct. 2009, published 3 Jul. 2013, https://keats.kcl.ac.uk/pluginfile.php/1402697/mod_resource/content/1/FCO percent20Witness percent20Seminar.pdf/ (accessed 23 May 2019); Deighton, *Germany and East-Central Europe*, 213.
4. British and French sources include Salmon, Hamilton, and Twigge, *German Unification 1989–1990*; Salmon, Hamilton, and Twigge, *Berlin in the Cold War 1948–1990*; Vaïsse and Wenkel, *La diplomatie française*; and Galkin and Tschernjajew, *Michail Gorbatschow*.
5. Research for this essay at the archives of the French Foreign Ministry have been possible thanks to the invaluable collaboration of Felix Schmidt.
6. See the Cold War International History Project, "Twenty-Fifth Anniversary of the Fall of the Berlin Wall," Wilson Center, http://www.wilsoncenter.org/article/twenty-fifth-anniversary-the-fall-the-berlin-wall/ (accessed 23 May 2019); "End of the Cold War" collection, Wilson Center, https://digitalarchive.wilsoncenter.org/collection/37/end-of-the-cold-war/ (accessed 23 May 2019); Blanton, *The Revolutions of 1989*; and Savranskaya, Blanton, and Zubok, *Masterpieces of History*.
7. These documents have been collected by the Margaret Thatcher Foundation or made available by scholars, as a result of FOIA requests in the United States and FOI requests in the United Kingdom and deposited in the digital archive of the Margaret Thatcher Foundation, http://www.margaretthatcher.org/ (accessed 23 May 2019).
8. Zelikow and Rice, *Germany Unified*.
9. Kettenacker, "Britain and German Unification," 100–3.
10. "It was British legal experts, in the 2+4 negotiations, who ensured that unification took place without damage to the structure of international relations." Salmon, "The United Kingdom," 183.
11. Salmon, "Préface," xii.
12. French embassy in London, memo on the British Foreign Policy, "Visite d'Etat du président de la République 23–26 Oct. 1984," 1 Oct. 1984, AMAE, Europe, Grande-Bretagne, 1981–85, box 5221.
13. M. Thatcher, Joint Press Conference with West German Chancellor Helmut Kohl, 18 Jan. 1985, Margaret Thatcher Foundation, http://www.margaretthatcher.org/document/105946/ (accessed 23 May 2019).
14. Memo of the director of political affairs to the minister of foreign affairs, 10 Jun. 1985; telegram from the French embassy in London, 3 Jul. 1985, AMAE, Europe, Grande-Bretagne, 1981–85, box 5209.
15. S. Boidevaix to R. Dumas, "Coopération germano-britannique," 6 Jan. 1989, AMAE, Europe, Grande-Bretagne, 1986–90, box 6283.
16. R. B. Bone, Anglo-German Summit: Report on Bilateral Relations, 1 May 1984, Margaret Thatcher Foundation, http://www.margaretthatcher.org/document/146810/ (accessed 23 May 2019).
17. Telegram of the French embassy in London, 3 Oct. 1988, AMAE, Europe, Grande-Bretagne, 1986–90, box 6270.
18. "It is the balance of nuclear forces which has preserved peace for forty years in a Europe." Margaret Thatcher, speech to the Conservative Party Conference, 10 Oct. 1986, Margaret Thatcher Foundation, http://www.margaretthatcher.org/document/106498/ (accessed 23 May 2019).
19. The prime minister to Pope John Paul II, 8 Jan. 1982, Margaret Thatcher Foundation, http://www.margaretthatcher.org/document/146265/ (accessed 23 May 2019).
20. National Security Council, Briefing for President Reagan on Thatcher visit, 27 Sept. 1983, Margaret Thatcher Foundation, http://www.margaretthatcher.org/document/109387/ (accessed 23 May 2019).
21. Memo of the Centre of Analysis and Prospection to the minister of foreign affairs, "Visite Howe: éléments de réflexion sur les "incertitudes anglaises," 6 Jun. 1986, AMAE, Europe, Grande-Bretagne, 1986–90, box 6219.

22. Savranskaya and Blanton, *The Reykjavik File*; memo from the U.S. embassy in London to the secretary of State, 23 Jul. 1986, Margaret Thatcher Foundation, http://www.margaretthatcher.org/document/143811/ (accessed 23 May 2019).

23. Bozo, *Mitterand, the End of the Cold War*, 17–18.

24. Telegrams from the French embassy in Bonn, on British-German cooperation, 5 Jan. 1989; letter from the French ambassador in Bonn, S. Boidevaix, 6 Jan. 1989, AMAE, Europe, Grande-Bretagne, 1986–90, box 6270, 6283.

25. Politique étrangère britannique, telegram of the French embassy in London, 6 Mai 1985, AMAE, Europe, Grande-Bretagne, 1981-85, box 5221; M. Thatcher, Joint Press Conference with West German Chancellor Helmut Kohl, 18 Feb. 1985, Margaret Thatcher Foundation, http://www.margaret thatcher.org/document/105946/ (accessed 23 May 2019).

26. Wenkel, "Overcoming the Crisis of Détente."

27. Thatcher, *The Downing Street Years*, 450-53. See also Braithwaite, "Gorbachev and Thatcher," 33; Brown, "Margaret Thatcher and Perceptions," 17–30; and Braithwaite, *Across the Moscow River*, 51–52.

28. Rey, "Europe Is Our Common Home."

29. Bozo, *Mitterand*, 11–13.

30. Bozo, "Mitterrand's France," 462.

31. On British Ostpolitik see the annual reports by British ambassadors, 1979–89. These have been released as result of FOIA requests submitted in view of Poggiolini and Pravda, "Britain in Europe in the 1980s." See also Poggiolini, "Thatcher's Double Track Road"; and the passage on Eastern Europe in M. Thatcher, Speech to the College of Europe, 20 Sept. 1988, Margaret Thatcher Foundation, http://www.margaretthatcher.org/ document/107332/ (accessed 23 May 2019).

32. Poggiolini and Pravda, "Britain in Europe in the 1980s"; Brown, "Margaret Thatcher and Perceptions of Change"; Braithwaite, "Gorbachev and Thatcher"; Grachev, "Political and Personal."

33. Savranskaya, "The Logic of 1989," 46.

34. Bullard, "Great Britain," 219.

35. Garton-Ash, "Britain Fluffed the German Question"; Salmon, "Préface," xii–xiii, n8.

36. Loth, "The origins of Stalin's note."

37. Letter from C. Mallaby, Bonn to J. Fretwell, 27 Jul. 1989 (Salmon, Hamilton, and Twigge, *German Unification 1989-1990*, 20–23).

38. Kettenacker, "Britain and German Unification," 103.

39. Bozo, *Mitterand, the End of the Cold War*, 21.

40. Salmon, "Préface," xii.

41. Minute from P. Wright to S. Wall, 30 Oct. 1989 (Salmon, Hamilton, and Twigge, *German Unification 1989-1990*, 78-80).

42. Bozo, *Mitterand, the End of the Cold War*, 66, 103.

43. Ibid., 99–101.

44. Letter from C. Powell to S. Wall, 2 Nov. 1989 (Salmon, Hamilton, and Twigge, *German Unification 1989-1990*, 84-85).

45. Record of conversation between M. Gorbachev and M. Thatcher, 23 Sept. 1989 (Savranskaya and Blanton, *The Thatcher-Gorbachev Conversations*).

46. The exchange was off the record but noted by A. S. Chernyaev. Record of conversation between M. Gorbachev and M. Thatcher, 23 Sept. 1989, Margaret Thatcher Foundation, http://www.marga retthatcher.org/document/112005/ (accessed 23 May 2019). However, there is no record of this conversation on the British side. In minutes from Sir P. Wright to S. Wall, The German Question, 30 Oct. 1989 (in Salmon, Hamilton, and Twigge, *German Unification 1989-1990*, 78-80), Wright writes, "I attach Mr. Powell's record of the conversation" (between Thatcher and Gorbachev) referring to Powell's letter of 24 Sept. 1989 on this subject, but the document is not there. As clarified by Salmon, Hamilton, and Twigge (footnote 4, 79, n3 of the same document), this letter is not attached to or found in the FCO files, though it is in PREM: Prime Minister visit to the Soviet Union. The PREM document records part of the talks on 23 September when both leaders agreed that notes should not be taken: "The Prime Minister then asked Mr Gorbachev's assessment of the prospects

in the GDR . . . Although NATO traditionally made statements supporting Germany's aspiration to be reunited, in practice we would not welcome it at all. She was not speaking for herself alone. She had discussed the matter with at least one other western leader. She would welcome some assurances about Mr Gorbachev's attitude" (Salmon, Hamilton, and Twigge, *German Unification*, footnote 4, 79). See also Thatcher, *The Downing Street Years*, 792; Braithwaite, *Across the Moscow River*, 135–36.

47. Letter from C. Mallaby, Bonn to J. Fretwell, Political Director and Deputy Permanent Under-Secretary, Bonn, 8 Nov. 1989 (Salmon, Hamilton, and Twigge, *German Unification 1989–1990*, 93–98).

48. C. Mallaby, Bonn to D. Hurd, 9 Nov. 1989 (ibid., 98–99).

49. Cradock, *In Pursuit of British Interests*, 105–6.

50. Thatcher, *The Downing Street Years*, 793–94.

51. Letters from C. Powell to S. Wall, Downing Street No 10, 10 Nov. 1989 (Salmon, Hamilton, and Twigge, *German Unification 1989–1990*, 101–4).

52. Extract from conclusions of a Cabinet meeting, 15 Nov. 1989 (ibid., 122–24).

53. D. Hurd to R. Braithwaite, 15 Nov. 1989 (ibid., 125–27).

54. Minute from D. Hurd to M. Thatcher, 17 Nov. 1989 (ibid., 128–29).

55. Helmut Kohl's Ten-Point Plan for German Unity, 28 Nov. 1989, German History in Documents and Images (GHDI), http://germanhistorydocs.ghi-dc.org/docpage.cfm?docpage_id=118 (accessed 23 May 2019); Kohl, "A Ten-Point Program." See the analysis in C. Mallaby, Bonn to D. Hurd, 28 Nov. 1989 (Salmon, Hamilton, and Twigge, *German Unification 1989–1990*, 139).

56. C. Mallaby, Bonn, to D. Hurd, 28 Nov. 1989 (Salmon, Hamilton, and Twigge, *German Unification 1989–1990*, 138–40).

57. Bozo, *Mitterrand*, 125; documents show secret messages from Moscow sparked West German chancellor to announce German unification plans on 28 Nov. 1989. See also Savranskaya and Blanton, *The Soviet Origins of Helmut Kohl's 10 Points*; on the question of Gorbachev's aversion to confrontational choices regarding the German question see Zubok, "German Unification," 268–71.

58. R. Braithwaite, Moscow, to D. Hurd, 8 Dec. 1989, Foreign and Commonwealth Office, National Security Archive, https://nsarchive2.gwu.edu/NSAEBB/NSAEBB296/doc07.pdf (accessed 23 May 2019).

59. Bozo, *Mitterrand*, 126.

60. On the controversy related to the interpretation of the Malta Summit within the framework of the end of the Cold War, see Shifrinson, *The Malta Summit*. Mary Sarotte makes this point in the introduction of her book on 1989; see Sarotte, *1989: The Struggle*, 3.

61. Kettenacker, "Britain and German Unification," 109.

62. Bozo, *Mitterrand*, 131.

63. Regarding the two sides of the same coin, see Haftendorn, "German Unification and European Integration," 139; and Haftendorn, "The Unification of Germany," 343.

64. Sarotte, *1989: The Struggle*, 82.

65. Bozo, *Mitterrand*, 132–33. I'd like to thank Sir Rodric Braithwaite for reading this essay and for the opportunity of accessing extracts from his diary. On Tuesday 19 December 1989, he wrote, "We have dinner in the evening with the Egyptian ambassador, Sayeed. Adamishin is the guest of honour. He draws our attention to the keynote speech delivered by Shevarnadze today in Brussels. It sets out the Soviet Union's definitive policy on Germany. In fact, it doesn't seem all that different from what the Soviets have already said clearly: They do not relish German reunification, hope the other Europeans and the Americans will cooperate in slowing down or stalling the process, but will not act unilaterally. Adamishin irritates me by saying that the French and the British are opposed to reunification but are relying on the Russians to pull their chestnuts out of the fire. I say he has no evidence. Our policy is that the Germans are entitled to self-determination in an orderly process, which respects their neighbour's interests. He persists. No doubt, some of the PM's attitudes have leaked through. But whatever the PM would prefer, our policy in practice will have to be as I (and for that matter Hurd) describe it." Braithwaite's diary is unpublished.

66. Charles Powell was private secretary to Margaret Thatcher 1983–90, and Stephen Wall was private secretary to the Foreign secretary 1988–91.

67. Thatcher, *The Downing Street Years*, 796–97; letter from C. Powell, Strasbourg to S. Wall, 8 Dec. 1989 (Salmon, Hamilton, and Twigge, *German Unification 1989–1990*, 164–66). A detailed report of this meeting has not been found in French archives; see Bozo, *Mitterrand*, 160, n147; Attali, *Verbatim*, vol. 3, 368–70; and minute from D. Hurd to M. Thatcher, 16 Jan. 1990 (Salmon, Hamilton, and Twigge, *German Unification 1989–1990*, 208–11).

68. Letter from C. Powell to S. Wall, 20 Jan. 1990, Margaret Thatcher Foundation, http://www.margaret thatcher.org/document/113883/ (accessed 23 May 2019). See the passage on prospect of unification that had allegedly turned the Germans into the "bad" Germans they used to be. See also Salmon, Hamilton, and Twigge, *German Unification 1989–1990*, 215–219.

69. In an interview with *Der Spiegel* on 26 Mar. 1990, Thatcher said that Kohl gave her the impression of being ready to put in question the Oder-Neisse border with Poland. An enraged Kohl totally denied this allegation.

70. C. Mallaby, Bonn to D. Hurd, 1 Feb. 1990 (Salmon, Hamilton, and Twigge, *German Unification 1989–1990*, 238–39).

71. Minute from C. Mallaby, Bonn to W. Waldegrave, 16 Jan. 1990 (ibid., 206–7).

72. E. Fergusson, Paris to D. Hurd, 5 Feb. 1990 (ibid., 256–58).

73. The distance between Thatcher's view and those of Sir Geoffrey Howe and Douglas Hurd on European issues and the German question was widening day by day, and this was certainly not a secret. See memo of the European department on British Foreign policy, 13 Feb. 1990, AMAE, Europe, Grande-Bretagne, 1986–90, box 6282 (accessed 23 May 2019).

74. M. Thatcher, interview for *Wall Street Journal*, 24 Jan. 1990, Margaret Thatcher Foundation, http://www.margaretthatcher.org/document/107876/ (accessed 23 May 2019).

75. Letter from S. Wall to C. Powell, 7 Feb. 1990 (Salmon, Hamilton, and Twigge, *German Unification 1989–1990*, 270–72).

76. Deputy chief of staff of the federal chancellery 1983–90.

77. Minute from C. Powell to M. Thatcher, 9 Feb. 1990 (Salmon, Hamilton, and Twigge, *German Unification 1989–1990*, 274–78).

78. Zelikov and Rice, *Germany Unified*, 193.

79. Neville-Jones to the Foreign and Commonwealth Office, 13 Feb. 1990 (Salmon, Hamilton, and Twigge, *German Unification 1989–1990*, 287–88).

80. Bozo, *Mitterrand*, 181–88.

81. Haftendorn, "German Unification and European Integration," 142. See also on this issue, Bush and Scowcroft, *A World Transformed*, 256.

82. Telegrams of the French embassy in London on a dinner with M. Thatcher, 13 Mar. 1990, AMAE, Europe, Grande-Bretagne, 1986–1990, box 6291.

83. Letter from C. Powell to S. Wall, 23 Feb. 1990 (Salmon, Hamilton, and Twigge, *German Unification 1989–1990*, 305–6).

84. For the French side of the argument see Bozo, *Mitterrand*, 170.

85. Garton-Ash, "Britain Fluffed the German Question."

86. See "Saying the Unsayable about the Germans," *The Spectator*, 14 Jul. 1990, 8–10. See also Cold War: Chequers Seminar on Germany ("Summary Record"), Margaret Thatcher Foundation, http://www.margaretthatcher.org/document/111047/ (accessed 23 May 2019).

87. P. Neville-Jones to the Foreign and Commonwealth Office, 16 Jul. 1990 (Salmon, Hamilton, and Twigge, *German Unification 1989–1990*, 433).

88. "Saying the Unsayable about the Germans," *The Spectator*, 14 Jul. 1990, 8–10, Margaret Thatcher Foundation, http://www.margaretthatcher.org/document/111535/ (accessed 23 May 2019).

89. Ibid.

90. European Community, Special Meeting of the European Council, Dublin, 28 Apr. 1990, European Council website, https://www.consilium.europa.eu/media/20571/1990_april__-_dublin__eng_.pdf (accessed 23 May 2019).

91. Letter from C. Powel to S. Wall, 8 Jun. 1990, Prime Minister's meeting with President Gorbachev in the Kremlin on Friday 8 Jun. (Salmon, Hamilton, and Twigge, *German Unification 1989–1990*, 416).

92. Ibid., 417.
93. Ibid., 411–17.
94. M. Thatcher, Speech to the Konigswinter Conference, 29 Mar. 1990, Margaret Thatcher Foundation, http://www.margaretthatcher.org/document/108049/ (accessed 23 May 2019).
95. Sarotte, *1989: The Struggle*, 8–9.
96. Ibid., 47.
97. Bozo, *Mitterrand*, 311.
98. Minute from P. Cradock to M. Thatcher, 19 Jun. 1990 (Salmon, Hamilton, and Twigge, *German Unification 1989–1990*, 423).
99. Salmon, "Préface," xxxiii.
100. Letter from C. Mallaby to J. Weston, 11 Oct. 1990 (Salmon, Hamilton, and Twigge, *German Unification 1989–1990*, 489).
101. Comments by R. Braithwaite to the author of this essay, 22 Feb. 2015.
102. Poggiolini, "Thatcher's Double Track Road," 298–311.
103. Bozo, "Thatcher's European Delusion."
104. Bozo, "France, German Unification."
105. Bozo, "Mitterrand's France," 466.
106. Savranskaya, "The Logic of 1989," 38.
107. Sarotte, *The Collapse*, 91–92; conversation between M. Gorbachev and D. Hurd, 10 Sept. 1991, quoted in Savranskaya, "The Logic of 1989," 47.

Bibliography

Attali, J. 1995. *Verbatim*, Vol. 3, *1988–1991*. Paris: Fayard.

Blanton, T., ed. 1999. *The Revolutions of 1989: New Documents from the Soviet/East Europe*. Electronic Briefing Book, No. 22, 5 Nov. National Security Archive, George Washington University, Washington DC. http://www2.gwu.edu/~nsarchiv/news/19991105/ (accessed 23 May 2019).

Bozo, F. 2007. "Mitterrand's France, the End of the Cold War, and German Unification: A Reappraisal." *Cold War History* 7, no. 4: 455–78.

———. 2008. "France, German Unification, and European Integration." In Bozo et al., *Europe and the End of the Cold War*, 148–60.

———. 2009. *Mitterrand, the End of the Cold War, and German Unification*. New York/Oxford: Berghahn Books.

———. 2009. "Thatcher's European Delusion." *Prospect Magazine* 165, http://www.prospectmagazine.co.uk/magazine/thatchers-european-delusions/.

Bozo, F., M.-P. Rey, P. Ludlow, L. Nuti, eds. 2008. *Europe and the End of the Cold War: A Reappraisal*. London: Routledge.

Braithwaite, R. 2002. *Across the Moscow River*. New Haven, CT: Yale University Press.

———. 2010. "Gorbachev and Thatcher." *Journal of European Integration History* 16, no. 1: 31–44.

Brown, A. 2010. "Margaret Thatcher and Perceptions of Change in the Soviet Union." *Journal of European Integration History* 16, no. 1: 17–30.

Bullard, J. 2002. "Great Britain and German Unification." In *Britain and Germany in Europe, 1949–1990* edited by J. Noakes, P. Wende, and J. R. C. Wright, 219–30. Oxford: Oxford University Press.

Bush, G. H. W., and B. Scowcroft. 1998. *A World Transformed*. New York: Vintage Books.

Cradock, P. 1997. *In Pursuit of British Interests: Reflections on Foreign Policy under Margaret Thatcher and John Major*. London: John Murray.

Deighton, A. 2014. "Germany and East-Central Europe, 1945–1990: The View from London." In *Imposing, Maintaining and Tearing Open the Iron Curtain: The Cold War and East-Central Europe, 1945–1989*, edited by M. Kramer and V. Smetana, 211–26. Lanham, MD: Lexington Books.

Galkin, A., and A. Tschernjajew, eds. 2011. *Michail Gorbatschow und die deutsche Frage. Sowjetische Dokumente 1986–1991*. Munich, Germany: Oldenbourg Verlag.

Garton-Ash, T. 2009. "Britain Fluffed the German Question. Now Britain Is Europe's Great Puzzle." *The Guardian*, 21 Oct.

Grachev, A. 2010. "Political and Personal: Gorbachev, Thatcher and the end of the Cold War ." *Journal of European Integration History* 16, no. 1: 45–56.

Haftendorn, H. 2008. "German Unification and European Integration Are Two Sides of One Coin." In Bozo et al., *Europe and the End of the Cold War*, 135–47.

———. 2012. "The Unification of Germany, 1985–1991." In Leffler and Westad, *The Cambridge History of the Cold War*, Vol. 3: *Endings*, 333–55.

Kettenacker, L. 2000. "Britain and German Unification, 1989/90." In *Uneasy Allies: British-German Relations and European Integration since 1945*, edited by K. Larres and E. Meehan, 99–123. Oxford: Oxford University.

Kohl, H. 1992. "A Ten-Point Program for Overcoming the Division of Germany and Europe." In *When the Wall Came Down: Reactions to German Unification*, edited by H. James and M. Stone, 33–41. London: Routledge.

Larres, K., and E. Meehan, eds. 2000. *Uneasy Allies: British–German Relations and European Integration Since 1945*. Oxford: Oxford University, 2000.

Loth, W. 2004. "The Origins of Stalin's Note of 10 March 1952." *Cold War History* 4, no. 2: 66–88.

Poggiolini, I. 2012. "Thatcher's Double Track Road to the End of the Cold War: The Irreconcilability of Liberalization and Preservation." In *Visions of the End of the Cold War*, edited by F. Bozo, M.-P. Rey, and P. Ludlow, 298–311. Oxford: Berghahn Book.

Poggiolini, I., and A. Pravda. 2010. "Britain in Europe in the 1980s: East & West. Introduction." *Journal of European Integration History* 16, no. 1: 7–16.

Rey, M.-P. 2004. "Europe Is Our Common Home: A Study of Gorbachev's Diplomatic Concept." *Cold War History* 4, no. 2: 33–65.

Salmon, P. 2008. "The United Kingdom and German Unification." In Bozo et al., *Europe and the End of the Cold War*, 177–90.

———. 2009. "Préface." In Salmon, Hamilton, and Twigge, *German Unification 1989–1990*, vii–xxxiii.

Salmon, P., K. Hamilton, and S. R. Twigge, eds. 2008. *Berlin in the Cold War 1948–1990. Documents on British Policy Overseas* (DBPO), series 3, vol. 6. London: Routledge.

———. 2009. *German Unification 1989–1990. Documents on British Policy Overseas* (DBPO), series 3, vol. 7. London: Routledge.

Sarotte, M. E. 2010. *1989: The Struggle to Create Post–Cold War Europe*. Princeton, NJ: Princeton University Press.

———. 2014. *The Collapse. The Accidental Opening of the Berlin Wall*. New York: Basic Books.

Savranskaya, S. 2010. "The Logic of 1989. The Soviet Peaceful Withdrawal from Eastern Europe." In Savranskaya, Blanton, and Zubok, *Masterpieces of History*.

Savranskaya, S., and T. S. Blanton, eds. 2006. *The Reykjavik File: Previously Secret Documents from U.S. and Soviet Archives on the 1986 Reagan-Gorbachev Summit*. Electronic Briefing Book, No. 203, 13 Oct. National Security Archive, George Washington University, Washington DC. http://nsarchive.gwu .edu/NSAEBB/NSAEBB203/ (accessed 23 May 2019).

———, eds. 2009. *The Soviet Origins of Helmut Kohl's 10 Points*. Electronic Briefing Book, No. 296, 18 Nov. National Security Archive, George Washington University, Washington DC. http://www2.gwu .edu/~nsarchiv/NSAEBB/NSAEBB296/ (accessed 23 May 2019).

———, eds. 2013. *The Thatcher-Gorbachev Conversations*. Electronic Briefing Book, No. 422, 12 Apr. National Security Archive, George Washington University, Washington DC. http://www2.gwu.edu/ ~nsarchiv/NSAEBB/NSAEBB422/ (accessed 23 May 2019).

Savranskaya, S., T. S. Blanton, and V. M. Zubok, eds. 2010. *Masterpieces of History: The Peaceful End of the Cold War in Europe, 1989*. Budapest, Hungary: Central European University Press.

Schabert, T. 2009. *How World Politics Is Made: France and the Reunification of Germany*, Columbia: University of Missouri Press.

Shifrinson, J. R. I., ed. 2013. *The Malta Summit and U.S.-Soviet Relations: Testing the Waters Amidst Stormy Seas*. http://www.wilsoncenter.org/publication/the-malta-summit-and-us-Soviet-relations-testing-the-waters-amidst-stormy-seas (accessed 23 May 2019).

Staerck, G., and M. D. Kandiah, eds. 2003. *Anglo-German Relations and German Reunification*. London: Institute of Contemporary British History. https://keats.kcl.ac.uk/pluginfile.php/1402696/mod_resource/content/1/ICBH percent20Witness percent20Seminar.pdf/ (accessed 23 May 2019).

Thatcher, M. 1995. *The Downing Street Years*. London: HarperCollins.

Vaïsse, M., and C. Wenkel, eds. 2011. *La diplomatie française face à l'unification allemande d'après des archives inédites*. Paris: Tallandier.

Wenkel, C. 2017. "Overcoming the Crisis of Détente, 1979–1983. Coordinating Eastern Policies Between Paris, Bonn, and London." In *The Long Détente: Changing Concepts of Security and Cooperation in Europe, 1950s–1980s*, edited by O. Bange and P. Villaume, 235–51. Budapest, Hungary: CEU Press.

Zelikow, P. D., C. Rice. 1995. *Germany Unified and Europe Transformed: A Study in Statecraft*. Cambridge: Harvard University Press.

Zubok, V. 2007. "German Unification from the Soviet (Russian) Perspective." In *Turning Points in Ending the Cold War*, edited by K. K. Skinner, 255–72. Stanford, CT: Hoover Institution Press Publication.

CHAPTER 12

FRANCO-SOVIET RELATIONS, GERMAN UNIFICATION, AND THE END OF THE COLD WAR

Frédéric Bozo

The suspicion of a Franco-Soviet understanding against German unification in 1989–90 has long contributed to fueling the narrative of France's alleged opposition to German unification.[1] Clearly, investigating the Soviet factor is key to understanding French policy in that context: if one country could be seen as a possible bulwark against German unification in 1989–90, it was the Union of Soviet Socialist Republics (USSR, or Soviet Union). Conversely, because France was seen in Moscow as the Western country most inclined to acknowledge the Soviet Union's security interests, any Soviet attempt at framing a German settlement to its liking would have involved an effort to reach out to François Mitterrand's France. So what was the relative importance of the Soviet factor in France's policies faced with the prospect of German unification in 1989–90? Was there convergence or cooperation between the two countries? And what were the effects of Franco-Soviet interactions on the course of events?

In order to answer these questions, we will briefly look at the role of the German question in Franco-Soviet relations from Charles de Gaulle to Mitterrand. We will then examine to what extent Franco-Soviet relations were a significant factor when the German question was dramatically reopened in the last few months of 1989, focusing on the December 1989 Kiev meeting between President Mitterrand and Soviet leader Mikhail Gorbachev. Third, we will investigate the role of Franco-Soviet relations against the backdrop of the new acceleration that took place in early January 1990 and the diplomacy that culminated in the spring over the international aspects of German unification, focusing on the May 1990 Moscow meeting between the two leaders. Finally, we will ask whether the two countries converged on the wider issue of the European order that would emerge against the backdrop of the end of the Cold War, an issue that is inseparable from that of German unification.

From de Gaulle to Mitterrand

In the mid-1960s President de Gaulle (1958–69) launched a policy of détente, entente, and cooperation whose aim was to overcome the logic of blocs and to allow for the reemergence of a Europe "from the Atlantic to the Urals."[2] For him, any long-term European settlement involved solving the German question. On the one hand, de Gaulle plainly recognized the fundamental legitimacy of the Germans' aspiration to regain their unity: "The reunification of Germany," he declared in 1959, is "the normal destiny of the German people."[3] On the other hand, solving the German question in his view should not be a cause for disruption—hence the need for certain preconditions. First, Germany must not once again upset the territorial and strategic status quo; this precondition entailed that Germany should recognize its borders (specifically the Oder-Neisse line) and renounce nuclear weapons. A second precondition was for the European security context to be transformed; German unity had to result from détente and not the other way around. (For de Gaulle, the pursuit of European construction was a central aspect of this necessary transformation and so Germany's continued European commitment was another key precondition for solving the German question.) And, last but not least, the Germans needed to show "unfaltering patience" with a process that was likely to last as long as a generation.[4]

By the time of de Gaulle's historic June 1966 USSR visit, Franco-Soviet relations had become key when it came to the German question. To be sure, the two countries disagreed on the core issue: whereas the Soviets claimed that the existence of the two German states was a historic reality, de Gaulle was adamant that the Germans should be granted the right of self-determination. Yet Paris and Moscow converged on the need to avoid a destabilizing handling of the German question. They saw eye to eye on Germany's necessary recognition of the Oder-Neisse line and its renunciation to any nuclear ambitions, and they agreed on the need for the European system to be deeply transformed as a prerequisite of a German settlement (though the actual compatibility of their views of such a transformation was doubtful.)[5]

Contrary to erroneous interpretations, however, there was no basic Franco-Soviet agreement on keeping Germany divided. True, while the Soviets made it clear that there was no possibility for reunification in the "foreseeable future," de Gaulle acknowledged that it was "unlikely immediately."[6] As a result, Moscow was prone to interpret de Gaulle's stance as an implicit acceptance of its view that Germany's division had to be kept permanent, if not as an admission of a shared responsibility to that effect. (Always suspicious of both countries in that realm, the West Germans were also inclined to detect a Franco-Soviet understanding at the expense of German unity.[7]) Still, under de Gaulle the German question was *not* a matter of Franco-Soviet active cooperation; the status quo, which was deeply entrenched, did not call for it anyway. Yet what would happen if the German question was effectively reopened remained to be seen, especially if either side came to see such a scenario as potentially disruptive. Would Paris and Moscow converge? While this question would remain hypothetical for more than two decades, both sides were willing to keep their options open. On the French side, relations with Moscow remained a virtual reassurance if not against German unity per se, then at least against a potentially problematic re-unification—one in which the necessary guarantees and the international conditions for a peaceful settlement were not met.[8]

The situation remained by and large unchanged after de Gaulle. True, while Georges Pompidou (1969–74) continued de Gaulle's line, Valéry Giscard d'Estaing (1974–81) marked an apparent departure, conveying as he did to the Soviets his attachment to the status quo.[9] Yet Mitterrand's coming to power in 1981 led to a return to a more Gaullist stance. Reunification, Mitterrand told West German Chancellor Helmut Schmidt in 1981, is "inscribed in history" and it would come about "in a generation" as a result of the loosening of the Soviet grip.[10] But he also confided to Gorbachev in 1985 that while he was pursuing a "fraternal understanding" with Germany and while he wanted to strengthen Franco-German cooperation and European integration, he "could not desire the re-emergence of a dominant power in the centre of Europe."[11] Mitterrand was in line with his predecessors' approach of accepting the legitimacy of reunification while guarding against upsetting European stability. For Mitterrand, his adviser Hubert Védrine later commented, relations with Moscow offered a "supplementary assurance" against any disruptive reopening of the German question.[12]

Still, by the mid-1980s the German question had lost much of its relevance in Franco-Soviet relations: the East-West status quo seemed to freeze it permanently, making it a less salient issue; and the increasingly close Franco-German relationship under Chancellor Helmut Kohl and Mitterrand and their joint willingness to build Europe diminished the French inclination to discuss it with the Soviets: the German question, the Quai d'Orsay noted before Mitterrand's June 1984 visit to Moscow, could no longer serve as "a factor in Franco-Soviet rapprochement."[13] When Mitterrand returned to Moscow in summer 1986, there was simply no mention of it.[14]

True, the progressive transformation of Soviet foreign policy under Gorbachev (and Mitterrand had been among the first Western leaders to salute that policy) was a potential game changer: Might a less bellicose Soviet Union become open to a gradual overcoming of the status quo? West German leaders certainly hoped so.[15] The French were sceptical, but they kept a keen eye on these developments. Mitterrand, Védrine later commented, understood that unification was again "at the center of Bonn leaders' thinking" and he "was going along with this slow movement," though "he did not imagine that he would actually see its result."[16]

The German question suddenly became central again as a result of the acceleration of history that took place throughout 1989. Coming on top of the East German refugee crisis, which culminated in September, the downfall of East German leader Erich

Honecker in mid-October raised the issue of the the German Democratic Republic's (GDR, or East Germany) future and of relations between the two Germanys. On 22 August Kohl declared, "The German question is once more on the agenda." While it was not yet reopened in diplomatic terms, by early November there was little doubt that it would reopen sooner rather than later.[17]

Moscow and Paris reacted differently to these developments. The Soviets continued to oppose any German reunification; Gorbachev told former Chancellor Willy Brandt in October that the German question was "not on the agenda."[18] Moscow believed that it could control events: there was no question of "letting down the GDR," the Soviets told the French.[19] At the end of October 1989 the bottom line seemed clear: Moscow's "primary concern remains the preservation of the European territorial status quo with the GDR as its keystone."[20]

The French attitude was different. As early as July 1989, Mitterrand had declared that unification was a "legitimate" goal, though it had to be attained "democratically and peacefully" and not "with forceps."[21] This was in line with the Gaullist approach: yes to German self-determination, but no to a disruptive process. The subsequent acceleration in the East did not make him change his stance: de Gaulle's vision of a gradual evolution that would allow combining self-determination with the maintenance of European stability did not seem invalidated by events.[22] Both the Elysée and the Quai d'Orsay, in the early fall of 1989, were wagering on a transition toward German unity that would take the form of a rapprochement between West Germany and a democratized GDR, in sync with the overall transformation of the continent.[23] "I am not afraid of German unification," Mitterrand declared on 3 November in a joint press conference with Kohl, highlighting "the will and determination of the people" while reiterating the need for a "democratic" and "peaceful" process.[24]

By early November 1989 the Soviet factor was nevertheless becoming significant again as seen from Paris. The Quai d'Orsay suspected that Moscow did not rule out an evolution in which German self-determination would at some point become inevitable; it was therefore important to be able to monitor a possible Soviet change of heart. In such a case, France and the Soviet Union would need to cooperate closely: France "is keen to reaffirm the Germans' right to self-determination," Quai officials noted, "yet our country, like the USSR, has a major interest in preserving stability."[25]

The fall of the wall on 9 November was a test. Would Paris keep a balance between German self-determination and European stability, or would the latter now prevail? Would Paris and Moscow converge in the name of avoiding a disruptive evolution of the German question, if not in preventing German unity? Be that as it may, Germany was again at the center of the interaction between Paris and Moscow.

Kiev: A Meeting of Minds?

The fall of the wall did not instantly change the conversation on the German question, yet Kohl's announcement of the Ten-Point Plan on 28 November at the Bundestag transformed the situation entirely. For the first time, the realization of German unity—still under an unknown form and within an indefinite timeframe—was back on the agenda, at least in West Germany, and it was given an operational content by those in charge in Bonn.[26]

Ironically, Kohl's move was the result of confusion in Moscow: we now know that Horst Teltschik's meeting on 21 November with the CPSU Central Committee's official and top German expert Nikolai Portugalov—which Teltschik took as a green light for Kohl's move—was not authorized at the highest level, hence Moscow's harsh reaction to the Bundestag speech: while Gorbachev after the fall of the wall thought he had received assurances from Kohl that he would calm things down, Kohl now seemed to renege.[27] The German foreign minister, Hans-Dietrich Genscher, experienced Gorbachev's ire in Moscow on 5 December: having complained to him about Kohl's move (Foreign Minister Edward Shevardnadze even evoked the policies of Hitler), Gorbachev once again put forward the "reality of two German states," adding that history would decide.[28] The Soviet Union's reaction to the Ten-Point Plan was "very negative," the Quai noted.[29]

The French were dismayed by the failure of the Germans to consult with them, or at least to give them prior notice. True, Kohl's plan envisaged German unity in an indefinite future, and the Elysée could live with it. Yet the French found Kohl's plan wanting with regard to two key issues: first, the Oder-Neisse line; and second, Germany's future engagement in the European project.[30] Mitterrand was concerned with Kohl's apparent vacillation at a key European juncture; he deplored his reluctance to firmly commit himself to the European Monetary Union (EMU), which he now saw as the litmus test of a unified Germany's enduring European commitment. While he wanted the forthcoming European Council meeting in Strasbourg to set a firm date for a future intergovernmental conference on EMU, Kohl, on the eve of his 28 November speech, had sent him a letter rejecting this.[31] The combination of Kohl's acceleration in German unification and procrastination in European integration was alarming, hence Mitterrand's strong words when he received Genscher on 30 November. His message was two-fold: German unification was "unstoppable" and he would not create "obstacles"; but there was a need for a "stable Europe," which meant a strengthened European community in which a unified Germany would remain engaged. Otherwise, he warned, the continent risked returning to "1913": the Soviet Union would "fight against a German reunification [that would take place] in isolation" and "individual countries" would turn to the Soviet Union," he said, implicitly evoking the hypothetical recreation of a Franco-Soviet alliance.[32]

Irrespective of Mitterrand's dramatization (no doubt aimed at influencing Kohl's attitude before Strasbourg), there clearly was a change of tone in Paris in the last few weeks of 1989. Of the two long-time French parameters for dealing with the German question—support for self-determination and avoiding a disruptive process—the latter was an increasing priority. German unity "is normal" and "it goes in the direction of history," Mitterrand told a foreign dignitary the day he met Genscher, yet that unity cannot ignore the pace of European transformations: "If the rhythms are different, there is [the danger of] an accident," he said.[33]

A week later, Mitterrand was scheduled to meet with Gorbachev in Kiev, as he had suggested during a telephone conversation on 14 November. As chairman of the European Community (EC) during the second semester of 1989, he wanted to prevent the EC Twelve from being sidelined in the rapidly changing East-West environment (Gorbachev and George H. W. Bush were scheduled to meet in Malta on 4 December). Mitterrand wanted to assure the Soviet leader that any precipitate move would be avoided: "There is a certain equilibrium" in Europe, he said, "and we should not disturb it." But he also wanted to gauge his counterpart's reactions to the Berlin events and find out if there existed any common ground: it is important for France and the Soviet Union to "understand each other," he said.[34] Kohl's Bundestag speech made the meeting between Gorbachev and Mitterrand on 6 December even timelier. Paris and Moscow still had different approaches to the German question (the right of self-determination vs. the reality of two states), but both—to different degrees—had shown nervousness with Kohl's initiative, which they saw as potentially disruptive. So was convergence becoming possible in practice, and might Mitterrand and Gorbachev decide, if not to coalesce along the lines evoked by Mitterrand with Genscher, then at least to cooperate actively?

Based on the thinking in both capitals at that time, this was, in retrospect, a possibility. Gorbachev, like his predecessors, was prone to minimizing basic differences with the French on German unity and he was, at least implicitly, eyeing the French president as a possible partner in order to keep a lid on the German question: "As far as I understand it, we have a mutual understanding on this really cardinal issue," he told Mitterrand on 14 November.[35] And, on the French side, diplomats were increasingly doubtful that Moscow's opposition to unification was durable.[36] This awareness of the fragility of Moscow's plain "no" to German unification should in itself dispel the notion that Mitterrand was traveling to Kiev in order to seek Gorbachev's help in opposing it, since such a blocking strategy could well be built on sand. Yet was there no room for convergence on imposing a German settlement that would be controlled internationally and spread over time?

Be that as it may, such an active cooperation did *not* materialize in Kiev. True, basic differences over the right of the Germans to unify their two countries now seemed blurred. Mitterrand appeared as a reluctant unifier, using a convoluted formula: "Of course, when one people expresses a strong will . . . it is difficult not to respect this," he said, repeating that he was "not afraid" of German unification. As to Gorbachev, while not explicitly recognizing the right of the Germanys to unify, he refrained from invoking his usual formula on the historic reality of the two German states. True also, both leaders appeared dismayed—though with different degrees of indignation—at the acceleration resulting from Kohl's speech. "Kohl's statement," Mitterrand said, "has turned everything upside down." Gorbachev agreed, repeating the harsh words he had used the previous day with Genscher: "In practise, it means a *Diktat*." Furthermore, the two leaders agreed on the need for profound European transformations to take place before German unification could be addressed; doing otherwise could threaten stability. Granted, they did not see eye to eye on these transformations—strengthening the EC for Mitterrand and the Conference on Security and Cooperation in Europe (CSCE) for Gorbachev. Yet while Mitterrand's priority was clearly West European and Gorbachev's pan-European, they agreed that events had to be brought again under control. "The German component should be but one of the elements of European politics, but in no way a dominant, leading element," Mitterrand said. Paris and Moscow "are in a position to preserve a normal evolution," Gorbachev replied, mentioning "an increasing mutual understanding" and a "new cooperation" between them.[37]

Yet while circumstances thus seemed to bring the French and the Soviets closer than ever and while the gist of the conversation in Kiev was, at least implicitly, the need to slow things down, nothing practical came out of the meeting. When Mitterrand asked Gorbachev what "he wanted to do concretely," there was no answer. When Mitterrand mentioned his forthcoming visit to the GDR, Gorbachev said, "Maybe I should go there too," to which Mitterrand replied, "Let's go together." But no formal decision was made, and the two leaders parted company without having agreed on any specific course of action.[38] The parallel meeting between Dumas and Shevardnadze in Kiev echoed the conversation between the two leaders, and it was equally inconclusive. Shevardnadze appeared agitated, mentioning the risk of a revanchist Germany and pushing for common action, in particular through the activation of the Four Powers' rights. Dumas appeared far more detached, rejecting Shevardnadze's historical parallel. While recognizing the need for vigilance, he refrained from agreeing to any specific strategy, including the use of quadripartite rights. One should react "appropriately," he said, adding that "a certain tone would only stir German susceptibilities."[39]

So why was there at Kiev no Franco-Soviet understanding on an active policy of slowing down German unification? One possible answer was that the French and the Soviets may have believed that the warning signs they had given Kohl in more or less harsh terms via Genscher and the calls for moderation expressed in that period by all major players—including the United States—would, for the time being, have sufficient effects. Since the international consensus seemed to reflect a shared desire—even by the Germans—to calm things down, there was no urgency to act. Mitterrand and Gorbachev may also have been confident that, if a new acceleration did take place, they would agree on what was to be done.

But the lack of any common Franco-Soviet action in the aftermath of Kiev was arguably more fundamental. In Moscow confusion reigned. As Shevardnadze's conversation with Dumas had showed, the Soviet leadership was split between an outright rejection of reunification and the feeling that the process was unstoppable. This left little room for any coordination with others, especially since Gorbachev refused any discussion of confederative ties between the two Germanys of the kind Kohl had mentioned on 28 November, which would have been the best way to control things.[40] And, on the French side, the main objective after Kiev was not to coordinate with Moscow: Mitterrand's goal was to obtain Kohl's final acceptance of EMU, for which he had exerted considerable pressure on Bonn. The pressure worked: at the Strasbourg European Council meeting on 8 December, Kohl finally agreed to Mitterrand's request that a firm date should be set for the future intergovernmental conference, making Strasbourg a success for French diplomacy. Because it alleviated earlier concerns that Kohl might be tempted to procrastinate, Strasbourg seemed to confirm Germany's European commitment, reinforcing the priority of Franco-German relations over any hypothetical—and potentially hazardous—Franco-Soviet entente.[41] True, Mitterrand used his visit to the GDR on 20–22 December to reaffirm the importance of a controlled process that had to start from the existing reality of the two Germanys. Contrary to a widespread misrepresentation, however, it was not an attempt to hinder unification by trying artificially to prolong the lease of life of the GDR—which no one at the time believed would disappear, as it would, in a matter of months. Kohl himself, at that time, believed that unification would take several years.[42]

Moscow: Kindred Spirits?

On 4 January 1990 Mitterrand and Kohl met at the French president's vacation home in the South of France. Kohl wanted to reassure Mitterrand: German unification would take time and take place under a European roof, and France remained Germany's key partner. Mitterrand agreed: German unity was on its way, and European unity had to proceed at the same pace. France, he repeated, would not create obstacles. But he warned Kohl against aggravating the "Russian problem": the Gorbachev experience, he argued, was not easily reconcilable with a rapid German unification, which might fuel resentment and trigger a dangerous backlash. At Kiev, Mitterrand had found Gorbachev worried of a possible German rush; unification, he advised, must not lead to Soviet sabre rattling.[43]

Whereas in the early days of 1990 German unification still seemed likely to stretch over a relatively extended period, things changed dramatically in the following weeks. By mid-January it was becoming clear that the disastrous economic situation of the GDR, combined with the political discredit of the reformist communist leadership, made the survival of the regime and even of the state increasingly doubtful. A rapid unification was now on the agenda, and it would likely be a takeover, not a merger. From Kohl's announcement on 6 February of his plan for economic and monetary union between the two Germanys to the Christian Democratic Union (CDU)–led alliance's victory in the GDR elections on 18 March the pace of events was hugely increased. By then, agreement had been reached in Ottawa on 13 February between the two Germanys and the four guarantor powers on a six-way diplomatic management of the external aspects of unification. This would lead in less than six months to the signing of the Moscow Treaty on 12 September, paving the way to the unification of Germany on 3 October.

Once again, Moscow and Paris were unsettled by this fresh acceleration, but they reacted differently. Moscow now accepted unification as a fact of life. When Modrow came to Moscow on 30 January, Gorbachev recognized that unity was the eventual endpoint of the rapprochement between West Germany and the GDR.[44] Yet Gorbachev was still wagering on a gradual process with intermediary steps, and he was hoping for France's support to impose it. In the wake of Modrow's visit, he wrote to Mitterrand that he wanted a "smooth," "step by step" evolution, and he warned against any "hasty impulses" toward German unification.[45]

Mitterrand was taken aback by the rapidity of Gorbachev's acceptance of German unity: Moscow "no longer has the psychological or political means to oppose anything," he remarked.[46] The risk of unification with forceps was again looming. Mitterrand aired his concerns during a 20 January meeting with Margaret Thatcher. Thatcher complained that "West Germany was constantly pressing forward toward reunification," causing "particular difficulties" for Gorbachev. Mitterrand concurred: the Germans were "concentrating on unification to the exclusion of everything else." They "had the right to self-determination," he continued, but one had "to take the concerns of the rest of Europe into consideration." Yet Mitterrand's reaction was not to try to hinder the process. He did not believe this was possible or desirable: "It would be stupid and unrealistic to say no to reunification," he said, because "no force in Europe . . . could stop it from happening," not even the Soviet Union. When Thatcher tried to convince him to joint efforts with her to "slow down reunification" by using the Four Powers' rights, he declined: "There would be nothing worse than to remind the Germans of their obligations but then find we had no means to enforce them," he said. [47]

While Mitterrand agreed to remain in close contact, nothing concrete came out of the meeting or of subsequent Franco-British consultations.[48] The French response to the January 1990 acceleration was, in fact, to press the Germans to accept the necessary international conditions for unification. This was in line with the French doctrine since de Gaulle: Germany had to finally recognize the Oder-Neisse line, to renounce nuclear weapons, and to reaffirm its commitment to European unification (Kohl's acceptance of EMU at Strasbourg had been a first step); and a solution had to be found regarding Germany's position vis-à-vis the military alliances.[49] While the French were still wary of Kohl's propensity to impose unification as a fait accompli in international terms, the Ottawa agreement came to them as a relief. Meeting Kohl again in Paris on 15 February, Mitterrand reaffirmed that France had "no reservations" on unification, but, he added "we do want to have a say on its international consequences."[50]

Now that the international conversation on German unification focused on how and when—rather than whether—it should take place, was there room for Franco-Soviet joint action? There was, in fact, quite little. At Ottawa Dumas had agreed with his Soviet counterpart on the need to "implement the two plus four formula very quickly."[51] Yet Franco-Soviet coordination, in the following weeks and months, proved remarkably limited in the framework of the Two Plus Four. The reason is simple: there was in fact very little convergence between Paris and Moscow on the international aspects of unification.[52]

The Soviets had a maximalist approach to the negotiation. They wanted the process to lead to a fully fledged peace treaty that would settle the scores dating back to 1945. On substance, they wanted the settlement to impose a restrictive international status on unified Germany, especially in politico-military terms: not only a confirmation of Germany's renunciation to nuclear weapons, but also Germany's neutralization, its demilitarization and denuclearization (meaning no foreign nuclear weapons on its territory), all of which had to be attained thanks to a synchronization between unification and an overall transformation of the European system that would lead to a prevalence of collective security over the existing military alliances—a process involving several years of transition during which the Four Powers would continue to exercise their rights.[53]

This left very little room for concerted action. True, Paris and Moscow agreed on the need for Germany to recognize the Oder-Neisse line and renounce nuclear weapons, but this led to remarkably little Franco-Soviet coordination in the Two Plus Four. True also, the French rejected a minimalist scheme in which the Four Powers—as the Germans, with the support of the Americans, clearly preferred—would have rubber-stamped Germany's unification without exercising their rights to extract the necessary conditions, particularly when it came to Oder-Neisse. Yet Paris also understood that there were limits to the role of the Four, if only because of the Germans' rejection of such a role. While the French were willing to make some formal concessions to the Soviets in order for them to save face—for example, by naming the end result of the Two Plus Four a peace settlement (in the end the notion of a final settlement was preferred), they were not keen on the Four Powers actually imposing a settlement.[54]

More crucially, Paris and Moscow diverged when it came to the issue of Germany's and—by implication—of Europe's future security status. For all the Gaullist rhetoric of moving beyond blocs, the fact of the matter was that the Soviet objective of a neutralized Germany embedded in a European collective security system—in essence resurrecting the Stalin Note of March 1952—ran directly counter to France's and the West's fundamental security interests. Paris wanted to avoid both a neutralization of Germany and a calling into question of the Western security system. "On all these issues," the Quai d'Orsay noted at the start of the Two Plus Four, "the Soviet vision does not in any way coincide with ours."[55]

The limits of Franco-Soviet convergence appeared in full light when Dumas met with Shevardnadze in Moscow on 30 March to discuss the incipient negotiation. Shevardnadze wanted to "synchronize German unification and the pan-European rapprochement," but Dumas did not take this up. And while Shevardnadze wanted the Four to rule out use of Article 23 of West Germany's Basic Law (i.e., unification by direct accession to West Germany of the East German territory, as opposed to the more convoluted procedure under Article 146, which involved the drafting of a new all-German constitution), Dumas rejected this: only Article 23, he said, "would not give the Germans the feeling that one tries to postpone unification."[56]

Dumas's stance confirmed that the French were not ready to join the Soviets in a policy of retarding German unification by embedding it in the larger transformation of European security: contrary to Article 23 (which essentially meant a West German takeover), Article 146 would indeed have entailed a protracted renegotiation of West Germany's existing international ties and would have allowed for the kind of synchronization desired by Moscow. Whatever his earlier wish of a more gradual process, Mitterrand was not willing to impose it in collusion with the Soviets (as Gorbachev had seemingly contemplated) or the British (as Thatcher had explicitly suggested) and, as a result, was going along the U.S.–West German push for a rapid unification on Western terms—albeit somewhat grudgingly as will be seen next.

Conversely, the French observed Moscow's impotence: Soviet diplomacy, the Quai concluded at the end of April 1990, finds itself isolated in defending a maximalist stance and "gives the paradoxical impression of wanting to play for time while passively watching the acceleration" of the unification process.[57] Shevardnadze's surprise suggestion, during the first ministerial meeting of the Two Plus Four on 5 May, to disconnect the internal and the external processes of German unification only confirmed, as seen from Paris, that Moscow was definitely no longer in a position to prevent a quick unification.[58]

By that time, any notion of a Franco-Soviet entente was at odds with Mitterrand's fundamental choice of addressing the challenge of German unification through a relaunch of the Franco-German couple and of the European project. True, the Oder-Neisse issue had led to frictions with Bonn at the end of winter; Mitterrand's strong insistence on the need for a definitive settlement of the border issue as part of any German settlement was met with irritation by Kohl.[59] Yet by mid-spring those frictions—exacerbated by domestic politics in West Germany—had essentially been overcome. Even more critically, Paris and Bonn, over the three months following their 15 February meeting, had reached a compromise on the need for a strengthened European construction in which a unified Germany would remain firmly embedded, as proclaimed by the Dublin European Council meeting on 28 April. It had taken "three or at most four months," Kohl's adviser Joachim Bitterlich later commented, for France and Germany to again unite in their "common responsibility for European unification."[60]

True, when he met again with Gorbachev in Moscow on 25 May 1990, Mitterrand was still ostensibly displeased with the pace and modalities of the process, which now appeared boosted by Washington's (and Bonn's) willingness to push for a rapid unification on Western terms—in other words, first and foremost within NATO. While Mitterrand did not disagree with the basic objective, he saw U.S. (and German) haste in achieving it as problematic: it could not only destabilize Gorbachev but could also contradict France's Euro-Atlantic strategic vision (on this more below). Yet Mitterrand skillfully used the meeting—dominated by the issue of Germany's NATO membership—to deter Gorbachev from trying to apply the brakes.

Gorbachev bitterly complained about Kohl's rush and lack of consideration for Soviet interests. Mitterrand did not conceal his own frustration: Kohl had accelerated again his pace in January, which had "turned things upside down." Now the United States and West Germany wanted unification "without delay." Yet this was a fact of life: "What means of influence do we have, excluding of course threats?," he asked.[61] While they had "good relations with the Germans," he went on, the French remained watchful. He did not want to set "preconditions," but he did want to discuss the "consequences" of unification and to obtain "guarantees." But when Gorbachev stressed the need to stretch the timelines, Mitterrand was dismissive: "You can harden your attitude," he said, but this "would lead to a destabilization of Europe."[62]

Similar to Thatcher four months before, Mitterrand, at this critical juncture, rejected any Franco-Soviet understanding in order to delay German unification; he wanted to dissuade Gorbachev from resorting to a last-ditch policy of obstruction. While ostensibly sharing his displeasure with the way the Germans had behaved over the past few months ("I feel more comfortable with you," he went as far as saying), he wanted to convince him that there was nothing to be done to slow down the process, most likely exaggerating the expression of his own frustration in order to make the point. By the time of Mitterrand's Moscow visit, the possibility of a Franco-Soviet entente—if it had ever existed—appeared definitively out of the question: "Obviously, there's no question of the two of us uniting against the Germans," Mitterrand hammered out.[63]

Mitterrand, Gorbachev, and the Future European Order

By the time of the Moscow meeting, ensuring unified Germany's continued NATO membership was at the top of Washington's and Bonn's agenda and had become the central bone of contention in the negotiation over German unification. Moscow rejected such an outcome vocally; Washington had stepped up its efforts at persuading the Soviets, but to no avail, as Baker's visit to Moscow on 18 May, one week before Mitterrand's, once again confirmed.[64]

The Soviets could have hoped for a measure of French support. France was a reluctant NATO member and a critic of U.S. dominance in it; now the U.S.-German determination to quickly impose a unified Germany in NATO—granted with some compensations for Moscow—was threatening to create a U.S.-German-dominated alliance and to perpetuate the Atlantic status quo. The French wanted to overhaul NATO in order to increase Europe's influence in it, so this was a potential blow to France's hope to strengthen the strategic role of the EC (soon to be the European Union [EU]).[65] All this could have led to Franco-Soviet convergence.

Yet the Soviets would soon be disappointed. True, the French believed that Moscow's security interests had to be taken into account; the Soviet Union should be given assurances that the former GDR territory would not become a NATO stronghold, and that the alliance's integrated machinery should not expand eastward: "The Soviet retreat should not correspond to a Western advance," Mitterrand told Kohl.[66] But Paris rejected any neutralization of the country: it would not only sap the Atlantic alliance—whatever the French frustration with U.S. dominance in it, the Alliance still represented for Paris the *ultima ratio* of Western security—but it would also prevent the emergence of a politically and strategically unified Western Europe, France's key objective: "We cannot allow the neutralization of Germany," Mitterrand told Bush.[67]

The French conundrum—keeping a unified Germany in NATO without perpetuating the Atlantic status quo—was the backdrop of Mitterrand's discussion with Gorbachev on 25 May. To be sure, the French president was annoyed with what he perceived as U.S.-German recklessness; still, Mitterrand's frustration did not lead to Franco-Soviet convergence. Gorbachev wanted to enroll Mitterrand in his attempt to oppose full NATO membership for united Germany, which he said would lead to a "serious disruption of the strategic balance." But Mitterrand's goal was to convince Gorbachev that there was no other alternative. "I know," he said, "that Germany's NATO membership creates very big problems for you," adding: "I also have difficulties in this regard, though of a different sort." But he rejected the other solutions put forward by Gorbachev, starting with Germany's belonging to both the Warsaw Pact and NATO, which the Americans would find nonsensical and the Germans would reject. As for Germany's belonging to the alliance but not the integrated structure (in other words the French model), he did not see objections, but he underlined that it was for the Germans to decide.[68]

The bottom line was clear: although Mitterrand understood Gorbachev's willingness to avoid a Soviet rollback and although he had his own reservations with regard to the U.S.-German approach, France was not willing to take the risk of being marginalized in its own camp by going along with the Soviet Union. "I simply do not see how you might impose your conceptions," he concluded, noting that the Germans and their NATO partners could simply go ahead and decide on Germany's NATO membership irrespective of Moscow.[69]

We now know that Mitterrand's arguments carried the day. Coming from the least pro-NATO of Gorbachev's Western counterparts, the notion that there was no viable alternative was hardly refutable.[70] Gorbachev recognized as much in his meeting with Bush in Washington one week later (though it took another few weeks before a deal was actually reached by Gorbachev and Kohl in the Caucasus in July). Then, he accepted the validity of the argument that Mitterrand had brought up in Moscow—in other words, that the 1975 Helsinki agreement recognized individual countries' freedom of choice of their alliances. The conclusion seems inescapable: not only were the French and the Soviets not in agreement on the basic issue of Germany's NATO membership, but also at a key juncture Mitterrand skillfully and successfully used France's anti-NATO posture to pressure Gorbachev to accept the West's stance.[71]

If Franco-Soviet agreement turned out to be impossible on the NATO issue, was it not possible in the pan-European dimension, where a shared aspiration to move beyond blocs prevailed? Ever since de Gaulle, apparent convergences had existed in that realm, and Paris and Moscow were keen to emphasize them as part of their bilateral dialogue. But they often did so at the price of overlooking substantial differences. While Mitterrand paid lip service to Gorbachev's concept of a European common home, disagreements persisted on concrete issues, starting with the role of the CSCE. While Paris did see the CSCE as an important framework for East-West rapprochement, it was also wary of its possible transformation into a collective security organization that would supplant the existing alliances, dissolve the transatlantic link, and prevent the emergence of a more autonomous Western Europe.[72]

True, the acceleration of events during the last weeks of 1989 seemed to lead to a meeting of minds. When in Rome on 30 November Gorbachev had called for a CSCE summit meeting in 1990, Paris had given its backing, and, at Kiev, Mitterrand had seemed to concur with Gorbachev's sense of pan-European urgency.[73] Yet the Soviets soon discovered that France's CSCE priority was at best relative and that Paris was not keen to give it a major role in channelling German unification. Because of the acceleration of the first weeks of 1990, making the latter conditional on the establishment of new pan European security structures was not in the cards, the French believed: "One needs to be pragmatic and not systematically make one process dependent on the other," the Quai d'Orsay director for political affairs, Bertrand Dufourcq, told his Soviet opposite number, Anatoly Adamishin, in mid-January.[74]

By the time of the beginning of the Two Plus Four negotiation in the spring, it was clear that French diplomacy was at odds with its Soviet counterpart's willingness to use the CSCE in order to frame the future security status of a united Germany, and that Paris disagreed with key Soviet ideas such as the CSCE's institutionalization and its role in transforming military alliances.[75] The Quai d'Orsay was wary of the Soviets' "attempt to propel their old ideas of pan-European structures" and their "hidden objective" of a Euro-American "decoupling." While French diplomats agreed the CSCE's role must be strengthened, they believed this could be done only "as a supplement, and not as an alternative, to the military alliances."[76] The Elysée concurred: "The key problem," a Mitterrand adviser wrote, is "the Soviet willingness to create a link between a final settlement [of the German issue] and an in-depth transformation of Europe's security structures."[77] In Moscow on 25 May Mitterrand's advocacy of a CSCE reinforcement was, accordingly, rather cosmetic: "One must give the CSCE a bigger weight," he said, mentioning a "permanent mechanism" and a "permanent secretariat."[78] By mid-1990 it was clear that the role of the CSCE summit (now scheduled to take place in Paris 19–21 November) would be to acknowledge German unity, and not to lay the groundwork for a new pan-European security system.

France's reluctance to transform the CSCE into an overriding pan-European institution may also be explained by Mitterrand's willingness to preserve his pet project: the creation of a European "confederation." Mitterrand's goal in launching his confederation idea on 31 December 1989 was to consecrate the soon-to-be EU as the cornerstone of the post–Cold War European order and to promote the emergence a Europe "from the Atlantic to the Urals" à la de Gaulle, in which Russia would be included. Mitterrand's concept was to a large extent a response to what he saw as the biggest challenge at Cold War's end: preventing the exclusion of the Soviet Union. As he flew to Moscow, he listed for himself the various avenues that existed to avoid the Soviet Union's isolation, including creating "links between the EC and the USSR," "strengthening the CSCE," and building the confederation.[79] "I will not take part in the manoeuver to marginalize the USSR," Mitterrand told Gorbachev in Moscow.[80]

Yet when the confederation was effectively launched in early 1991, Soviet participation proved to be a major hurdle. The new Eastern democracies saw the project as a ploy to indefinitely postpone their future EC/EU membership, motivated by Mitterrand's fear that a rapid EC/EU enlargement would lead to the dilution of the European project. But the new Eastern democracies were also wary of a concept that combined Soviet participation and U.S. exclusion, a combination they disliked all the more as they were increasingly leaning toward NATO membership as a reassurance vis-à-vis the potential resurgence of a Soviet threat.[81] By the time of the June 1991 Prague meeting, during which the creation of the confederation was to be sanctioned, support for the project was found only in Moscow, where it was seen as a lifeline against the political marginalization and economic breakdown of the Soviet Union.[82]

The project all but collapsed in the aftermath of the Prague meeting. The attempted coup against Gorbachev in August was the final blow. By then, the Soviet Union was seen as a strategic liability, and any notion of including it in Western institutions was seen as reckless, sapping the rationale for Mitterrand's confederation. By the time the Soviet Union effectively disintegrated at the end of the year, it was clear that the French objective of keeping it firmly anchored to the West in general and to Western Europe in particular in order to prevent a backlash of the 1989–90 events from causing a backlash in the Soviet Union had failed.

Conclusion

In spite of the close relationship that prevailed between Gorbachev and Mitterrand, France and the Soviet Union failed to cooperate actively against the backdrop of German unification. Beyond apparent convergences, the two countries did not see eye to eye when it came to the fundamental issue of German self-determination, they did not share a full understanding of the international conditions required for German unification, and, even more crucially, they had different visions of the transformation of the European security system that should accompany it. While Mitterrand was, initially, unsettled by the pace and modalities of the process, at times projecting the image of a reluctant unifier in his conversations with Gorbachev, he was not ready to coalesce with him to oppose German unity. On the contrary Mitterrand, ever the tactician, skillfully used his sympathy for the Soviet conundrum and his ostensible dissatisfaction with some aspects of German (and U.S.) policies in order to convince Gorbachev that there was no point in opposing it or in trying to prevent it from happening along the lines that were emerging in the spring of 1990—in other words, with a unified Germany firmly anchored in Euro-Atlantic institutions.

The bottom line is clear: at no point were Franco-Soviet relations seriously seen as a substitute to the Franco-German partnership that, by the end of the 1980s, had become the alpha and the omega of French policy. An active Franco-Soviet cooperation (let alone a most improbable return to the bygone pattern of an *alliance de revers*) could only have materialized in the worst-case scenario of a serious disruption caused by an ill-managed, uncontrolled unification process. This is not to say that the Soviet factor was not important in French eyes. Yet at the end of the day it was not—and arguably it could not be—about using the Soviet Union as a reassurance against German unification, a policy that would likely have failed given Moscow's inability to oppose it and would have endangered the Franco-German partnership perhaps irremediably. Mitterrand's efforts, rather inversely, were aimed at giving the Soviet Union assurances with regard to the consequences of German unification. By doing so, he effectively helped to bring Moscow around to accepting its realization on Western terms.

Frédéric Bozo is professor of contemporary history at the Sorbonne Nouvelle (University of Paris 3, Department of European Studies). He was educated at the École Normale Supérieure, at the Institut d'Études Politiques de Paris, and at Harvard University. He received his PhD from the University of Paris-Nanterre (1993) and his habilitation from the Sorbonne Nouvelle (1997). His publications include *Mitterrand, the End of the Cold War, and German Unification* (2009), *Visions of the End of the Cold War in Europe, 1945–1990* (coedited with N. Piers Ludlow, Marie-Pierre Rey, and Bernd Rother; 2012) and *French Foreign Policy since 1945: An Introduction* (2016), all with Berghahn Books. His most recently published book is *A History of the Iraq Crisis: France, the United States, and Iraq, 1991–2003* (2016).

Notes

This chapter draws in part from my earlier article "'I Feel More Comfortable with You': France, the Soviet Union, and German Unification," *Journal of Cold War Studies* 17, no. 3 (Summer, 2015): 116–58. © 2015 by the President and Fellows of Harvard College and the Massachusetts Institute of Technology. Used with permission from the *Journal of Cold War Studies* and the MIT Press.

 1. For works conveying such a narrative, see, e.g., Hutchings, *American Diplomacy*; and Weidenfeld, *Außenpolitik für die deutsche Einheit*. For an account stressing the constructive character of French policy, see Bozo, *Mitterrand*.

2. See his press conference of 4 Feb. 1965 in de Gaulle, *Discours et messages*, vol. 4, 338–42. On de Gaulle's concept for overcoming Yalta, see Bozo, "France, 'Gaullism.'"

3. Press conference of 25 Mar. 1959 (de Gaulle, *Discours et messages*, vol. 3, 84–85).

4. See de Gaulle, *Mémoires d'espoir*, vol. 1, "Le Renouveau," 1958–62, 191.

5. See, e.g., the de Gaulle-Brezhnev meeting in Moscow, 22 Jun. 1966, DDF 1966, vol. 2, 133–36.

6. Ibid., 134.

7. See, e.g., Bonn telegram no. 3662-75, 17 Jun. 1966, ibid., 103–5.

8. See, e.g., MAE, Centre d'analyse et de prévision, note, "Caractères du dialogue Franco-soviétique au sommet (1966–1980)," 16 May 1984, Secret, AMAE, Europe, URSS 1986–90, box 5694.

9. On this, see Soutou, "Valéry Giscard d'Estaing."

10. Meeting between Mitterrand and Schmidt, Latché, 7 Oct. 1981, AnF, 5AG4/CD 72, dossier 2.

11. Meeting between Mitterrand and Gorbachev, Paris, 2 Oct. 1985, AnF, 5AG4/CD 76.

12. Védrine, *Les Mondes*, 374.

13. Note, "Caractères du dialogue Franco-soviétique au sommet (1966–80)," 16 May 1984.

14. Meeting between Mitterrand and Gorbachev, Moscow, 7 Jul. 1986, AMAE, Europe, URSS 1986–90, box 6684.

15. See Grachev, *Gorbachev's Gamble*, 133–34.

16. Védrine, *Les Mondes*, 406.

17. On the chain of events that led to the reopening of the German question in the fall of 1989, see in particular Zelikow and Rice, *Germany Unified*; Sarotte, *1989: The Struggle*; Rödder, *Deutschland*; and Bozo, *Mitterrand* (Kohl's quote is on p. 88).

18. Gespräch Gorbačevs mit dem Vorsitzenden der Sozialistischen Internationale, Brandt, am 17 Oct. 1989 (Galkin and Tschernjajew, *Michail Gorbatschow*, 211).

19. Moscow telegram no. 5933, 21 Sept. 1989, AMAE, Europe, Allemagne 1986–90, box 6125. See also Grachev, *Gorbachev's Gamble*, 139.

20. Fiche, A/S attitude de nos principaux partenaires occidentaux à l'égard de la "question allemande," 30 Oct. 1989, AMAE, Europe, URSS 1986–90, box 6681.

21. Mitterrand interview with five European newspapers, 27 Jul. 1989, PEF, Jul.–Aug. 1989, 78–82.

22. On this, see Bozo, "Mitterrand's Vision."

23. Hubert Védrine, Note a/s Réflexions sur la question allemande, 18 Oct. 1989, AnF, 5AG4, CD177; MAE, le directeur d'Europe (Jacques Blot), Réflexions sur la question allemande, 30 Oct. 1989, AMAE, Europe, Allemagne 1986–90, box 6119.

24. Mitterrand-Kohl joint press conference, Bonn, 3 Nov. 1989, PEF, Nov.–Dec. 1989, 4–6.

25. MAE, Fiche, A/S Conception française du rapprochement des deux Europe et de la "question allemande," 8 Nov. 1989; Fiche, A/S: Les relations l'URSS et la RFA, 9 Nov. 1989, AMAE, Europe 1986–90, URSS, box 6681.

26. On this, see Rödder, *Deutschland*, 137; and Zelikow and Rice, *Germany Unified*, 118.

27. See Grachev, *Gorbachev's Gamble*, 142 *ff*.

28. Gespräch BM mit GS Gorbatschow am 05.12.1989 in Moskau (Hilger, *Diplomatie*, 76).

29. MAE, Fiche, A/S Les réactions des pays voisins de la RFA et de la RDA au "plan en dix points" du chancelier Kohl, 30 Nov. 1989, AMAE, Europe 1986–90, URSS, 6681.

30. MAE, Fiche A/S: Déclaration du Chancelier Kohl (Bundestag, 28 Nov. 1989), [no date but from context late Nov. 1989], AMAE, Europe 1986–90, URSS, box 6681.

31. On this issue, see Bozo, "France, German Unification."

32. Gespräch von Bundesaussenminister Genscher mit dem französichen Staatspräsident Mitterrand am 30 Nov. 1989 in Paris (Hilger, *Diplomatie*, 59). Dumas delivered the same message. see diplomatic telegram 25193-4, 4 Dec. 1989, AMAE, Europe, Allemagne 1986–90, box 6800.

33. Mitterrand-Roh-Tae-Woo meeting, 30 Nov. 1989 (private papers).

34. Record of the telephone conversation between Mikhail Gorbachev and François Mitterrand, 14 Nov. 1989 (Savranskaya, Blanton, and Zubok, *Masterpieces of History*, 593–94).

35. Gorbachev-Mitterrand telephone conversation, 14 Nov. 1989.

36. Moscow telegram no. 7079-80, 4 Dec. 1989, AMAE, Europe 1986–90, URSS, box 6681. On French diplomats' assessment of Moscow's opposition to unification, see Bozo, *Mitterrand*, 114, 134–35.

37. Gespräch Gorbačevs mit dem französichen Staatspräsidenten Mitterrand am 6. Dezember 1989 (Galkin and Tschernjaew, *Michail Gorbatschow*, 266 *ff*).

38. Ibid.

39. Ambassade de France en URSS, Note A/S Compte-rendu de l'entretien entre M. le Ministre d'Etat et M. Chevardnadze à Kiev le 6 Dec. 1989, 15 Dec. 1989, AMAE, Europe 1986–90, URSS, box 6674.

40. On this, see Grachev, *Gorbachev's Gamble*, 152.

41. See Bozo, "France, German Unification."

42. Schwarz, *Helmut Kohl*, 534.

43. Kohl-Mitterrand meeting, Latché, 4 Jan. 1990, AnF, 5AG4/CD 73, dossier 1; Gespräch des Bundes-kanzlers Kohl mit Staatspräsident Mitterrand, Latché, 4 Jan. 1990 (Küsters and Hofmann, *Deutsche Einheit*, 685).

44. See Grachev, *Gorbachev's Gamble*, 152; and Adomeit, *Imperial Overstretch*, 474 *ff*.

45. Letter, Gorbachev to Mitterrand, 2 Feb. 1990 (private papers).

46. Council of Ministers, 31 Jan. 1990 (private papers).

47. Letter from Mr. Powell (no. 10) to Mr. Wall, 20 Jan. 1990 (Salmon, Hamilton, and Twigge, *German Unification* 215–19); and Mitterrand-Thatcher meeting, 20 Jan. 1990 (notes by Loïc Hennekinne) (private papers).

48. Letter from Powell to Wall, 20 Jan. 1990; Mitterrand-Thatcher meeting 20 Jan. 1990. See also Thatcher, *The Downing Street Years*, 797–98.

49. Védrine note for President Mitterrand, 8 Feb. 1990 (private papers).

50. Mitterrand-Kohl meeting, 15 Feb. 1990 AnF, 5AG4/CD 73, dossier 1; Gespräch des Bundeskanzlers Kohl mit Staatspräsident Mitterrand, Paris, 15 Feb. 1990, (Küsters and Hofmann, *Deutsche Einheit*, 843 *ff*).

51. Paris telegram no. 3170, 14 Feb. 1990, AMAE, ASD 1985–90, box 15.

52. On France's role in the Two Plus Four negotiation, see Bozo, *Mitterrand*, 209 *ff*.

53. MAE, ASP, note a.s. Ordre du jour des réunions des "Six." Positions de nos partenaires et premières conclusions du groupe, 20 Mar. 1990, AMAE, ASD 1985–90, box 16. See also Dufourcq, "2+4," 467–84.

54. MAE, directeur politique, Note pour le Cabinet du Ministre d'Etat a./s. Entretien avec M. Chevard-nadzé (Moscou, 30 Mar. 1990), "groupe à six," 28 Mar. 1990, AMAE, Europe, URSS 1986–90, box 6683.

55. Note pour le Cabinet du Ministre d'Etat a./s. Entretien avec M. Chevardnadze (Moscou, 30 Mar. 1990), "groupe à six," 28 Mar. 1990. See also MAE, note pour le directeur des affaires politiques, a.s. Quad du 13 Mar. 1990. Ordre du jour commenté (questions de sécurité), 12 Mar. 1990, and note a.s. Ordre du jour pour les réunions à Six, secret, 20 Mar. 1990, AMAE, ASD 1985–90, box 16); and Dufourcq, "2+4."

56. Moscow telegram no. 2501-2, AMAE, ASD, 1985–90, box 16.

57. Berlin telegram 1172-3, 1 May 1990, ibid.

58. Paris telegram no. 8907, 7 May 1990, ibid.

59. Teltschik, *329 Tage*, 171. See also Rödder, *Deutschland*, 241.

60. Bitterlich, "Frankreichs," 123. On this, see Bozo, *Mitterrand*, 233 *ff*.

61. Gespräch Gorbačevs mit dem französichen Staatspräsidenten Mitterrand am 25 Mai 1990 (Galkin and Tschernjajew, *Michail Gorbatschow*, 419–20); and Attali handwritten notes.

62. Zweites Gespräch Gorbačevs mit dem französichen Staatspräsidenten Mitterrand am 25. Mai 1990 (Galkin and Tschernjajew, *Michail Gorbatschow*, 420 *ff*); and Attali handwritten notes.

63. Ibid. See also Grachev, *Gorbachev's Gamble*, 159.

64. Gespräch Gorbačevs mit dem Amerikanischen Außenminister Baker am 18. Mai 1990 (Galkin and Tschernjajew, *Michail Gorbatschow*, 406 *ff*).

65. On this, see Bozo, "France, the United States."

66. Mitterrand-Kohl meeting, 15 Feb. 1990.

67. Bush-Mitterrand telephone conversation, 27 Jan. 1990, George H. W. Bush Presidential Library, http://bushlibrary.tamu.edu/research/pdfs/memcons_telcons/1990-01-27—Mitterrand.pdf.
68. Gespräch Gorbačevs mit dem französichen Staatspräsidenten Mitterrand am 25. Mai 1990 (Galkin and Tschernjajew, *Michail Gorbatschow*, 418); and Attali handwritten notes.
69. Zweites Gespräch Gorbačevs mit dem französichen Staatspräsidenten Mitterrand am 25. Mai 1990 (Galkin and Tschernjajew, *Michail Gorbatschow*, 420 *ff*); and Attali handwritten notes. Mitterrand's dilemma—how to keep Germany in the Alliance without confirming the U.S. dominance—remained acute in the following months; on this, see Bozo, "France, the United States."
70. See Moscow telegram no. 4097, 1 Jun. 1990, AMAE, Europe 1986–90, URSS, box 6682. Mitterrand's impact is also confirmed by Gorbachev's memoirs; see Gorbatschow, *Wie es war*, 135–36; see also Grachev, *Gorbachev's Challenge*, 158–59.
71. On this, see Grachev, *Gorbachev's Gamble*, 158–59.
72. On this, see Bozo, *Mitterrand*, 64–65; and Rey, "'Europe Is Our Common Home."
73. Gespräch Gorbačevs mit dem französichen Staatspräsident Mitterrand am 6. Dezember (Galkin and Tschernjajew, *Michail Gorbatschow*, 269).
74. Paris telegram no. 1253, 17 Jan. 1990, AMAE, Europe 1986–90, box 6674.
75. MAE, Note pour le Cabinet du Ministre d'Etat, Entretien avec M. Chevardnadze (Moscou 30 Mar. 1990). Groupe à "Six," 28 Mar. 1990, AMAE, Europe 1986–90, box 6683.
76. MAE, Schéma d'entretien, Visite officielle de travail du président de la République à Moscou (25 mai 1990), 21 May 1990, AMAE, Europe 1986–90, box 6682.
77. Caroline de Margerie, note pour le président de la République, "Les négociations Est-Ouest en cours: l'exercice 4+2, le désarmement, la CSCE," 23 May 1990, AnF, 5AG4/CD412.
78. Zweites Gespräch Gorbačevs mit dem französichen Staatspräsidenten Mitterrand am 25 May 1990 (Galkin and Tschernjajew, *Michail Gorbatschow*, 422); and Attali handwritten notes.
79. Mitterrand handwritten notes on Védrine's note of 23 May 1990. The other options listed were bilateral relations, relations between the G-7 and the Soviet Union, as well as the GATT and the EBRD.
80. Gorbachev-Mitterrand Moscow meeting, plenary session, 25 May 1990, handwritten notes [no author but from handwriting and file probably Caroline de Margerie], 5AG4/CDM48. On the European Confederation project (and its demise), see Bozo, "The Failure."
81. Memorandum for the president from Hubert Védrine, Problèmes de sécurité en Europe centrale et orientale, 26 Mar. 1991, AnF, 5AG4/EG70.
82. Moscow telegram no. 2652, AMAE, ASD 1985–90, Questions multilatérales, box 20.

Bibliography

Adomeit, H. 1998. *Imperial Overstretch: Germany in Soviet Policy from Stalin to Gorbachev.* Baden-Baden, Germany: Nomos Verlag.
Bitterlich, J. 1998. "Frankreichs (und Europas) Weg nach Maastricht im Jahr der deutschen Einheit." In *Schwierige Nachbarschaft am Rhein: Frankreich-Deutschland*, edited by W. Rouget, 112–23. Bonn, Germany: Bouvier.
Bozo, F. 2008. "France, German Unification, and European Integration." In *Europe and the End of the Cold War: A Reappraisal*, edited by F. Bozo, L. Nuti, N. P. Ludlow, and M.-P. Rey 148–60. London: Routledge.
———. 2008. "The Failure of a Grand Design: Mitterrand's European Confederation, 1989–1991." *Contemporary European History* 17. 391–412.
———. 2009. *Mitterrand, the End of the Cold War, and German Unification.* Oxford: Berghahn Books.
———. 2010. "France, 'Gaullism,' and the Cold War." In *Cambridge History of the Cold War*, Vol. 2, edited by M. P. Leffler and O. A. Westad, 158–78. Cambridge: Cambridge University Press.
———. 2012. "Mitterrand's Vision and the End of the Cold War." In *Overcoming the Iron Curtain: Visions of the End of the Cold War, 1945–1990*, edited by F. Bozo, N. P. Ludlow, M.-P. Rey, and B. Rother, 280–93. Oxford: Berghahn Books.

————. 2013. "France, the United States, and NATO: between Europeanization and re-Atlanticization, 1990–1." In *European Integration and the Atlantic Community in the 1980s*, edited by K. K. Patel and K. Weisbrode, 265–84. Cambridge: Cambridge University Press.

De Gaulle, C. 1970. *Discours et messages*. Vol. 3, *Avec le Renouveau*. Paris: Plon.

————. 1970. *Discours et messages*. Vol. 4, *Pour l'effort*. Paris: Plon.

————. 1970. *Mémoires d'espoir*. Vol 1, *Le renouveau 1958–1962*. Paris: Plon.

Dufourcq, B. 2000. "2+4 ou la négociation atypique." *Politique étrangère* 2: 467–84.

Galkin, A., and A. Tschernjajew, eds. 2011. *Michail Gorbatschow, und die deutsche Frage. Sowjetische Dokumente 1986–1991*. Munich, Germany: Oldenbourg.

Gorbatschow, M. 1999. *Wie es war: die deutsche Wiedervereinigung*. Berlin: Ullstein.

Grachev, A. 2008. *Gorbachev's Gamble: Soviet Foreign Policy and the End of the Cold War*. Oxford: Polity.

Hilger, A., ed. 2011. *Diplomatie für die deutsche Einheit*. Munich, Germany: Oldenbourg.

Hutchings, R. 1997. *American Diplomacy and the End of the Cold War: An Insider's Account of U.S. Policy in Europe, 1989–1992*. Washington, DC: Woodrow Wilson Center Press.

Küsters, H. J., and D. Hofmann, eds. 1998. *Deutsche Einheit. Sonderedition aus den Akten des Bundeskanzleramtes 1989/90*. Munich, Germany: Oldenbourg.

Rey, M.-P. 2004. "'Europe Is Our Common Home': A Study of Gorbachev's Diplomatic Concept." *Cold War History* 4, no. 2 (Jan.): 33–65.

Rödder, A. 2009. *Deutschland einig Vaterland. Die Geschichte der Wiedervereinigung*. Munich, Germany.

Salmon, P., K. Hamilton, and S. Twigge, eds. 2009. *German Unification 1989–1990: Documents on British Policy Overseas* (DBPO), series 3, Vol. 7. London: Routledge.

Sarotte, M. E. 2009. *1989: The Struggle to Create Post–Cold War Europe*. Princeton, NJ: Princeton University Press.

Savranskaya, S., T. Blanton, and V. Zubok, eds. 2010. *Masterpieces of History: The Peaceful end of the Cold War in Europe*. Budapest, Hungary: Central European University Press.

Schwarz, H.-P. 2012. *Helmut Kohl: Eine politische Biographie*. Munich, Germany: DVA.

Soutou, G.-H. 2013. "Valéry Giscard d'Estaing and the German Problem." Contribution to the conference on "France and the German Question." Paris, 7–9 Feb. 2013.

Teltschik, H. 1991. *329 Tage. Innenansichten der Einigung*. Berlin: Siedler.

Thatcher, M. 1993. *The Downing Street Years*. New York: HarperCollins.

Védrine, H. 1996. *Les Mondes de François Mitterrand. A l'Elysée, 1981–1995*. Paris: Fayard.

Weidenfeld, W. 1998. *Außenpolitik für die deutsche Einheit. Die Entscheidungsjahre 1989/1990*. Stuttgart, Germany: Deutsche Verlags-Anstalt (DVA).

Zelikow, P., and C. Rice. 1995. *Germany Unified and Europe Transformed: A Study in Statecraft*. Cambridge: Harvard University Press.

PART VI

ENDURING CONCERNS
ANSCHLUSS, BORDERS, AND THE TWO GERMANYS

CHAPTER 13

TOWARD A NEW ANSCHLUSS?
FRANCE AND THE GERMAN AND AUSTRIAN QUESTIONS, 1945–1955

THOMAS ANGERER

At first glance it might seem anachronistic to include the Austrian question in a volume on France and the German question during the Cold War. By the end of World War II, Austria's union with Germany from 1938 to 1945 (the so-called Anschluss) had disillusioned a large number of Austrians. At their Moscow Conference in late 1943, the Big Three had declared Germany's annexation of Austria null and void (a similar declaration by the French Committee of National Liberation followed soon thereafter). In late April 1945, after Soviet troops had liberated Vienna, Austrian representatives had proclaimed the country independent. And, after 1949, neither the Federal Republic of Germany (FRG, or West Germany) nor the German Democratic Republic (GDR, or East Germany) would ever challenge Austrian independence in Western or Eastern talks on the German question. Meanwhile independence from Germany became a basis for Austria's national identity. Austria, in other words, had seemingly ceased to be part of the German question in 1945.

This picture, however, is too simple. Analyses of French attitudes with regard to the German question during the Cold War are arguably too narrow when they focus exclusively on the so-called three Germanys—the contemporary expression for the FRG, the GDR, and Berlin. This is especially true (though it is not only true) for the first postwar decade. After all, ever since the dissolution of the Austro-Hungarian monarchy at the end of World War I, France's insistence on Austrian independence was an integral part of its policy to minimize Germany's potential for a new hegemony in Europe: hence its wide-ranging policy of Austrian de-annexation after World War II—a policy that used ostensibly friendly means that were seemingly opposite but in fact closely related and complementary to the means used in Germany. As such, France's policy toward Austria in the decade after 1945 was part and parcel of its German policy, and the emergence of the Cold War complicated the scheme without changing it fundamentally.[1]

This chapter will concentrate on three other reasons for including Austria when examining French positions on Germany during the Cold War. The first is occasionally mentioned by historians but still waiting for a systematic analysis: depending on circumstances, the French regarded an Allied agreement on Austria as a test for Soviet goodwill in German affairs—or as a trap for the West. Whether by prolonging or ending occupation in Austria, the Union of Soviet Socialist Republics (USSR, or Soviet Union) might set dangerous examples for Germany: in the former case, Austria would show how Soviet delaying tactics could make permanent a four-power control that would be only provisionally acceptable for a reunified Germany; in the latter, a sovereign and neutral Austria might prepare the ground for a neutral Germany and, by the same token, for a new Anschluss. Conversely, a partial, Western Anschluss was expected if the Soviet Union were to split Austria as it had done with Germany—with or without a possible complicity of the United States and Great Britain.

This leads to a second reason for considering the Austrian problem when discussing French dealings with the German question during the Cold War: fears of a new Anschluss were widespread and various among French observers. As explained in the second part of this chapter, political developments in both Germany and Austria were seen to undermine Austrian independence, especially during the first half of the 1950s.[2]

Finally, there is a third reason why historians should not ignore Austria when analyzing France's handling of the German question during the Cold War. Since its origins in the early nineteenth century, the German question had always been more than about national unity—whether unification was desirable, within which borders, and by which means. For other key powers, the German question—or what they rather called the German problem—was fundamentally about German power: about how to avoid Germany becoming either a power vacuum *in* or the gravitation center *of* Europe.[3] As the third part of this chapter will argue, the latter scenario became a concern when French observers gained the impression that, against the backdrop of West Germany's rapid economic reemergence, gradual political emancipation and growing power of attraction, Austria was perhaps about to become a West German satellite. From the French point of view, an economic Anschluss—a dominant West German share in Austrian capital and trade, making the small country's formal independence a pretense—was then already in the making and could lead to compromising the balance of power in Western Europe, especially within the newly formed Europe of Six.

The Interplay between the Austrian and the German Problems: Anschluss Again?

The initial French approach after the end of the war was to dissociate the Austrian question from the German question by solving the Austrian one first and as quickly as possible. Favorable treatment by the Allies was seen as likely to boost the Austrian's will for independence.[4] Yet Allied negotiations over an Austrian treaty ran into repeated deadlock, precisely because "the shadow of the German question has fallen on the Austrian problem," as Austria's Foreign Minister Karl Gruber put it.[5] Obviously, Soviet obstructions and overtures both related more to German than to Austrian developments; to a certain extent, this was also true of Western attitudes. In the case of France, one can identify two basic ideas about the way in which the solution of the Austrian problem should—or should not—affect the answer to the German one.

The first idea was that the Austrian question, being comparatively minor, could serve as a test for Soviet dispositions on Germany. If the Soviet Union was not even ready for concessions on Austria, how could Moscow be expected to be more conciliatory on Germany? Conversely, if the Soviet Union agreed to solve the Austrian problem, could this not be a promising sign for a more general détente, including a softening of the Soviet attitude on Germany? These were particularly topical questions when the Soviet Union countered Western moves for arming West Germany with proposals for new talks on Germany, as Moscow did during and after negotiations of the Paris and Bonn Treaties of 1952, or the Paris Protocol of 1954.

Testing the Soviet Union on Austria could serve two purposes. One was defensive: to evade East-West talks on Germany that would block the conclusion or ratification of treaties with West Germany; this motive was clear when defenders of the European Defence Community (EDC), close to the French government, launched the idea of an Austrian test in late 1951 and mid-1952.[6] Another purpose was more offensive: a possible Soviet move on Austria would belie critics who maintained that arming West Germany made further East-West talks impossible. In this case, the Austrian test would prove that Western strength paid off or, at least, did no harm. Both approaches, the defensive and the offensive, were reflected in French Prime Minister Pierre Mendès France's UN speech of November 1954, in which he proposed agreeing on Austria after ratifying the Paris Treaties.[7]

A limit had soon been reached, however. Starting in spring 1953, Paris expected Moscow to promote a neutrality clause in the Austrian treaty, believing "this would be the Austrian test turned against the Westerners."[8] The second French idea on how developments in Austria could affect Germany was, indeed, a negative version of the test: instead of setting a good example, Austria could set a negative one. The idea appeared in two variants.

Following one variant, Austria exemplified the perpetuation of a problematic interim, in which the Soviet Union obstructed a definitive solution through delaying tactics. Accordingly, French diplomats pointed to the "Austrian precedent" or "Austrian trap" when opposing negotiations on the basis of the Stalin Notes on Germany of spring 1952. Once Germany unified while at the same time being dissociated from the Western bloc and provisionally returned to Four Power control, the Soviet Union could freeze the situation as it did in Austria.[9] A year later, the French high commissioner in Vienna interpreted spectacular Soviet gestures easing occupation in Austria as further attempts to make the Austrian example attractive for Germany, in the hope of "austriacizing the German problem."[10] Yet by that time most officials of the foreign ministry (including Foreign Minister Georges Bidault) had already lost such apprehensions: following the East Berlin revolt of June 1953, they no longer expected the Soviet Union to accept free elections in Germany.[11]

Another variant of the Austrian trap scenario was a definitive, yet unacceptable, solution: sovereignty at the price of neutrality—which leads us back to the "Austrian test returned against the Westerners."[12] French governments and diplomats notoriously opposed the idea of a sovereign, neutral, unified Germany and worried about sympathies with the idea both in West Germany and in parts of the French public and political class. The fear of a negative Austrian precedent for Germany therefore largely explains why they continued harboring strong reservations against Austria accepting neutrality in return for sovereignty right until the finalization of the Austrian State Treaty in 1955.[13]

One further aspect needs to be taken into account: French diplomats expected the neutralization of the two countries to lead, sooner rather than later, to their unification. Bad enough as a contagious example for Germany, Austrian neutrality was thus considered as further entailing the possibility of a new Anschluss. Significantly, when French diplomacy began suspecting leading figures in Bonn and Vienna of playing with the idea of neutrality in late 1951, the French high commissariats in Bonn and Vienna linked an alleged secret complicity of Adenauer and Gruber on that issue to widespread intentions of "preparing the ground for an Anschluss."[14] A few months later, after the first Stalin Note on Germany, officials at the French Foreign Ministry were convinced that, with Germany unified and both countries neutralized in one way or another, "one would end up de facto with an Anschluss."[15] "De facto" would be replaced by "soon" in later warnings, making them even more categorical.[16]

Apprehensions came from a perceived inclination toward a new Anschluss both in West Germany and Austria; in addition there was the suspicion that the Soviet Union might sacrifice Austrian independence in order to bring a unified Germany to dissociate itself from the West or even to cooperate with the Soviet Union. Speculations had been publicly launched by General de Gaulle in late 1949: "Think of all that the East would one day have to offer to Germany. . . . Above all, unity. Then the Eastern borders. Who knows, the Anschluss?"[17] The conjecture returned in another variant in the wake of the Stalin Notes of spring 1952: "Does one not think secretly . . . , on the Soviet side, that the attachment of the whole of Austria to a unified Germany could compensate it for the loss of the territories on the other side of the Oder-Neisse?"[18]

Suspicions that the Soviet Union might quietly play with Anschluss scenarios may help to explain why French diplomats long considered it mere propaganda when Moscow accused Austria, West Germany, and the United States of preparing an Anschluss by covertly remilitarizing Western Austria. It took the fresh look of a new high commissioner in Vienna, Jean Chauvel, one of the most prominent French diplomats at the time, to suggest in autumn 1954 that, far from secretly considering it an option, "the Russians were in fact fearing the Anschluss" and that "our concerns and fears meet those of the Russians."[19] Until then, however, suspicion of Soviet Anschluss plans was one more reason for France's particular apprehensions about Soviet demands for Austrian neutrality.

On the other hand, French decision makers—from Pierre Mendès France to Edgar Faure and Antoine Pinay—could envisage Austrian neutrality if certain conditions were met, most importantly that West Germany was previously locked within the Western defense system.[20] Accordingly, a new French approach could develop after the original strategy for dissociating the Austrian from the German question (i.e., solving the Austrian question first) had failed and even become counterproductive: the new approach consisted of securing a partial answer to the German question—tailor-made for West Germany and leaving open the question of unification—before Austrian neutrality could have damaging effects. In turn, a rapid four-power solution for Austria might limit the harm to East-West relations caused by the Western deal with West Germany. The scheme succeeded narrowly, with the Paris Treaties in force only a couple of days before the conclusion of the Austrian State Treaty.

While the Paris Treaties avoided a possible spillover of neutrality from Austria to Germany, the Austrian State Treaty ended fears that Germany's division might extend to Austria. During the late 1940s and early 1950s, the split of Germany had loomed large as a portent of what might happen to Austria if East-West cooperation were to break down there as well. For the French, this would have meant more than the Sovietization of Eastern Austria, including Vienna: as the chief French negotiator of the Austrian treaty had already warned in June 1947, a split of Austria "would bring shortly the Anschluss of Western Austria with Germany."[21] An internal note detailed the threat after insurrectional strikes in Austria in autumn 1950 had been openly sponsored by the Soviet occupation forces, fueling the impression that the Soviet Union was now prepared to split the country: "The breakdown of quadripartism would sooner or later lead to the idea of an Anschluss of Western Austria with the FRG." This would be the likely consequence of "the unfavorable economic situation of Western Austria and the fact that Austrian nationalism is not unfailing."[22] It became conventional wisdom among French observers that a partition of the country would "inescapably" bring Western Austria into West Germany's fold.[23]

In comparison with a complete Anschluss, the inconveniences of a partial Anschluss were considered "of a lesser degree but still significant."[24] Most explicit was an internal note of October 1952: ". . . [T]his Austro-German union [i.e. the union of Western Austria with West Germany] would still represent a heavy danger for France and for the Western community . . . , as it would consecrate German prepotency and have as a corollary the absorption of a part of Austria by the USSR. Faced with this danger, the French government must protect itself by all means at its disposal."[25] The then junior minister for foreign affairs, Maurice Schumann, instructed French diplomats to explain in Washington and London that "[t]he possible reappearance of an Austro-German union would compromise above all the construction of Europe."[26] By that time, the European Coal and Steel Community (ECSC) was in place and the EDC was on track. Concerns about the balance between France and the FRG were a major reason for the mounting opposition to the EDC in France, and also help to explain why alertness to perceived risks of a new, if partial, Anschluss, increased during the period. The perspective of West Germany's accession to NATO and the Western European Union in 1955 only compounded the problem: even a partial Anschluss would seriously increase the military potential and geopolitical weight of the FRG.[27]

French diplomats and politicians saw the risk of an Anschluss by partition heightening as the United States proposed a controversial short treaty for Austria in March 1952. Even more risky, in the eyes of French diplomacy, was the U.S. covert remilitarization of Austria's Western zones and their use for strengthening NATO defense and transit lines. In both cases, France criticized the United States for useless provocation, potentially leading to Austria's division and a partial Anschluss.[28] Internally, diplomats even suspected the Americans and the British of hidden thoughts: "Does one not think secretly, on the Anglo-Saxon side, that in case of a division of Austria the Western part could be offered, under certain conditions, to Western Germany in compensation for the quasi definitive separation from East-Germany . . . ?"[29]

Whether correct or not, thus, French diplomats suspected both the Anglo-American Allies and the Soviet Union of being conditional Anschluss accomplices by retaining the option of a partial or complete Anschluss in a partial or full solution of the German problem. By contrast, France excluded any option of the sort and insisted on Austrian independence unconditionally. This not only explains why France, among the four, had the most to fear from certain interplays between the German and the Austrian question, but also why it considered itself so isolated when worrying over perceived Anschluss tendencies in Austria and the FRG at the height of the Cold War.

Perceived Anschluss Tendencies in Austria and in the FRG: The Political Dimension

French observers considered Austrian independence to be put at risk by a variety of political developments that, for the sake of analysis, can be divided into push and pull factors. While push factors turned Austrians away from independence, pull factors revived attraction by Germany, if not German appetite. Perceived as mere tendencies and not clearly separated from each other at the time, both push and pull factors had, in French eyes, a dangerous potential, especially but not only when the Allies would end their control of the country.

The main push factor was discouragement. While one source was the fear of partition, another was frustration with the mere status quo. Even if Allied control could be seen as "the best guarantee against Anschluss . . . in the short term," occupation was "dulling the patriotic sense of the country" and hence counterproductive in the long term.[30] The French expected ongoing four-power occupation and the ensuing uncertainty over the country's future to impede Austrians' preference for independence, leading them to place their hopes into a new Anschluss.

Concerns arose in three waves. A first wave occurred in spring 1946 when it be-came clear that, for the time being, the Soviet Union would at best negotiate on reducing Allied control—not on lifting it. A brochure orienting French occupation forces warned, "If we . . . were forced to . . . prolong an occupation this would not fail to exasperate the population. . . . We will play in the hands of the pan-Germanists and throw Austria sooner or later in the arms of Germany."[31] The high commissioner, General Antoine Béthouart, gave a similar warning in a speech in Paris.[32] A second wave of anxieties came in early 1950. By then, negotiations on an Austrian treaty had run into a new deadlock. The foreign ministry worried that "in the face of the impossibility to acquire their independence [i.e. full sovereignty] . . . the Austrians are at risk to definitively lose confidence in the future of Austria and may be tempted to turn to West Germany . . . ; a new Anschluss cannot be without seduction."[33] French apprehensions reached a new peak in late 1954 and early 1955 when the quarrels about the Paris Treaties appeared to block any prospect of resuming Austrian treaty negotiations. Chauvel, who had witnessed Austria's annexation during his first mission in Vienna, in 1938, repeatedly insisted after his return as high commissioner in autumn 1954 that "stagnation in the current situation and regime risks undermin-ing more and more profoundly the national spirit of the population" and thereby increased the Anschluss risk.[34]

Related to discouragement was a certain revival or re-emergence of pan-Germanism in Austria. Since late 1949 a new Austrian party appealing especially to former Nazis and demanding close cooperation with the FRG, the Federation of Independents (Verband/Wahlpartei der Unabhängigen), was fueling French skepticism about the long-term attitudes of the Austrian population at large. Parts of the Socialist Party were presumed to hold true to its traditional pan-Germanism, and industrialists were suspected of remaining nostalgic of their former German connections.[35]

Hidden agendas were supposed to drive influential circles, including leading gov-ernmental figures in Vienna and especially in Bonn. A particular suspicion was raised in autumn 1951 when Vice-Chancellor Karl Blücher complained to a French official of "advances" made on the German government by unnamed Austrian socialists and Foreign Minister Gruber (a conservative) advocating "a truly German community" between the blocs.[36] This seemed to give credit to information gathered in the early summer of the same year but originally not taken seriously, along which Adenauer had told an intimate about having "a reliable friend" in the Austrian government (suspected to be Gruber) with whom he could work toward "a Greater Germany . . . with complete peace of mind as the Allies were not at all suspecting him [Adenauer] of such sentiments."[37] In May 1953, when Gruber first visited Bonn, an ambiguous phrase in a communiqué alarmed the French high commissioner in Bonn, André François-Poncet, who was notoriously suspicious: "What confidence can one have in Mr Gruber? He is an expert in hiding his ulterior motives. No less is Mr Adenauer. . . . [Gruber's] visit in Bonn is for him, like for his interlocutor, the first step on the path that should conduct to Anschluss if conditions lend themselves one day."[38] Adenauer remained under suspicion for being "open-minded" about a possible Anschluss until, at least, early 1954.[39] Positions in West Germany, in fact, were much more important for French observers than Austrian attitudes. The most trenchant verdict, as usual, came from François-Poncet: "[I]n the minds of the West German leaders, Anschluss is by no means buried. If one never speaks of it, one ever thinks of it." And going even farther: "[I]f the Germans do not pronounce the word Anschluss . . . they nevertheless behave as if they were preparing the thing."[40]

Even more difficult to control than suspected ulterior motives in the Bonn government was another pull factor drawing Austrians toward West Germany: the spectacular rise of the Bonn Republic. While the phenomenon created anxiety in France, it was followed in Austria with a mix of enthusiastic interest and jealousy. From late 1951 on, French reports were regularly and insistently describing the mounting "prestige" and "attractive power" of the young FRG in Austria, where one realized that, except for German division, the status difference between the two countries was shifting in favor of West Germany.[41] Faced with the ascent of the Bonn Republic, Austrians were reportedly losing the impression of being treated favorably by the Allies while returning to their traditional inferiority complex vis-à-vis Germany. That complex was nourished in particular by the FRG's successes in negotiating an easing of Allied control and its related progress in European integration. Although Austria was a founding member of the Organisation for European Economic Co-operation (OEEC) and excluded participation in military organizations, economic and political circles in Vienna feared marginalization from other European organizations, notably the ECSC and the Council of Europe. German pulling, thus, triggered Austrian pushing.

An Economic Anschluss in the Making?

Since spring 1952 even moderate French newspapers were repeatedly warning against the danger of a new Anschluss.[42] Chauvel put Paris on guard after the signature of the Paris Treaties: "[I]f the Anschluss is currently neither in the spirits nor in the hearts, it is in the logic of facts."[43] Chauvel's warnings were among the reasons behind Mendès France's proposal for finalizing the Austrian State Treaty as soon as the Paris treaties would be ratified.[44] Apart from the political developments mentioned above, Chauvel pointed to "the German economic hold" over Austria.[45] This was a delicate issue, as influence on third countries was part of the economic balance between France and Germany, a balance notoriously considered to be a key security factor in postwar France. The Austrian case was even more sensitive because the French high commissariats in Bonn and Vienna described Austrian politics as remaining under the sway of economics: "Since 1918 Austrian politics has been determined by the economy. By reason of its economic fragility, this country is more than others condemned to following the political trail of the country that helps it to survive."[46]

Three problems were particularly critical and had already been extensively exposed by Chauvel's predecessor, Jean Payart. The first was the uncertain future of the so-called German assets—in other words, the confiscations, the (more or less proper) acquisitions, and the investments Germany had made in Austria during the annexation period. The perspective of the FRG putting Austria under pressure after the Allies had left and getting even parts of what it claimed worried not only the Austrian authorities but the Allies too, especially the French. If the German assets were not liquidated before the conclusion of the Austrian State Treaty, the high commissariat warned in March 1954, "the economic Anschluss would be a fait accompli and Austria would have ceased to be independent."[47]

The second problem was the FRG's massive investments since the early 1950s. Following the same report, political more than economic motivations seemed to explain their importance since the FRG was expected to run sooner or later into capital shortages and other foreign investors were discouraged by the uncertainty over Austria's future. Yet whatever the motives of West German investors, Austrian industry was already about to become "a branch of [West] German industry."[48]

The third problem was West Germany's rising part in Austrian foreign trade. As the high commissariat explained, the FRG benefited most from the reorientation of Austrian trade from the now communist-dominated Danube area toward the West. Therefore, Austria had come into a "flagrant and abnormal reliance" on West Germany, especially for its imports—much more so than other small neighbors of the FRG like Switzerland, Denmark or the Netherlands.[49]

The conclusion of the high commissariat was gloomy: "The development of Austro-German relations in trade and finance has already reached a stage of potential economic Anschluss." If France wanted to protect "Austria's economic independence," it was "high time to act."[50] Even though general economic indicators were contrasting favorably with the interwar period, Payart added: "The 'special case' of Austria has only changed in character. The question is no more whether Austria's national economy is viable as such but whether, on a slippery slope, it does not tend to integrate itself more into the German economy every year, in a word, whether the economic Anschluss is not in the making."[51]

By warning against an "economic Anschluss," Payart could be sure of triggering associations with the Austro-German customs union plan of 1931 for which the term had been coined at the time, suggesting that a customs union would serve as a preliminary step for political unification like the German customs union had done in the nineteenth century. As junior minister and deputy delegate to the Society of Nations, François-Poncet had been in charge of combatting the Austro-German plan.[52] In addition, as ambassador to Berlin, he had closely monitored German-Austrian relations all the way through to the Anschluss. François-Poncet thus seemed authoritative when backing Payart's alarm call in 1954 and insisting that Austria's trade dependence on Germany had already become higher than before 1938, which was bound to have political consequences.[53] An economic Anschluss being traditionally considered in France as a potential prelude to political union, the FRG's growing grip on the Austrian economy was thus received as an additional and particularly dangerous pull factor toward a new Anschluss—a warning to be found even in the moderate press.[54]

There was more. Even if it stopped short of being a fully fledged Anschluss, a "mere" economic Anschluss seemed dangerous enough: "At the end of such a development," Payart suggested, "it would not even be necessary any more to envisage an act of violence from Germany's part. With or without the suppression of borders, Anschluss would become a fait accompli, without the word having been pronounced."[55] France, however, did not want Austria to "slide into the German orbit" by any way or in any form.[56] Indeed, as much as Austria's possible annexation, the country's potential satellization by the FRG was, for French diplomacy, a question of "maintaining a certain balance in Europe" or, more precisely, of avoiding a "German preponderance."[57]

The Austrian example also shows how worries about the FRG's economic rise interfered with French European integration policy, which, among other things, was an answer to the German (power) problem. In French eyes, European integration presupposed an FRG whose power was limited, both formally, in terms of sovereignty; and practically, in terms of political, military, and economic weight. These limits would be circumvented, however, if the FRG began dominating other countries, bringing them into its dependence, thereby boosting not only its national economy but also its influence in Europe. As a consequence, watching over Austria's "economic independence" (i.e., its "economic autonomy vis-à-vis [West] Germany") was seen as necessary in order to "save the future of European cooperation."[58] In a conversation with the Austrian chancellor, Payart insisted, "[E]verything that exceeds normal [commercial] relations" with the FRG "indicates a sliding toward Anschluss" and "impedes the process of West European integration."[59]

French anxieties about a possible West German preponderance in the Europe of the Six become even clearer when looking at Austria's possible ECSC membership, once occupation ended.[60] Should France welcome Austria into the club and perhaps even invite the country to join before the FRG might do so? French officials were embarrassed when raising the question for the first time, in September 1953. True, by opposing Austria's ECSC entry, France "would play into the hands of the Germans," as Austria could then but turn to the FRG for improving its access to the common coal and steel market. But would Austria, if admitted into the ECSC, not "strengthen the German element?" Would its accession not amount to "a sort of Anschluss"?[61] The answer by the head of the European division of the foreign ministry, François Seydoux (later Chauvel's successor in Vienna), was initially evasive.[62] Half a year later, after the high commissariat had sent its analysis of the "economic Anschluss in the making," the situation became quite forthright: "Any membership of Austria in the Europe of the Six" contained "a number of dangers" because "Austria would only tend to become a province of Germany. . . . Austria's presence at the heart of the European Community would risk tilting the balance in favour of the German element."[63]

Hence, French anti-Anschluss policy, which was already in trouble since continuing Allied occupation risked undermining Austrian independence, had come into a new dilemma against the backdrop of the fledgling European integration process: on the one hand, Austria's exclusion from the Europe of the Six was an additional push factor driving Austria into West Germany's arms; on the other, Austria's possible participation in the Europe of the Six risked propelling the "economic Anschluss" even farther.

Conclusion

To be sure, the above findings require further research. French perceptions of Anschluss dangers and tendencies need to be compared with those of other powers, namely the Big Three and the countries concerned—Austria, the FRG, and the GDR. In addition, possible differences in perception among French actors need to be investigated. It is also necessary to analyze how French perceptions were rooted in French political culture and memory in order to determine domestic sources and implications of Anschluss fears and their possible instrumentalization, including by other powers like the Soviet Union. Yet some preliminary conclusions can already be drawn.

Most striking is the permanency of a broad notion of the German problem in France, even after the reestablishment of Austrian independence and the split of Germany. For the French, the German question went beyond the unification of the FRG with the GDR and the possible recovery of the Eastern territories (or the Saarland until 1955). Austria was a critical aspect too, at least during the first decade after World War II. From the outset, French observers and decision makers were far from optimistic about the future of Austrian independence from Germany, and the Cold War made them even more pessimistic. In their view, a range of factors pointed to new Anschluss dangers: the discouragement of the population by the continuing occupation and the ensuing uncertainty about the country's future; a certain reappearance of pan-Germanism in Austria and its permanence in the FRG, including at the top of Bonn's government; the growing attraction of the FRG; the excess of Austrian reliance on West German investments and trade; and last but not least the risk of Austria splitting into nonviable entities or of both countries turning neutral and unifying thereafter. All these perceived Anschluss dangers influenced French assessments of the German problem during the early Cold War. During that period, at least, the German question in French eyes continued to include a potential and unwelcome Austrian dimension.

Moreover, the Austrian case relates to another dimension of the German problem in the French perspective: the German question was not only about Germany's territorial limits but also and more fundamentally about its potential power. Power, not borders, was the heart of the German issue, precisely because power does not end at borders but affects other countries. The German problem was also and most importantly about German influence abroad, with the neighboring small countries and particularly Austria seen as the most vulnerable geographically, culturally, economically, and politically. Accordingly, France perceived the growing West German influence in Austria as dangerous to the balance of power in Western Europe. In its view, there was no need for a fully fledged, formal Anschluss for compromising France's position. West German dominance of the Austrian economy was threatening enough. Compared with the FRG's economic and (one could expect) political influence in Austria, French observers considered it almost secondary whether or not the Austro-German border remained formally intact, a fortiori if Austria were to join the Six and hence to remove its customs with Germany. In French eyes, thus, Austria's possible satellization by West Germany was a further, if wider, dimension of the German problem. More generally, future investigations on France and the German question during the Cold War should address the rivalry between France and the FRG for influence on smaller European countries, both within and outside the European communities, and in both Western and Eastern Europe.[64]

It might be helpful here to draw on Glenn Palmer's and Clifton Morgan's concept of "foreign policy portfolios." Palmer and Morgan define a "foreign policy portfolio" as a "set of policies a state adopts to meet its foreign policy objectives."[65] We may better understand France's German policy if we look at it as a policy portfolio. France's German policy portfolio would consist of different but complementary policies, all aiming at preventing Germany from becoming dominant and potentially dangerous again. Securing Austrian independence, formal and real, would be one of these policies. To prevent Austria from rejoining (West) Germany in a common state or group of states was part and parcel of French strategies for dealing with the German problem after World War II as much as it had been after World War I.

Thomas Angerer is assistant professor at the Department of History of the University of Vienna. Educated in Austria, the Federal Republic of Germany, and France, he has widely published on Franco-Austrian relations and on Austria's position in Europe since 1918. He is working on a book on France and the Austrian Question since 1918.

Notes

1. For further literature, see Angerer, "Kontinuitäten und Kontraste"; and Angerer, "Französische Freundschaftspolitik."
2. This has passed unnoticed, for instance, in the valuable book Miard-Delacroix, *Question nationale allemande*.
3. Geiss, *The Question*, 15–20; Gruner, *Deutschland*, 97–99; Wolff, *The German Question*.
4. For previous literature, see Angerer, "Französische Freundschaftspolitik," 132–33.
5. Stourzh, *Um Einheit und Freiheit*, 103 (an English edition is forthcoming). See also Bischof, *Austria*; Steininger, *Austria, Germany*. Unless otherwise noted, all translations are my own.

6. "L'Autriche—un test pour la paix," interview by the prominent Christian Democrat Pierre Schneiter, in *Le Figaro*, 27 Dec. 1951, 1, 3; statement by the general secretary of the foreign ministry, Alexandre Parodi, in a meeting of 14 March 1952 dealing with the first Stalin note, in "Compte-rendu de la réunion tenue chez M. Parodi", AMAE, Europe 1944-1960, Allemagne, box 936; meeting of the Foreign Affairs Committee of the National Assembly of 18 and 25 Jun. 1952, especially the statements by Pierre Schneiter (rapporteur) and Jean Michel Guérin de Beaumont, AnF, C 15591.

7. Angerer, "Re-launching East-West Negotiations."

8. Note by the Central European Office, 22 Jun. 1953, AMAE, Europe 1944-1960, Autriche, box 284.

9. Sources quoted in Soutou, "La France et les notes soviétiques," 266-68; N. Meyer-Landrut, *Frankreich*, 44; Gehler,"Kurzvertrag für Österreich?," 257; Maelstaf, *Que faire de l'Allemagne?*, 401, 455.

10. Jean Payart, 12 Jun. 1953, quoted in Gehler, *Modellfall für Deutschland?*, 244. If not indicated otherwise, the telegrams or dispatches from French representatives abroad are always addressed to the French foreign minister.

11. Maelstaf, *Que faire de l'Allemagne?*, 393, 402, 405; Soutou, "La France et les notes soviétiques," 271.

12. Note by the Central European Office, 22 Jun. 1953, AMAE, Europe 1944-1960, Autriche, box 284.

13. Lohse, *Östliche Lockungen*, 177; Gehler, "The Austrian Solution," 45-46; Gehler,"Österreich und die deutsche Frage," 104, 117; Gehler, *Modellfall für Deutschland?*, 687-91, 777-78.

14. Deputy high commissioner Armand Bérard, 23 Nov. 1951, T. 8218/8220 (quote); Payart, 12 Dec. 1951, AMAE, Europe 1944-1960, Autriche, box 251.

15. Statement by the deputy political director of the foreign ministry, Roland de Margerie, during the internal meeting of 14 Mar. 1952, AMAE, Europe 1944-1960, Allemagne, box 936. See also Meyer-Landrut, *Frankreich und die deutsche Einheit*, 81.

16. Notes by the head of the Central European Office, Jean Sauvagnargues, 15 and 22 Apr. 1953, quoted in Maelstaf, *Que faire de l'Allemagne?*, 397-98; note by the Central European Office, Oct. 1954, DDF 1954, vol. 2, 637-38.

17. Press conference of 14 Nov. 1949 (de Gaulle, *Discours et messages*, vol. 2, 328).

18. Note "Autriche–Allemagne," in "Dossier pour le voyage du Secrétaire d'État à Vienne," 28 Aug. 1952, AMAE, Europe 1944-1960, Autriche, box 260.

19. Chauvel, 27 Oct. 1954, DDF 1954, vol. 2, 623-25, here 624. See also a personal letter by Chauvel to Mendès France, 7 Jan. 1955, IPMF, Accords de Paris; Jardin, "Österreich wird frei," 318-21; and Soutou, "France," 117-18.

20. Angerer, "Besatzung, Entfernung," 97-98; Gehler, *Modellfall*, 778-79.

21. General Cherrière to Chauvel, then secretary general of the foreign ministry, 24 Jun. 1947, DDF 1947, vol. 1, 1063-65, here 1065.

22. Note by the Central European Office "L'attitude soviétique en Autriche et de la politique alliée à l'égard de ce pays," 28 Oct. 1950, AMAE, Europe 1944-1960, Autriche, boxes 230 and 266.

23. Note by the Political Directorate, "L'Autriche et les risques d'un Anschluss," 22 Mar. 1954, AMAE, Europe 1944-1960, Autriche, box 255.

24. Personal letter by Chauvel to Mendès France, 7 Jan. 1955, IPMF, Accords de Paris.

25. Note by the Political Directorate on Austrian-German relations, 20 Oct. 1952, AMAE, Europe 1944-1960, Autriche, box 253. The word "*prépotence*" (prepotency) was old-fashioned and gendered French diplomatic language, appealing to traditional conceptions of diplomacy learned at the École libre des sciences politiques where most of French diplomats had been trained in diplomatic history.

26. Schumann, 23 Oct. 1952, AMAE, Europe 1944-1960, Autriche, box 253.

27. Personal letter by Chauvel to Mendès France, 7 Jan. 1955, IPMF, Accords de Paris.

28. Angerer, "Besatzung, Entfernung," 92-94. Notwithstanding limited French cooperation in secret remilitarization; see Koppensteiner, "Béthouarts Alpenfestung."

29. Note "Autriche–Allemagne" in "Dossier pour le voyage du Secrétaire d'État à Vienne," 28 Aug. 1952, AMAE, Europe 1944-1960, Autriche, box 260.

30. Note of the Central European Office, "État actuel du problème autrichien," 30 Oct. 1954, AMAE, Europe 1944-1960, Autriche, box 287. As an exception this document does not mention the risk

of partition (and, by implication, partial Anschluss) posed by Allied occupation. Gehler, "Österreich und die deutsche Frage," 85, quotes "the best guarantee against the Anschluss," though without considering the context—an analysis of short-term perspectives—and the same document's critical assessment of the long-term risks of occupation, including new Anschluss tendencies following protracted occupation.

31. Commandement en chef français en Autriche, *Le problème autrichien actuel. Pourquoi la France est-elle en Autriche?*, undated brochure (probably May 1946), 20, AMAE, Bibliothèque, AU/D (4).

32. Lecture by General Béthouart "Les problèmes autrichiens d'après-guerre" at the École libre des sciences politiques, 22 Jun. 1946, Österreichisches Staatsarchiv, Archiv der Republik, BKA-AA, II-Pol./1946, box 5. Béthouart would later become an outspoken opponent to ending occupation, arguing that "a single danger" remained in Austria: "the Soviet one"; see Auriol, *Journal du Septennat*, vol. 1, 152. His setting aside of the German danger was probably one of the reasons why his advice would finally not be followed by decision makers in Paris, even though he contributed to making Bidault hesitate in spring 1948 and obtained the support of the head of the Foreign Affairs committee in the Chamber of Deputies, Édouard Bonnefous, in late summer and autumn 1949.

33. "Note au sujet d'une politique française à l'égard de l'Autriche, en cas d'échec des négociations des suppléants," by the Central European Office, 19 Jan. 1950; see a similar passage in notes of 20 and 27 Jan. 1950, AMAE, Europe 1944–1960, Autriche, box 274.

34. Chauvel, 13 Dec. 1954, AMAE, Europe 1944–60, Autriche, box 288. A similar passage in his farewell dispatch from Vienna of 1 Feb. 1955, DDF 1955, vol. 1, 139–43, here 143, cited by Stourzh, *Um Einheit und Freiheit*, 583, n16.

35. See, e.g., *Le Monde*, 12 Apr. 1952; and *L'Aurore*, 12 May 1952.

36. Bérard, 23 Nov. 1951, Telegram no. 8214/8217, AMAE, Europe 1944–60, Autriche, box 251. Payart, 12 Dec. 1951, ibidem, faithfully reproduced Bérard's information on Gruber, apparently without having been able to check it with Viennese sources.

37. Bérard, 23 Nov. 1951, T. no. 8218/8220, AMAE, Europe 1944–60, Autriche, box 251.

38. François-Poncet, 22 May 1953, AMAE, Europe 1944–1960, Autriche, box 254.

39. Bérard, 18 Jan. 1954, AMAE, Europe 1944–1960, Autriche, box 255. There is not enough space to cover French apprehensions about the "usual suspects" like Adenauer's deputy in the Christian Democratic Union and Minister for Questions Concerning Germany as a Whole, Jakob Kaiser, or prominent members of the Liberal party like Justice Minister Thomas Dehler.

40. François-Poncet, 27 Jun. and 21 Oct. 1952, AMAE, Europe 1944–1960, Autriche, boxes 252 and 253. "If one never speaks of it, one ever thinks of it" was an obvious allusion to Gambetta's famous guideline for French revanchism after Germany's annexation of Alsace-Lorraine in 1871: "Y penser toujours, n'en parler jamais."

41. For this and the following, Deputy High Commissioner Roger Lalouette, 6 Oct., and Payart, 12 Dec. 1951, AMAE, Europe 1944–1960, Autriche, box 251. The quotations appear in both sources.

42. See, e.g., *Le Monde*, 12 Apr. 1952; *L'Aurore*, 12 May 1952; and "Vienne: pour l'Anschluss: 30 percent des Autrichiens," *Paris-Match*, 19 Sept. 1954.

43. Chauvel, 27 Oct. 1954, DDF 1954, vol. 2, 623–25, here 624. See also letter by Chauvel to Mendès France, 7 Jan. 1955, IPMF, Accords de Paris; Jardin, "Österreich wird frei," 318–21; and Soutou, "France," 117–18.

44. For further literature, Angerer, "Re-launching East-West Negotiations," 266.

45. Chauvel, 27 Oct. 1954, DDF 1954, vol. 2, 623–25, here 624. See also a personal letter by Chauvel to Mendès France, 7 Jan. 1955, IPMF, Accords de Paris.

46. Payart, 23 Jun. 1952, and approval by François-Poncet, 27 Jun. 1952, AMAE, Europe 1944–60, Autriche, box 265.

47. Dispatch by Payart, signed by Lalouette, 16 Mar. 1954, AMAE, Europe 1944–60, Autriche, box 255.

48. Ibid.

49. Ibid.

50. Ibid.

51. Telegram by Payart, 16 Mar. 1954, AMAE, Europe 1944–1960, Autriche, box 255.
52. Heyde, *Das Ende der Reparationen*, 151–60.
53. François-Poncet, 28 Apr. 1954, AMAE, Europe 1944–1960, Autriche, box 255.
54. See, e.g., "L'Autriche en marche vers l'Anschluss," in the economic weekly *Les Échos*, 16 Sept. 1954.
55. Payart, 28 May 1953, AMAE, Europe 1944–1960, Autriche, box 254.
56. François-Poncet, 27 Jun. 1952; and Payart, 28 May 1953, AMAE, Europe 1944–1960, Autriche, boxes 252 and 254.
57. Dispatch by Payart, signed by Lalouette, 16 Mar. 1954, AMAE, Europe 1944–1960, Autriche, box 255.
58. Ibid.
59. Payart, 16 Aug. 1952, AMAE, Europe 1944–60, Autriche, box 252.
60. For this and the following see Angerer, "Integrität vor Integration," as well as other contributions in Gehler and Steininger, *Österreich*; and Gehler, "Annäherung auf Raten."
61. "Remarques sur le problème autrichien," note without letterhead, date, or signature but referred to in a later note ("Note pour la Direction des Affaires économiques et financières" by the Central European Office, 12 Sept. 1953, signed with the initials of François Seydoux, AMAE, Direction économique, Commerce extérieur, box 558), and therefore to be identified as emanating from the German and Austrian Office of the Economic and Financial Directorate of the foreign ministry, 4 Sept. 1953, and probably drafted by the Sous-directeur in charge, François Valéry, AMAE, Direction économique, Commerce extérieur, box 558.
62. "Note pour la Direction des Affaires économiques et financières" by the Central European Office, 12 Sept. 1953, signed with the initials of François Seydoux, AMAE, Direction économique, Commerce extérieur, box 558.
63. Note by the Political Directorate, "L'Autriche et les risques d'un Anschluss," 22 Mar. 1954, AMAE, Europe 1944–1960, Autriche, box 255, with special mention of the opinion of the directeur d'Europe.
64. Studies on triangular relations between France and Germany with small states are rare and have hitherto concentrated on issues like transborder cooperation, cultural transfers, or national perspectives. See, e.g., Dumoulin, Elvert, and Schirmann, *Encore ces chers voisins*.
65. Palmer and Morgan, *A Theory of Foreign Policy*, 3.

Bibliography

Angerer, T. 1994. "Besatzung, Entfernung . . . Integration? Grundlagen der politischen Beziehungen zwischen Frankreich und Österreich seit 1938/45." In *Frankreich–Österreich seit 1918*, edited by F. Koja and O. Pfersmann, 82–100. Vienna, Austria: Böhlau.

———. 2005a. "Französische Freundschaftspolitik in Österreich nach 1945. Gründe, Grenzen und Gemeinsamkeiten mit Frankreichs Deutschlandpolitik." In *Die Gunst des Augenblicks*, edited by M. Rauchensteiner and R. Kriechbaumer, 113–38. Vienna, Austria: Böhlau.

———. 2005b. "Re-launching East-West Negotiations while Deciding West German Rearmament. France, the Paris Treaties, and the Austrian State Treaty, 1954/55." In *Der Österreichische Staatsvertrag 1955/The Austrian State Treaty*, edited by A. Suppan, G. Stourzh, and W. Mueller, 265–333. Vienna, Austria: Österreichische Akademie der Wissenschaften.

———. 2007. "Kontinuitäten und Kontraste der französischen Österreichpolitik 1919–1955." In *Von Saint-Germain zum Belvedere*, edited by K. Koch et al., 129–57. Vienna, Austria: Verlag für Geschichte und Politik.

———. 2014. "Integrität vor Integration. Österreich und 'Europa' aus französischer Sicht, 1949–1960." In *Österreich und die europäische Integration 1945–1992*, edited by M. Gehler and R. Steininger, 183–208. Vienna, Austria: Böhlau.

Auriol, V. 1970. *Journal du Septennat*. Vol. 1, *1947*. Paris: Colin.

Bischof, G. 1999. *Austria in the First Cold War 1945–55*. New York: Palgrave.

De Gaulle, C. 1970. *Discours et messages*. Vol. 2, *Dans l'attente*. Paris: Plon.

Dumoulin, M., J. Elvert, and S. Schirmann, eds. 2014. *Encore ces chers voisins. Le Benelux, l'Allemagne et la France aux XIXe et XXe siècles*. Stuttgart, Germany: Steiner.

Gehler, M. 1994. "Kurzvertrag für Österreich? Die westliche Staatsvertrags-Diplomatie und die Stalin-Noten von 1952." *Vierteljahrshefte für Zeitgeschichte* 42, no. 2: 243–78.

———. 1995. "The Austrian Solution in 1955 as a 'Model' for Germany?" In *Austria in the Nineteen Fifties*, edited by G. Bischof, A. Pelinka, and R. Steininger, 39–78. New Brunswick, NJ: Transaction.

———. 1998. "Österreich und die deutsche Frage 1954/55." In *Bericht über den 20. österreichischen Historikertag in Bregenz 1994*, edited by L. Mikoletzky, 83–134. Vienna, Austria: Verband Österreichischer Historiker und Geschichtsvereine.

———. 2008. "Annäherung auf Raten. Österreich und die Europäische Gemeinschaft für Kohle und Stahl 1950–1972." In *Geschichte und Identität*, edited by F. Schausberger, 383–452. Vienna, Austria: Böhlau.

———. 2015. *Modellfall für Deutschland? Die Österreichlösung mit Staatsvertrag und Neutralität 1945–1955*. Innsbruck, Austria: Studienverlag.

Geiss, I. 1997. *The Question of German Unification 1806–1996*. Abingdon, Great Britain: Routledge.

Gruner, W. D. 2009. *Deutschland in Europa 1750 bis 2007*. Cluj-Napoca, Romania: Presa Univ. Clujeană.

Jardin, P. 1992. "'Österreich wird frei.' Le traité d'État autrichien du 15 mai 1955." *Relations internationales* 71, 311–25.

Heyde, P. 1998. *Das Ende der Reparationen. Deutschland, Frankreich und der Youngplan 1929–1932*. Paderborn, Germany: Schöningh.

Koppensteiner, B. W. 2000. "Béthouarts Alpenfestung. Militärische Planungen und Verteidigungsvorbereitungen der französischen Besatzungsmacht in Tirol und Vorarlberg." In *Österreich im frühen Kalten Krieg 1945–1958*, edited by E. A. Schmidl, 193–237. Vienna, Austria: Böhlau.

Lohse, E. 1995. *Östliche Lockungen und westliche Zwänge. Paris und die deutsche Teilung*. Munich, Germany: Oldenbourg.

Maelstaf, G. 1999. *Que faire de l'Allemagne? Les responsables français, le statut international de l'Allemagne et le problème de l'unité allemande (1945–1955)*. Paris: Ministère des Affaires étrangères.

Meyer-Landrut, N. 1988. *Frankreich und die deutsche Einheit 1952*. Munich, Germany: Oldenbourg.

Miard-Delacroix, H. 2004. *Question nationale allemande et nationalisme. Perceptions françaises d'une problématique allemande au début des années cinquante*. Lille, France: Presses du Septentrion.

Palmer, G., and T.C. Morgan. 2004. *A Theory of Foreign Policy*. Princeton, NJ: Princeton University Press.

Soutou, G.-H. 1988. "La France et les notes soviétiques de 1952 sur l'Allemagne." *Revue d'Allemagne et des pays de langue allemande* 20, no. 3: 261–73.

———. 1994. "France." In *The Origins of the Cold War in Europe*, edited by D. Reynolds, 96–120. New Haven, CT: Yale University Press.

Steininger, R. 2008. *Austria, Germany, and the Cold War*. New York: Berghahn.

Stourzh, G. 2005. *Um Einheit und Freiheit. Staatsvertrag, Neutralität und das Ende der Ost-West-Besetzung Österreichs 1945–1955*. Vienna, Austria: Böhlau.

Stourzh, G., and W. Mueller. 2018. *A Cold War over Austria: The Struggle for the State Treaty, Neutrality, and the End of East-West Occupation, 1945–1955*. Lanham: Lexington. (This updated English version of Stourzh, *Um Einheit und Freiheit* was not yet available to the author of this chapter.)

Wolff, S. 2003. *The German Question since 1919*. Westport, CT: Praeger.

CHAPTER 14

FRANCE, POLAND, AND GERMANY'S EASTERN BORDER, 1945–1990

THE RECURRENT ISSUE OF THE GERMAN QUESTION IN FRENCH-POLISH RELATIONS

PIERRE-FRÉDÉRIC WEBER

Because it involved the future of the two German states and the possibility of their reunification as well as the final drawing of their borders, the German question was of paramount importance for the neighbors to the east of the Federal Republic of Germany (FRG, or West Germany) and the German Democratic Republic (GDR, or East Germany). Among them, Poland was certainly more preoccupied by German affairs than any other country, including even Czechoslovakia. Its particular geographic position as well as burning postwar border issues fostered Warsaw's diplomatic efforts to influence the discussion about the German question. Its main concern was linked to the Oder-Neisse line, which had been defined at the Potsdam Conference (17 July–2 August 1945) as Poland's Western border, at least pending a final settlement.

Of all European states, it was France with which Poland's diplomats most frequently sought dialogue. There existed between the two countries a tradition of relatively good relations, exemplified in particular by interwar cooperation through the French Military Mission to Poland (1918–39), including a specific moment of densification during the war against Bolshevik Russia (1919–21), followed by the signature of the Franco-Polish alliance treaty in February 1921. Already in the interwar period, French diplomacy had showed strong interest in Central European border issues.[1] In Polish-French relations the question of the Oder-Neisse border was a recurrent topic throughout the postwar period and the Cold War, with zeniths at almost every time when changes in East-West relations or in the FRG's foreign policy were noticable—in other words, 1945–47 (in the pre–Cold War period); 1959–63 (as France and the FRG got closer); 1967–70 (with the onset of the FRG's Neue Ostpolitik); and 1989–90 (in the closing stage of the Cold War).

Those periods always intensified French-Polish activities with regard to the German question and revealed the entanglements of France's multiple loyalties as well as Poland's particular interests. Hence the traditional French-Polish friendship would come into conflict with the process of French-German reconciliation. Poland's diplomatic activity over the border issue forced France to offer a clearer definition of both its interest in the European integration process and its concern for the European order. Poland, on the other hand, appeared not only as a speaker of the Eastern bloc but also as a state trying to maintain contacts with the West and a central position in European affairs. Our purpose is thus to highlight this trans-European dimension of the German question by looking at French-Polish relations especially around the key issue of Germany's Eastern border during the whole Cold War period. The following reflections are chronologically structured around the four zeniths above mentioned.

French-Polish Relations in the Aftermath of World War II: 1945–47

By the end of World War II the French and Polish provisional governments were eager to resume the tradition of good bilateral contacts, a difficult endeavor given the Poles' bitter experience with the French-Polish military alliance at the beginning of the war—in other words, in 1939. Although initially, even during the difficult negotiations for the signing of the French-Soviet Treaty (December 1944), General Charles de Gaulle refused to recognize the Polish Committee of National Liberation (PKWN),[2] a Communist ad hoc institution supported by the the Union of Soviet Socialist Republics (USSR, or Soviet Union) and formed in Lublin in July 1944, the Provisional Government of the French Republic (GPRF, created in Algiers on 3 June 1944) was one of the first Western executive authorities to recognize the Polish Provisional Government of National Unity (TRJN, founded in Warsaw on 29 June 1945) as Poland's official representative organ—on the very day after its establishment.[3] France was not present at the Potsdam Conference, but the other Allies informed the French government about the decisions made at the conference. As far as the German-Polish border was concerned, the French stated that they "have no objection to the takeover by the Polish administration of the territories situated East of the Oder and of the Western Neisse." However, final decisions regarding Germany as a whole could be made "only after a general examination of the question by the Powers concerned."[4]

In the first stage of the postwar period, when the tensions between the Soviet Union and the Western Allies were arguably not as irreversible as they would become in 1947 with the beginning of the Cold War,[5] France and Poland would even try to restore their interwar relations: both governments were planning to sign a bilateral assistance treaty and negotiations between them were quite intensive, albeit not easy, especially between summer 1946 and February 1947. Nevertheless, already by the end of November 1945, the French noted the Poles' hurry in trying to obtain an official French recognition of the Oder-Neisse border; this hurry made Paris keep a certain distance, as it seemed clear that the Polish attempt went "together with the overall Soviet policy in Europe."[6] The French position was marked by some hesitation concerning the evaluation of dangers in postwar Europe: the foreign policy of the GPRF and later of the young French Fourth Republic went through a "dialectic phase where the consciousness about the Soviet danger would cohabitate with [the perception of] the German one."[7] In the end, the division of Europe and the stiffening bipolar world system made it impossible to conclude an agreement. This was all the more true because dominating Stalinism on the one hand and anti-Communism on the other hand would contribute to create an atmosphere of mutual distrust and suspiciousness, sometimes leading to paranoid spy-hunting campaigns in the Eastern bloc (but also in the West). In this respect, French-Polish relations were not different from other tense East-West contacts: in March 1949 the Robineau case, named after an employee of the French consulate in Szczecin supposedly spying for France,[8] brought about a major diplomatic crisis between the two states that ended in a general freezing of their relations almost until the end of the Bierut period (1948–56).[9]

Yet even during the inauspicious period of the late 1940s and early 1950s, scarce meetings and talks between diplomats would be used by the Polish side to reaffirm the traditional link between Warsaw and Paris, especially with regard to a potential German threat. This was true in particular in the context of the Western Allies' discussions about a possible (re)armament of the FRG at the beginning of the 1950s. The recurrent motive could be summed up as follows: "Apart from any other difficulties in [French-Polish] bilateral relations due to certain factors, there is one fundamental issue that unites both nations, no matter what kind of policy is being pursued by some short-sighted politicians. It is the question of the rebirth of German imperialism, threatening both nations."[10]

A few years later, in autumn 1953, Warsaw undertook steps to exert influence on the Assemblée nationale (the lower house of the French parliament) during the debates on the project of a European Defence Community (EDC). With Soviet acquiescence, the Polish embassy in Paris helped a group of French deputies to organize a visit to Poland planned in December 1953. Whereas the initiative came from the French side, the Polish Ministry of Foreign Affairs rapidly saw the benefit of instrumentalizing the visit to promote the (once German) recovered territories and to seek contact with French members of Parliament who were basically hostile to the EDC, or still hesitant, in order to influence them and thus contribute to French-Polish diplomatic rapprochement.[11] The French visitors had the opportunity to see progress made by Polish authorities in rebuilding and re-Polonizing Wrocław (formerly Breslau, Lower Silesia) since the border change.[12]

French-Polish Relations during the Period of French–West German Rapprochement: 1959–63

The end of the French Fourth Republic and the return of de Gaulle to power in 1958 provided an opportunity to strengthen French-Polish relations, which remained excellent throughout the 1960s. Both de Gaulle's concept of international relations (in particular his desire to overcome the bipolar Cold War system) and his European project (a nonfederal Europe of nations) led to enhanced contacts with Eastern European satellite states. Among those states Poland certainly had the highest diplomatic potential, based on long national traditions. During a press conference on 25 March 1959, ten months after having returned to power, de Gaulle made an important declaration about Germany's borders, stating that reunification would be "the normal destiny of the German people, provided they did not contest their current Western, Eastern, Northern and Southern borders."[13] Of course, it should not remain unmentioned that this statement was made in the context of the beginning of the second Berlin crisis. In a secret conversation with the Soviet ambassador in Paris, Sergei Vinogradov, on 6 March, the French president had already made his point very clear about Europe's postwar borders: "For France, the Oder-Neisse issue is settled, all the more so as reopening that question would be against the interests of Poland. . . . We do not look favorably at all upon an Anschluss either and for us the borders of Czechoslovakia are not at stake. [However,] although the reunification is not an urgent problem, nothing should be done to exclude it forever. . . . We should not drive the Germans into despair."[14]

France was not the only power trying to link the solution of the Berlin crisis with a more general settlement of the German question, including the problem of the Oder-Neisse border. Internal discussions in the U.S. State Department took this direction, too. In October 1959 Martin J. Hillenbrand of the Office of German Affairs prepared a memorandum for discussion regarding the possibility of connecting the border question with the Berlin issue.[15] However, only de Gaulle expressed his concern and support for the Oder-Neisse border so clearly. Although they did consider the new border as a definitive settlement, the United States (and the United Kingdom) made no equivalent public declarations.[16]

Paris was in a delicate situation because both the FRG and Poland were keen to monitor the evolution of France's bilateral relations with each of them: the FRG wanted to obtain French confirmation that the German question was still unsettled, while Poland wanted to win Paris over for the Polish (and Eastern European) position: not only should the Oder-Neisse border be confirmed, but Germany's division should be acknowledged, too. From 1961 to 1963 and, in particular, at the time of the signature of the Elysée Treaty (22 January 1963), these competing West German and Polish demands or expectations were becoming increasingly obvious: whereas the West German Ministry of Foreign Affairs (Auswärtiges Amt) anxiously registered every single French statement regarding the German question in general and the border issue in particular,[17] its Polish counterpart (Ministerstwo Spraw Zagranicznych, MSZ) expressed its concerns with regard to the announced French–West German "pact"—as they would call it, interpreting it as a potentially threatening military alliance. Poland feared that the completion of the treaty might lead to changes in France's foreign policy, with possible negative consequences for Polish interests, first of all regarding the intangibility of the Oder-Neisse border. Already after de Gaulle's first public statement regarding Germany's borders (in March 1959), the MSZ had given its embassy in Paris a short instruction about how to underpin Poland's position: "a/ work patiently towards a rapprochement with France and exploit every discord in its relations with the German Federal Republic [*sic*], b/ have France firmly adhere to the position adopted by de Gaulle in the border issue."[18] Similar steps were made in the following years. In its annual report on the international position of the FRG, the MSZ regretted in 1961 the "waning sensitiveness of the [French] public opinion to the problem of West German revisionism and militarism."[19]

After the conclusion of the Elysée Treaty, Poland would not stop its efforts. On 25 February 1963, only about a month after the treaty had been signed in Paris, the MSZ sent to the Quai d'Orsay a memorandum that included an analysis of the new situation created by the treaty and the risks entailed as perceived in Warsaw. Paris could not but disagree with that interpretation. In its official response to the Polish memorandum, the French stressed the fact that the treaty had also been signed to "preserve the possibilities of a settlement of the German question, respecting the right of self-determination."[20] In further bilateral meetings France repeatedly tried to reassure Polish diplomats that the Elysée Treaty was not a threat against the Eastern bloc in general nor against Poland in particular. Moreover, de Gaulle's position concerning the Oder-Neisse line had been clear enough at least since 1959, and the fact that the FRG accepted a rapprochement with France despite the latter's declarations about the German question could already be seen as West Germany's "tacit acceptance" of those previous statements (as French Ambassador Pierre Charpentier suggested).[21] Of course, the Poles were not prepared to accept such a minimalist interpretation. Facing France's polite but firm statements with regard to its cooperation with the FRG, Poland realized that much lobbying would be necessary in order to bring Paris possibly closer to Warsaw's position. Even a few months before the signing of the Elysée Treaty, the MSZ had started reevaluating its own action abroad: "We need to modify the contents and forms of our propaganda activities about the FRG hitherto developed, especially as far as France is concerned. Stressing such aspects as war martyrology and German revisionism does currently not seem to be sufficient. Obviously, the real character of West Germany's policy as a threat to world peace needs to be made clearer than done so far."[22]

France, Poland, and the New West German Ostpolitik: 1967–70

Beyond the traditional friendship with Poland and the Poles, regularly mentioned and repeated sometimes like a leitmotiv, France was interested in closer relations with Warsaw also because the French wished to find partners for their policy of opening toward the east, but also due to Poland's relatively autonomous and dynamic diplomacy within the Eastern bloc. This approach became particularly obvious during the second half of the 1960s, when de Gaulle made his interest public through an official visit to the Union of Soviet Socialist Republics (USSR, or Soviet Union) in June 1966, later completed by his trips to other socialist countries, including Poland in September 1967, and Romania in May 1968.[23] De Gaulle's "politique à l'Est" (policy to the East) partly revived interwar trilateralism between France, the Soviet Union and third states in Central Europe,[24] but it was also meant to avoid Soviet suspicion: France did not want to appear as an instrument of U.S. diplomacy aiming at a division of the Eastern bloc's unity through bilateral contacts with satellite states without prior concertation with Moscow.[25] In Poland, the French president was very clear about his position concerning the postwar decisions with regard to Poland's Western border: during his visit in Upper Silesian Zabrze (formerly Hindenburg), his public greetings to the population, stressing the Polishness of the city and the region,[26] were warmly welcomed in Poland—and reluctantly, but rather silently, registered in the FRG.[27] Although de Gaulle's declaration did not really bring anything new, it took a particular significance in the context of the difficult birth of a new, cautiously more realistic West German Ostpolitik.

On 27 January 1967, in a conversation with the Polish foreign minister, Adam Rapacki,[28] de Gaulle repeated and developed the arguments he had already exposed to the Soviet ambassador eight years before, in March 1959. He also gave several indications about his own vision of the future of Germany in Europe:

> As far as the border is concerned, we have given our view: it is the Oder-Neisse. This is not at stake, there is no other border. We do not want any Anschluss, and neither do we want a Czech issue. . . . Nevertheless, that undefined situation in the heart of Europe cannot last forever. It has several disadvantages—for Germany as well as for the others. . . . It is no good to have this unsolved problem in the middle of Europe. We have to find a way to resolve it, though it will be long and difficult. The solution will be brought about by a European settlement, a European agreement about Germany, with the Germans—they need to be included. As for their unity, well, they will not be a Reich! We do not want that, and neither do you. It will rather be a rapprochement, a conjunction, maybe some day a confederation. . . . As for your problem, especially concerning the border, they [= the Germans] will not tell you today nor tomorrow: "we recognise it, we accept it." They will say so one day, because it is a fait accompli and it will be so more and more, as the years go by. They do have refugees in Germany, but as time goes by these will not be refugees any more, they will integrate themselves and they will lose their habit of looking beyond the Oder-Neisse line. This way, little by little, the problem shall lose its acuteness."[29]

Indeed, at that moment the FRG had already started developing alternatives to its hitherto adopted position in its relations with the East along a step-by-step approach (Egon Bahr).[30] West Germany would try to defuse bilateral conflicts with the Soviet

Union, Poland, and Czechoslovakia in particular. Bonn wanted to build normal diplomatic relations with Warsaw, too, a project that became realistic after 1969 and the
political change in Bonn, once Willy Brandt had taken office as chancellor. In Paris
that evolution was both welcomed and thoroughly observed.[31] On the one hand, neither de Gaulle nor his successor Georges Pompidou wanted to give up any element
of France's Great Power status concerning the German question, and Pompidou was
uneasy about the possible near-term realization of German unity through the Neue
Ostpolitik.[32] As a consequence, France would keep an eye on West German efforts to
improve relations not only with the GDR, but also with the Slavic neighbors. On the
other hand, Poland's repeated pleas for intermediation during the Polish–West German negotiation process (1970) to have the FRG recognize the Oder-Neisse border
as part of a final settlement would of course give France the opportunity to underline
its special status. But it would also put its diplomacy in a delicate situation, revealing
the above-mentioned double-bind: France committed itself to respect the principle
of *Friedensvertragsvorbehalt* (the peace treaty reservation), while simultaneously re-
assuring Poland that France had had and would still have a favorable position concerning the Oder-Neisse line as Poland's Western border. That French guarantee with
reservation given to Poland was called after Pompidou's Foreign Minister Maurice
Schumann the Schumann solution,[33] or, referring to France's and the other Western
Allies' similar statement with regard to Kaliningrad, the Kaliningrad solution. In
case of a peace treaty with Germany, France would not be against a confirmation of
the hitherto existing postwar status quo concerning borders in Europe as decided
in Yalta in 1945. President Pompidou took the opportunity to show his continuity
with de Gaulle's position while receiving the letter of credence from the new Polish
ambassador, Tadeusz Olechowski, in July 1969. At this occasion, he stressed the role
of Poland in Europe within its current borders.[34] A similar statement was transmitted
to Poland in a written note in spring 1970.[35] Paris clearly informed Bonn about this
step, without any fallout for West German–French relations.[36] One month before
the final signature of the Warsaw Treaty, the Quai d'Orsay appeared quite confident
and satisfied with the result of the negotiations, stressing the fact that "the quadripartite rights and responsibilities, including those concerning Germany's borders,
will remain intact after the signature of the German-Polish treaty."[37] All in all, the
Schumann solution did not mean a major concession to Poland in the French position regarding the border; in fact it was rather a clarification of the general purpose
statement de Gaulle had made in March 1959.

France's will to be active and present in the Eastern bloc, both as a companion and
a chaperone of the FRG, was understood as such not only by the Poles but also by
the West Germans themselves. The West German decision makers were conscious of
a certain spirit of competition present in French policies toward the East: as reported
in a West German note to the Auswärtiges Amt six years after the conclusion of the
Elysée Treaty, the Quai d'Orsay made it clear that "[the French] want to show Eastern
Europeans, that not only Germans are good at science and modern technology, and

that France does not stand out only in the field of fashion and perfumes."[38] Although Paris did not make political concessions in its project in order to present France as valuable economic partner to Eastern Europe, it tried to show more understanding for the Eastern bloc's approach concerning the security dimension of the German question.

As a member of the Warsaw Pact and the Council for Mutual Economic Assistance, Poland was eager to actively participate in the overall bloc policy developed by the Soviet Union in its relations with the West. As far as France's policy of opening toward the East was concerned, the Soviet Union saw it as an opportunity to play on the observed competition between France and West Germany. Moscow wanted to gain more French support and exert a stronger pressure on the FRG during its negotiations about signing the Moscow Treaty with the Soviet Union (August 1970) and the Warsaw Treaty with Poland (December 1970). In a teletype message sent from Moscow in May 1970, the Polish ambassador informed the MSZ of a meeting with his counterparts from the Soviet Ministry for Foreign Affairs: "The Soviets stress the fact that the USSR is interested in a further development of its relations with France. . . . In its contacts with France and the FRG, the USSR will continue to exploit the contradictions existing between those two Western European partners in order to play them against each other."[39]

The question of French support for the Polish postulate concerning the German-Polish border, which had been settled—at least officially—between Poland and the GDR through the Görlitz Treaty signed in July 1950, was only part of Poland's interest in deeper relations with France. Beyond the game consisting in playing on France and the FRG for tactical purposes, the Polish-French relations had an eminently strategic dimension (as had the Soviet-French relations). Seeking to obtain a final settlement of the border issue, but also to postpone German reunification ad kalendas Graecas, Poland at the same time wanted to avoid becoming dependent on the FRG's economic power. Bearing in mind the comparatively advanced level and the likely further development of the French economy and its technological achievments, Poland saw France as "one of the best partners in Western Europe for commerce . . . and industrial cooperation, especially in the field of motorisation, engineering and shipbuilding."[40] In spite of the broader Cold War antagonism, the 1970s marked a high point in Polish-French relations between 1945 and 1989–90. Notwithstanding tensions concerning specific issues (such as interpersonal and intersocietal contacts in the context of bilateral cultural exchange programs), France and Poland managed to get closer to each other economically—for example, in areas like the sale of turnkey plants or the exploitation of coal mines.[41] Generally speaking France also proved to be an important source of capital for investments in Poland, while Poland was able to provide the French industry with several kinds of ores. After the FRG's acceptance of the Oder-Neisse line in December 1970, which was ratified in May 1972, the two states would try to further develop their friendly relations, quite in compliance with the beginning of the Conference on Security and Cooperation in Europe (CSCE).[42] The personal contacts between President Valéry Giscard d'Estaing and the First secretary of the Polish United Workers' Party, Edward Gierek, were a good example of the warming up between Paris and Warsaw. Cooperation between France and Poland would then be justified not because of a potential German threat for peace, but rather based on some shared apprehension of West Germany's economic potential and the obvious expansion of its influence in the Eastern bloc. These fears would be confirmed by the FRG's rise in Poland's external trade: in 1975 imports of West German products already exceeded those from the GDR, and only the Soviet Union exported more to Poland than the FRG.[43]

France, Poland, and the Denouement of the German Question, 1989–90

As we have seen, Polish activities to win France's support for the recognition of the Oder-Neisse line were also part of an overall strategy aiming at creating closer French-Polish relations on several levels. The recognition of the border was of course an essential goal of post-1945 Poland, but it was also intrumentalized to stress the idea of a German threat to peace—an aspect the Polish regime never really gave up in its attempt to win France over to its approach of the border issue. So to what extent did Warsaw manage to secure Paris's support for Polish arguments? Here we need to look at two important events when the border issue was at stake, at least de jure: during the already mentioned negotiations for the Warsaw Treaty between the FRG and Poland in 1970, and during the discussions for the Two Plus Four Agreement (or Treaty on the Final Settlement with Respect to Germany) in 1990.

In 1970 a trilateral dialogue took place among France, the FRG, and Poland about the possibility that Bonn might recognize the Oder-Neisse line as the current and inviolable Polish Western border. Or one could call it perhaps a triple dialogue, as in fact there were never any joint French–(West) German–Polish meetings, but rather parallel German-Polish, French-German, and French-Polish discussions. They followed more or less the same pattern: German-Polish negotiations (marked by six main meetings before coming to a solution) would regularly lead to deadlocks, be it on the question of how to formulate the passage concerning the border issue or whether to include or not particular aspects of the expected subsequent normalization process—like additional rights for the German minority in Poland for instance. As a consequence, Poland would try to secure French support, asking French decision makers to exert some influence on the West German position.[44] Difficulties would arise because of sometimes diverging German and Polish interpretations of positions expressed by French diplomacy, either due to misunderstandings or to the negotiators' tactics on the German side and on the Polish side. True, France was ready to give some discreet support to some of Poland's desiderata, sometimes by default. For instance, the Quai d'Orsay reported to the Polish ambassador in Paris that the

French side had not conveyed to the West German Foreign Minister Walter Scheel the need for a repatriation clause in the prepared Polish–West German Treaty project for those Germans eager to leave Poland and emigrate to the FRG: "That issue does not concern France and has only little significance for Poland,"[45] was Schumann's answer to Scheel. Nevertheless, whatever the French moral support for Poland (and France's fear of a West German rise of economic weight in the East), Paris would not act against Bonn nor endanger the West German line of argument.[46] One should bear in mind that the FRG and France were closely allied, whereas the latter had no treaty with Poland.

France was one of Poland's main partners in Western Europe twenty years later when the border issue became current again. There was, of course, a certain convergence faced with a rapidly evolving unification process that nobody seemed to be able to delay. From November 1989 onward, concerns were detectable not only in the United Kingdom (not least in Margaret Thatcher's abrupt declarations), but also in France, where decision makers were taken aback by the pace of events. Yet even if French President François Mitterrand had not foreseen such a process (as certain authors have suggested) other than in general terms,[47] he was not opposed to German unification in principle (a misinterpretation often made as a result of Mitterrand's official visit to the GDR in December 1989).[48] In that context, the border issue was only one aspect, but France considered it as a question of utmost importance. Again Poland wanted France to take a position, and again France sought a middle course. Paris exerted strong pressure on Chancellor Helmut Kohl who, for domestic and electoral reasons, was reluctant to make any public commitment regarding the confirmation of the German-Polish border before unification. This reluctance caused short-term tensions between France and West Germany that were finally eased thanks to an official statement made by both the West German and the East German parliaments in June 1990. Moreover, with Mitterrand's help, the idea of inviting Poland's Foreign Minister Krzysztof Skubiszewski to attend the Paris meeting of the Two Plus Four negotiations in July 1990 (for the discussions concerning the border issue) was accepted by the German side—both FRG and GDR.[49] Nevertheless, despite the fact that Mitterrand was sympathetic to the Polish will to have the Oder-Neisse border guaranteed,[50] he did not entirely share the Polish view: France would not insist on having Bonn confirm the border legally (by a treaty) before a German reunification; the French support was instead limited to asking for an official political statement, and leaving open the possibility of a bilateral German-Polish agreement after reunification. Here again Paris did not take any step to oppose the West German side or even to interfere with its policy and legal doctrine. Poland's efforts did not succeed in altering any of the core principles of France's German and European policies, but Warsaw was for sure successful in its attempts to draw Paris's attention to its expectations. Tactically the presence of Foreign Minister Krzysztof Skubiszewski in Paris was undoubtedly (and justifiably so) a point of satisfaction for Poland.[51] Although France did not necessarily represent the voice of Poland in the West, it should be recognized that given Paris's interests and Warsaw's endurance, France helped at least to amplify Poland's own voice.

Conclusion

The fact that beyond the border issue France and Poland never shared a complete unanimity with regard to the German question can easily be explained: both nations were part of two opposite camps in a bipolar world system. Even if French decision makers tried to develop a dialogue with the Eastern bloc, that did not offset fundamental ideological divergences. Despite good relations with Poland, French government regimes remained basically hostile to communism—both as a program and as a system. Similarly, France and Poland's official relations with West Germany were qualitatively different between 1949 and 1989.

In "Deutschland, ein Wintermärchen" (1844), the German poet Heinrich Heine expressed his critique against German militarism and nationalism. The title is usually translated into English as "Germany. A Winter's Tale," but in an edition of the 1980s a translator opted for a more liberal translation: "Deutschland. A Not So Sentimental Journey."[52] Paraphrasing that expression, we could sum up our point of view as follows: Poles and French (both decision makers and societies) had not the same emotional background concerning Germany; in other words, the path leading to peaceful relations with the Germans was not an equally emotional journey. Instead, it depended very much on whether it was seen from the Seine or from the Vistula. Past experiences of conflict and war (especially the period 1939–45), but also political factors made it much more difficult for Poland to gain confidence in Germany (even East Germany). This was all the more so as the fear of West Germany and the West Germans was also used as an instrument of domestic politics and power by the socialist states in the whole of the Eastern bloc, particularly in those countries where propaganda strongly used patriotism and even nationalism as a means of legitimizing the dominating ideology or party.[53] There the fear of Germany, already more present than in Western Europe after Hitler's total war against his Eastern neighbors, was constantly stirred to weld together as many social groups as possible around the leading party presented as the only shield—with the help of the "Soviet brothers."

This element of controlled social mobilization was part of a specific "emotional regime—[a] set of normative emotions and . . . official rituals, practices, and emotives that express and inculcate them; a necessary underpinning of any stable political regime."[54] Even if communication between the Polish and the French emotional regimes were possible and actually happened, those were basically different. In France the fear of Germany worked as an instrument of domestic political debates only in very specific situations, such as the EDC case, but not as a permanent instrument of stabilization for any given French president or government after 1945 (and even less after 1963). It was not so much that the French would not again have been ready to "die for Danzig" (if they ever were),[55] but that such a need appeared simply improbable to most of them. In France, as in other Western countries, the fear of Germany, albeit diffusely present and sometimes—rather tactically and somehow artificially—reactivated, was overlaid to a large extent by anxieties concerning the overall threat of communism.

Pierre-Frédéric Weber, born in 1980, studied German and European Studies in France, at the universities of Angers and Paris III—Sorbonne Nouvelle. PhD (2006) on German-Polish relations in the 1960s and early 1970s. Currently associate professor at the University of Szczecin, Poland. Research fields: history of twentieth century's international relations and postwar processes in Europe—reconciliation, normalization, and conflicts; history and sociology of emotions. His latest book is about the fear of Germany in Europe since 1945: *Timor Teutonorum: Angst vor Deutschland seit 1945. Eine europäische Emotion im Wandel* (2015).

Notes

1. See Dessberg, "La France et la question."
2. Stalin first wanted to force de Gaulle to recognize the PKWN as a precondition for the USSR's acceptance of a French-Soviet Pact of mutual assistance against Nazi Germany; see F. Levêque, "Le général de Gaulle à Moscou."
3. See Soutou, "La place de la Pologne," 250.
4. Circular letter by Foreign Minister Georges Bidault, 8 Aug. 1945, quoted in DDF 1945, vol. 2, 238–41. Unless otherwise noted, all translations in this chapter are my own.
5. Usually the East-West discord about the European Recovery Program (ERP) presented by U.S. secretary of State George Marshall on 5 June 1947 is seen as the beginning of the Cold War period. Concerning ERP, see Milward, *The Reconstruction.*
6. Note from the Quai d'Orsay (Department for Eastern European Affairs), 26 Nov. 1945 (quoted in DDF 1945, vol. 2, 796–98).
7. Maelstaf, *Que faire de l'Allemagne?,* 22.
8. See Jarosz and Pasztor, *Robineau, Bassaler.*
9. As the first secretary of the Polish United Workers' Party (PZPR) from 1948 to 1956 Bolesław Bierut was the main representative of Stalinism in Poland; see Garlicki, *Bolesław Bierut.* French-Polish relations were complicated especially in 1951–52; see several letters by French ambassador Étienne Dennery stressing the embassy's worsening working conditions in Warsaw in that period, due to disruptive actions by the Polish authorities (AMSZ, z.8, w.29, t.383).
10. Note about a meeting between Polish prime minister Józef Cyrankiewicz and French ambassador Étienne Dennery in Warsaw, 13 Oct. 1950, AMSZ, z.8, w.13, t.193.
11. See encrypted telex from the French embassy in Warsaw to the French Ministry of Foreign Affairs, 15 Nov. 1953, AMAE, Europe, Pologne, 158.
12. See Weber, "Édouard Daladier." In Potsdam the Allies had decided the expulsion of about 8 million Germans from the territories attributed to Poland at the East of the Oder-Neisse line. For an overall presentation in English see Douglas, *Orderly and Humane.*
13. See de Gaulle, *Discours et messages,* vol. 3, 84–85.
14. DDF 1959, vol. 1, 291–94.
15. See Allen, *The Oder-Neisse line,* 219.
16. "President Kennedy and the State Department continued the approach begun during the second Eisenhower administration of publicly maintaining that the final solution to the border problem

awaited a peace conference, while confidentially discussing the possibility of pressuring Bonn to recognize the Oder-Neisse in order to foster closer Bonn-Warsaw relations." Ibid., 239.

17. That kind of sometimes slightly fault-finding accountancy was provided by the Auswärtiges Amt throughout the 1960s, see, e.g., list of de Gaulle's public statements concerning the German question, realized by Dept. I (A-3), 5 Apr. 1967 (PA/AA, B24, 607, 307). In the document, the Auswärtiges Amt reports nineteen (!) such declarations made by the French president between 1959 and 1967. For each of them the report laconically mentions only dates, related events, and places.

18. Top secret note sent by the MSZ to the Polish embassy in Paris, 13 May 1959, AMSZ, Dept. IV, z.17, w.15, t.133.

19. MSZ annual report FRG 1961, Jan. 1962, ibid..

20. DDF 1963, vol. 1, 397.

21. MSZ note after a meeting with French ambassador Pierre Charpentier, 10 Aug. 1962, AMSZ, Dept. IV, z.17, w.18, t.152.

22. MSZ note, 14 Sept. 1962, AMSZ, Dept. IV, z.17, w.20, t.162.

23. See Vaïsse, *La puissance ou l'influence?*, 242–50.

24. See Dessberg, *Le triangle impossible*.

25. See Brzezinski, *Alternative to Partition*.

26. De Gaulle said, "Long life to Zabrze, the most Silesian city in Silesia, thus the most Polish of all Polish cities." See the original quotation in a television program for the French broadcast as presented in *Charles de Gaulle, paroles publiques. Voyage en Pologne*, Institut national de l'audiovisuel, http://fresques.ina.fr/ (accessed 23 Mar. 2016).

27. See analysis of de Gaulle's official visit in Poland by Dept. I(A-3), 14 Sept. 1967, PA/AA, B24, 610, 96–103: "With his comments he has gone beyond his previous declarations. . . . He has tried to equate 'Silesian' with 'Polish.'" In fact, as the French embassy in Bonn remarked in a note sent to the Quai d'Orsay on 12 Oct. 1967, Chancellor Kurt Kiesinger did not make any statement about de Gaulle's faux pas, but words of protest and surprise were to be heard in the media, in particular by some Social Democratic Party (SPD) leaders: Foreign Minister Willy Brandt considered that de Gaulle's words were "incomprehensible," whereas West Berlin's future mayor Klaus Schütz said they could "jeopardize Germany's interests." DDF 1967, vol. 2, 461–65.

28. Rapacki was well known after his plan for a nuclear-free zone in Central Europe comprising Czechoslovakia, Poland, GDR, and FRG, presented at the United Nations in 1958.

29. DDF 1967, vol. 1, 162–70.

30. See Vogtmeier, *Egon Bahr*.

31. See Weber, "La France."

32. See Soutou, "L'attitude de Georges Pompidou."

33. Maurice Schumann was foreign minister from 1969 to 1973.

34. See DDF 1969, vol. 2, 267–71.

35. See encrypted telex from the MSZ to the Polish embassy in Paris, 5 Jun. 1970, AMSZ, z.6/77, w.248, t.1166, 158–60.

36. See encrypted telex from the MAE to the French embassy in Bonn, 15 Sept. 1970, AMAE, Europe, Pologne, 352, 27/23/9.

37. Encrypted telex from the MAE to the French embassy in Bonn, 10 Nov. 1970, AMAE, Europe, Pologne, 353, 27/23/9.

38. See encrypted telex from the West German embassy in Paris to the Auswärtiges Amt, 22 Jan. 1969, PA/AA, B24, 637, 21.

39. Encrypted telex from the Polish embassy in Moscow to the MSZ, 2/ May 1970, AMSZ, GM, O, 197–70.

40. Report from the Polish embassy in Paris to the MSZ, about the perspectives of the French foreign policy in the 1970s, 16 Aug. 1971, AMSZ, Dept. IV, z.27, w.77, t.6.

41. See Jarosz and Pasztor, *Polska-Francja*, 177–82.

42. See AMSZ, z.31/82, w.8, t.86, 236–242. Report from the Polish embassy in Paris to the MSZ, 16 Jun. 1976. See also Jarosz and Pasztor, *Polska-Francja*, 49–104.

43. See Główny Urząd Statystyczny, *Rocznik statystyczny*, 36.
44. This was true especially as far as the Western powers' notes of reply were concerned. Poland was afraid such notes could relativize the meaning of the FRG's recognition of the Oder–Neisse border. See encrypted telex from the Polish embassy in Paris to the MSZ, 10 Jun. 1970, AMSZ, z.6/77, w.248, t.1165, 190.
45. Encrypted telex from the Polish embassy in Paris to the MSZ, 2 Nov. 1970, AMSZ, z.6/77, w.248, t.1165, 338–39.
46. Encrypted telex from the MAE to the French embassy in Bonn, 22 Aug. 1970, AMAE, Europe, Pologne, 351.
47. See Schabert, *Wie Weltgeschichte*.
48. See Bozo, *Mitterrand*, 163–67.
49. See Borodziej, *Polska wobec*, 270–74; Bozo, *Mitterrand*, 237.
50. The Oder-Neisse border was the main issue discussed during the visit of the Polish delegation in Paris (with President Wojciech Jaruzelski, Prime Minister Tadeusz Mazowiecki, and Minister of Foreign Affairs Krzysztof Skubiszewski) on 9 March 1990. See Bozo, *Mitterrand*, 233.
51. See Skubiszewski's note quoted in ibid., 392–99.
52. Heine, *Deutschland*.
53. For Poland see Zaremba, *Komunizm*. For Hungary see Mevius, *Agents of Moscow*. For Romania see Tismăneanu, *Fantoma*.
54. Reddy, *The Navigation*, 129.
55. See Déat, "Faut-il mourir," 31.

Bibliography

Allen, D. J. 2003. *The Oder-Neisse line: the United States, Poland, and Germany in the Cold War*. Westport, CT: Praeger.

Borodziej, W. 2006. *Polska wobec zjednoczenia Niemiec 1989–1991. Dokumenty dyplomatyczne* [Poland and the German reunification process 1989–1991. Diplomatic documents]. Warsaw: Wydawn. Naukowe Scholar.

Bozo, F. 2005. *Mitterrand, la fin de la guerre froide et la réunification allemande: de Yalta à Maastricht*. Paris: Odile Jacob.

Brzezinski, Z. 1965. *Alternative to Partition: for a broader conception of America's role in Europe*. New York: McGraw-Hill Book Company.

De Gaulle, C. 1970. *Discours et messages*. Vol. 3, *Avec le renouveau*. Paris: Plon.

Déat, M. 1939. "Faut-il mourir pour Dantzig?." *L'œuvre*, 4 May, reprinted in *Perspectives françaises*. Paris: Editions de L'œuvre n.d. [1940].

Dessberg, F. 2007. "La France et les frontières de l'Est européen dans les années 1920." In *Sécurité européenne: frontières, glacis et zones d'influence de l'Europe des alliances à l'Europe des blocs (fin XIXème siècle-milieu XXème siècle)*, edited by F. Dessberg and F. Thébault, 23–39. Rennes, France: Presses universitaires de Rennes.

———. 2009. *Le triangle impossible. Les relations franco-soviétiques et le facteur polonais dans les questions de sécurité en Europe (1924–1935)*. Brussels, Belgium: Lang.

Douglas, R. M. 2012. *Orderly and humane: The expulsion of the Germans after the Second World War*. New Haven, CT: Yale University Press.

Garlicki, A. 1994. *Bolesław Bierut*. Warsaw: Wydawn. Szkolne i Pedag.

Główny Urząd Statystyczny [Polish central statistic office]. 2009. *Rocznik statystyczny handlu zagranicznego 2009/ Yearbook of foreign trade statistics of Poland*. Warsaw: Główny Urząd Statystyczny.

Heine, H. 1986. *Deutschland: A Not So Sentimental Journey*. Translated into English with an introduction and notes by T.J. Reed. London: Angel Books.

Jarosz, D., and M. Pasztor. 2001. *Robineau, Bassaler i inni. Z dziejów stosunków polsko-francuskich w latach 1948–1953* [= Robineau, Bassaler, and others. Chronicles of French-Polish relations 1948–1953]. Toruń, Poland: Marszałek.

———. 2006. *Polska-Francja 1970–1980. Relacje wyjątkowe?* [= Poland-France 1970–1980. Exceptional relations?]. Warsaw: Oficyna Wydawnicza.

Levêque, F. 1994. "Le général de Gaulle à Moscou (décembre 1944)." *Espoir* 99.

Maelstaf, G. 1999. *Que faire de l'Allemagne? Les responsables français, le statut international de l'Allemagne et le problème de l'unité allemande (1945–1955)*. Paris: Ministère des Affaires étrangères.

Mevius, M. 2005. *Agents of Moscow: The Hungarian Communist Party and the Origins of Socialist Patriotism 1941–1953*. Oxford, UK: Clarendon Press.

Milward, A. S. 2006. *The Reconstruction of Western Europe 1945–1951*. Berkeley: University of California Press.

Reddy, W. M. 2001. *The Navigation of Feeling: A Framework for the History of Emotions*. Cambridge: Cambridge University Press.

Schabert, T. 2005. *Wie Weltgeschichte gemacht wird. Frankreich und die deutsche Einheit*. Stuttgart, Germany: Klett-Cotta.

Soutou, G.-H. 1995. "L'attitude de Georges Pompidou face à l'Allemagne." In *Georges Pompidou et l'Europe*, edited by Association Georges Pompidou, 267–313. Brussels, Belgium: Complexe.

———. 2007. "La place de la Pologne dans la politique extérieure française pendant la guerre froide." In *La Pologne et l'Europe. Du partage à l'élargissement (XVIIIe–XXIe siècles)*, edited by I. Davion, J. Kłoczowski, and G.-H. Soutou, 249–74. Paris: Presses de l'université Paris-Sorbonne.

Tismăneanu, V. 1995. *Fantoma lui Gheorghiu-Dej [The Spectre of Gheorghiu-Dej]*. Bucharest, Romania: Editura Univers.

Vaïsse, M. 2009. *La puissance ou l'influence? La France dans le monde depuis 1958*. Paris: Fayard.

Vogtmeier, A. 1996. *Egon Bahr und die deutsche Frage. Zur Entwicklung der sozialdemokratischen Ost- und Deutschlandpolitik vom Kriegsende bis zur Vereinigung*. Bonn, Germany: Dietz.

Weber, P.-F. 2007. "La France et le Traité de Varsovie (1970). Entre aval et appréhension." *Allemagne d'aujourd'hui* 179, no. 4: 100–16.

———. 2009. "Édouard Daladier en Pologne (décembre 1953). Chronique des contacts officieux franco-polonais sur la question allemande et la CED." *Allemagne d'aujourd'hui* 187, no. 4: 62–80.

Zaremba, M. 2001. *Komunizm, legitymizacja, nacjonalizm. Nacjonalistyczna legitymizacja władzy komunistycznej w Polsce* [Communism, legitimization, nationalism. The nationalist legitimization of communist power in Poland]. Warsaw: Wydawn. Trio.

CHAPTER 15

A SURPRISING CONTINUITY

THE FRENCH ATTITUDE AND POLICY TOWARD THE GERMAN DEMOCRATIC REPUBLIC, 1949–1990

CHRISTIAN WENKEL

During the autumn of 1989, while the situation in the the German Democratic Republic (GDR, or East Germany) changed rapidly, French diplomats were somewhat surprised that for more than twenty years—in other words, since the end of the de Gaulle era—the French attitude with regard to the German question had not really changed.[1] However, since Charles de Gaulle had clarified elements of an existing policy rather than developed a new French policy with regard to the German question during his presidency from 1958 to 1969, one could assume that the fundamentals of this attitude did not change from the very beginning of the 1950s until the German unification in 1990.[2] A significant illustration of this continuity is the French attitude and policy toward the GDR during these four Cold War decades.[3] Founded in 1949 as the Federal Republic of Germany (FRG, or West Germany), the German Democratic Republic was considered by French officials and diplomats during the whole period as an artificial construction.

Even the formal recognition of the East German state and the establishment of official diplomatic relations in 1973 did not break this continuity. This step had become necessary in the context of the détente process, fostered in particular by French foreign policy since 1963. The opening of the Conference on Security and Cooperation (CSCE) in 1973 required the participation of the GDR and thus its formal recognition by all other participants. The signing of the Basic Treaty between both German states in December 1972 was a precondition for the Helsinki conference as well as for the establishment of official Franco–East German relations some weeks later.[4] The German unification, or more precisely the framed return to a unified German nation, remained however a long-term goal of French policy. Any uncontrolled return to this unity was in contrast considered as one of the most important dangers to France in terms of international security. From the viewpoint of French foreign policymakers for the whole duration of the Cold War, the second German state was an essential part of the German question. As such, the attitude toward the GDR depended on the attitude toward the German question in general and the issue of German unification in particular.

Looking at how French officials and diplomats dealt with the GDR, as one of the most particular issues of the German question, thus enables us to understand how they dealt with the German question in general. In order to explore French policy toward the German question through the lens of the GDR issue, this contribution analyzes the attitude of French officials before 1973, studies the highly complicated establishment of official relations between both states during the 1970s, and concludes with François Mitterrand's visit to East Berlin and Leipzig in December 1989.

From Robert Schuman to Charles de Gaulle: The Definition of the French Official Attitude toward the GDR during the 1950s

In the public political discourse in France, the GDR was taboo during the 1950s and during most of the 1960s. One of the rare exceptions was Charles de Gaulle's press conference on 25 March 1959, where, in the context of the second Berlin crisis, he explained the French position with regard to three closely linked issues relating to the German question: the status of Berlin, especially the access to West Berlin; the future of Germany; and Germany's eventual neutralization. Dealing with these issues, he also necessarily dealt with the East German state. However, in order to avoid the terms "GDR" or "German Democratic Republic," de Gaulle spoke only of the "system of Pankow": "As a matter of fact, we are not prepared to recognize this system ["the Pankow-system," i.e., the GDR; author's note] as a sovereign and independent state, as it has not emerged and still exists only because of the Soviet occupation and a harsh dictatorship. Regarding the Foreign policy of the French Republic as a whole, we could not put on the same level this arbitrary construction on the one hand and the Federal Republic of Germany on the other."[5]

This attitude corresponded to the Western viewpoint in general, yet it also reflects a specificity of the French approach to the German question. In fact, the French approach to the German question as well as to the GDR was determined by a specific understanding of the nation. The foreign policy of the founder of the Fifth Republic was even based on what could be called a national principle.[6] The recognition of two German states was clearly in contradiction with this principle. De Gaulle also defended the idea of self-determination, based on a congruence of citizenship and nation as conceptualized in the French understanding of their own nation.[7] According to these ideas, the East German state possessed neither sovereignty nor legitimacy.

Thus, the press conference of March 1959 provided a definition of the French attitude and policy toward the German question, including the GDR. Moreover, Charles de Gaulle was the first French leader to give such a definition in public, but what he said about the GDR was in accordance with what the French Foreign Ministry considered at the time as the "traditional" French position.[8] All he did was to put together and to formalize different elements of the existing French policy in a comprehensive position concerning the second German state and the future of the German nation. His quite simple and useful definition became a sort of guideline for French diplomats over more than thirty years. As a result, the equal treatment of the two German states by French diplomacy, formally excluded by de Gaulle, was strictly avoided until 1989–90.

Considering the division of the German nation as a phenomenon limited in time, the French diplomats and officials had to address the question of how to control the expected movement that would tend to overcome that artificial division. Following the tradition of the policy on Germany, inaugurated by Robert Schuman in 1950 with the plan for the future European Coal and Steel Community (ECSC), Charles de Gaulle considered European integration as the necessary frame for the German nation and its future. The integration of Germany as a whole was indeed raised as an ideal for French foreign policy from the early 1950s. According to this scheme the overcoming of the European division was considered a decade later in the context of French détente policy as the best framework for overcoming the German division.[9]

From March 1959 onward de Gaulle approved and demanded in public the intensification of inner-German relations, especially on the economic and the cultural level: "Until this ideal is achieved [the unification of Germany and its integration in a European organization; author's note], we believe that those two separate parts of the German people should have and practice multiple contacts and relations in all fields."[10] Other French statesmen, like Edgar Faure as prime minister, had already since 1955 been asking for an intensification of East-West relations in order to foster détente. De Gaulle was able to translate his ideas of détente policy into concrete action only after the end of the Algerian War and the Cuban Missile Crisis. He started by normalizing Franco-Soviet relations from 1963 on, symbolized by his spectacular Moscow visit in 1966. During those years, French diplomats also normalized gradually the relations with the other East European countries, except the GDR. The normalization of the Franco–East German relations depended on a paradigmatic change of the German Ostpolitik that took place only after the election of Willy Brandt in 1969.[11] His new policy toward the Soviet Union, Eastern Europe and the GDR in particular made it not only possible but also strongly required for the Quai d'Orsay to adapt the French relationship with the GDR.

Nevertheless, any decision in this domain continued to be determined, as before 1969, by the French aim to do nothing that could weaken the position of the FRG toward the GDR. The motivation to do so was clearly a French one, because the normalization of the inter-German relations was considered as a precondition for the normalization of the East-West relations in Europe in general and thus for the settlement of the German question in particular, which the French diplomacy worked for.[12]

Recognizing the GDR without Recognizing the German Division during the 1970s

On 9 February 1973 the French government established diplomatic relations with the GDR. However, French officials and diplomats scrupulously avoided mentioning in this context the term "recognition." In order to satisfy the East German side, they simply acknowledged afterwards the Common Declaration of the Four Allies of 9 November 1972—a declaration to support the candidature of both German states to become members of the United Nations—as the formal recognition of the East German state. In contrast with a usual recognition or with a usual establishment of diplomatic relations, the establishment of diplomatic relations between the French Republic and the GDR was neither a unilateral nor unique act.[13] It was much more part of a multilateral process that lasted more than ten years from the end of 1960s up to the signing of different bilateral conventions in 1980. The principal reason for this particular situation was the unwillingness of the French diplomacy to fully recognize a second German state in terms of international law and thus the German division.[14]

The FRG's New Ostpolitik initiated by Willy Brandt in 1969 launched this process, while changing completely the framework of the Franco–East German relations. In previous years, the normalization of economic and cultural relations with the GDR had been constantly postponed with respect to the inter-German relations and in accordance with the French attitude toward the German question. The only exception was the selling of the French SECAM technology (séquentiel couleur à mémoire) for color television to the GDR during the first months of 1969 despite an urgent request of the federal government to stop it. French Foreign Minister Michel Debré used this decision to remind Bonn that French political solidarity with Germany required reciprocity and to urge the West German partner to change its policy on Eastern Europe.[15]

Once this change had taken place in autumn 1969, many Franco–East German projects, adjourned since the intensification of the Berlin crisis in 1960, could now be realized within a very short time frame of about two years. On the cultural level, a performance of the state opera of East Berlin took place in Paris, for instance, as did a week of East German film. On the economic level, the relations reached a new stage thanks to a five-year trade agreement, the changing of credit guidelines following a French initiative at the level of the European Economic Community (EEC) in Brussels, and the opening of an office of the French industry in East Berlin. In 1970 were also created friendship societies in the French National Assembly and in the French Senate in order to formalize contacts with East German parliamentarians.[16] During those years, the Franco-German Exchange Society (Échanges franco-allemands), an unofficial society that had organized the Franco–East German relations on the cultural and on the parliamentarian level in the absence of official relations during the 1960s, even became a partner to the Quai d'Orsay. However, the rhythm of normalization between France and the GDR still depended on the evolution of the inter-German relations. The principal guideline for French diplomats in the relationship with the GDR was still to do nothing that could undermine the ongoing negotiations and the rapprochement between the two German states. This limit was not motivated by the special relationship with the FRG, but rather by the French quest for a solution to the European question, including the German question. The normalization of the inter-German relations, as well as of the Franco–East German relations, was considered as a crucial condition for any solution of the overall European question, instead of a full recognition of the GDR.

From the moment the question of a possible establishment of official relations with the GDR arose in 1970 for the first time, French diplomats were clear about excluding a complete recognition, especially because of the repercussions on the status of Berlin, a status, that precisely conferred on France a lever to retain influence on how to solve the German question in the future: "A complete recognition of the GDR by the three Western allies would necessarily have consequences on their rights regarding Germany as a whole. . . . In addition, such a recognition, sanctioning the division of Germany, would undermine as a consequence the possibility of a peace treaty with a unified Germany, one of the most crucial elements of the quadripartite responsibilities."[17]

However, in order to get ahead with the détente in Europe and to start the CSCE process, France had to recognize the existence of a second German state and to establish official relations. One of the most important conditions for the French diplomacy to embark on those negotiations was the signing of the Four Power Agreement on Berlin on 3 September 1971.[18] By signing this agreement, France gained an official confirmation not only of the status of Berlin but also of the Allied rights and responsibilities concerning Berlin and Germany as a whole. The other condition that had to be fulfilled before the beginning of negotiations between France and the GDR was the signing of the Basic Treaty between both German states on 21 December 1972. In order to clarify the larger multilateral framework of East-West negotiations, Foreign Minister Maurice Schumann reinforced the Allied rights and responsibilities while announcing the French willingness to start talks in a telegram to East German officials on 22 December 1972: "Underlining that the very object of a diplomatic relationship was to enable the increase of discussions between two countries on political, economic and cultural subjects, the French delegation firmly rejected the suggestions of their interlocutors, who tended to confer a privileged character on the future relationship between France and the German Democratic Republic."[19]

Thus, the establishment of diplomatic relations some weeks later on 9 February 1973 was considered in Paris only as a consequence and a part of a large process, and not linked to the state of the Franco–East German relationship. Moreover, the French attitude toward the GDR and to the German question did not change in 1973. Consequently, this step of a broader normalization process of East-West relations did not respond to the East German attempt at recognition. The recognition issue was only replaced and reappeared during the following years within a broad range of related problems for French diplomacy, as for instance the exchange of the ambassadors between both capitals, or the problem of denomination of the French embassy in East Berlin. Dealing with these issues, France had above all to repel the constant East German attempt to undermine the status of Berlin after 1973 within the bilateral relationship. In a conversation with his East German colleague, the French foreign minister left no doubt on the French position concerning the Berlin status and the German question: "As in the quadripartite agreement, the only option was to put aside divergences between theoretical views. There is no interest in looking behind and raising controversies on a legal level. France does not wish to enter into these controversies: to avoid not only affecting its good relationship with the Federal Republic, but also an impact on European stability, a permanent feature of its policy."[20]

The most significant example of the conflict between an unchanged French attitude in general and the evolving context of East-West relations, however, was the conclusion of a bilateral consular convention. For French diplomats the recognition of an East German nationality was clearly inconceivable, but in terms of international law, a recognition of a state implies the recognition of its citizens. For this reason, France had to deal with a contradiction that could actually not be solved, since the recognition of two German states was fundamentally not compatible with the responsibility for Germany as a whole: "Considering on the one hand that we never subscribed *expressis verbis* to the extensive conception of the Federal Republic, and on the other hand that, pursuant to our quadripartite rights and the Paris agreement, we should do nothing that might endanger the concept of Germany as a whole, we have kept to our constant practice according to which the definition of nationality has no place in a consular convention and have removed any definition of the nationality of the nationals [nationalité des ressortissants] on both sides."[21]

While Great Britain could quickly conclude such a convention with the GDR, due to the different British concept of nation, France was involved in these negotiations during nearly seven years. Only after a compromise agreed between the United States and the GDR on this issue France could conclude with the GDR a consular convention in 1980.[22] The French reluctance to define a position in this matter was also motivated by the reactions expected from the federal government in Bonn. Foreign Minister Jean Sauvagnargues however missed no opportunity to assure the West German diplomats that the French position concerning a possible recognition of the East German nationality was necessarily determined by the French attitude toward the German question in general, and thus excluded: "We will largely take into account the well-known point of view of the French government on the German question and will do nothing that might be incompatible with our position concerning Germany as a whole."[23] In contrast, the East German aim was to officialize as much as possible its relationship with France. The GDR did nearly everything to raise the frequency of political contacts on a governmental level—still led by the desire of a complete recognition in terms of international law. French diplomacy did its best to slow down this type of normalization but could not prevent such contacts in the end.

In return, Paris asked for more substantial efforts on the economic and the cultural level: "But this should not prevent us from establishing a thorough and constructive relationship, by following the example of the cooperation between France and the Soviet Union, inaugurated ten years ago by General de Gaulle. For you as for us, it is a question of how to give a concrete content to the Détente policy to which we are both equally committed."[24]

Beginning with the visit of French Foreign Minister Jean François-Poncet to the GDR in 1979, the Franco–East German relations are characterized during the 1980s by a growing number of official visits, up to those of Prime Minister Laurent Fabius in East Berlin in 1985 and of GDR head of state Erich Honecker in Paris in 1988.

François Mitterrand, His Visit to East Berlin, and French Interests with Regard to the GDR and the German Unification in 1989–90

While establishing diplomatic relations with the GDR, the French side was quite insistent on the principle of reciprocity as a basis for the future bilateral relations. Hence, after the official visit of the head of the East German state, Erich Honecker, to Paris in January 1988, the next step on the way toward normalizing Franco–East German relations was necessarily an official visit of the president of the French Republic to the GDR. At the beginning of his second mandate in 1988, François Mitterrand wanted to revitalize French Ostpolitik. In order to achieve this aim, official visits to different states of the Eastern bloc were planned, among them the Soviet Union, Czechoslovakia, Bulgaria, Poland, and the GDR. According to French interests within the CSCE process, the main objective of these journeys was the promotion of European détente by strengthening economic and cultural relations with these countries.[25]

In the case of East Germany, another important aim was to replace the inter-German bilateralism, especially on the economic level, by a European multilateralism. In order to enhance the French share of the East German market, the Quai d'Orsay was now even ready to foster political consultations with East Berlin. Moreover, in order to improve the East German perception of France and the diffusion of French values, language, and culture in the GDR, French diplomats suggested also the strengthening of the French cultural presence in the East German province.[26]

At the beginning of 1989, the project of Mitterrand's visit to the GDR reemerged. During the following months French diplomats assessed the appropriateness of maintaining or not this visit—just as they apprehended the Franco–West German relations—according to their criticism of the exclusive bilateralism, practiced by the FRG in dealing with different East European countries. For the in-house think-tank of the French Foreign Ministry, the Centre d'Analyse et de Prévision, the visit thus seemed to be a way of bringing the FRG to formulate a real vision for its foreign policy and to feel that the West Germans had a place in the French conception of Europe.[27]

But given the political evolution in the GDR during 1989, the project could not be carried out. Only after the dismissal from office of Erich Honecker on 18 October could the project take shape, as well as German unification, both once again conceivable. It was at this very moment the diplomatic advisers of François Mitterrand also became convinced that German unification should not be realized quicker than the ongoing European unification, but as a part of the latter: "If the trend of rapprochement between both Germanys seems inevitable, the outcome of this process is not a foregone conclusion. . . . Everything is manageable, provided this movement up to the end of the division of the German people does not move forward faster than the European construction and the general suppression of barriers between Eastern and Western Europe."[28]

Asked to choose a concrete date for his GDR visit, Mitterrand seemed however to hesitate. Only a few days after the Berlin Wall came down, the French ambassador in East Berlin, Joëlle Timsit, received concrete instructions.[29] Now he hurried in order to make this visit not only as president of the French Republic but also as president of the European Council, an office he held until the end of December 1989. Consequently, Mitterrand rejected a date during the month of January 1990, which would have been much more convenient for the GDR as well as for his own administration.[30]

The preparation for the visit is characterized by a hectic rush, due to the constantly changing political landscape in the GDR. Right up to a couple of days before the beginning of the journey, the East German interlocutors of Mitterrand were unknown.[31] Nonetheless, the journey was prepared with as much care as French diplomats deemed necessary to preserve French positions concerning Berlin or the future of Germany. The first official visit of a head of state of one of the three Western allies indeed required particular efforts on the part of French protocol. In terms of Berlinology, it was for example necessary to avoid the presence of the East German minister of defense during the visit, because the whole city of Berlin was considered to be under the military authority of the Allies. From a French perspective, the particular status of Berlin after World War II even made a visit outside Berlin—in other words, on the proper GDR territory—mandatory.[32] Mitterrand therefore spent a part of his visit in Leipzig and he refused an invitation to the congress of the Social Democratic Party (SPD) held in West Berlin at the same time. From a legal viewpoint, such a trip on the other side of the city would produce as a result the formal equality of both German states—a situation that French diplomats tried to avoid under any circumstances.[33] A complete recognition of the GDR was still not on the agenda. These details may seem trivial, but it was precisely on this legal level that French diplomacy demonstrated its unchanged attitude toward the German question and defended the Allied rights and responsibilities that would allow France to have control over the settlement of the German question in the future.

Mitterrand and his diplomats also had to deal with different attempts at political exploitation of this visit by both Germanys. The East German leaders especially expected that the French president might contribute to enhance the international status of the GDR—an East German aim that was misunderstood in Bonn as the French position itself. For this reason, Mitterrand did not authorize the broadcast of an interview he gave to the East German television before Helmut Kohl had carried out his visit to Dresden on 19 December. In return, he refused to open a new border crossing-point close to the Brandenburg gate together with Kohl. Mitterrand indeed did not appreciate the FRG's demonstration of power in Berlin, especially as this gesture was liable to undermine the Allied status of Berlin.[34]

Among the concrete subjects of the visit figured at the top of the agenda the strengthening of economic relations, illustrated by the huge presence of economic and industrial representatives within the French delegation. The GDR still represented in a French perspective an interesting and even solvent trading partner. Since the 1950s the most important challenge for French enterprises consisted in competing with companies from West Germany.[35] As a consequence, the political changes and the expected period of transformation were considered as a good opportunity to enhance the French presence on the East German market and to avoid in particular a sort of economic takeover of the GDR by the FRG.[36] The focus on economic issues was a response to the feared solo effort of the federal government and part of the French strategy that tended to Europeanize the German unification process.

French diplomacy in general and François Mitterrand in particular did not question the legitimacy of German unification, but the way Helmut Kohl proceeded during the weeks and months following 9 November was considered too hasty, and therefore as undermining the process of European integration as well as the stability of the European continent:

> If the unification of the German people [unité du peuple allemand] is put forward without having a strategy on this issue, we will accumulate all the concerns. . . . We should go forward toward European unification and German unification. . . . We should find a status as well as structures with the European countries which are becoming more democratic. Let us build agreements, even political ones. I do not exclude the USSR experiencing the same evolution. . . . Until 95, we have to strengthen the EEC. After 1995 we have to set up a series of increasingly strong agreements with the Eastern European countries.[37]

Instead of enhancing the international status of the GDR, the stabilizing of the situation in the Eastern part of Germany seemed to be an important issue for French diplomacy. Going ahead with the concept of a European framing of Germany, proven since the 1950s, Mitterrand pleaded in 1989–90 for a European frame of the German unification-process and the need to invent new structures: "With Bonn, I have always linked the evolution of the German problem with that of the EEC. We are preparing the next century and not the last one. I imagine perfectly your country, if it wants to do so, entering this process one day."[38]

One of the most important issues of his visit was therefore the announcement of a decision about the establishment of regular political consultations between the EEC and the GDR—a decision taken by the EEC foreign ministers in October 1989, but not announced to the East German government because of the uncertain situation in the country. From a French perspective, these consultations were to favor the European framework, hinder West German solo efforts, and thus facilitate the French economic engagement on the East German market. The consultations were also considered as a key to link the German and the European unification process.[39]

The French aim to Europeanize the German unification process, to achieve European unity as a bigger framework for German unity, was also the leitmotif of Mitterrand's speech during his stay in East Berlin, addressed not only to his East German hosts but also to the federal government in Bonn, who followed closely any of Mitterrand's steps in East Berlin. Aware of this special attention, Mitterrand used this stage to confirm the Franco-German solidarity, combined with a clear request to put this solidarity in the service of overcoming the European division: "I am not one to dread ongoing history. The message I am bringing to you, is a message of friendship France has for the German people, the entire German people. This is also a message of confidence in its maturity, in the East as well as in the West. This is finally a message of solidarity, because we have the will to build together a peaceful, open, and free Europe."[40]

And even if at the end of his speech he raised his glass in honor of the GDR—anything less would be hardly conceivable during an official visit—he did not refer to the GDR as a state. He spoke rather about the "peuple allemand" (German people), synonymous with the German nation, which can be understood as an allusion to de Gaulle and his remarks on the destiny of the German nation and thus as an affirmation of German unity. Excluding formally the equality of both German states, he defended the equality of both German societies—in his opinion the right to self-determination should be a right of all Germans in the West as well as in the East. At the same time, he also spoke about the "other Germany"—a Germany that stands since the nineteenth century in the French perception for Aufklärung, philosophy, literature, and culture, and that served as a role model, despite numerous military conflicts:

> How could we not emphasize the contribution of your country to European civilization? The artistic creation, the ferment of ideas nourished the work and the thinking of Bach, Handel, Leibniz, Lessing, Luther, Nietzsche and many other German geniuses, universal geniuses. How could a French person forget the Edict of toleration which, more than 300 years ago, opened the Brandenburg to those of our compatriots who were condemned to exile as a result of the cancellation of the Edict of Nantes? How could he forget what the philosophy of the Enlightenment owes to Berlin, owes to the Prussia of Frederick the Great? Getting back to

the present, we know that during the last forty years this intellectual and artistic dynamism never faltered. The tragedy that deeply touched great minds, and that led to thinking about the future and about the identity of the GDR, was transformed, thanks to the determination and the initiative of some people, into a huge movement of liberation that emerged from the work of writers, artists, and in the theatres. . . . Two centuries later, it seemed to us that the impetus coming from the depth of your people responded to the impetus of our people in 1789 and travelled around the world. I want to pay tribute to those who were able to express their aspiration, those who let them express these aspirations, and those who understood that moral or physical violence could not stop history.[41]

To this day, his visit to the GDR in December 1989 seems to be disastrous for the image of François Mitterrand. For his critics, it symbolizes the failure of his policy toward Germany in 1989–90.[42] How to explain that he hastened to East Berlin just some weeks after the wall came down if not by the wish to stabilize the East German state and to hinder German unification? Considering the long-term perspective, Mitterrand did nothing but apply the policy toward Germany, initiated by Robert Schuman and raised into a political doctrine by Charles de Gaulle. With the Franco-German initiative, taken at the European summit in Dublin on 28 April 1990, Mitterrand had at least partly reached this goal, as formulated by his predecessors.

With his visit to East Berlin that was indeed addressed to both parts of Germany, he declared the French will to take part in the unification process and to create a corresponding European framework. He did not come precisely to preserve the status quo, but to take part in the ongoing evolution, wishing, as all his predecessors since the 1950s, to have an influence on the final settlement of the German question. Given the uncertainty of the situation in the GDR, his double authority as French president and as EEC president should confer to his visit a double legitimacy. To the president of the East German State Council, Manfred Gerlach, Mitterrand declared that he was coming to prepare the next century, rather than being stuck in the last one.[43]

Right from the beginning of the project, the visit might be considered as the peak of normalization of Franco–East German relations, but it was rather the dawn of a new era. In fact, no one could have foreseen at this moment that German unification would happen not later than 3 October 1990.

Conclusion

Was François Mitterrand obliged to follow the path of his predecessors with regard to the German question in general and the GDR in particular? According to Roland Dumas, his foreign minister at the end of the Cold War, Mitterrand's policy toward Germany was clearly influenced by the Gaullist philosophy to such an extent that he had even no scope to diverge from the path laid out since the 1950s.[44]

In early May 1989, two days after the Hungarian government had announced the opening of the Iron Curtain, Mitterrand commented on German unification: "Any reunification, achieved in a peaceful and democratic way, would be a matter of course. But you know perfectly well that the problems are not exactly these today."[45] During the following months, he confirmed on several occasions the legitimacy of German unification, but also the hypothetical character of his own reflections. During the visit of Michael Gorbachev in July 1989, he stated, "I will not adopt an attitude that is more imprudent than those of the German leaders themselves, who are however very patriotic Germans. But, nobody is turning history upside down, a history that was founded at the end of World War II, simply following an inspiration, be it an excellent one."[46]

The acceleration of the evolution in East Germany in September and October 1989, however, brought French diplomats to reflect intensively on the French attitude with regard to the German question. Jacques Blot, director for European affairs at the Quai d'Orsay, in a very long memo of about sixty pages tried to adapt the traditional, so-called Gaullist position, while maintaining it as a benchmark. He proposed for instance to maintain the framework of parallel bilateral consultations with Bonn and Moscow. He also referred to the Gaullist legacy with regard to the conception of Europe, suggesting that the existing West European Community should be the ground on which a pan-European community was to build in the future: "The new German organisation should come within a global vision of the European future. . . . In compensation for a satisfying arrangement of the German question, France could accept the creation of a pan-European organisation as an outcome of the Helsinki process."[47]

French efforts to place the ongoing German unification process in a European frame can be considered as a consistent continuation and implementation of the French policy toward Germany since the 1950s. That François Mitterrand defended a specifically French position in the context of 1989–90 can be shown by comparing his statements not only to those of Charles de Gaulle, but also to those of Valéry Giscard d'Estaing, who accused Mitterrand of being too quick in supporting German unity.[48] Preparing the official visit to East Berlin in December 1989, Mitterrand read some pages of de Gaulle's *Mémoires d'espoir* concerning the French policy toward the German question.[49] Some of the official statements made during his stay seem to reflect this reading, especially when he evoked the destiny of the German nation: "The aspiration to become unified is rooted in history and has become topical once again. This aspiration is, first, a matter for those who have a culture, a tongue, and a long history in common. I would like to say that it is, first, a matter for the Germans, who will have to decide freely how they envisage their destiny."[50]

The Gaullist definition was a reference not only for Mitterrand, but for all French diplomats, too. Thus, the report made by Bertrand Dufourcq, director for political affairs at the Quai d'Orsay and head of the French delegation to the Two Plus Four negotiations on the final settlement of the German question in 1990, at the end of these negotiations can be understood as a sort of response to the requirements for German unification mentioned by Charles de Gaulle thirty years earlier in March 1959:

> The French position arose from the double concern about purifying history in a way that prevents any possibility of calling things into question, on the legal as well as on the political level, about refusing any arrangement that might hinder the future European construction. . . . We attached particular importance to the confirmation of the final nature of the German borders, to the confirmation of its commitment to renouncing ABC [atomic, biological, and chemical] weapons, and to an orderly settlement of the questions concerning Berlin. As for the rest, we refuse any neutralization of Germany or any special political or military status, in order to avoid creating a pole of instability in the centre of Europe, and to avoid signing away the future of a European option in the field of defence.[51]

Christian Wenkel is associate professor for contemporary history at Artois University. After receiving a PhD from the University in Munich and SciencesPo Paris, he was a senior research fellow at the German Historical Institute in Paris from 2009 to 2016. His research interests cover the Franco-German relationship, French foreign policy, the Cold War, and European integration. Relevant publications in the context of this book include *Auf der Suche nach einem "anderen Deutschland"* (2014) and *La diplomatie française face à l'unification allemande* (with Maurice Vaïsse, 2011).

Notes

1. Memo of J. Blot, 30 Oct. 1989, AnF, series 5AG4, box CDM33; see also Vaïsse and Wenkel, *La diplomatie française*; Bozo, *Mitterrand*; Schabert, *How World Politics*. See also the memoirs of different French actors: Mitterrand, *De l'Allemagne*; Védrine, *Les mondes*; and Dumas, *Le fil*.
2. The use of the term "unification" seems much more appropriate than that of "reunification," since there was no return to an older Germany, but instead a unification of three parts of Germany created after the end of World War II. By the way, François Mitterrand himself preferred the use of "unification" for this very reason, too.
3. On Franco–East German relations, see Wenkel, *Auf der Suche nach einem*; and Pfeil, *Die "anderen."*
4. On Europe and the CSCE process, see Romano, *From Détente in Europe*; on French détente policies, see Badalassi, *En finir avec la guerre froide*; and Heyde, *Frankreich im KSZE-Prozess*.
5. De Gaulle, *Discours et messages*, vol. 3, 84. Unless otherwise noted, all translations are my own.
6. On Charles de Gaulle and the idea of nation, see La Gorce, "La nation"; M. Cazenave. 2000. "La nation chez de Gaulle," *Cahiers de la Fondation Charles de Gaulle* 7, 5–12; and Maillard, "La nation."
7. On the French conception of nation, see also Krulic, *La nation*, 69–82, 126–36; and Billard, *La France*, 180–85.
8. Memo of the Division of Central European Affairs for the cabinet of the minister, 2 Dec. 1960, AMAE, series RDA, box 33, folio 135.
9. De Gaulle, *Discours et messages*, vol. 4, 338–42. See also the contributions of Benedikt Schoenborn and of Garret Martin in this volume.

10. De Gaulle, *Discours et messages*, vol. 3, 85.
11. On Willy Brandt, the New Ostpolitik, and France, see Hiepel, *Willy Brandt*; Möller and Vaïsse, *Willy Brandt*; and Fink and Schaefer, *Ostpolitik*.
12. Memo of the Division of Central European affairs, 6 May 1970, AMAE, series RDA 1971–76, box 3081; minutes of the Foreign Affairs and Defense Committee of the French Senate, 13 Dec. 1972, 8, AP, séries Sénat, box 48S15; Wenkel, *Auf der Suche nach einem*, 410–21, 468–69.
13. Paech and Stuby, *Machtpolitik*, 292–300.
14. Wenkel, *Auf der Suche nach einem*, 426–48.
15. On SECAM, see Chantriaux, "SECAM"; Fickers, "*Politique de la grandeur*," 257–63; and Wenkel, *Auf der Suche nach einem*, 395–99.
16. Wenkel, "La marge de manœuvre."
17. Memo of the Division of Central European Affairs, 6 May 1970, AMAE, series RDA 1971–1976, box 3081.
18. Osmont, "La négociation."
19. Memo of the Division of Central European affairs, 31 Jan. 1973, AMAE, series RDA 1971–1976, box 3101.
20. Memo of conversation between J. Sauvagnargues and G. Götting, 19 Feb. 1975, AMAE, series RDA 1971–1976, box 3100.
21. Memo of the Division of Central European affairs, 29 Dec. 1975, AMAE, series RDA 1971–1976, box 3105.
22. Wenkel, *Auf der Suche nach einem*, 435–42.
23. Memo of the Division of Central European affairs, M. Plaisant, 23 Jan. 1972, AMAE, series RDA 1971–1976, box 3102.
24. Draft for a toast of the minister during the visit of O. Fischer in Paris, 12 Dec. 1975, AMAE series RDA 1971–1976, box 3100.
25. Memo of C. de Margerie to F. Mitterrand, 23 Jan. 1992, AnF, series 5AG4, box CDM33.
26. Memo of J. Timsit, 16 Jan. 1989, AnF, series 5AG4, box CD187.
27. Memo of the Centre for Analysis and Strategy, J. Guéhenno, 30 Apr. 1989, AnF, series 5AG4, box CDM33.
28. Memo of H. Védrine, 18 Oct. 1989, AnF, series 5AG4, box CD177; with a handwritten remark of F. Mitterrand: "The issue of comparative rhythms is essential."
29. Telegram from the French embassy in Berlin, J. Timsit, 13 Nov. 1989, AnF, series 5AG4, box CD187; with a handwritten remark of F. Mitterrand: "Set the nearest date."
30. Memo of H. Védrine, 18 Oct. 1989, AnF, series 5AG4, box CD177; see also the memo of conversation between F. Mitterrand and M. Gorbachev, 6 Dec. 1989, AnF, series 5AG4, box CD67.
31. Report on a preliminary delegation to East Berlin from 3 to 5 December, C. de Margerie, 6 Dec. 1989, AnF, series 5AG4, box CD187. De Margerie concludes her report by saying that nobody would be able to predict the future of the GDR: "No one knows towards which regime, towards which state, the increasingly chaotic transition in the GDR will be directed."
32. Memo of J. Timsit, 16 Jan. 1989, AnF, series 5AG4, box CD187.
33. Memo of L. Hennekinne for F. Mitterrand, 12 Dec. 1989, AnF, series 5AG4, box CD187.
34. Interview of the author with R. Dumas, 5 Feb. 2007.
35. Memo of the Bank of France, 12 Nov. 1953, CAEF, series Trésor, box B55827; report of the commercial counselor at the French military government in Berlin on the spring fair in Leipzig, 29 Mar. 1969, AMAE, series RDA 1961 70, box 94; memo of Boudier for Mitterrand, 19 Dec. 1989, AnF, series 5AG4, box EG204; see also Wenkel, *Auf der Suche nach einem*, 149–75.
36. Telegram from Bonn, commercial counselor, to the French Ministry of Economic Affairs, Division of Foreign Trade, 24 Nov. 1989, AnF, series 5AG4, box CDM33.
37. Memo of conversation between F. Mitterrand and H. Kohl, 4 Jan. 1990, AnF, series 5AG4, box CD68.
38. Memo of conversation between F. Mitterrand and M. Gerlach, 20 Dec. 1990, AnF, series 5AG4, box CD67.

39. Memo of E. Guigou, 18 Dec. 1989, and memo of the Division of Central European Affairs, 13 Dec. 1989, AnF, series 5AG4, box EG204.
40. Telegram from the French embassy in Berlin, J. Timsit, 23 Dec. 1989, CADN, series Berlin-Est, box 149; see the French original in Vaïsse and Wenkel, *La diplomatie française*, 179.
41. Telegram from the French embassy in Berlin, J. Timsit, 23 Dec. 1989, CADN, series Berlin-Est, box 149; see the French original in Vaïsse and Wenkel, *La diplomatie française*, 175. See also Wenkel, "'L'autre' dans le rapport."
42. Lappenküper, *Mitterrand*, 261–77.
43. Memo of conversation between F. Mitterrand and M. Gerlach, 20 Dec. 1989, AnF, series 5AG4, box CD67.
44. Interview of the author with R. Dumas, 5 Feb. 2007.
45. Quote according to a memo of the Centre for Analysis and Strategy, 12 Sept. 1989, AnF, series 5AG4, box CDM33.
46. Ibid.
47. Memo of J. Blot, 30 Oct. 1989, AnF, series 5AG4, box CDM33.
48. V. Giscard d'Estaing during an interview with D. Vernet published by RTL and *Le Monde*, 12 Nov. 1989, AnF, series 5AG4, box CDM33.
49. Copies of pages 183, 186 and 187 from the first volume of de Gaulle, *Mémoires d'espoir*, were assembled by H. Védrine in order to prepare Mitterrand for his trip to East Berlin. The markings and notes allow the conclusion that Mitterrand not only actually read these pages, but that they also served as an inspiration for him (AnF, series 5AG4, box CD177).
50. Telegram from the French embassy in Berlin, J. Timsit, 23 Dec. 1989, CADN, series Berlin-Est, box 149; see the French original in Vaïsse and Wenkel, *La diplomatie française*, 176. See also De Gaulle, *Discours et messages*, vol. 3, 84–85: "The reunification of the two factions into a single Germany, which would be entirely free, seems to us to be the normal destiny of the German people ['le destin normal du peuple allemand'], provided that they do not question their current borders, in the West, East, North and South, and that they tend to integrate."
51. Telegram of B. Dufourcq, 17 Sept. 1990, CADN, series Berlin-Est, box 225; see also Vaïsse and Wenkel, *La diplomatie française*, 363–70.

Bibliography

Badalassi, N. 2014. *En finir avec la guerre froide. La France, l'Europe et le processus d'Helsinki 1965–1975*. Rennes, France: Presses universitaires de Rennes.
Billard, J. 1997. "La France et l'idée de nation, Philosophie politique." *Revue internationale de philosophie politique* 8, 161–98.
Bozo, F. 2011. *Mitterrand, the End of the Cold War, and German Unification*. New York: Berghahn Books.
Dumas, R. 1996. *Le fil et la pelote. Mémoires*. Paris: Plon.
Cazenave, M. 2000. "La nation chez de Gaulle." *Cahiers de la Fondation Charles de Gaulle* 7, 5–12.
Chantriaux, O. 2005. "SECAM, dossier pionnier de la coopération franco-russe." *Revue d'histoire diplomatique* 119, no. 1: 75–91.
De Gaulle, C. 1970. *Discours et messages*. Vol. 3, *Avec le renouveau*. Paris: Plon.
———. 1970. *Discours et messages*. Vol. 4, *Pour l'effort*. Paris: Plon.
———. 1970. *Mémoires d'espoir*. Vol. 1, *Le renouveau. 1958–1962*. Paris: Plon.
Fickers, A. 2007. *"Politique de la grandeur" versus "Made in Germany."* Munich, Germany: Oldenbourg.
Fink, C., and B. Schaefer, eds. 2009. *Ostpolitik, 1969–1974. European and Global Responses*. Cambridge: Cambridge University Press.
Heyde, V. 2017. *Frankreich im KSZE-Prozess. Diplomatie im Namen der europäischen Sicherheit*. Munich, Germany: Oldenbourg.
Hiepel, C. 2012. *Willy Brandt und Georges Pompidou. Deutsch-französische Europapolitik zwischen Aufbruch und Krise*. Munich, Germany: Oldenbourg.

Krulic, B. 1999. *La nation. Une idée moderne*. Paris: Ellipses.

La Gorce, P.-M. de. 2002. "La nation selon Charles de Gaulle." In *Charles de Gaulle et la nation*, edited by Fondation Charles de Gaulles, 193–200. Paris: François-Xavier de Guibert.

Lappenküper, U. 2012. *Mitterrand und Deutschland. Die enträtselte Sphinx*. Munich, Germany: Oldenbourg.

Maillard, P. 2000. "La nation et les autres nations chez Charles de Gaulle." *Cahiers de la Fondation Charles de Gaulle* 7, 56–73.

Mitterrand, F. 1996. *De l'Allemagne, de la France*. Paris: O. Jacob.

Möller, H., and M. Vaïsse, eds. *Willy Brandt und Frankreich*. Munich, Germany: Oldenbourg.

Osmont, M. 2008. "La négociation de l'accord quadripartite sur Berlin 1969–1971. Le rôle du groupe de Bonn." *Relations internationales* 135, 37–52.

Paech, N., and G. Stuby. 1994. *Machtpolitik und Völkerrecht in den internationalen Beziehungen*. Baden-Baden, Germany: Nomos.

Pfeil, U. 2004. *Die "anderen" deutsch-französischen Beziehungen. Die DDR und Frankreich 1949–1990*. Cologne, Germany: Böhlau.

Romano, A. 2009. *From Détente in Europe to European Détente: How the West Shaped the Helsinki CSCE*. Brussels, Belgium: P. Lang.

Schabert, T. 2009. *How World Politics Is Made: France and the Reunification of Germany*. Columbia: University of Missouri Press.

Vaïsse, M., and C. Wenkel, eds. 2011. *La diplomatie française face à l'unification allemande. D'après des archives inédites*. Paris: Tallandier.

Védrine, H. 1996. *Les mondes de Mitterrand. À l'Élysée 1981–1995*. Paris: Fayard.

Wenkel, C. 2012. "La marge de manœuvre des parlementaires en l'absence de relations officielles. Le cas de la RDA 1967–1976." *Parlement[s]* 17, 72–87.

———. 2012. "L'autre" dans le rapport franco-allemand." In *50 ans de relations franco-allemandes*, edited by R. Marcowitz and H. Miard-Delacroix, 43–73. Paris: Nouveaux mondes.

———. 2014. *Auf der Suche nach einem "anderen Deutschland." Das Verhältnis Frankreichs zur DDR im Spannungsfeld von Perzeption und Diplomatie*. Munich, Germany: Oldenbourg.

INDEX